For Cole Anne

Keep

CLICKING

Many Thanks
Much Love,

FAITH POPCORN
AND
LYS MARIGOLD

CLICKING

16 TRENDS TO FUTURE FIT YOUR LIFE, YOUR WORK, AND YOUR BUSINESS

Illustrated by Gerti Bierenbroodspot

HarperCollins*Publishers*

If you're interested in subscribing to BrainReserve's newsletter, CLICK-TIME ($199 per year bi-monthly in U.S.), please send a postcard with your name and address to BrainReserve, One Madison Ave., New York, NY 10010. Please, only written inquiries can be processed.

HarperCollins books may be purchased for educational, business, or sales promotional use. For information, please write: Special Markets Department, HarperCollins Publishers, Inc., 10 East 53rd Street, New York, NY 10022.

FIRST EDITION

Designed by Alma Hochhauser Orenstein

Library of Congress Cataloging-in-Publication Data

Popcorn, Faith.
    Clicking : 16 trends to future fit your life, your work, and your
business / Faith Popcorn & Lys Marigold.
      p. cm.
    ISBN 0–88730-694-2
    Includes index
    1. Success in business.   2. Success.   I. Marigold, Lys.   II. Title.
HF5386.P754   1996
650.1—dc20   96-379

96 97 98 99 00 ❖/RRD 10 9 8 7 6 5 4 3

For my sister, Mechele Flotkin Flaum,
who has been the constant Click of my life.
Always fair, always there, with love.

. . . FAITH

For the two generations so cherished and central in my life—
my mother, Virginia Davis Ackerman,
and my warrior-baby daughter, Skye Qi.

. . . LYS

C O N T E N T S

PART THREE   **HOW TO CLICK**

ACKNOWLEDGMENTS

Dear Reader:

Before we go on to recognize the many who helped us with this book: a moment for my co-author, and best friend, Lys Marigold. Her uncanny genius lies in her ability to search out the "right" stories, reveal the emerging trends, follow the bread crumbs of new directions, express them eloquently and support them logically. Even after all these years it's always startling. Her gift is extraordinary; to weave, to wander, to invent, to shape, to create with humor and irony, and then paint a big, broad, and brilliant societal vision. A trillion thanks, Lys.

Love, Faith

Thanks to the BrainReserve family, who, as well as running a full time consultancy, helped support the creation of this book. It's a credit to our shared passion for brailling the culture and their brilliant ability to be an ensemble. They are the best people-to-have-around-you people every day.

Ash DeLorenzo, who made sure that our concepts were supported, relevant and current. His endless reading and commenting on this manuscript was done without complaint. Michele Cruz, who kept us financially (and rationally) balanced. And thanks to John Shin, who was her balance. Gordon Matz, who patiently taught computer-illiterates to be somewhat literate. Carmen Colon-Medina who cheerily greeted us each morning, saying her mantra, "It's going to get done." Erica Nathanson, our young Project Coordinator who brought in Generation-Xers to share their insights on the culture and the Trends; to David Hardcastle, our talented Creative Designer whose visual sense added something special. For Ada Basabe-Cruz, who endlessly printed out revise after revise. Our wonderful TrendView Director, Suki Diamond, who is going on to create our Clicking Seminar. Janet

Siroto, our Creative Director, whose thoughtful contributions are in many chapters, and Joanne Serling, Janet's able assistant, who helped proof and provoke. To Jenny Noonan, our upbeat, tenacious Project Director who kept us moving forward. To Lisa Antinore, whose fresh thinking provided trend-perfect examples. Carrie Macpherson, who gave us the British sense of humor, the dry, the wry, to get this bloody thing done. To the staff of the Newlin Company, especially Daniel Urbas and Jackie Widrow, who came in to do a TrendPull, ripping, clipping, snipping, accessing all kinds of information. Rosemary Cardona, for her ability to run reception with warmth while minding Ms. Miyake. For Jennifer Confrey, who took care of the staff. And to Mechele Flaum, who took care of us: encouraging, creating and again watching the store, while we watched the book. Extra, extra special thanks to Mary Kay Adams Moment, whose loving loyalty got us through. Her calm wisdom, her patience, her instincts, her insights, her ability to anticipate, helped make every page perfect.

To all the publishing pros whose support and advice helped achieve our dream: Jack McKeown, Seer and Prince of Patience; Binky Urban, universal negotiator, friend; Gladys Carr, superlative playful editor; Joseph Montebello, creative curator; Lisa Berkowitz, p.r. spark; Cynthia Barrett, diligent overseer; Linda Dingler, diva of design; Alma Orenstein, book architect extraordinaire; Ruth Lee, perfect picture placer; Joel Avirom, cover sorcerer; Jason Snyder, the sorcerer's support source.

Gratitude to Ayse Manyas Kenmore, the brightest light: her intelligence, her humor, her good spirits, her constant comments were a source of strength.

And significantly, to Gerti Bierenbroodspot, whose support to Lys and this project never wavered. Month after month, she gave the spark of her boundless energy, her creative genius, her unparalleled imagination, and her loving soul.

A special and separate thanks to Dr. Ethel Person for her ongoing and beautiful belief in this book and in me; and for bringing her analytic powers to bear.

To my good friend Adam Hanft, for his 'thereness;' his ideas, logic, cultural comments, insight, and foresight.

Lastly, but importantly, to Kate Newlin, who spent many of her weeknights and weekends contributing her clear, keen mind, marketing prowess, astounding strategic thinking, and her heart. The center held.

W e also want to thank all of the people whose insights, memories, and wisdom permeate this book. Whether they're directly quoted or not, their stories are here. They shared their time, their ideas, their childhood dreams: Their stories are emblematic of our society . . .

A lot of books are written from an internal voice, but a book like this can only be written by listening to the cultural voice, the real experiences of real people.

Patricia Allen, M.D.

Ted Athanassiades, Vice Chairman of the Board, MetLife

Margaret J. Barrett, President, Consumer Direct, GE Capital

Lynn Beasley, Senior Vice President, R.J. Reynolds Tobacco Company

Jeffrey Berg, Chairman & CEO, International Creative Management

Chuck Braverman

Michael Braverman, Braverman Newbold Brennan Real Estate

Jennifer Brook, Executive Vice President, Creative Director, Earle Palmer Brown

Vera Brown, Vera's Retreat in the Glen

Dennis Carey, Co-Managing Director, SpencerStuart

Tom Chappel, President, Tom's of Maine

Cher

Deepak Chopra, M.D.

Stephen Covey

Laurel Cutler, Vice Chairman, FCB/Leber Katz Partnership

Susan Davis, Executive Director, WEDO

Jerry Della Femina, Chairman, Jerry & Ketchum

Robert F. DiRomualdo, President & CEO, Borders-Walden Group

Jeremy Dorosin

Kevin J. Doyle, President, Wassall USA, Inc.

Thomas M. Fallon, Vice President, Advertising & Publicity, The Carlisle Collection

Richard D. Fairbank, CEO, Capital One Financial Corporation

David Fink, Esq.

James A. Firestone, General Manager, Consumer Division, IBM

Peter Flatow, President, CoKnowledge

Sander A. Flaum, President/CEO, Robert A. Becker, Inc., EURO/RSCG

Frederick Frank, Senior Managing Director, Lehman Brothers

Marcia & Gene Garlanda

Peter A. Georgescu, Chairman & CEO, Young & Rubicam Inc.

Vikki & Gary Gralla

H. John Greeniaus, President & CEO, Nabisco, Inc.

Amy Gross, Editor in Chief, *Mirabella*, Editorial Director, *Elle*

Flora Hanft

Mike Harper, Chairman, RJR/Nabisco, Inc.

Neil D. Hart, Director of Marketing/Creative Services, Corning Vitro Corporation

J. Tomilson Hill, Senior Managing Director, The Blackstone Group

Isabelle Hupperts, Conseiller du Groupe Suez pour le Japon, Compagnie de Suez

Robert E. Ingalls, Jr., Vice President, Consumer Marketing, Bell Atlantic

Carole Isenberg, Writer/Producer

Jerry Isenberg, Professor/Executive Director Electronic Reading, USC School of Cinema-Television

James W. Johnston, Chairman & CEO, R.J. Reynolds Tobacco Company

Eric Jonsson

Thomas J. Kalinske, President & CEO, Sega of America

Robert H. Kenmore, President, Equivest Partners, Inc.

Clark Kinlin, Vice President Marketing, Corning Consumer Products Company

Calvin Klein

Jesse Kornbluth

Lenore Kundrat, President, Mahwah Tax Service

Rick Kundrat, Vice President & General Manager, Thomas J. Lipton Co.

Linda Lanz, Director of Research, Ameritech

Carl Levine, Carl Levine Consulting & Licensing

Mike Lorelli, President, The Americas, Tambrands Inc.

Gina Louie, M.D.

Doug R. Lunne, Director of Corporate Communications, Standard Register

Elaine Lunne

Ellen Malcolm, President, EMILY's List

Gayle Morris, Sharper's Pot Trading Company

Colleen May, Chairman, Intervine Incorporated

Marnie McBryde, Senior Director, SpencerStuart

Rip McEldowney, Vice President, Consumer Education Center, MetLife

John J. McLaughlin, President & CEO, DAP Inc.

David Mixner, DBM Associates

James Morgan, President & CEO, Philip Morris U.S.A.

Edward Myer, President & Chairman of the Board, Grey Advertising

Fran Myers, Senior Director, Integrated Marketing, Nabisco Biscuit Company

Robert J. Myers, President, Carnegie Council on Ethics and International Affairs

Jerry Noonan, Senior Vice President of Marketing, Nabisco Biscuit Company

Jessye Norman

Richard C. Notebaert, Chairman & CEO, Ameritech

Torie Osborn, Author

Carol Peters, daVinci Time & Space

Robert Pritikin, M.D.

Paul F. Rickenbach, Jr., Mayor of East Hampton

Leonard Riggio, CEO, Barnes & Noble Inc.

Cynthia Rowley

Diane Sawyer

Lori Schiaffino

Andrew J. Schindler, President & COO, R.J. Reynolds Tobacco Company

Toni Schmitt

Wolf Schmitt, Chairman of the Board & CEO, Rubbermaid Incorporated

Jeffrey Schwager, Sales Manager, Mevisto

Marsha Scott, White House Deputy Assistant to the President

John Sculley, CEO, Live Picture

Vivian Shapiro, Vice President, David Geller & Associates

Bernie Siegel, M.D.

Patti Walton Silver

Jacqueline Albert-Simon, Associate Editor, U.S. Bureau Chief, "Politique Internationale;" Sr. Resident Scholar, Inst. of French Studies, New York University

Pierre F. Simon

Ove Sorensen, Executive Vice President Marketing, R.J. Reynolds Tobacco Company

Bill Smail, General Manager, The Smail Family Dealerships

Ray Smith, Chairman of the Board & CEO, Bell Atlantic

Liz Smith

John Stegeman, White House Watch

Linda Stegeman, Vice President Marketing, Octel Communications

Gloria Steinem

William E. Storts, Managing Director, Andersen Consulting

Deidre Sullivan

Mary Tanner, Managing Director, Lehman Brothers

Susan Thomases, Partner, Willkie Farr & Gallagher

James A. Valentino, Senior Vice President, Market Planning & Coordination, MetLife

Tony Van Hook

Rusty Warren

Leslie Wexner, CEO, The Limited

PART ONE

CLICKING

SAFECRACKING THE FUTURE

SAFE-CRACKING THE FUTURE

The future belongs to those who believe in the beauty of their dreams.
—ELEANOR ROOSEVELT

First, you lightly brush your fingertips against what you're wearing. Then, ever so gently, you turn the dial to the right. With your ear pressed to the surface, you listen as the tumblers slip into place. Next challenge, you move it counterclockwise, slowly to the left. Finally, you spin it again to the right. All your numbers seem to be on the mark. Have you cracked it? Yes, you can hear the mechanism as it settles into the final groove. Click. Perfect. It opens.

How many times in your life have you Clicked into place? Like opening a safe, it's searching and finding the right combination to Future Fit into a new life. Mastering control, becoming clear. Too many people spend their whole lives feeling slightly off-kilter, slightly out-of-step with their expectations. Something doesn't work—a job, a place, the totality of what you're doing.

Many times, it's not a monumental change that's needed. Often it just takes a minimal adjustment of the parts—until you get to that zoom zone of the all-over Click.

You can describe Clicking as a thunderbolt, a surge. There's a wonderful seismic word, "tsunami," meaning a gigantic ocean wave caused by an underground earthquake or volcano. That's how it feels when you do something that Clicks—like a groundswell is sweeping over you and everything in your sight.

In the dictionary, "to click" literally means "to fit together," to become suddenly clear or intelligible. The slang definition is "to succeed, make a hit," such as when the older Boston Celtics player, Robert Parish, recalled the days when he and teammate Larry Bird "played absolutely effortlessly and clicked on the court." In computer-ese, Clicking is all-powerful: single clicks, double clicks, sending commands, moving icons. Click and a light goes on (or off).

But think of all the controls in modern life that you Click with. Click and your television comes on. Click, Click, you play with your remote to channel-surf when you're restlessly looking for something interesting to watch. You Click your camera every time you want to capture a moment. Click, that's the sound you hear when a phone call gets interrupted; Click, Click, you can switch over and talk to the caller who's waiting.

Click, the very sound, the very word, wakes people up, shakes people up—like snapping your fingers—and makes them aware and alert to the chance for a brave new future.

Clicking, in that sense, is about being ready to be in synch with what's coming tomorrow. To survive now, one has to bend, to be flexible. It sometimes feels like déjà vu—only it didn't happen before. Although Clicking can make you feel at ease, it isn't passive. It doesn't revolve around luck (although that helps) or being struck by lightning (that only hurts). Giving you the combination to Safe-Crack the Future is what this book is all about. Think of it as if you're standing at the intersection of who you are and who you want to be. Our goal is to push you in the right direction (only in our book, all arrows point the same way: forward) and provide you with the right tools to Click into Next.

Where Clicking Came From

The idea for the book that you hold in your hand grew out of the enormous outpouring in response to our first book, *The Popcorn*

Report. Judging by the 40,000 people responding to the last line, "call me, fax me, write me, beam me up," we recognized that regular people used a "business book" to change their lives.

A similar inkling came from my seminar, TrendView. Although the talk is geared to the business community, most of the audience questions would invariably be personal. "What are the jobs of the future?", "What should my kids be studying?", "Will the economy be kind to small companies?" (usually a disguise for "Should I open . . . ?").

These queries are the modern-day equivalent of the "note in a bottle" that shipwrecked sailors would set adrift. Except these come from average, everyday Americans who are marooned (or stuck) in one phase of their lives—and unsure of what tomorrow will bring. This makes sense. Clearly, it's getting harder to achieve personal and professional success. Too many of us are trapped in dead-end jobs that offer little in the way of financial or emotional rewards. Hundreds of thousands have actually seen their positions callously eliminated by the mergers, acquisitions, and outright closings in the late '80s and early '90s and haven't yet been able to find their personal centers of gravity.

Our answer? To show how to use the BrainReserve Trends as concrete formulas for change. The same Trends that we have successfully applied to hundreds of small and large Fortune 500 companies will work equally well with an individual. The Trends are a way to look at the growth markets of the future and help spark ideas for those legions of people who've created blueprints (on paper or in their dreams) for starting their own business.

It seems as if we hear the same story from every part of society.

- From single-parent households who tell us they have the imagination and energy to make a mark in society—but don't know where to begin.
- From the mislabeled Generation-Xers who tell us they need help getting started on their career paths and are desperate to find a first job. (Did you know that over 50% of the 1993 Ivy Leaguers looking for work were still unemployed six months after they graduated?)
- From a forced-into-early-retirement middle manager who wanted to know, "Where else could my skills be needed?" Or flippantly, "I gave 33 years to a Blue-Chip company and

it gave me a Pink Slip in return" (sounds like the title of one of our favorite Country Western songs—"She Got the Gold Mine, I Got the Shaft").

But most of all, we heard from people who wanted confirmation of an idea they'd been grappling with that would either alter—or better—their own future. Such as a nurse and single mother who read the Trends and decided to start a phone service for physicians in her area . . . or a socially conscious grad who didn't want to enter the Jurassic Park of American business, instead starting a reforestation service . . . or a fifty-ish manager, downsized out of his aircraft job, but who has more energy than ever before, and has opened a health-oriented seafood shop.

All these strands of the tapestry of the future began to come together. As divergent as these individuals were, they were linked by common threads: A search for a way to end the frustration, the disappointments. A plan to jump over any personal obstacles and clear any fears. A dedication to seize all new opportunities and see the future clearly. One single word seemed to sum up for us what all these smart men and women are looking to do—and that word is . . . Click.

When we stared at those five letters, we found that they each contributed to a process that described many of the experiences people shared with us. Although we're not great fans of acronyms, this one seemed to work:

C is for *C*ourage.
L is for *L*etting Go.
I is for *I*nsight.
C is for *C*ommitment.
K is for *K*now-how.

It's a major theme in all the stories ahead. Very often, the act of Clicking starts out with an act of **C**ourage.

Take Jerry Della Femina, who needed **C**ourage to get out of the rough, tough section of Brooklyn he grew up in (called the #1 "breeding place for crime in the U.S."). He learned about "getting out" in a lesson in life from his mother. She took him along when she paid their monthly rent bill, pointing up to the landlord's big house, saying "Isn't it beautiful? Don't ever hate someone because they have more; just get yourself in a position to get there." Jerry looked for a job in advertising in 1954, landed one in 1961, and started on his star-studded, award-laden career. Then came the Letting Go. He sold his agency, along with the rights to his name. Jerry jokes, "I'm the only Italian who lost his last name without being part of the witness protection program." Insight came with an understanding of his success: "I will it and it has to happen."

The Commitment and Know-how parts are obvious. He plunged back into the advertising world (big-time) with Jerry, Inc., and also plowed that same energy into the still-sleepy Hamptons. Now a local tycoon, Jerry spends his days and nights running from one restaurant, Della Femina's, to the dockside restaurant and marina, East Hampton Point, to a gourmet emporium, Jerry & David's Red Horse Market (with partner David Silver). At this last place, he can be seen on Saturday mornings slicing the smoked salmon. Plus, in whatever spare time is left, he writes a weekly column in his daughter's newspaper, *The Independent*, in which he alternates blasting the local administration and declaring his love for wife, Judy Licht, and his kids. In a moment of utter contentment (and supreme modesty), Jerry told us, "I feel like I've gone from Cluck to Click."

Or take the story of Lori Schiaffino, renegade single mother with a stripe of white hair and eyes of two colors (both characteristics due to a rare childhood malady), who had the Courage to move to Long Island's East End from western Massachusetts to raise her daughter, Nicole, in a more job-promising environment. (Click places *can* make a difference.) She worked double shifts as a waitress, Letting Go when her strength and ambition were noticed by the parents of Niki's best kindergarten friend (well, it helped that they were Steve and Courtney Ross, who just happened to be looking for an assistant on a Quincy Jones documentary). Her Insight came when she realized how good she was at organizing *anything and everything*. The next job tested her Commitment.

Lori was asked by Steven Spielberg to set up his family's move to Krakow for the filming of *Schindler's List*: everything from a house, multiple phone lines, special food flown in from Vienna, endless airline reservations, arranging for friends' visits. With her Know-how and bloodhound instincts, she did the job flawlessly. Now she's put her special talent to smart use, in her own company, Details, and she's been hired to handle all sorts of challenges, from public relations to specialized travel backpacks. Those organizing skills are also much in demand for fund-raising, such as helping find the money needed to build a new $4-million youth center in East Hampton. A real Click.

Click stories pop up in the strangest places. For example, one came out of the experience when my sister Mechele and I spent a weekend at Tony Robbins's Date with Destiny seminar in San Diego. In this incredibly intense gathering, we were all charged with discovering "a life mission statement" (mine, "to lift myself and others into our best futures"). During one exercise, I was partnered with a young auto mechanic named Tony Van Hook, who found the Courage to attend this meeting to gain some clues about what would happen to him if he tried Letting Go. He was unhappy fixing cars, but didn't know what he should do next. Although we've kept in touch occasionally, it's only now (two years later) that Tony has had the Insight about a future venture. His recent letter (Commitment) said, "I have this idea that I believe has great potential . . . I call it 'Cross the Line' actionwear. Cross the Line meaning to take a chance, risk something, pursue your dreams, quit wishing and start doing. To face your fear, stand on the edge and see what you are really capable of doing. The power is inside all of us. That is the message I hope to promote with phrases and sayings on T-shirts, such as Nothing Big comes from Small Dreams." That's Tony's Know-how (fixing people instead of cars) and his steppingstone to a Click.

Then, there's the Click of building on the experience of your life. My co-author, Lys Marigold, had taken the law boards, loved the detective aspect of legal research, but at the last moment, instead of plunging into more schooling, she opted for a life in New York as a magazine writer (Courage). Except for the one year driving a little blue humpbacked Volvo around Europe, she pounded the typewriter keys as a copy chief for many of the major women's magazines. Reasonably happy, until one fateful day at *Ladies' Home Journal* when a workman came by to brick up the window in her office, explaining that a new high-rise building was being built flush against it. That wall suddenly seemed symbolic of her job—too closed in, too confined to writing about food, fashion, beauty, and decorating.

Letting Go meant joining BrainReserve as its Creative Director, expanding into the world of business, learning a new marketing lingo, developing the Trends. Twelve years later (another **Letting Go**), a move to Europe, but tethered to BrainReserve by the eternal search (more detective Insight) for new products, new Trend signs. Lys came back as the writer of the first book, *The Popcorn Report* (she knew the case histories, the biography of BrainReserve better than anyone else).

But Lys's Heart Click came when she went to live with the Bedouins in the ancient red-rock city of Petra in Jordan. She found and photographed the writing of its early inhabitants, the Nabateans, carved in the deep ravines. And on high cliffs, she discovered little carved indentations, in rows, and realized that these were gaming boards from 1 B.C. to A.D. 2. She deduced that the wealthy caravan tax collectors must have had lookout stations and that those sentries, when bored, played games. Next on her agenda, Lys is investigating the development of similar games for CD-ROMs (good for children worldwide—no language skills are needed) or creating Virtual Reality adventure treks through the caves and temples of Petra's archaeological wonders. Her business experience (**Know-how**) will continue to prove invaluable. And she might even write the libretto of an opera on Queen Zenobia of the desert. A global Click.

*   *   *

Lys Marigold, Nikon in hand,
on a mountaintop in Petra, Jordan.

Thus was born the concept of Clicking. It's what happens when your unique DNA meets up with a clear and sharp vision of the future.

For a handful of people, Clicking comes easily, intuitively. Those are the gifted and fortunate among us, those who can honestly say, "From the time I was four I knew I would be a painter," or "I'm completely happy running this hardware store my whole life." This book isn't for that dedicated group, or for the lucky few who've just won a lottery. Even though the odds are 12,913,583 to 1, when one lone ticket holder hits the jackpot, as happened this year to a young college student who won $87 million-plus, we all get our hopes up.

But for most of us—99.9%, in fact—Clicking requires soul-searching and a commitment to have the Courage when the Insight smiles on us.

Or, as Calvin Klein said, when we talked about the Click of his life, "For me, the 'C' signifies Confidence. My advice would be, 'Even if you're not confident, act it.' If I believe in something, I can make others believe in it."

As we approach the millennium, the need to Click intensifies. Why? Because as the odometer of the century begins to turn (even though Trends don't change by the calendar and people don't Click by the calendar), even things we take for granted as secure may become unsettled. The gaps will continue to widen—between winners and losers, between the Haves and Have-Nots. What we're talking about goes beyond money. We're talking about the vast division of Techno-Haves, Education-Haves, Family-Haves, and Happiness-Haves with their counterparts, the sadly Have-Nots.

As part of the research for this book, we interviewed about a thousand individuals to gain insight into what worked—or didn't work—as one moves along the path to Clicking. Some of the people we talked to were business legends or household names. For example, John Sculley talked about Clicking in the computer industry: "It's not necessarily only having the leading technology, but it's more about how you put it together with very good marketing. In reality, Macintosh wasn't an instant success, neither was Windows. Even fax machines and cellular phones had several lives before they caught on." Sculley went on to talk about his general philosophy: "I think there are two Clicks. The most important one is in your own head. The second Click is for others. For instance, Frank Lloyd Wright Clicked for himself, but not with most of the world. Only now is he universally appreciated." "Yet," Sculley concedes, "if you spend too much time worrying about how other people perceive you, you'll never break the rules."

Others who were interviewed were not celebrity-famous—but people who have Clicked rather famously. Two rule-breakers who come to mind are Fred Frank, Senior Managing Director at Lehman Brothers, and his wife, Mary Tanner, Managing Director at Lehman Brothers. Fred, a mega-merger mogul, and Mary, the first female partner at the firm, had successfully worked together, with a team of twenty reporting to them, before they decided to marry. Although it was against the rules of the investment banking house to have spouses working together, Fred's boss, Peter Cohen, said, "Whatever our policy was, it just changed." Proving our point that when you're worth it, the rules often bend. Or, conversely, that following the rules can be a framework for failure. What would be worse for a corporation? Having a Clickable team continue on or disrupting it and having one partner go outside to a competing firm?

Words of wisdom can come from someone close to you (see "ClickGuides: Mentoring") or occasionally from something you overhear or read that just Clicks. In "Why Follow the Trends," where we explain the importance of tracking the Trends, we've excerpted some of the letters and faxes that came flying in after our last book. We met Chip Conley, the owner of the Nob Hill Lambourne Hotel in San Francisco, who made a decision to let the BrainReserve Trends add a new dimension to his concept of comfort and service. Guests are offered business equipment/help as well as unusual nurturing opportunities: a health bar in every room, aromatherapy, yoga, and reflexology (foot massage).

What we're trying to do by detailing the Trends is to force you to think differently. Find new patterns in things. Question the obvious. Because Clicking is about breaking clichés, ripping apart refrigerator philosophy—comforting "words to live by" that don't necessarily hold true anymore. There used to be a very smart marketing person at BrainReserve who followed the teachings of a guru. At her apartment, she had notes taped on every mirror, saying, "Remember to Love." If it's in your heart, do you need a note?

Don't Believe Everything You've Believed
. . . or Click-out the Clichés

You might want to reconsider the adage, "All publicity is good publicity, as long as they spell your name right." In this age of ultra-muckraking "journalism," we can think of hundreds of people who would have been better off *not* having their names spelled correctly in the news. Certainly one of the most outdated catchphrases has to be, "Life begins at 40." This first surfaced in the early '30s in a book about "adult reorientation" that postulated that at age 40, "Work becomes easy and brief; play grows richer and longer; leisure lengthens." Nowadays, this description would be about life beginning at 85 or more.

Yet we can see an inherent value in "putting all your eggs in one basket." It's not that risky (who drops a basket?) and it's very tidy. It's also another way of saying "focus." We can also show you how Humpty Dumpty can be put together again. If you like to glue (as Lys does), it's possible to repair almost anything— from fragile eggshells to broken friendships to smashed business hopes.

Another cliché that we don't trust is "Tomorrow is the first day of the rest of your life." You don't always have to start from scratch. Some people who have Clicked have incorporated the worst of their past into their future. There can be something healthy, even cathartic, in the recognition of your nemesis. From going beyond facing your fear to actually embracing or living with it.

Nelson Mandela not only invited his jailer of twenty-six years to his inaugural ceremonies (shades of *Les Misérables*), but one week later, he also asked for a copy of the floor plan of the house where he had been incarcerated to use as the basic design for his new house. Coco Chanel, too, reached back to re-experience a painful memory from her past. Later on in life, when she was worldly and wealthy, she supposedly reconstructed the austere bedroom she occupied while growing up in a convent orphanage. Maybe that's where both Mandela and Chanel learned to Click through adversity.

Of course, at the heart of the Clicking message are the Brain-Reserve Trends. The Trends are what are shaping our society and what will shape the future. *You can't Click on yesterday's news.* Each Trend chapter will show you what others who are on the front lines are doing now as well as present new ideas of what needs to be done.

Neither life nor the Trends have stood still in the few years since *The Popcorn Report.* We've refocused the Cocooning Trend from being a cozy snuggled-up at home to being as scared-as-a-hare-in-a-chair, and fortifying our armored home.

We're reporting on the new Trend of Icon Toppling, which documents the anti-big feeling (fear and loathing) that's going on in the world today.

We delve into the fascinating Trend called Anchoring, a spiritual exploration in which we ground ourselves by looking back at the past—to prepare for the millennium and beyond.

We identified another new Trend, FemaleThink, which is important to business planning. FemaleThink explains the very different way women see, hear, sense, want, approach, view, and purchase things. Women are familial and process-interested, while most men are hierarchical and action-oriented. Because men and women are basically so different, we're offering a simple, but shocking theory: Market to them differently.

There are various ways women cope with this inherent difference. Some fight it, some join it. For instance, columnist Liz Smith talked about her "So That's It" enlightenment of Clicking when she overcame a mind barrier as a young woman in the man's world of early television. "I was a struggling hardworking production assistant, a 'good right arm,' in the old days of NBC-TV. I remember studying the faces of these dynamic men whenever I, Liz, had to tell them that one of their impossible demands was, indeed, impossible. And then one day, I Clicked. I was being part of the problem, not the solution. From then on, I began to really *try* to do the impossible. With this Click, I began to climb steadily. Every job advanced me, every experience helped me." And today, her "good right arm," Saint Clair Pugh, wordsmith and games-master, continues to help Lizzie Click.

Many of the men and women we interviewed gave us a rarely talked-about slant on success—that it's not always a steady uphill climb. In a chapter called "Zero-to-Hero: Clicking Through Failure and Success," we've documented many who started up the ladder, Clicked, and then crashed back on their collective bottoms—only to brush themselves off and start another business, another relationship, another venture. Barry Diller summed it up succinctly, without whining or blaming, when QVC lost the bid for Paramount: "Our current position demands brevity: They won. We lost. Next." And if the Next Attempt didn't Click (in spite of trial and error, error, error), somehow they found the drive to try, try, try again. Sometimes, life is about making tough choices or taking a big risk.

If anything, this success-failure-success syndrome means we need to erase any old mindsets about careers-for-life. And concentrate on the new concept of Re-Careering (see "Careers and Clicking"). According to the U.S. Bureau of Labor Statistics, most Americans will probably have three careers in their lifetimes. When you think about being in an unClick job, you need to unStick. In our neck of the woods (and ocean), a perfect example of a three-career person (who may even go on to four) is handsomely rugged Paul F. Rickenbach Jr. of East Hampton, Long Island (both my weekend place and Lys's home turf). Even though he gave us this humble quote, "I think I've Clinked more times than I've Clicked," still he went from fourteen years in the Village Police Department to top estate management to be elected mayor of one of the highest-profile little towns in this country.

Clicking is also about timing (see "ClickTime"). Or taking advantage of a coincidence. Think about Fran Drescher, the creator and star of the hit television show "The Nanny." Apparently, no one wanted to take a chance on the scratchy, nasal-voiced, Queens-accented, chutzpah-driven actress, until she spotted the president of CBS Entertainment on her flight to London. Not one to let a golden opportunity slip through her fingers, Fran sat next to him and chatted nonstop across the Atlantic. Click.

Another chapter is concerned with Kids and Clicking. How to guide your little ones on the right path for the next decade. It's time to examine the necessity of the obligatory college route, in light of certain success stories of the '90s. Did you know that Steve Jobs was so bright that they let him attend Stanford engineering classes when he was still in high school? Then one time, when he was tinkering with integrated circuits in his family's garage, his father supposedly gave him an ultimatum: Make something salable or get a job. Two months later, the first Apple computer was sold and the computer industry was set on fire. Bill Gates is a college dropout (Harvard). You know the rest.

We have also looked inward in a chapter called "HadTo[3]: Visionary Clicking." This is about people who were driven to do something for the outer good. Opera star Jessye Norman talked about taking the ultimate responsibility for one's own life, about bringing honesty and commitment to whatever one does. "Even if one takes advice, everyone needs to realize ultimately that this is your life, this is your decision. You just have to be confident in what you have to contribute—and have faith that you can make a real contribution." Jessye went on to make a very strong point about where she derives some of her strength: "There is no future in selfishness. We can only be successful if we are willing to make an investment in something outside of oneself and one's own interests. Because I grew up in rural Georgia, I understand the importance of breathing fresh air. Therefore, I support the Fresh Air Fund. It's so important to give back. In order not to become overwhelmed by the needs, you need to find your own niche. Certain things become priority: AIDS, education, children, the homeless—they're a part of my life." On Clicking, Jessye pointed out, "I can recognize someone who's Clicked by their body language. If they enter a room openly vs. sneaking into it. And it doesn't matter how old they are. My brother George's godson, Josh, is only four, but you can already tell that he's comfortable with life."

Feeling comfortable with yourself and your surroundings is the essence of Clicking. How you get there reminds us of a questioning quote taken from everyone's favorite, *The Tao of Pooh*:

> *How can you get very far,*
> *If you don't know Who You Are?*
> *How can you do what you ought,*
> *If you don't know What You've Got?*
> *And if you don't know Which To Do*
> *Of all the things in front of you,*
> *Then what you'll have when you are through*
> *Is just a mess without a clue*
> *Of all the best that can come true*
> *If you know What and Which and Who.*

This book is dedicated to nothing less than helping you Click into the What and Which and Who.

So, brush your fingertips against your shirt. Give the dial a spin, listen to the tumblers as they whirl. Pay attention. It's your future *firma*.

Let's begin it.

FUTURIST, CLICK THYSELF

Sometimes I feel like a figment of my own imagination.
—LILY TOMLIN

"It's all in my head. And sometimes something just clicks . . .
sometimes you just know. Know what? I asked. If it's a fit . . ."
—SUSANNA MOORE, *IN THE CUT*

f I had to describe myself in a Click exercise (as you should
do), I'd write down a summary of who I think I am (in
essence) and what has led me, Click-wise, to today. As founder
and head of my company, BrainReserve, I get to work on diverse
and challenging projects for clients, all based on a mixture of
ideas, societal trends, and a vision of the future. Then I have the
fun of airing my views and predictions on television and in the
press. And of giving my seminar, TrendView, to thousands of audiences all over America and Canada, and frequently in far-off
countries around the globe. I've finally moved from my first studio apartment to live and work in a townhouse, and retreat on
weekends to a tiny, rose-covered cottage on a serene swan pond in
East Hampton.

I have a warm, nurturing family of friends. My sister,
Mechele, is the President of BrainReserve, so I get to see her
every day. My very best friend, Lys, understands my sense of
humor when we talk (constantly), work together, and shop, and

has the ability to capture my true voice when she writes. I have the best little character dog in the world, Miyake, a dynamic black and white Japanese Chin from the north of Holland who was born on my exact same Taurus birthday, May 11.

I've Clicked into our culture and become what I've always wanted to be. But it wasn't always a fit. In fact, far from it.

The first full-color picture I can remember from my childhood is of my maternal grandparents, Rose and Isaac (whom I adored), standing on a Manhattan pier and waving farewell to my mother and me. We were headed for Shanghai, China, on the *Queen Mary*, to join my father, who was stationed over there as a Captain in the Army's Criminal Investigation Division (pre-CIA). My mother, a working lawyer, was not thrilled that her life was being uprooted. And me? No one had asked, but I wasn't overjoyed either.

China was not exactly heaven for little girls, and certainly not for Jewish-American little girls. (Even today, it's not a culture that reveres women: witness the 400,000 Chinese baby girls abandoned at orphanages each year.) And, added to my run of "luck," the only safe school (less chance of kidnapping) was at the Convent of the Sacred Heart, where I was, to put it mildly, "nun" too familiar with the daily litany.

This feeling of being displaced didn't disappear, even when we returned to New York several years later. Because of my travels, I felt different from my classmates in P.S. 63, and because of the strict and excellent education in Shanghai, I was totally bored in class. I had also developed a habit at Sacred Heart of crossing myself and genuflecting in front of every church I passed, which so horrified my Orthodox grandparents that my grandmother immediately enrolled me in a five-day-a-week Hebrew School. Instead of being allowed to run outside and play with the other kids, I had to go to "horrible-Hebrew."

I made it clear that I hated every moment of it. And in rebellion, I refused to learn Hebrew. In fact, the only time I was really happy was when I'd sit around with my grandparents and talk shop. They lived right above their small haberdashery store on Fifth Street and Second Avenue, where we'd spend endless hours discussing such matters as whether the windows were set up to maximize the attention of passersby (my first "positioning" lesson), how to improve sales, how to make sure the customers were satisfied, and how to earn their loyalty for life.

Shop talk is not exactly what turns on the average 12-year-old, but it felt right to me. My first Click. It's not surprising that I've chosen to live like my grandparents "above the shop," still debating the very same kinds of questions, still combining home and work and life.

But back to earlier times. No matter what, I always felt out-of-step with my own age group. Never in the right crowd, never in the right school. Not athletic or particularly popular. When my mother tried to help out, her good intentions almost guaranteed my sense of being a perennial outsider. Ignoring my pancake-flat feet and the curvy body shape I'd inherited from her side of the family, she decided that I should take ballet lessons—not from a local teacher, but from one of the country's best ballet companies. With the tenacity of a Jack Russell terrier, she begged, bothered, and cajoled my way into the Metropolitan Opera School of Ballet. A perfect place for future prima ballerinas—but not for me. Visualize this terrible moment: a Russian teacher, brandishing a thin rod, practically foaming at the mouth at my very unswanlike attempts to go *en pointe*. Classical ballet was a study in classical humiliation.

It seemed that life was a safe that I was never going to crack. My mother's next bright idea for developing my social skills was through piano lessons. But by now, I had learned some subtle tactics—and distracted my piano teacher with some of the Talmudic questions I'd overheard in Hebrew class (a lesson learned here— good things *can* come out of bad experiences). It was so successful that she frequently didn't notice how little I'd practiced. Although my music skills stayed around zero, my talking and thinking skills had improved immensely.

By the time I'd reached my early teens, I had turned into the '60s version of today's computer nerd (in those days, a "beatnik"). I was suddenly cool, hanging around the fountain in Washington Square Park, playing bongo drums. I'd perfected a serious and dramatic look, dressed from head-to-toe in black, with kohl-black eyeliner and my hair pulled tightly back in a long braid. In fact, no one saw me smile for the next five years.

It was the perfect attitude for my next stage: acting. It seemed to me that actors had an ideal profession. They had writers to tell them what to say, directors to show them where to stand, and a script to turn them into "someone else." And, of course, acting would put me where I wanted to be—right at center stage.

At age 13, I decided to apply to the High School of Performing Arts for their drama department. Since I was competing for a place against kids with impressive theatrical résumés, they turned me down flat. (Did you ever see the movie *Fame* or the subsequent TV show? It was based on the show-biz kids at Performing Arts.) Undaunted, I applied again a year later. This time, I partially Clicked, but instead of the coveted drama courses, they admitted me into a newly formed department of playwriting. Still, I learned voice and diction (getting rid of any New York accent). Later on, this turned out to be important for my future Trend seminar.

When it came time to leaf through college catalogs, what I dreamed about was heading far from home to some place with ivy-covered towers and small-town movie theaters. In reality, my middling-to-minus-C average landed me exactly four blocks from home—at my parents' alma mater, New York University. They had both gone to law school there and hoped I would follow in their footsteps. However, when I was 19, my father tragically died in an automobile accident on the Taconic Parkway. Besides taking away my mentor and best friend, this life-catastrophe abruptly put an end to our endless discussions, our favorite being one on how to pull off the perfect crime (he was a criminal lawyer, well-known for his pro bono work). Any plans I had about studying law were squashed, and to help me get through the rest of my college days, I fell back on my old "piano teacher" trick: diverting my professors' minds to other things: questions, hypotheses, arguments.

Instead of staying on in school for some advanced degree, I took a detour. My steady boyfriend was Alan Kupchick (even then I encouraged another last name for him: Kelwyn), who had just started out as an art director at Grey Advertising (he's now president of the L.A. office). In my quest to be his perfect "mate," I decided to learn about what he did and signed up at the School of Visual Arts for a course in advertising concepts with one of the best copywriters around, Frankie Cadwell. Almost immediately afterward, she guided me to my first job: copy chief of a small agency, Salit & Garlanda.

This small step parlayed into a self-changing leap for me. My boss, Gene (Gino Constantino) Garlanda, had a profound influence on my life. He showed me how to write advertising-ese—strong, sharp, riveting—and how to recognize really good design. He's since gone on to Click as a serious and deeply funny photographer—of such things as defunct handball courts; people's inner spaces; and his wife, Marcia, nude on hotel/motel beds around the world. More important for my immediate life, Gene gave me the nickname of "Popcorn." One day at work, he simply decided that it was easier on his Italian tongue and more playful than saying "Plotkin."

This was a Click. Suddenly I had a name that fit me: Fun. Funny. Funky. Alive. Weird. Liberating. Unforgettable. What more could I have asked for? Although there were a few detractors (including my then-therapist), who tried to convince me that it was too "kooky," this time I didn't listen.

My fledgling job in advertising was the first of four. I was actually fired from the next one (for writing poetry instead of copy) and the one after that (for wearing a rabbit-fur micro-miniskirt to a maxi-client meeting). But my fourth job, at Smith/Greenland, was an unqualified success. In retrospect, it seems perfectly logical that promotions came swiftly and I was given the title of Creative Director by the age of 26. I loved my bosses (Leo Greenland, a master of PR, and Marty Smith, who showed me a company can be run creatively), and my clients loved me for creative-directing award-winning ads, such as the two mansions with "Can I borrow a cup of Johnnie Walker Black" and "As long as you're climbing your way to the top, it helps to have a taste of what's up there" (both for Johnnie Walker Black) and "Own a Bottle" (for Tanqueray Gin). I had lots of good support from my creative partner, Stuart Pittman, and a Creative Department of twenty talents (four of whom later started their own agencies). I thought I had Clicked at last.

But one day, after an executive roller-coaster ride (would I be promoted to president? would I not?), I burned out of agency life. It was too compartmentalized, too departmentalized. After those informal "Mom and Pop" years with my grandparents, I craved my own small shop. It was 1974, and I and my creative partner from the agency, Stuart Pittman, opened BrainReserve—even though we didn't have a clue what a "BrainReserve" was or would be or could be. What we knew was that clients needed future-supported, long-term strategies rather than a series of quick-fix commercials. And that it was far better to solve tough problems by brainstorming with the smartest creatives (thus the name, BrainReserve) than alone. So we set out to sell our brainpower.

Looking back now, we could be a case history for How Not To Start A Business. Although we were smart, enthusiastic, and reluctantly willing to struggle, we didn't have a business plan . . . and we didn't have any business. We couldn't get a marketing assignment, because we had no track record in marketing. And we couldn't afford to staff up until we were reasonably established.

The old Catch-22.

Determined to succeed, our three-person company (Stuart, me, and a third, Ginny Danner, who kept us organized) decided to think big and act big. Sometimes you simply have to project yourself into your own future. When one senior VP of marketing from a large company asked to check out our staff and tour our offices before he would assign us a project, we instantaneously created a "Virtual office," well ahead of its time. Our real offices were located in a ground floor professional suite at 3 E. 66th St., but we often rented the impressive Gothic, wood-paneled library in the Lotos Club next door whenever we needed a conference room.

This time, we rented the whole top floor of rooms; brought in desks, typewriters, drawing tables, telephones connected to nowhere (we crossed our fingers that the client wouldn't ask to make a call); and peppered the place with freelancers and friends. Even though we didn't get that assignment, the story had an eventual happy ending in my mind. The visualization of what BrainReserve "could be" came true. We were motivated to sign a lease for "non-boutique-y" office space on 57th and Madison and staffed up with qualified people. Now, twenty years later, the core of us are in a limestone building of our own, just two blocks from that club. Best of all, the phones are very much connected, and even better, they're busily ringing.

"If the vision is there, the means will follow" was the valuable lesson I learned from that makeshift episode. And I began to understand that if my company, BrainReserve, was going to make it in marketing, I was going to have to make it by marketing myself. It occurred to me that I needed to figure out what was going to happen and how to base my business on it. To find the person I needed to become. To Click into my own best future.

What happened next would appear to fall under the category

of a lucky break, but it really came from that tenacity gene I got from my mother (also a Taurus, 5/18). Send a letter, call, send a follow-up letter, call again and again—until someone listens. Finally, about six years after we first opened, our name was getting some recognition and people had begun to spread the good word. Then Isadore Barmash, the summer replacement for advertising columnist Phil Dougherty of the *New York Times,* called to say that he was intrigued by the names Popcorn and Brain-Reserve, and wanted to set up an interview. Pandemonium and panic set in. What should we do? What should we say?

I rang up my friends and family, casting about for the way to maximize this tremendous opportunity. My thoughts ran like this: "If we get a favorable mention in that column, we'd be made." (Today, I'd phrase it differently: "We would Click.") But there were no major success stories to brag about. Nothing concrete that we could point to and say, "Here's a product we've launched, a campaign we've developed." Since I couldn't impress him by spinning tales of recent triumphs, I decided to describe what we talk about every day at our office. Predictions of *what* we thought was going to happen and *why.* It was as simple as that: a big, beautiful Click.

"Since we'd be cutting back on salt for health reasons," I told him, "we'd be looking for alternatives—say, fresh herbs and spicier foods." "Flashy American cars would come back," I said "to replace the bland, boxy look." "With an aging population, gray will be more than okay; even beyond that, middle age and older will be viewed as sexy." "Fidelity will be popular again" (remember, this was 1980, pre-AIDS explosion). "And there'll be a renewed interest in the family" (pre–Republican values–push). Instead of writing me off as a "flake," Barmash was a first-class reporter who wrote it right. Furthermore, the article served as a benchmark, proof positive that everything we predicted happened.

BrainReserve was recognized as a futurist marketing (or a marketing futurist) company, and I was its fearless leader. It had Clicked. And I consider that I've finally Clicked. After so many scared, friendless, uncomfortable, hard years, I had figured out what I could do that was unique: channeling problems into solutions through a future vision. I'd Clicked into the right combination—out of my cage, out of my rage, into a new age.

The next forward giant step came out of a New Products assignment we were hired for by the gutsy, creative Tony Adams, then Research Director at Campbell's. Assignments like this can be sheer pleasure, a chance to build on our future projections of what Americans would be buying/eating three to five years down the road. Lys came up with an astounding one hundred viable new products. But instead of just handing over an alphabetized copy of these original ideas (too many to grasp), we figured out a way of grouping them into Trends. Each Trend section was organized with a set of icons depicting (1) the kind of person the product would be targeted to, (2) what lifestyle each group led, and (3) what occasions the product would serve. In other words, we linked each new product idea to a specific societal movement that we believed would continue to grow over the next ten years.

The people at Campbell's gave us high marks. They said that it was the first time any marketing company had ever put new products into the perspective of the consumer of the future. At that presentation, BrainReserve's TrendBank was born. The Trends served as a platform to leap from, creating a fusion between what is now and what will be.

Because Trends never end (they mutate, snake, spin, metamorphose), neither can the quest for Clicking ever stop. Every time we meet someone with an interesting job or slant on life, we ask him or her to become part of BrainReserve, in an informal way, by joining our TalentBank. So far, more than 5,000 "talents" have filled out brief questionnaires or "bios" that are entered into our main computer, so that we can readily tap into each person's unique perspective. As my company evolved, so did the definition of who and what we are. We're constantly round-tabling to reposition ourselves. Over the years, we've gone from being a Think Tank to a Marketing Consultancy to a "Small, Caring Clinic for Future Thinking" (thought up by our former New Biz whiz, Nadja Bacardi). At the BrainReserve of today, we've changed the way we describe ourselves, adopting the motto of "Cool, Hot, Visionary and Fearless." That's what it takes for us to stay on top of the Trends.

If you pay attention to what's Clicking in the Trends today, you'll learn ways to profit from them tomorrow. Pay special attention, too, to the personal anecdotes of the many people we've interviewed who have Clicked. In doing this, you'll pick up the common theme of the book: If I Clicked and they Clicked, so can you. If my company has Clicked, so can yours. Our goal is to help you find your own best Future. And that Future starts now.

PART TWO

TRENDS

FROM THE BRAINRESERVE TRENDBANK

Imagine a language with *only* a future tense. That's TrendTalk.
—*THE POPCORN REPORT*

A brief and handy reference guide to BrainReserve's 16 Trends so that you can quickly understand the essence of each one—and check this list whenever you have a question about a Trend's meaning anywhere throughout this book— or throughout your life.

Cocooning: The stay-at-home Trend, reflecting our strong desire to build soft and cozy nests in order to protect ourselves from the harsh, unpredictable realities of the outside world.

Clanning: The inclination to join up, belong to, hang out with groups of like kinds, providing a secure feeling that our own belief systems will somehow be validated by consensus.

Fantasy Adventure: As a break from modern tensions, we actively seek excitement in basically risk-free adventures, whether it be via travel, food, or Virtual Reality.

Pleasure Revenge: Consumers, tired of all the rules and regulations, want to cut loose and have secret bacchanals with a bevy of forbidden fruits.

Small Indulgences: Stressed-out from ever-increasing expenses, consumers are finding ways to reward themselves with affordable luxuries.

Anchoring: A new Trend that tracks the recent phenomenon of reaching back to our spiritual roots, taking what was comforting from the past in order to be securely anchored in the future.

Egonomics: In a direct reaction to the sterile computer era, we are looking for new ways to make more personal statements. Thus, businesses that market to the "I" and provide exceptional service should excel.

FemaleThink: A Trend that reflects a new set of business and societal values, encouraging us to shift marketing consciousness from the traditional goal-oriented, hierarchical models to the more caring and sharing, familial ones.

Mancipation: A NewThink for men that goes beyond being "strictly business" and warmly embraces the freedom of being an individual.

99 Lives: A new look at the modern motto of "Too Fast a Pace, Too Little Time," which forces us all to assume multiple roles in order to cope with busy, high-tech lives.

Cashing Out: Working women and men, questioning the intrinsic value of a high-powered career, are opting for more fulfillment in a simpler way of living.

Being Alive: There's a growing awareness that a new concept of "wellness" can add generous years of good health, giving us an overall better quality to our lives.

Down-Aging: Nostalgia for a carefree childhood lets us introduce a new sense of lightness into our often-too-serious adult lives.

Vigilante Consumer: A scanning of the various ways the frustrated, often angry consumer can manipulate the marketplace through pressure, protest, and politics.

Icon Toppling: A new socioquake has transformed mainstream America and the world, forcing us to question and often reject our monuments of business/government, the long-accepted "pillars of society."

S.O.S. (Save Our Society): In order to protect our endangered planet, we must rediscover a social conscience based on a necessary blend of ethics, passion, and compassion.

WHY FOLLOW THE TRENDS?

We must use time as a tool, not as a couch.
—JOHN F. KENNEDY

The future is called "perhaps."
—TENNESSEE WILLIAMS

People who Click are naturally on-Trend. Their ideas, their actions, their passions, and their pursuits fall effortlessly and target What People Want. For marketers, Trend knowledge is invaluable. To get to where the consumers are just before they get there, offering these consumers what they didn't even know they wanted, spells success. In reading the Trends, you'll start to see that there are patterns to follow, ideas and suggestions to aid you in finding a new Click profession, a new Click product, a service that will Click into a bigger business or more satisfying life.

By charting the 16 Trends that are driving America and the rest of the consumer world, it's possible to gauge in advance if something will Click . . . or not Click. Note: We're constantly being asked if BrainReserve's Trends apply to everyone, everywhere. The answer is a qualified no. If a region or part of the world is under severe financial hardship, and people have no money to buy what they would like, they can't be considered an active and viable part of the Trendscape, the consumer scene.

Otherwise, we feel comfortable in saying that the Trends are not only national, but global in scope.

Using the Trends as a screen (and as a screen *test*) can save you from false starts, misguided attempts, or outright failures in whatever venture you have in mind. The strongest way for us to make the point of exactly why *you* should follow the Trends is to give you examples of how others have taken our Trends and used them as a jumping-off place . . . or confirmation. If you read each of the Trends carefully, you'll be able to zero in on the relevant details that make up the larger picture of society today. And find a fit or an expansion of any of your plans.

Tracking the Trends can guide you both in your life and in your business.

Just visualize being on a plane that's soaring higher and higher. As it lifts off, you begin to get a picture of how the nearby streets and houses, then the towns and farms, finally the bigger spread, all relate to one another. A true bird's-eye view. The Trends will build up a painting of the landscape of the future. Many times when I explain it this way, clients and seminar attendees Click into a clearer understanding of what we're doing. Telling me: "Although the Trends have felt comfortable and familiar, I never understood how they fit together and how many of them we're living today."

Taken together, the trends give you a clear profile of the marketplace, both what's starting to happen now and what will be happening in the near and far future. They serve as early predictors of how people are feeling, what new products and services will be sought after (as well as which ones will be rejected), and where any present need-gaps are located. Success is, for the most part, not just an accident or a matter of blind "luck," but a result of having a clear picture of the future.

We often are asked about the difference between a Trend and a fad. If you're going to launch an entire business based on an idea, it's important to understand the distinction. A fad is a flash in the pan, a quick trick you can turn to make your money and run. Pogs are a fad. These milk-bottle tops made a fun game, but kids collected them, played with them, and tired of them—all too quickly. They were too mass-produced to become collectibles. Stores that bought heavy inventories of them are sitting with tons of the colorful stacks. Also, had you banked a long-term business on signing up celebrities specifically to feature them on Pogs, you would probably have lost your investment.

Yogurt makers, too, were a fleeting fad. You could have leaped to the conclusion that because people are concerned about their health and natural goodness, making yogurt at home would be an ongoing project. But you have to add in the impact of the 99 Lives Trend (our busy-lives Trend) to see that it wouldn't work. Few people have time to make their own yogurt culture when a store down the block sells every kind of variation of yogurt, from mango/banana/passion fruit to low-fat coffee with chunky granola.

Fashion merchandising is notorious for following fads. Neon colors are in/out; wide lapels, wide ties, and bell-bottoms redux and redux. However, if you have the wherewithal to turn your manufacturing/marketing capabilities around on a dime and get out as quickly as you got in, it's possible to make a fast buck (or a fast million) on a fad.

On the other hand, Trends are big and broad. This may sound Forrest Gump–ish, but it's the easiest way to describe Trends. Although they start off as small seedlings (we call them Drifts), scattered here and there, they have a way of gathering strength until they make up a whole forest. Unshakable by the winds, impossible to ignore. And when you're in the midst of these towering Trend trees, if you were there early, you can say smugly, "Of course, I saw them growing." Conversely, if you arrived late, you'll probably say, as many critics do, "How obvious." Timing makes the difference between reading the Trends for pleasure . . . or for profit.

For example, in 1981, we saw Cocooning coming. Although it was the era of sex, drugs, and rock 'n' roll, we believed that the future consumer would be yearning to curl up in bed with a friendly pizza, raise a couple of kids, maybe even start a business at home. Many laughed. The few who listened immediately took action to get ready for future Cocooners. Some smart folks in the food service business reconfigured their fancy restaurants into family-style cafes/pubs, and the even smarter ones began offering home delivery of dinners. Others designed home theaters with larger-screen televisions and state-of-the-art music systems; or put out a shingle for home office design; or got interested in upstart personal computer companies and started investigating the possibilities of shopping online.

To test if you're on-Trend (or if a business idea is right), our rule of thumb is that four or more Trends have to apply, have to make a "fit." Otherwise you might be picking up on a fad, or reaching a too-small segment of the marketplace. For example, if you decide that you love planting and gardening more than you like your job of sitting in a bank all day, try testing the concept of growing herbs as a business—against the current Trends.

We're not talking peanuts here. Gardening has long gone beyond the small-town-ish, flowered-hat clubs to Baby Boomers' obsession, big-time. The National Gardening Association estimates that more than 75 million people are involved in mulching and mudding the soil, many in the highly marketable, college-educated, 30–49 age group. Literally hundreds of new businesses have been started around the concept of general gardening: greenhouses, tools, clothing, composters, birdhouses, grape arbors, follies, and so on.

But let's concentrate on the business of raising herbs. Fresh, green, and healthy herbs are now being sold in most supermarkets, year-round, in small clumps or packaged in clear bags. Some catalogs, such as *Gardener's Eden*, offer wreaths and kitchen bouquets of herbs to dry on your door, display on your kitchen walls, or hang from the beams of your house. Or there's the other route of dried herbs, either whole or crumbled—or distilled and essenced for the oils. Herbs are not just culinary accompaniments, but are also considered a bedrock of the miracle-growing area of holistic medicines (as we predicted, "You'll be buying herbs to cleanse and purify your body").

The Trends that support a business in herbs are Cocooning (people staying home, improving their nest, weekend chefs); Fantasy Adventure (herbs are still considered somewhat exotic, nonthreatening outdoor adventure); Cashing Out (a retreat to being countrified, a quest for the simple life, realness); Being Alive (herbs are good for you, part of growing interest in holistic alternatives); Anchoring (a return to spirituality and a knowledge of the past, other cultures' reliance on herbology); and a less important fit with Egonomics (herbs can make things individualistic); FemaleThink (women have always cleverly used them for cooking, perfuming, and curing ills); Small Indulgences (they add something nice for little pocket change); and finally, S.O.S. (environmentally correct).

With just that amount of Trend analysis, you could determine that if you ran a herb business right, it could Click. You could sell flats of herbs in season and fresh bunches to restaurants/general stores/farm stands or mail-order them by Fed Ex; freeze-dry them for yearlong sales; or design and make herbal papers, books, and assorted paraphernalia. We've seen beautiful chintz-covered small pillows called Sweet Dreams by Harvey & Strait, which contain "a sleep inducing mixture of herbs and spices to ward off insomnia and cheer the soul." Or another pillow idea of almost-sheer silk with golden tassel edges and an aromatic herb filling. To push the idea even further, you could set up a brainstorming session to come up with new uses for traditional herbs or whole new directions to explore for a unique business.

Following a slightly different course of greenery action, a teacher in Houston started growing a vegetable garden with his fifth-grade class as an exercise in both working together and economic feasibility. It was such a hit that they've launched the idea into a full-blown organic vegetable business.

Or how about two Casher Outers from urban madness, Pamela Serure and Nancy Sorkow, who started a small organic juice company in Bridgehampton, New York, with a great name, Get Juiced. They quickly branched out from a delivery system of expensive fresh juices into a three-pronged operation: opening a chain of retail stores with juice/elixir bars; selling their blends of organic juices wholesale; and the one with the biggest potential, offering a body-detox-cleansing program, a three-day $99 "Juice Fast" kit that anyone, anywhere, can use (and rumor has it, which Donna Karan, Barbra Streisand, and Christy Brinkley go on regularly). Imitators have sprung up, ones copying the juice system (sincere flattery or business smarts?), but none has accomplished the total health package. And Pamela will be coming out with her own Get Juiced, get-well book soon (for more info. 800-537-7010).

Close to this is another idea that uses fresh juices but adds an extra-special overlay of health benefits. A concerned company named Odwalla from California had originally brainstormed with twelve women to hear about real grown-up concerns: osteoporosis, PMS, menopause. With this knowledge, it created a preservative-free drink, Femme Vitale, blending five fresh fruit juices with such beneficial things as iron, calcium, B vitamins, herbs, and dong quai (a Chinese herb with mild estrogen properties). The products are going cross-country, sent into stores in their own cold cases. Wouldn't it be great to find them in the Gap or Barnes & Noble bookstores?

There's also a small company called Juice Plus that gives you fruits and vegetables in capsules. It's a healthy patented process that captures five servings of the essence of the whole foods—an answer to those who hate to clean their juicers. As daily preventive insurance, you can take a fruit cap in the morning, a veggie cap at night.

We're mentioning these New Age juice concepts to bring up another point about the consumer Trends: If you read the Trend directions and come up with an inventive new product idea, chances are, someone else somewhere will be thinking along the same lines. Maybe not exactly the same product at exactly the same time, but close enough for comfort.

We had coined a new word, "Foodaceuticals," in *The Popcorn Report*: "Food combined with drugs, 'foodaceuticals,' will enhance the dynamics of the body and the mind. Foods prescribed in doses, foods to keep you alert and younger." We went on to say that the edges will be blurred between drug therapy and nutrition, "daily-dose soups or drinks will give you prescribed doses of anti-oxidant beta-carotenes, or therapeutic doses of anti-disease nutritives" and predicted, "Engineered-for-health foods are the future."

Those words led to working with Dr. Scott Connelly, a nutritional expert and the inventor of MET-Rx, who came to Brain-Reserve with Blade Thomas and his marketing team. At the first meeting, one of his executives mentioned, "It's as if you dreamed us." Their nutrient-dense, low-fat products were already labeled, "Engineered Foods . . . for the Best Shape of Your Life." Their new advanced nutrient bar packs vitamins, minerals, and trace elements, including 120% RDA calcium, making it a great way for women to get that much-needed bone strengthener.

Actually, we had outlined ways in *The Popcorn Report* to market "foods" to different segments of the population and then some. "Egonomics hasn't hit the food arena yet—but it will. Customized food will be next. It will be recognized that your body's nutritional needs are different from your husband's. You'll be serving foods for mood—to reduce stress, enhance energy, induce sleep. A certain bread to quiet you; a special beef to stimulate you.

Foods by age, by stage of life—teen menus, menopause meals. Traditionals/medicinals—to aid breathing, to boost you when you're nursing or have PMS. Serious foods. Survival foods. Healing foods. Soon to be available for you and your family." Still viable, still waiting.

So, now, we'd like to ask: Who will be the first to create a bag of chips or crackers with healthy additions? Targeted to specific age groups and their needs, from toddlers to elders. This would be the first step in answering one of our eternal marketing questions: Why, if so many people like salty tastes as well as sweet, do so many things come in dessert flavors? Why are all frozen ice pops sweet? Instead of marshmallow fudge or cherry coconut, why not frozen V-8 on a stick? Why are most yogurts fruit-based with sweet globs of jam? Why not copy the Mediterranean taste of cool cucumber/mint or crunchy vegetable yogurts for lunch or a snack? And those diet shakes that are a substitute for meals. Why should you have to drink a sweet chocolate, vanilla, or strawberry dinner? Why not tomato-basil, herbal chicken, or wild mushroom, all closer to regular soup flavors? We're still waiting for some Trend-savvy on these ideas. Anyone?

In looking back over some of the 40,000 letters, faxes, and phone calls received from readers of *The Popcorn Report* we found that the Trends inspired many budding entrepreneurs who were on the brink of "should I, should I not?" One letter came from Donald Gammon of Andover, Massachusetts, who wrote: "Here are the results of you as a catalyst. After a series of 'Aha!' reactions in me, I'm making all-natural, personal care products for the hotel industry, called Nautilus Naturals. They're based on water hyacinths from Florida and I'm donating some of the profits back to protect the environment."

Besides the Trends, we had peppered the book with some ideas for new businesses based on Trend application. A well-thought-out letter came to BrainReserve from a reader who totally grasped the concept of how to use the Trends. In fact, Daniel Houck of Baltimore, who had just finished graduate school, even volunteered additional new business ideas:

> At one point in your book, you gave brief examples of possible companies or ideas for existing ones, and asked us to think about more. I have. Here are a few:

- Swatch watch: customized individual watches you could
  design on a computer at in-store kiosks or Swatch boutiques.
  Trends: Egonomics, Small Indulgences, Down-Aging, even
  Cocooning, if done online.
- Speedy Muffler/Jiffy Lube: why not do this at night? Marketed toward suburban communities—you drop off your
  car, get a mini-van shuttle home. In the morning, the car is
  magically at your door, having been worked on and
  returned while you slept. Trends: 99 Lives, Cocooning, Egonomics.
- Sony: why not design stereos with extraordinary sound that
  can be controlled with just two buttons or slides, for those of
  us who do not want to take the time to learn all the complicated functions. Or, we'll go to Sony stores where they'll evaluate our listening habits, tastes (lots of bass, etc.) and they'll
  pre-program the system geared to our preferences. At home,
  we'll push a single button or better yet, simply say "Stereo
  On." Trends: Egonomics, Cocooning, 99 Lives.

Now, that's a person who understands how the Trends can
put an idea in a larger context.

One reader specifically focused in on the chapter, "Ask Not
What Your Consumer Can Do for You, but What You Can Do
for Your Consumer" in which we had talked about having to go
beyond packaging, beyond style, beyond hype, to build a business. This concept applies directly to those people who own
stores where the traffic has slipped because of the many people
staying at home (Cocooning) and mail-ordering by phone, TV,
or computer. This small-appliance store owner wrote that he
was trying specific "Cocoon Penetration Systems," such as cross-
marketing with other local stores (delivering homemade bread
with every toaster oven; a basket of cleansing products with
every washer), personalizing his service, offering routine at-
home tune-ups to penetrate the Cocoon and earn customer loyalty.

A clever man named Jonathan Lewis remarked that he and
his two partners were very grateful to Lys and me. They had
since leveraged the Fantasy Adventure Trend into three successful restaurants, basing their concept on the Trend premise of
offering "an experience beyond dining." Jonathan had been

sparked by the specifics of what we wrote, "What is Fantasy Adventure exactly? It's vicarious escape through consumerism . . . a momentary, wild-and-crazy retreat from the world into an exotic flavor, a 'foreign' experience. . . . It's adventure-by-association . . ." All of this translated into action for Jonathan as he conceived of a Southern Florida restaurant, and called it Cafe Tu Tu Tango, which serves tantalizing *tapas* and is decorated with Latinesque props—a far cry from a traditional dining experience. With its crazy rhythms and witty fun, going to Tu Tu Tango is like dropping into a private party that happens every night.

Another thanks came from O. Alex Mandossian, COO of Rodell Research Inc. He sent us samples of his whitening toothpaste and mouthwash, called Supersmile. Very on-Trend (Being Alive, Small Indulgences, Fantasy Adventure/Wildering, 99 Lives). The products are made with Calprox, a non-invasive whitener, baking soda, and fluoride; no alcohol or sugar; and the packet the mouthwash comes in opens up as the cup (good for travel). His note said, "Thank you for teaching me simple ways to eliminate many frustrations and uncertainties in my business and personal life. I'm grateful for your work."

Brock Green took the time to describe his Trend-based concept, Designs for Education, for us in detail. "It's a marriage of capitalism and activism. We allow teenagers to design the clothes they wear and at the same time raise money to support the art programs in American schools." Sixty-five schools participated and entered 6,000 designs. The final selections were made into unusual, stylized T-shirts and sweats, sold through department stores (Dayton-Hudson, Macy's, etc.), and $1 per item was contributed back to the art/design programs in those schools. Trends? S.O.S. (doing good, cause marketing); Egonomics (personal clothes); Cashing Out (small business idea); and Fantasy Adventure (artistic, not run-of-mill). Very good Trend understanding.

The Trends can really help a person switch gears out of one profession into a better Click, or at least isolate a promising idea for the future. Barbara McQuiston, who works at Research & Development in the field of computers/engineering, told us: "Your book started me thinking in all other directions. For instance, after a long conversation with my son, I suddenly real-

ized that there were no good science magazines for children."
That's all it takes to Click into a new pathway.

Marsha Wagner from Minneapolis was inspired by a specific
idea in *The Popcorn Report*, in which we described a new profession called "Dream Architects: A new consulting business will
help individuals identify and implement their dream life. We'll
learn how to make our 'dreams come true' over short, medium,
or long periods of time, in business, the arts, sciences." She now
has a personal and career consulting company called Castle-
Visions (Making dreams come true), which does everything to
assist you on a new road to Clicking, from résumé writing to creatively helping you identify, clarify, and implement a change in
your life.

Kathy Barr-Pape, Director of Business Development for Best
Upon Request in Cincinnati, wrote, "You have guided us from
conception and continue to serve as a lighthouse as we continue
to evolve." This organization, a "task management" company,
was the first in the Midwest to combine concierge and personal
errand services for tenants and their employees in commercial
office buildings. The long-range plan is to roll out a national
network of service-based operations. The company's mission
echoes the Egonomics, Small Indulgences, and 99 Lives Trends,
"Everybody just wants a little attention, a little recognition" and
"Why not provide services in offices themselves? What we really
want is to buy back time."

Trends spark the not-for-profit area, too. Reverend Mark
Pranaitis of St. Fidelis Church in Chicago received the book as an
ordination present. "I could not help but think that these Trends
affect my church (and all religions). And I'm thinking how I can
make churchgoing more Fantasy Adventure or Small Indulgences." That's putting your faith in Trends. We don't know what
exactly was done, but can think of many suggestions, such as having foreign-theme suppers (Fantasy Adventure), keeping wool
shawls on hand for drafty days (Small Indulgences), making more
home calls (Cocooning), offering yoga or meditation classes
(Anchoring), organizing a Clean-Up-Our-Neighborhood Day
(S.O.S.), and so on.

Nowadays, one question that slightly mistrusting or cynical
reporters love to ask is: "Can you personally start a Trend?" I usually shake my head and say, "I suppose it's possible for one human

being to start a fad, but certainly not a Trend. One could influence 400,000 people to buy a hula hoop, but when I coined the word 'Cocooning' and outlined the concept, did I make 250 million people suddenly stay home?"

We believe that you can't create a Trend, you can only observe it. And you can't change a Trend, you can only change people's minds about believing in it. Trends are lines of energy. At BrainReserve, we isolate these lines to make them easier to identify, but each person is affected, in some way, by all the Trends.

The art is in Trend-predicting, scanning today's culture for signs of the future. The seeds are everywhere—you just have to open your eyes and look: in the restaurants, bars, and clubs; on the streets; in the music we're listening to; in the magazines we're reading; in the television programs we're watching. Watch what government is telling us and what business is selling us.

In the early '80s, when we first started telling corporate America about this new disease called AIDS and what it would mean to our mindset and to our world, they snickered nervously in disbelief. The same group has now been breaking into guffaws at the mention of Virtual Reality and our belief that there will be a VR room in every American home by the early 2000s. We're so sure about the Trends and the future that we can now say, "Wait and see."

As for the Trends we wrote about in *The Popcorn Report,* we have a large category that we refer to as "We Told You So." We're not telling you this to blow our own horns but as a reminder that what sounds outlandish in the Trend chapters could be just around the corner. And ready for you to Click on.

For instance, we mentioned, "Imagine the possibilities of applying the Egonomics Trend quite literally to fashion. You go to a mall, pick the components you want for a pair of jeans . . . the compu-tailor measures your body . . . and for the first time in your life, you have a pair of jeans that are made exactly how you want them, in design and in body-fit." Now, in 1994, the world's largest manufacturer of jeans has done just that: selling computer-customized "Personal Pair" jeans for women. At certain Levi's stores, a customer's taped measurements are fed into a computer to create a digital blueprint. BrainReserve's lanky Assistant to the Chairman, Mary Kay Moment, reported that the computer first indicated the closest correct size and style, then waited while she tried on a prototype pair from an extensive "library of off-sizes." A description of any area that was the slightest bit off was fed back into the computer, which spewed out another suggestion. When the perfect sample was found, specialized instructions were electronically transmitted to a computer-robot tailor to make up a custom pair that will be shipped to the customer's home.

Although the jeans took two weeks and cost about $20 extra, Mary Kay was happy with the customization. "Before, my jeans were always either too big in the waist or too short or too something," explained Mary Kay. "Now, they fit me exactly." Consumer happy—and company happy, too. Since the Original Levi's Stores started doing this in select stores, the one in Cincinnati reported a sales increase of 300% in women's jeans. Next? Customized blazers, bras, shoes?

We also made another computer prediction: "The biggest technological achievement of the 99 Lives era will be a way to *edit down* all the information that assaults us daily. Maybe a computer that scans selected publications and edits out information we want or need to know, based on intimate knowledge of our lives, our tastes, our inclinations." Who knew it would happen so fast? A company called Individual offers an online service, NewsPage, that comes close to what we described for the future. You can pick your topics from a master list on your screen, then NewsPage scans around 500 sources each day to bring you one short news brief. If you want to read about a single topic in more depth, you can request the full text. Otherwise, it's the editing job we wanted, asked for.

We concentrated on How People Buy in a chapter entitled "The End of Shopping," in which we created a futuristic innovation called "InfoBuying." This idea streamlined the shopping experience (crowded, slow, frustrating) into a way to ask the "InfoBank" in your computer for answers to such questions as: "What are the three best cars on the market for long-term maintenance? The three easiest-to-use VCRs? The nearest places to buy them at the lowest price? . . . Then you can make your decision from the screen and computer-order your choice at once. (The end of advertising as we know it.)" The future is already here. It's now possible to log onto CompuServe, ask for information on the car you're considering, and obtain a printout of that detailed invoice that new cars have stuck to one of the windows. Ready for you to order.

More evidence that the Trends steer you right—and more fodder for thought. We've talked a lot about the importance of pure water as an ingredient, about even knowing where the water in our soft drinks comes from. We spelled out a potential, put-the-consumer's-mind-at-rest area, saying, "New Product idea: Baby Springs, pure water for babies from the Arctic Alaskan glacier springs." Now, Beechnut, Heinz, and Gerber have all introduced special bottled waters for babies.

One little suggestion we mentioned in the Small Indulgences Trend has come partially true. We wrote, "And thinking trend-smart can inspire Big Indulgence-makers to rethink, scale down, make their luxury accessible to a whole new 'deserver.' How about, for example, a Mercedes motorbike? Or a Maserati mountain bike?" When Lys and I were recently in Copenhagen on a business trip, we saw an unbelievable leather-covered Hermès bicycle. And a sharp reader from Down Under, M. J. (Mike) Martin of Perth, Western Australia, sent a fax: "When I read my *Sunday Times* of London (a nice yearly subscription from my mother-in-law), lo and behold, there was a mountain bike—not a Maserati, but a genuine James Bond Aston Martin Mountain Bike." Are you listening, L.L. Bean or Orvis?

It was in 1992 when we talked about what the more entrepreneurial Trend of Cashing Out was going to mean to the strict business world. "Even if a new company can't handle a four-day schedule or flex time, the new trend will be to let the staff relax on Fridays. Wear jeans and tees, bring in the kids . . . Infusing a Mom-and-Pop feeling in the office-place helps to break down title hierarchies and makes everyone feel that someone cares." If you followed the Trends, plus had a retail clothing store (or were a manufacturer), this would have been a clue to lighten up on the navy suit and tie look. In January 1995, the *New York Times* did a story on outdoors-specialty retailer Eddie Bauer's move into a new line of indoor casual clothing. "The chain hopes to cash in on what it sees as a consumer trend toward the wearing of more casual clothing on the job." We once dubbed the upscale outdoorsy look "Log Cabin Chic." Banana Republic calls their Friday-to-the-office line "Cabinwear."

In "The Trends Lens," we said, "Imagine the possibilities for a Virtual Reality Supermarket—a super high-tech shop-at-home-for-home-delivery system . . . This means putting capital spending into warehousing and delivery systems . . . to build a strong, believable foundation for the Virtual Reality supermarket . . . in the future." We guess Dick Notebaert, Chairman and CEO of Ameritech, agreed when he invested in Peapod, an online grocery service that delivers food, liquor, medicines, and just about anything you need to more than 10,000 homes. As we foresaw, shoppers can stroll up and down virtual aisles, via their PCs, seeking out the best buys or foods designed for a special diet (low-fat, low-salt) or hard-to-find ethnic ingredients. If you live in Chicago or San Francisco (Boston, next), you can have your order delivered to your kitchen door in around three hours.

A decade before *The Popcorn Report*, *The New York Times* wrote an article about BrainReserve that we can point to as early proof of the correctness of our predictions. We refer to it not necessarily as "look how smart we are," but to show that if you listen to the early directions, you can be there first. One good idea that feels right (the Click into place), one improvement on "what is," can lead down a very lucrative path. Since then, we've been quoted as predicting such diverse items as lean beef and grocery shopping by computer.

Once upon a time, we gleaned an idea that Disney later developed into a resort for mind expansion. We foresaw the non-Mickey, non-Goofy, non-Donald Duck Disney Institute as a path to Fantasy Adventure: a wish-fulfillment center where you can go and learn what you'd always wanted (to draw, to speak Italian, to crack the Minoan code), a magic place where dreams come true. In early 1995, Disney formally announced its plan for a new vacation/learning center for adults/older families.

We dreamed up a Breath-a-lyzer attachment for a car that would prevent an engine from starting up if the driver had too much to drink (it's been made, as well as a device that tells parents where a kid went the night he borrowed the car). We lamented that running shoes had to be so heavy and cumbersome that they are a burden to travel with ("these enormous shoes take up almost a quarter of a suitcase")—and now Nike has created 6.1-oz., pared-down, slimmed-down, lightweight-mesh, and less-foam athletic shoes.

We suggested that an excellent use of Virtual Reality would be to put on your goggles and headset to live certain experiences—before you committed to them. Like moving to another state. Like having elective surgery. Or experiencing the first day on a new job. Or, for instance, if you think babies are cute and cuddly, you could find out what it would actually be like to have one. Wouldn't that be a painless way to determine if you're a likely candidate to be a good parent? Since VR is not yet advanced enough for such a procedure, here's the next best thing. An engineer named Richard Jurmain designed a doll called Baby Think It Over, which is being bought by schools and clinics to counter teen pregnancy. Lifelike, the "infant" is pre-programmed to shriek and wail at random times day and night. The five- to thirty-five-minute crying jags can only be stopped when the student participant actively plugs into the baby's computer. If the cries are ignored or, even worse, if the "kid" is slapped—it will be so recorded. A weekend of this ragged "realism" probably works better than all the sex education courses ever devised.

However, at BrainReserve, the main thrust of our daily business is not the fun of predictions, but the nitty-gritty work on substantive, long-range vision for our assignments. Besides consulting our TrendBank, we regularly (and globally) interview about 4,000 consumers per year on twenty different product categories; read about 350 publications monthly in several languages; go to movies/theater/concerts, listen to the top-ten music hits, keep up with the best-seller list; and BrainJam (brainstorm) new ideas with our staff, our clients, and our Talent-Bank of thousands worldwide. We also go on TrendTreks around the planet, looking for new stores, new formats, new product ideas wherever we go. These activities help us Braille the Culture and become the basis for what BrainReserve is known for: getting our clients and our readers ready for the future.

We have had many tough consulting assignments over the years, which ask us to FutureFocus—forcing us to project into the far future and then backtrack into the viable near future. One such task was for Eastman Kodak in 1987, entitled "The Future of Film." For that, we created a world, based on the Trends, that pushed the direction of technology as far as we could imagine.

Our answer for what "film" will be: Simply, it won't be. "In the future," we reported, "there may not be a need for emulsion film, as we know it, in the little yellow canisters." Now, less than ten years later, Kodak has introduced a computerized camera that uses no film. It stores digital images and transfers them to computers for viewing or printing. For those few who don't have a computer setup, in-store kiosks can do the job. One of the best features of digital imaging is that it can be sent over phone lines—instant grandma gratification.

Coincidentally, John Sculley is CEO of a private company called Live Picture, which is working with Kodak as a strategic partner to dramatically change the quality of digital photography. This could be an important building block for interactive advertising, digital catalogs, and zines on the World Wide Web . . . Sculley is also involved in other digital startups, in such areas as children's educational interactive games and tools for the Internet. As we once said, "The practical application [of an idea] basically goes like this: From a trend prediction . . . to a trend production . . . to a trend product."

For if you study the culture (as we do), you get good at spotting those early indicators, those subtle signals of change. All that is required then is to capitalize on them. True, it's possible for a crisis such as an energy shortage, a natural disaster (hurricanes, earthquakes), or a war to make slight alterations or shifts in the Trends. But even those unforeseen occurrences do not make sweeping changes in the life of a Trend. Trends are rock-steady enough to last an average of ten years or more; certainly long enough to base a business plan on them. You can rely on the integrity of the Trends to read the climate now and project into the decade beyond.

As you embark on reading the Trends, look for ideas that call to you. Or ask yourself and *note* down how many of these Trends support an idea that you've been thinking about for a new product or a life change. One of the reasons we point out fledgling businesses around the country and world is to stimulate you into thinking whether such an endeavor would work in your locale. There's nothing wrong with taking a sound idea and adapting it to your present situation. We truly believe, "Let the best man/woman win." Even though one supermarket, dry cleaners, copy shop, hardware store, hour-photo place is in your neighbor-

hood, you can glean creative suggestions from the Trends and figure out a way to do things better, faster, friendlier, more satisfying
to the consumer. That's the final answer to our original question,
"Why Follow the Trends?"

If you Click into working with the Trends, you'll be able to
Click into the future. And make the Trends work for you.

CLICKING THROUGH COCOONING

I wish that I was where I am.
—GERTRUDE STEIN

Bless these walls, so firm and stout,
keeping want and trouble out.
—CHRISTIAN PRAYER

When we first coined the Trend name "Cocooning," we talked a lot about hunkering down, ordering in, and watching our favorite shows on TV. Cocooning conjured up warm images of hanging out. Nestling. Cuddling. Enjoying ourselves in our own homes. Clicking with those we love.

For these past years, we've enjoyed huddling under the warmth of our covers. We liked tilling the soil on our own side of the fence. Home Sweet Home meant Home Safe Home. But today, while we weed our gardens and channel-surf on our entertainment centers, anxiety creeps in. Where we once Cocooned because it was fun, we now Cocoon out of fear.

It's almost impossible to move from Cocoon to Cocoon without tension. When we venture out, we venture out carefully. Places in our lives where we once felt secure have all but disappeared. Forget Cocooning at work. Workplace homicide is the fastest-growing kind of murder in the United States. Forget safety in schools. One in four junior high students say that they've seen a gun on school property. Violence is said to be "the high of the '90s."

To get a handle on how this Trend has changed, picture a turtle tentatively peering out from under its shell. Instead of looking eagerly at the world, the turtle is wary, scared. At the first sign of trouble, that turtle dives back inside for cover. We are those turtles. So are many of our friends. For as much as we want to venture out, learn more, try new things, even the bravest of us are intimidated—or at least worried on some level that violence could strike at any moment. To protect ourselves from going crazy from distress-overload, we are building more psychological and emotional cocoons around ourselves every day.

You know you're a turtle when you forgo honking at someone for cutting you off on the freeway (who knows if the other driver may have a shotgun?). You know you're a turtle when you smile and try to pacify, rather than argue with, an aggravated postal worker (doesn't it seem as if a disproportionate number of violent crimes happen in the post office?), a scowling salesperson, a short-tempered waiter. You know you're a turtle when you stop going to rock concerts or basketball games because of the hordes of people . . . and you know that hordes of people mean that trouble could start at a moment's notice. Some may call it the new paranoia. We call it common sense.

This is a time in history when the word "unexpected" should be struck from the dictionary. Nothing surprises us anymore. A gunman on the commuter railroad. Stray bullets. Severed parts. Cannibalism. Office explosions. Random fire bombings. Men who stalk their extramarital girlfriends, women who stalk their dates. Kids who kill their parents. Serial murderers.

In the '80s, we freaked out about "wilding," when out-of-control gangs of teenagers mugged or raped anyone in their frenzied sweep (the Central Park Jogger). More recently, there's something new to worry about, "dis" (short for disrespect) crimes. "Dis" is when someone pulls out a gun and *bam*, you're dead, for nothing more than the expression on your face or the fact that you stared too long or that you accidentally bumped into someone's shoulder. That's considered disrespectful (you've dissed them) and therefore, you deserve to die. The alarming part is that it's so offhand-ish, so unpredictable, so unpreventable.

Making matters worse is that so many crimes are committed

by supposedly "normal" people. Prisons are filled with individuals who had "respectable" jobs, came from "nice" families, then one day flipped out and committed a heinous crime. When the neighbors are interviewed on local TV, they all say the same thing: "He was so quiet." And then the family writes a book (Gary Gilmore's brother, John Wayne Gacy's father).

We've lost patience. We're fed up and we want control even if it means getting extreme. It's not surprising that a majority of Americans supported the Singapore government in its decision to cane an American teenager for spray-painting cars. In complete agreement with this disciplinary measure, local leaders from all over America—from San Antonio and St. Louis, as well as all of Orange County, California, and the state of Tennessee—have introduced bills to sentence young vandals with up to ten whacks with hardwood paddles for their crimes. Public opinion in California has been running 40 to 1 in favor of instituting walloping as punishment, with those interviewed adding such enthusiastic comments as "Make it hurt."

The most hale, hearty, and hospitable of us are taking extra precautions. A recent survey said that 33% of consumers have changed their shopping habits because of fear of crime. Of these, 43% no longer shop after dark. Even on college campuses, the days of *Animal House* are over. Fraternities and sororities are getting stricter about whom they let roam into their parties. At Penn State, there are no more "open house" parties; guest lists are now the norm on Fraternity Row.

An obsession with crime is even creeping into our vocabularies. "Don't pull a Tonya" means "Don't hurt me because I might do a better job than you." And thanks to the movie *Fatal Attraction,* the word "fatal" has crossed over from an adjective to a noun. A fatal is someone with an obsessive crush who won't leave you alone. A fatal calls you all the time, tracks you down, finds you wherever you are. A fatal might show up unexpectedly at your job or health club. Fatals are annoying. But worse, a fatal could be dangerous. Only after umpteen attacks or even deaths by fatals, we're just beginning to create strict "stalker" laws, and have them taken seriously, *before* there's another innocent victim.

We've also heard of a new aggressive verb that's come from the "Most Frightening to Males" domestic violence case on the crime logs: Lorena vs. John Wayne Bobbitt. A typical example of its usage: Slightly annoyed wife says in a mock-threatening voice to husband, "Be nice . . . or I'll Bobbittize you." Husband laughs nervously, protecting groin area.

Here's a big Click in the realm of Cocooning: anything that smacks of extra safety or security. Bodyguards are the "techno-butlers" of the '90s, armed with the latest beepers and 007 tricks. Private security firms employ two and a half times the number of people that public law enforcement services do. The National Institute of Justice estimates that by the year 2000, we will spend $104 billion on private security annually versus $44 billion on public services.

Uniformed cops have to fight to keep up with what criminals are packing. Automatic weapons and fragmenting bullets have become commonplace. In our relatively peaceful village of East Hampton, the relatively peaceful police department had requested that they be allowed to trade in their six-shooters (.357s) for the more powerful Glock 9-mm semi-automatic pistols. The upgrade was more for peace of mind than for precautionary measures, since one village officer admitted that in his twenty-eight years on the force, no one had actually fired a weapon in the line of duty (except for encountering the occasional badly wounded animal). The need for protection is not just an American phenomenon. Another bastion of civilization has fallen: Scotland Yard has bent its nonviolent attitude, authorizing some of London's police bobbies to carry Smith & Wesson revolvers for self-protection.

Better safe than sorry is the credo of Cocooners today. Mace sales are soaring. Today, one in three homes is built with an in-house alarm system. Home and car security business is now a $1.5-billion industry and growing. Since statistics show that a car gets swiped at the astounding rate of one every twenty seconds, the whole area of auto theft prevention is a definite Click.

The Mobile Cocoon

With cars getting more and more customized and accessorized, it's harder to shrug off a stolen vehicle and say, "My insurance company can pay to replace it." Loaded with a 6-disk player and a stack of CDs, a fax outlet, a fancy car phone, bad-back Shiatsu cushions, and football team vanity plates, your car is really your mobile nest. Coffee cup holders are now a given, so can mini-microwave ovens, refrigerators, and fold-down trays be far behind? As your home-away-from-home, your car is something you want to protect from harm.

Go down any street in any city and look at the steering wheels on parked cars. Most will be securely locked with an easy-to-spot red gizmo. Last year, sales of the Club (or look-alikes) doubled to about $120 million, as car theft went up and prices went down. For those who want to catch the criminal in the act, there are sneaky products like the Smoke Defense Dragon, a device that fills a car with smoke when someone tries to break in. But if all else fails and your car heads off to the chop shop, just hope that it's been forearmed enough to have a tracking device installed, such as the Lojack Recovery System.

Using an idea we first heard about in Holland (land of bicycles), the city of Portland, Oregon, has come up with a clever idea to stop the theft of bikes: leaving some free ones out for grabs. The catch is that they're all highly recognizable, being painted bright yellow (versus Amsterdam's white). They're purchased through donations and maintained by corporate sponsors, and the goal is to set out a thousand on the streets. The program takes away the impetus of stealing, provides low-cost, no-fuel transportation, gives poor kids the fun of biking, even offers adults an easy way to exercise. Copenhagen has joined in with one thousand free bikes, each loaded with a built-in tracking device (just in case). Other cities might take a look at this Click idea.

Personal Safety

One of the most effective ideas of how to use a traditional weapon (guard dogs) in a new way comes from Shelley Reecher, a woman who was once brutally attacked. Shelley channeled her pain into creating Project Safe Run, now a forty-five-station network that provides ferocious-looking dogs to accompany women and the elderly on shopping trips, walks, and runs around the park. The program now boasts over 18,000 safe excursions and not one attack.

For exercise buffs without a pooch, there's always a canister of Jogger Fogger Counter Assault Red Pepper Spray. Or for pricier peace-of-mind, you can spring for the hand-held Air Taser, which flings barbed probes up to fifteen feet away, knocking any aggressors off their feet. It works via electrical signals that block neuromuscular control. Police can also track the perps, if they run off, by following the micro-dotted barbs. For a semblance of control, Taser owners are all registered.

A magazine called *Safe and Secure Living* shares such targeted articles as "Police Secrets You Can Use" to enhance your protection. Certain how-to-be-violent handbooks are popular now as a way to channel anger (or are read out of sheer curiosity). George Hayduke's multivolume *Get Even* series offers nasty ways to seek revenge.

For those who want to order products from inside their Cocoons to protect themselves, the catalog *Safety Zone* sells products for this dog-eat-dog world, such as motion sensors that wake up and bark like a don't-tangle-with-me dog. Night vision goggles, popularized during the Gulf War, are the latest defensive fad. With one called Moonlight NV-100 that amplifies light ten thousand times, you'll be able to peer into your darkened basement, if you hear a suspicious noise, without turning on the lights. *Perfectly Safe*, another mail-order catalog, geared especially for parents, has a reassuring Baby Watch Video Monitor for $299.95. And nervous parents can implant "nannycams," video recording devices, into their kid's teddy bear, to spy on the baby-sitter. We're seeing some First Amendment rights and federal regulation backlash in this gray area, as sensitive devices developed for law enforcement have been turned to personal use.

The phone, our primary connection to the outside world, is also helping us feel safer, smarter, and more protected. But poor old Alexander Graham Bell never thought of all the terrible, harassing, invasive, intrusive uses of his simple sweet invention. Talk about security paranoia: Just look at what the local New York company, NYNEX, offers as "protective" basics. Even though we're familiar with most, if not all, of these features, when you put them together as a group, they seem menacing. Repeat Dialing, the service that keeps endlessly dialing and redialing a number, and Caller ID, the feature that lets you snoop at the incoming call number. Yet to keep the person you're calling from knowing that it's you, it is possible to block the display of your number with Call

Restrict (*67 displays a "P" for private, instead of revealing your call number). Interestingly, 20 million households have unlisted phone numbers, almost 1-in-5 phone numbers. Caller ID services arc also uscd in thc rcvcrsc by businesses, to surreptitiously snare your home phone number when you call in, even to an 800 number, to build up and potentially sell a telemarketing list.

For a surefire way of knowing the local someone who keeps calling and hanging up, you can just hit Call Return (*69) and the last incoming number will be automatically redialed. This has squashed the age-old kids' phone prank of calling and saying, "Do you have Prince Albert in a can? . . . Well, let him out." For even more control, Call Trace can be enlisted to fight obscene phone calls. Hook it up to put an end to the annoying heavy breather. The date, time, and phone number of the last caller will be forwarded to the phone company's Annoyance Call Bureau. Too bad there isn't Call Revenge, to give those nuisance callers a mild electric shock.

In toto, it seems as if a new safe phone service comes with every bill. And with every service, a new warning. "Your home security system is only as good as the telephone line . . . " "If your line is cut, so is the communication between your home and your alarm company, leaving your home vulnerable to burglary and fire." "Pulsenet offers cut line protection." If your line gets severed, beep, beep, your alarm company is alerted. Something to worry about that you hadn't even thought of.

Inner city crime rates have made people desperate. In an effort to "take back" a neighborhood, some schemes have gone beyond the "StreetWatch" idea. There's been talk about "cordoning" off whole sections of the so-called better neighborhoods. Bringing back more uniformed cops to the beat, more clean sweepers to the streets. Property owners would foot the bill for a privatization, or basic upping of sliding city services—security, sanitation, tree care, holiday lights, etc. One such mapping has defined a section of New York's Upper East Side, where between 350 and 500 private security guards will be patrolling the streets.

According to the *New York Times*, the violent crime rate of Five Oaks, Ohio, fell by 50% after the installation of metal gates "designed to rebuff prostitution and drug dealing and the automotive traffic that often supports them." The barriers create a safer inner community, all part of a plan called Crime Prevention

Through Environmental Design, known as CPTED. Nearly 4 million Americans now live in gated communities—with ever taller, thicker, higher walls being built each week.

Lawmakers, in response to our pressure, are among the most security-obsessed of us all. The Associated Press observed that an unusually high proportion of state laws with security-related themes went into effect in 1994. California banned "gang attire" in class and New York has forbidden video stores from selling customer names and rental history records. In Illinois, telemarketers aren't allowed to make sales pitches during the hours of 9 P.M. to 8 A.M. (letting Cocooners get their sleep). Legislation in New Hampshire, Tennessee, and Oregon mandates that schools must check all new teachers for potential criminal records.

What's the world coming to? Not every writer is sanguine. In *Elect Mr. Robinson for a New World*, novelist Donald Antrim depicts a United States where seemingly reasonable Americans build moats around their homes and commit barbaric acts of torture in the name of civic responsibility. Will Cocooning get to that? Who knows, but . . . it's not too far a reach between "gated communities" and the castlelike fortifications of walls and moats.

If we're going to keep the outside world out, we're going to want magic within. We're deeply concerned about what surrounds us each day. Soon, we'll be able to call up Picasso's *Les Demoiselles* or a Diego Rivera fresco or a Louise Nevelson black box: art masterpieces on computer that can be changed at whim. Bill Gates of Microsoft already has such capabilities. One reads (with fascination) snippets about his $35-million lake-front house where display screens will be hitched to a central database holding untold thousands of works of art. He simply "owns the digital rights" to much of our visual heritage.

Cocooning at the Office

One of BrainReserve's clients, Ameritech, has made a basic change in the standard workplace. When you enter the sleek steel and glass headquarters of Ameritech's Consumer Services in Hoffman Estates, Illinois, you can hear the soothing sounds of Gregorian chanting or the ruckus of Snoop Doggy Dogg rap. As you get closer to the source of the music, the area starts to look curiously residential. In fact, it looks like a cozy family room with overstuffed furniture, a small dining room, a work-at-home area, and a home entertainment center. There's not a fluorescent light bulb in sight.

The idea behind this "home," dubbed the "Cocoon," created by Linda Lanz, Director of Research at Ameritech's Consumer Business Unit, is that the latest communications products should be tested in some place similar to a consumer's environment, rather than in a sterile lab. Real live customers are sometimes asked to come into the Cocoon to try out Ameritech's state-of-the-art wireless and switching technology. Company employees can use the Cocoon for relaxing, checking out the latest best-sellers or magazines, surfing on the Internet, listening to the music, watching the large-screen TV. It's also a terrific place for holding meetings, although business presentations take on a different tone when co-workers are stretched out on sofas or have their feet up on the plush ottomans. That's an office Click, '90s style.

For a more cosmic method of Cocooning, people are delving into *feng-shui* (pronounced fung-shway), the ancient Chinese art of placement (how to juxtapose man's things with nature). In Hong Kong and Singapore, and growing here, *feng-shui* is not treated like going to a storefront psychic for a reading, but it's a major business. Consultants can help design your space to work with the building's *qi*, or life force, minimizing conflict and encouraging spiritual growth. To prosper, you have to be situated the right way in the universe. An architect we know hired an expert in *feng-shui* to design and balance his office in a way that would foster creative thinking. Mirrors are used strategically to channel energy flow. The *feng-shui*-ers believe that where a desk is placed in relation to a chair or a table in any room sets up an aura of harmony and orderliness. In fact, Oriental wisdom seems to be tempered with a Mafia overlay: Never sit with your back to the open door. Advice we follow stringently, especially in busy restaurants.

Thomas Moore, the best-selling author of *Care of the Soul,* also connects spirituality to the everyday values of caring for one's home. How you treat the space around you, he says, affects your mental and spiritual health.

One thing is certain: Care of the home is part of Clicking now. For as chaotic and unpredictable as it is outside, we still want our Cocoons to be cozy and well-equipped. We're remodeling at a record pace, up 8% from last year. Sales at Home Depot, the do-it-yourself emporium, were up 36% in the third quarter of 1994. It's sheer heaven to be able spend hours there, as Lys does, filling up carts with green marble tiles, outdoor lampposts, sinks, and $9.99 orchid plants. The whole bed-and-bath business grew to $16 billion a year, up $2 billion from the year before. We're four-postering and four-pillowing our beds with Italian linen sheets, cashmere throws, pleated silk dust ruffles. And changing our utilitarian bathrooms into luxurious spas with RainStorm showerheads that spray 127 separate streams of water, automatic hand dryers, heated towel racks for our three-initialed monogrammed towel sets.

Sales of lawn and garden products hit over $25 billion in 1994. Gardening is the perfect pastime for Cocooning—a place to burrow in and feel healthy, creative, and wise. We're spending small fortunes on gingerbread gazebos, wisteria arbors, dig-your-own pond kits for lilypads and koi, and underground sprinkler systems for ever-greener grass. We're getting our hands in the muck and our feet in calf-high Wellies, turning over compost; planting topiary and weeping spiral evergreens; and building multi-tiered birdhouses. The circulation of magazines like *Martha Stewart Living, Garden Design, Horticulture,* and *Organic Gardening* is growing faster than a honeysuckle vine on a hot summer's day.

Serious gardeners are getting on the plane, to jet over to the English gardening shows, to hear lectures about mossy stones, spotty mildew, and the palest Victorian roses. One such enthusiast, Marjorie G. Rosen, returned with the idea of designing strong, simple wrought-iron hanging baskets (she scouted Europe for them, in vain). Result: Georgica Baskets, made in Southampton, New York, by old-world craftsmen at La Forge Francaise, at about $200 each. There's even the Home and Garden Television Network (HGTV), which reaches about 10 million viewers, offering hands-on features on gardening, home repairs, and crafts.

You may want to dust off the Singer sewing machine and get out your needles and threads. Home sewing is making a comeback. Fueled by the vintage clothing stores and flea markets, antique fabrics (luxurious and funky) are soaring in value. Old buttons, too, are getting to be expensive collectibles. Tender Buttons in New York is a treasure trove of unique oldies. To whip up/zip up a new fashion creation, top designers, such as Isaac Mizrahi of the movie *Unzipped*, are getting into the act, making patterns at the same time they present their haute couture collections. In Paris, the Marche Saint Pierre, a wholesale fabrics market, is jammed with both foreign and French home sewers Crafts are heading into cyberspace. CompuServe has a section called Go Crafts, where you can log onto a quilting bee on Tuesday nights.

Part of our precious home time is spent poring over the deluge of catalogs we receive in the mail every day. In 1995, more than 10,000 mail-order companies shipped out about 12.8 *billion* books. It's mind-boggling. And the saturation point is nowhere in sight. New people as well as tried-and-true catalog shoppers are still being tempted to buy from the pages; a total of $58 billion in sales now and growing. As we write, Lys is waiting for her new slip-covered sofabed to be delivered, sight unseen, from Ballard Designs. And then there's Cher's Sanctuary, the singer/star's ambitious venture into High Gothic home cataloging. Most catalogs Click, some maybe won't.

Since America's mailboxes are in a state of being overstuffed, the general catalog industry is smartly looking elsewhere. Although some (example: The Linen Source) refuse to send overseas, others welcome the challenge, just adding more in postage costs. Such traditional outfitters of American sportswear as Lands' End, L.L. Bean, J. Crew, and Eddie Bauer are going one better, starting to mail directly in the emerging markets of Japan (up 15–20% a year) and Europe. Now that credit card ordering is getting more familiar, foreign armchair shoppers should get ready for shipments of plaid flannel shirts and shearling slippers.

Are there any changes in the actual houses we're Cocooning in? Homes of the future are inching toward being more user-friendly. We're right on the cusp of some major changes (changes that can inspire new areas to Click into). Already there are about a thousand so-called Smart Houses in the United States preprogrammed to make our lives easier (for about $20,000 in added costs). By car phone, you can give verbal commands to open doors; turn on the lights, the security system, and appliances such as your washer, dryer, and VCR; or even run a bath, There are Smart Ovens that can be turned on and off, told to cook a 14 lb. turkey, even talk back and tell you how your dinner is doing or call the repair service if a problem occurs. Soon, Smart Fridges and Pantries will be able to scan and self-monitor their internal food supplies. You'll be reminded, or better yet, your store charge will be alerted when you are almost out of chunky peanut butter or black bean soup or when more 1% milk needs to be pumped into the cold storage tanks. What about a Smart Video Screen, on which you could see your baby and baby-sitter, from your car, or even better, on your wrist?

Smart Cookware could have built-in testers to evaluate the safety and purity of food. No more guesswork on whether the pork or chicken is well-enough done or if all the bacteria has been neutralized. There'll be a countertop with hand-scanning technology to take your daily temperature, prescribe drugs (or vitamins), and tell each member of your family what nutrients they'll need for energy. Water distillation systems will be commonplace, as we'll have grown to distrust even bottled waters. (The Hampton Jitney, the sleek and well-thought-out commuter bus, used to serve containers of spring water from Brazil. "Is tropical Brazil really known for the absolute purity of its water?" we were always asking ourselves.)

At BrainReserve, we've also been daydreaming about unified appliances: Kitchen tools and equipment rolled into one. Wouldn't it be nice to have a refrigerator with a built-in video screen complete with a CD-ROM recipe drive? What if the door space that houses your icemaker also held a can opener, a coffeemaker, and a sealer for leftover food? Teresa Riordan's *New York Times* Patents column featured a future-planner, Ellis D. Gordon, who came up with a "computerized appliance that can mix ingredients together and chill or cook them to create a wide range of foods, from chocolate mousse to fried chicken." Just insert a recipe on CD-ROM and this machine will make it, a kind of techno-chef. Want one, you say? It's only an idea in the mind of the inventor (not even a prototype has been built yet).

Some 38% of American households already have personal computers, and the numbers are jumping daily. Every nanosecond, these PCs are getting smaller and faster, faster and smaller. And prices are dropping into the realm of the possible for more people. In 1993, some 62% of the owners of home computers made over $75,000 a year. And twice as many whites as minorities owned them.

Televisions, conversely, are getting bigger and bigger. But

both computers and TVs are feeding into the armchair ease of electronic shopping. We're just starting to comparison-shop online or by CD-ROM, going through catalogs and clicking an order. At BrainReserve, since we read so many books, we used to make daily treks to the nearest bookstore. Now we log onto Book-stacks on Pipeline, type in the title, get an onscreen display of pertinent information, and credit-card order as many books as we want sent. That's it. No walking, no waiting, no phoning. We're also ordering from infomercials, the Home Shopping Network, and QVC, as a more comfortable way of mall shopping. In 1994, QVC's phones rang 55 million times, and the company sold over $1.2 billion in merchandise in this country alone. But as reports of falsely inflated price values keep surfacing, will the luster continue to shine on the sale of cubic zirconias? Stay tuned for a totally interactive vision for television.

The next generation of TVs will probably be the science-fictionalized, four-walled room of screens. We will be surrounded by stimuli. Each wall could screen the same show or four totally different ones (with hundreds or thousands of channels to choose from, it's still hard to find four you want to watch). Music systems, too, will be boomier and roomier. As you play any CD or audiotape, you'll be able to see the performers as well as hear them.

Bottom line: Whether we're laying low from being scared or being stressed, from being a turtle or being a couch potato, the future of Cocooning is still driving us home. For home is where the heart is. And home is definitely where the Click is.

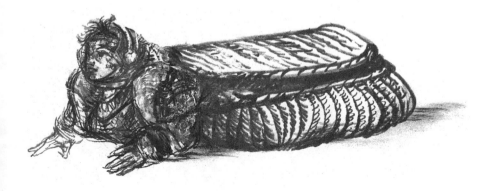

CLICKING THROUGH CLANNING

I think it would be terrific if everybody were alike.
—ANDY WARHOL

Whenever anyone visits our BrainReserve offices, they're likely to notice what we sport on our lapels. On any given day, most of the staff members are wearing a small enameled pin of a planet, with glittery little stars and Saturnesque rings. Some of us wear the original blue pin, others the following year's pin in red, green, or white, or the latest, blacks . . . and some of us wear all of them. Often, guests ask where they can buy one, and our answer is, "Sorry, you can't. They're just for those in the BrainReserve constellation" (our team, clients, friends).

The pins, you see, resemble the image on the cover of *The Popcorn Report*, and we have them made up every New Year in a different color. Wearing the pins is our gesture of unity and group pride . . . and a perfect example of Clanning.

Clanning hitches us up with those who share our interests. Our ideas. Our aspirations. Our addictions. Consider it the flip side of the Egonomics Trend. Instead of insisting, "I'm an individual," Clanning is the Trend that asserts, "I'm part of a group, and proud of it. I *belong.*" Not surprising given the way Cocooning has swept—and is sweeping—America: All that huddling in the safety of our homes has made us want to reach out and connect to people of like kind. Another way to look at Clanning: It's a rebound reaction to our overcommitted lives. The more fragmented our identities and fractured our days, the more we need to ground ourselves. Declare our "us-ness" versus "them-ness." Network with those of the same minds . . . and similar needs.

BrainReserve's planetary pins are just a drop in the Clanning bucket. The identifying badge of belonging that's seen in our thirty-person office is also seen in the larger planned communities that are springing up across America. You don't have to look too far for the swelling Clanning feeling. Previously in *The Popcorn Report,* we'd mentioned a drift called the Great Divide, about how this country's "melting pot" is no longer being stirred. Traditional marketing ploys are not working; communities (by and large) are polarized into separate and distinct little groups. Even the almighty *Good Housekeeping* Seal of Approval has been challenged by the Hispanic-American Group's Calidad Confiable, a seal that identifies good products and also contributes to programs that help Hispanic youths and families.

It's easy to find people of like leisure activities amid the sudden upsurge in memberships at private clubs in every city and state, from the Princeton Club to the Maidstone to the Bel-Air Country Club. Waiting lists and exorbitant initiation fees are commonplace; having a professional membership consultant to advise on admissions is a new and necessary component for selective clubdom. There's a smugness, an aura of safety when you belong to a bastion of sameness—whether it's based on a shared interest in golf, tennis, or squash; on being college alumni; or simply on keeping the rest of the world out.

A modified clubby feeling is being recaptured at both the mega-bookstores and the strong independents such as Powell's in Portland, Oregon (whose airport-shop manager, Chequeta Nutt, actually sent Lys a refund check for cash accidentally left on the counter) and the two popular Tattered Cover bookstores owned by Joyce Meskis in Denver, Colorado. Meskis describes the "living room style" she's been working at creating since 1974. With sink-in-able sofas, wing chairs, warm woody shelving, wall-to-wall carpeting, poetry readings, hot coffee and sweet buns, today's bookstores have become communal hangouts.

In an interview, Robert F. DiRomualdo, President and CEO of the Borders-Walden Group, expressed his passion for "continuous improvement." "Whether teaching or running a chain of bookstores, the important aspect is to instill an interest in learning for learning's sake. We all need to develop a store of knowledge and an ability to turn our knowledge to practical use. For instance, I've encouraged my daughters to learn how a car works. Then, to pass on what they've learned. That's the best I can do."

In these Clanning bookstores, the warm atmosphere makes people feel secure enough to talk to one another, whether it's about the occult, Oceanus, or the ocarina. It feels like a safe haven, because you can be almost certain everyone who comes there is reasonably literate, and is there to sit and browse through the same titles as you are.

Our wish? That other businesses would take a lesson. We'd certainly spend more time (and money) in the drugstore chain that offered a reading area stocked with the latest health news, Q&A forums with doctors, or even video monitors by the checkout line that broadcast wellness tips.

Clans can spring up around a singular interest. Even the lonely writer can come forth from his/her ivory tower to exchange ideas while Clanning with fellow creatives during a stint at one of the writing colonies, such as the legendary Yaddo. Specialty clubs hone in with a common focus, giving members an immediate rapport; such as the Diving Dentists Society (DDS) or the Moles, not CIA or animal lovers, but a grouping of tunnel and subway workers. In Baltimore, there's the Johns Hopkins Hospital Bone Marrow Transplant Reunion, where survivors of this harrowing medical procedure gather to give thanks and trade war stories. In L.A., one can find LADIES (Life After Divorce Is Eventually Sane), a Clanning meet for ex-wives of Hollywood stars, who find strength in getting together to rehash custody battles, betrayals, and alimony settlements. And squeaking in as a rather narrow Clan, there are the subscribers to *Paranoia,* a zine that will network you with other conspiracy-theory aficionados across America.

Examples of the Clanning Trend range from the sublime to the ridiculous to the frankly frightening. Young adults are responding to the call of the Greeks: fraternity membership has been revived and sororities likewise. We've noticed that the Grateful Dead, with its self-destructive late leader Jerry Garcia, wasn't the only touring rock band to command a fanatic Clan of devotees. These days, roving groups troop after Spin Doctors and Phish, for months on end. Those who made it through the mud for Woodstock '94 will be part of a subculture, a Clan. Call-in radio shows fill a niche, a *simpático* haven for the lonely and the verbose, a new kind of Verbal Neighborhood.

On a more somber note, lawless gangs and dangerous cult Clans are also on the rise. Roving "crews" or "posses" spray-paint graffiti signatures or rush stores to shoplift in groups. Such groups are not confined to only the inner cities; suburban "yuppie" gangs around Denver, San Antonio, Omaha, Phoenix, and White Plains, New York, are mimicking L.A.'s notorious Crips and Bloods, indulging in vandalism and violence. Uglier still are the hate groups, white supremacists, and skinheads who threaten racial holy wars, using the newer technologies of cable TV and the Internet to spread their venom. This is the destructive side of Clanning.

Clans can be political, economic, communal, spiritual, or virtual in nature. Clans can have 20 members or 20,000 members. Some are rigidly structured with an undisputed leader and a flock of followers. Others are models of equality. Still others are free-floating and amoeba-like, shifting and changing shape, as well as ground rules, daily. The importance of Clanning is to understand the power of special interest groups; and figure out what's the driving force behind these gatherings, so that you can decide whether to Click into the Clan, either personally or as a business-building opportunity.

Off-Hours Clanning: Salooning & Saloning

"But what if everyone is Cocooning?" is a question we're constantly fielding. "If we all stay at home, play at home, and now work at home, won't we get too insular?" Always a good question to ponder. Especially since we know that Americans won't be abandoning the combination of refuge, creature comforts, and startup of home-based businesses any time soon. Yet life encapsulated within a Cocoon could border on being lonely—not to mention claustrophobic. That's when we need an escape hatch—a reassuring exit that puts us in contact with something other than the same four walls.

Off-hours Clanning is the perfect answer: going to a place

where the faces are familiar and the conversation is easy. Think of how we all fell in love years ago with that cozy little bar known as Cheers. Some Clans are no more complicated than that; Clicking into a neighborhood bar, luncheonette, diner, cafe—or even a local gym—that's as friendly and as protected as your own Cocoon.

Some watering holes speak to specific preferences and predilections. In Manhattan's East Village, the Résumé Cafe posts job listings, helping its bohemian clients find work, as well as serving them pizza and gelati. In Beverly Hills, a Clan of cigar aficionados has emerged at Havana, a nightspot where people get together to light up stogies and share the not-so-politically-correct pleasures of a good smoke. We've heard about a Clanning/singles event on Christmas Eve, at which Jewish-Americans, who possibly feel left out of the Santa loop, can attend one of nine "Matzoh Balls" across the country. Started in Boston, the inexpensive dance party has spread to Washington, D.C.; San Francisco; and Boca Raton, Florida, where about 1,500 celebrate their alikeness on a traditionally low-key night.

And we've been hearing reports from friends about ways to Click with a '50s retro twist. Seems that sewing circles, bridge clubs, and roving poker games are attracting a new, nostalgic generation of enthusiasts. Says a 20-ish designer in Indiana who's joined a quilting group: "It's creative, calming—and a great excuse to get together with some friends and gossip."

Another Clanning diversion is a poker hangout in San Bruno, California, called Artichoke Joe's, which is open 24 hours a day and attracts up to 300 people at a time, everyone from college professors to slingers of hash at local eateries. Our ever-clever friend Ayse Kenmore figured out a way to lure back her card-playing husband, Robert: by bringing the game home and nicknaming their house Broccoli Bob's. She explained the draw: "You can get to know someone better playing one night of penny-ante hold-'em poker than countless evenings of cocktails and dinners." The regulars, fluctuating between eight and twelve friends, meet once a week, all decked out in "Broccoli Bob" T-shirts, made up to proclaim that they're members of the same Clan.

Clanning can even offer the opportunity to link you with people who'd rather live in another era. Ever hear of the Society for Creative Anachronism? These fanciers of medieval culture gather, often in period dress of flowing velvet robes, to mine the pleasurcs of 11th-ccntury verse, music, and culture. Other Clans stay firmly rooted in the modern world. On Monday nights, from Spokane to St. Petersburg, "Melrose Place" fanatics gather to watch the show, placing bets predicting which characters will sleep together (or try to kill each other) in the evening's episode, and repeatedly screaming, "Jane, get a life!" at the TV screen.

In keeping with the fear-of-crowds, going-out-but-still-Cocooning mentality, many in the disco scene have discovered the quieter joys of saloning: book-reading literary salons, cooking-course evenings, art-film viewings. Even formerly noisy nightclubs have dimmed the din, filling in the open dance floor with small round tables, comfortable chairs, and soft lights to encourage their patrons to sit around and talk to one another.

Communal Clanning: Family by Choice

Suppose that when you stuck your toes out of your Cocoon, you saw only people you had hand-picked to live near. That's the ultimate in Clanning. Whether you find the concept comfortable or scary is another issue. It's splintering the melting-pot fabric of our society, creating new definitions of extended family. There's a new wave of collaborative communities, allowing you to choose "family" members by common bond, rather than determining family by blood. We call this Communal Clanning.

In both communes and co-housing, what you give up in privacy, you make up for in community spirit. If you get a chance to live with large, extended families (as Lys did with the Bedouins in Jordan), in which everyone takes care of the other generations, the American way of having so many lonely people living solo in a house or apartment seems societally backward.

Communes were big in the '60s, with a kind of pot-smoking, free-love, search-for-utopia mindset. But the more middle-of-the-road aspects of communes—togetherness, sharing jobs and resources, the sense of responsibility—have stayed valid. Co-housing, a newer kind of community living that was pioneered in Denmark, Sweden, and the Netherlands (the sensible countries) about twenty years ago, is finding acceptance here. Popping up from Rhode Island to Bainbridge Island, Washington, it's based on cluster housing, with an average of about thirty units. Generally, residents (a mix of young professional families with some older singles) have separate living quarters, but enjoy communal facilities, such as play areas, gardens, laundry rooms, and often a dining room. These places are like a return to small-town life, when you knew—and helped out—all your neighbors. Plenty of baby-sitters, someone to get your kid off to school if you have the flu, one lawn mower to buy and fix—that's what it's all about.

What attracts the co-housers varies: Sometimes they're simply like-minded people who want to pursue the homesteading spirit. Generally they are eco-minded, but instead of tackling the global concept of "changing the world," they attempt the narrower idea of "changing *my* world." Other times, co-housers are united by their demographics or "life circumstances." Often, for people who don't have a mate or are empty-nesters, co-housing offers a way to Click with others. One small tribal village in northern California was formed by a group of mainly long-term friends (four married couples and three single women, all in their 50s and 60s) who ardently believe that they will have longer, more active lives if they stick together. They fish, make wine, pool computers, and stay ultra-busy concocting successful cottage industries, such as a local bookstore/bakery. And they're happy.

The Oklahoma City bombing has focused a harsh spotlight on the scores of anti-government, militia-oriented Clans that are tucked into the wilder corners of America's least-inhabited areas. Mainly right-wing survivalists, residing in so-called covenant communities, they share a strong anti-government fervor as their common denominator. They're against paying taxes and basically want to be left alone to live "off the grid." Or to become nonexistent, as far as the government is concerned. It was fairly easy to disappear (off the federal tax rolls) down a long dusty road in sparsest Idaho or Iowa, but now the fringe movement is spreading into the more populated parts of New York and Pennsylvania. A 4/10/95 article in New York City's trendy weekly newspaper, the *Observer*, talked about the emerging concept of moderate "sovereign citizens." A woman named Sharon Biggs teaches a "three-phase, 40-week course . . . on how to successfully remove oneself from the system." The sovereign path begins by banishing Social Security cards, driver's licenses, marriage contracts, voter registrations, insurance policies, credit cards, and bank accounts.

Actually, if more of these groups would pack up their secret weapons and protest openly through a trail of paperwork, they'd be doing things not much different from the starting premise on which this country was founded. There is a similarity in the talk about what it means to be a state "citizen" in a "republic," what our "inalienable rights" are, and how one expresses discontent with "the system" through tax defiance. So we can only expect more of this acting out of the frontier fantasy. Starting over, being totally self-reliant. Able to close the wagon-train circle to protect yourself and your neighbors. Who hasn't at least daydreamed about this? (I once sat around with our Burton's client, Stuart Rose, and bandied about the idea of purchasing a few hundred acres somewhere, like Montana, selling off ten-acre plots to friends, sharing a central library and community house, and living in peace and quiet.)

In a larger sense, all of the Communal Clanners are engaging in a form of social secession, much like the Pilgrims who came to Massachusetts to create a better life and escape forces of oppression. How one community member put it: "The way we have been living doesn't work. Due to the small size of today's families and the scattering of families, our kids have no chance to experience the joys of a big support system. We rarely see their grandparents and most of the elderly are treated like pariahs. The whole notion of borrowing a neighbor's ladder, or even a cup of sugar, has all but disappeared. We're craving some deep, meaningful contact. Co-housing is our solution."

At BrainReserve, we think co-housing will Click in the decade and century ahead. In place of real estate agents, we'll have Co-housing Counselors, akin to certified social workers, who will match up would-be neighbors or housemates. We'll have Co-housing Clearinghouses on the Internet or 900-number phone lines, where people can post openings in co-housing communities and screen applicants. And maybe someday we'll be watching the evening news on Election Night and hear reports on how the "co-housing vote" is swinging. Because co-housing—and the tightly knit new Clans it creates—promises to be that big a phenomenon.

Healing Clans: Therapy Through Togetherness

How many people do you know who are in some sort of support group or twelve-step program? Maybe you're in one yourself. The National Institute of Mental Health, in fact, has estimated that more than 500,000 different kinds of support groups are meeting in communities throughout the country. Just open the phone book or call your local community center; under the first letter "A" alone, besides Alcoholics Anonymous, there are Alien Abduction victims, Airplane Phobics, Artificial Limb Patients, and Asthma Sufferers. It's hardly an exaggeration to say that for every problem, there is a meeting. Whatever your vice, from overeating to nail biting to gambling to liking sex too much, there are others with the same problem to talk to. Other groups gather not for long-term compulsions, but for timely support for an illness or death. (A strong and lovely woman we know whose husband of forty years, Finn, died of cancer, went to a local bereavement group and was asked out by both of the two other attendees, men who had just lost their wives. Clara is happily marrying one of them later this year.)

We call the whole phenomenon of therapeutic meetings Healing Clans. Even junior high and high schools are organizing their own groups by age. If you're a student at Austin High in Austin, Texas, you can chose to attend a meeting—during the school day—of AA, NA (Narcotics Anonymous), Cocaine Anonymous, or Survivors of Incest. Austin High also recently started a program for girls who've been battered by their boyfriends and another for the boyfriends who've done the battering.

In the best of all possible worlds, therapeutic Clans—especially 12-step meetings—are a place to come to grips with your problems and find a commonality with others. The meeting rooms for these Clans are where people share their struggles and joys. They arc a place to talk and to listen, to Click into a healing dialogue. It's free group therapy; you get your moment to shine in the spotlight. Plus you get the added comforts of cookies and milk, as well as a round of applause and a wedge of cake on your anniversary. What could be bad about that? For millions of Americans, these Clans represent the equivalent of a sacred space—a "family" that's more caring, sharing, and supportive than the one they were born into.

But for many people, therapeutic Clans have evolved into so much more. How many people do you know who'd rather miss work than miss a meeting? Who become "addicted" to the meetings, going to two a day? Who wear the jewelry, give the medals, send the cards, needlepoint the slogans, read the recovery books and magazines, go on the cruises or off to rehabs and places like Chitchat in Pennsylvania? Who make it a rule not to make friends or even socialize with others unless they belong? In isolated breakdowns of the AA code of silence, gossip can be repeated outside the Clan, especially if the person is famous.

Some AA individuals might even join up to partake in what's known familiarly as the 13th step. Every major metropolitan area has them: possible 13th-step groups, meetings where people go hopefully to get a date, have an affair, maybe even fall in love. The added aspects of socialness, friendship, and action aren't limited only to your locale. People who travel frequently can call for a detailed listing of all the various meetings wherever they may go and use the program as a way of meeting like-minded people in strange cities. We know one New York woman who practically makes a beeline from the L.A. airport to the Malibu women's AA meeting as an efficient way of announcing "I'm here" to her West Coast social circle. She then opens her Filofax and gets booked up for lunches and dinners (but not drinks). It's faster than multiple phoning.

Since AA is a rather anonymous Clan, it is amazing how deeply 12-step thinking has seeped into our everyday vernacular. Everywhere from the car sticker that says "One Day at a Time," to Sinead O'Connor reciting the motto, "God grant me the patience to change what I can, and the serenity to accept what I cannot" at the beginning of one of her songs. We even have a group of local electricians who call their small company The Higher Power. How many times have you heard someone exclaim, "Oh, he is so dysfunctional!" Could we be taking ourselves, our problems, and our Healing Clanning just a little bit too seriously? Al Franken, the "Saturday Night Live" comedian, certainly seems to think so. His Stuart Smalley character, a self-described "caring nurturer," uses all the buzzwords in a funny/silly way, and his book, *I'm Good Enough, I'm Smart Enough and Doggone It, People Like Me,* has sold over 400,000 copies.

Virtual Clanning: Seeking in Cyberspace

When a 40-year-old hacker died, his friends held a wake for him online. Although they'd never met him face to face, his cyberspace family mourned him for weeks on the computer networks. These individuals were a Virtual Clan; the people he communicated with on a daily basis via his computer and modem in Santa Fe. His wake was a fitting symbol for Clanning in the Information Age.

Have you noticed how common it is for executives now to include an e-mail or Internet address, along with their phone/fax numbers, on their business cards? Maybe you even telecommute to work or buy your airline tickets via your PC. Or plug into a chatty virtual lounge by click-clacking away at the keys of a laptop rigged up at your favorite coffee bar. It's estimated that over 20 million people are hooked into cyberspace. Can an online U.S. Census be far behind?

And these fine lines pulsing with information are revolutionizing the way we network. We know proud first-time fathers who scan the requisite just-born baby photos into the PC and modem them to far-flung relatives within hours. Granddads who communicate online with their grandchildren. Talking about the future, our Ameritech client, Jim Firestone (now at IBM), said, "The cost of technology is plummeting to the point that I think we are on the threshold of really revolutionizing certain social interactions. Today, you talk to your close relatives only periodically and rarely as a group, except at isolated family reunions. Not too far away, we'll all have a 'window' in our kitchens, a flat-screened television monitor which will mostly show a pleasing picture. However, on Sunday mornings, from 8 to 10, it's just 'on.' It's also 'on' in my mom's kitchen, my sister's kitchen, my brother's kitchen and so on, at the same time. If you walk by, you say 'Hi.' It's real time, like leaning out of a window or talking over the fence in the old days. You could do the same thing with any sort of community of interest."

Meanwhile, the very Clannish are making do with today's computer tricks. Fraternity brothers are sending out party announcements through campus e-mail, radio talk hosts answer their listeners online, and people with AIDS are using the information superhighway to communicate with doctors and fellow patients. These people are the new CyberClanners. They use information to Click and connect with one another.

If you still don't have a modem and maybe suspect (as so many people do) that CyberClanning is for computer wonks or people who live in Silicon Valley, think again. Everybody from Madonna, who reads "bedtime stories" to Keith Richards (stones@delphi.com), to the Dalai Lama has scooted onto the online ramp of the information superhighway. In fact, the over-abundance of users has created the biggest annoyance, netlag, better known as a traffic jam. The most popular features online? We wondered, "What's attracting as many as 100,000 new members per month? Is it the stock trading function? The weather service? Online shopping?"

Answer: The main online attractions, by far, are the interactive chat channels and news groups (including alt.sex.stories and KinkNet) and e-mail. Let's say your particular bent is a curiosity about tropical fish and you want to Clan with like-minded others to talk about an esoteric topic. If you log onto CompuServe, you may choose from more than 600 forums. The Well even runs a group devoted to the scope of virtual communities. The kinds of topics that are regularly discussed are: Is online communication a conversation or a community? How can electronic networks reach out to women and people of color? What do you do about people who are rude? Who decides what's right and wrong?

What's it like to communicate online? CyberClanners say it's the ultimate Click. Their reasoning goes like this: In an age rife with prejudice and hate, online communication is a nobler, purer expression. It's not about what you look like, how you dress, or where you're from. It's all about what you say. And how you say it.

It's no surprise that romances, known as netlove, flourish. We read about a Virtual Marriage, where the bride who lived in Washington and the groom who was in the Amazon rain forest in Brazil met electronically, and fell in love through discussions of international ecology. They have floppy disks documenting their full courtship. Rush Limbaugh, too, found his true love through his e-mail. In mid-1994, he married a young woman who boldly messaged him over his bulletin board. But not everyone is ready to open his/her heart to the great unknown electronic network. After all, how do you really know whom you're talking to over the computer lines? Gender-bending is rampant. Beyond "she"s masquerading as "he"s, there are other forms of deception at work. The 32-year-old black-Irish male movie producer you're chatting with might be ITRW (cyberslang for In The Real World) a gutsy 80-year-old grandmother looking for some fun.

That, actually, might be a best-case scenario. Because life on the info highway isn't always nice. CyberClans have their codes of conduct . . . and people who violate them. It's common for women to complain of being "flamed" or given the PC equivalent of a tongue-lashing over their modems. Sexual harassment, or what we call Virtual Rape, over the Internet seems to be a given for any woman who logs on on a Friday night. Obviously, there's a growth area for the future: patrolling the Internet. Although there are already "bouncers" being posted, they're mainly against software violations and commercialism. Here at BrainReserve, we think many parents would pay a little extra to know that there's an online "chaperone" who's watching over their kids' communications.

Corporate Clanning: Bonding at the Office

Of course, we don't just Clan on weekends and after the nine-to-five day is done. The workplace allies and aligns us in ever more powerful ways. There's a group of enthusiastic employees at Nike who call themselves Ekins (that's Nike spelled backward) that are so fervent in their commitment to the company that they've each had the Nike logo tattooed on their body. (Would you tattoo *your* employer's name?) At Microsoft's Seattle headquarters, the boundaries between work and family have all but dissolved. The same little groups of employees (known as MicroSerfs) who toil round-the-clock as a team wind up sharing houses together, where they occasionally crash for a few hours on the weekend.

This kind of professional passion is wonderful. But we think the Corporate Clans that will survive and gain strength in the future will have deep emotional bonds. Managers will gain loyalty not just by financially rewarding their employees, but by making them friends, if not family. An example to consider? Seattle's Paul Allen, a high-tech magnate who also owns Ticketron. He invites employees to his compound on Monday nights to swim laps in his Olympic-sized pool and watch movies in his personal screening room (complete with candy stand). Smart thinking. When employer and employee play together, they're more likely to stay together.

Future Clanning

Support. Connection. Intimacy. Healing. Conscious choice. Compatibility. The language of Clanning indicates that as a culture we're yearning to Click into something more. Something we haven't found in our Cocoons. The need for community is like a gravitational pull. In the next decade, this pull is only going to become stronger and more pronounced. Clanning reminds us of something very important: that we're all on this planet together.

CLICKING THROUGH FANTASY ADVENTURE

Wide-awake, I can make my most fantastic dreams come true.
—LORENZ HART

I'm still hungry for every sensation I can get.
—MARTHA GRAHAM

Okay, so we're sitting in our favorite chair and thinking about where we'd like to go, what we'd like to do for fun . . . if only we weren't sitting in our favorite chair.

Truth is, the Fantasy Adventure Trend relies more on the airy flights of Fantasy than on the hard-core risk of high Adventure. Nothing could sum it up better than this quote by writer Thornton Wilder: "When you're safe at home, you wish you were having an adventure; when you're having an adventure, you wish you were safe at home."

It's about seeking thrills and chills in small doses. Veering, but not too far, off the well-traveled path. We want to live dangerously, but still wake up precisely at 7:30 to get to work on time. Even daredevil flier Amelia Earhart wistfully said, "Someday I would like to write a piece about the fun of voyaging with maps . . . without ever leaving home." Perfect Fantasy Adventure will come with home-based Virtual Reality: Armchair travel on a safari to Africa, with Paul Newman or Demi Moore as your tour guide.

The essence of Fantasy Adventure is in its safe passage. And in its fleetingness. There has to be a beginning and a foreseeable end. We don't want to be on a high road forever. This trend can be about something as minor as a delve into the exotic (eating Indonesian lumpias, instead of the usual Chinese egg rolls), the strange (bison, instead of steak), and the forbidden (flashing a dragon tattoo on your biceps). It's such wild-and-bizarre business combinations as coolest-of-the-cool Harley Davidson cross-licensed with slapsticky Looney Tunes (Bugs Bunny, a biker?). It's traveling around Vietnam on your American Express card. Or rising with the dawn to practice *t'ai chi,* a combination of mind/body martial art.

Fantasy Adventure is choosing a Breitling chronograph watch that was made to track a pilot's cruising speed. Or a rugged Tag Heuer that smoothly ticks to a depth of 200 meters. (You might say, when was the last time you went diving with dolphins? But, on the other hand, the underwater world might be your next conquest.)

Fantasy Adventure can be as simple as donning a Canadian Mounties jacket or a U.S. Cavalry coat to go to the movies. It's when you get bored with plain aerobics, and instead of stopping, switch to high-spirited reggae aerobics or soul-spirited gospel aerobics. It's wearing tree climber boots to work. And playing street-recorded rap on your superb Bang and Olufsen sound system. It's also about letting your fantasies run free—after learning about the importance of freeing up your secret hopes and dreams in Dr. Ethel S. Person's book, *By Force of Fantasy: How We Make Our Lives.*

Fantasy Adventure embraces our need to experiment, to scramble the neatly arranged molecules of our mundane lives. Consider it an access route to life as a chameleon, with the way back to reality guaranteed. One of the most natural paths is through outdoor adventuring. Fantasy Adventure explains why in-line skating is the fastest-growing recreational sport in America. When you're Rollerblading (or just blading) down a sloping country lane, so in control, you feel like a pioneer with the wind in your hair. The Trend accounts for the over 9 million mountain bike owners in the United States (Coolest: BMW's folding mountain bikes. Beautifully engineered, they're sturdy, speedy, easy to fold.)

Fantasy Adventure is the incredible Click in America of the

new Land Rover. This tough four-wheel-drive vehicle, originally made to forge the sand dunes of the Sahara and ford a mountain's muddy streams, is now content to cruise the asphalt of city streets (the Southampton dealership rents out a racetrack one day a year and fills it with hills and puddles, so owners can play tough).

Fantasy Adventure can be those few nights when you bypass your favorite chilled bottle of white wine or cobalt blue-bottled Skyy Vodka and reach instead for Wild Spirit, Drink of the Frontier, which proclaims in print on the bottle, "Paddle Your Own Canoe."

Wildering

We need the tonic of wildness.
—HENRY DAVID THOREAU

A subcategory of the Fantasy Adventure Trend is called Wildering. It's about modern man and woman breaking out of the monotony and pitting their cityselves against the wild. Wildering is the reason why 275,000 people per year have decided to raft down the river in the Arkansas Headwaters. Or why 5 million visitors circle around the Grand Canyon and peer into its multihued gorge. And for all those travelers who are ho-hum about yet another five-star hotel, there's the increasingly popular category of "tough lux." Many travelers are spending many thousands of dollars to trek in New Guinea with local tribesmen, walk with the elephants in India, hike to an outback bush camp in Australia. On-target Fantasy Adventure. Rough, but safe. Testing your mettle, pushing your level of endurance, but having a warm shower waiting at the end of the day.

For quieter Wildering, there's the growing sport of orienteering (called the "thinking" sport). Being left in the forest with only a map and a compass. This can be a solitary challenge or a competition—a race among peers to see who can navigate his/her way out the fastest. There's a five-day meet in Sweden, the O-Ringen, that attracts about 25,000 Orienteers. The United States has about 10,000 members so far, according to the sport's federation. Another way to respond to the call of Wildering is a sport called tracking. In this activity you are forced to be close to nature by spending days or a week in unknown terrain. You can prepare for tracking with yoga to improve your balance and meditation for concentration. Somewhat like pretending that you're an Indian scout; keen of eye, light of foot.

Native American lore holds sway over many of us. To imagine what this country was like as an unspoiled wilderness. Majestic and powerful. In fact, in a related way, one of my personal cultural Clicks happened when I started collecting artifacts from the Old West for my former house in East Hampton: fine American Indian and prairie paintings, horse blankets and antique Western saddles, a horseshoe firescreen, and wagon wheel made into a chandelier. Muralist Jane Thurn faux-painted one large room, its bathroom, and the entrance hall of my house in a subtle range of adobe colors, complete with arrowheads, Indian symbols, and fiery sunsets.

When asked why I wanted to surround myself with this theme, I would explain that the West was where I felt most at home. "But Faith," some friends would snicker, "isn't that strange for someone who grew up on Manhattan's Lower East Side?" True. But it didn't matter to me that I had never heard the sound of thundering hooves outside my window, I was creating the environment where I felt I Clicked. It may not be the real Wild West, but it's where my spirit wants to dwell. Besides, a channeler once told me that I had been a scout, a trailblazer, in a former life. I'm certainly trying to be one now. So whether this counts as a life-altering Click is up for debate, but the moral of my story seems clear. It's no longer enough just to dream about how we want to live; we want to live the dream. No more delayed gratification for us, thank you.

Gratification can even be totally of the instant, for the instant. Consider the seduction that Japanese women say they feel when they sign up for a "try a new you" tour called "Dress-up Tokyo." The Hato Bus Company whisks them to a posh hotel, where they each get to choose an extravagant evening gown or frothy white wedding dress and are photographed as a souvenir. More than 700 women became queen-for-a-day in the first month the tour was offered. Another such makeover escape in Japan is a bullet-train ride called Transform-into-Maiko (apprentice geisha) Package. A few thousand women per year get to leave their routines and play-act in a geisha role.

It seems that the Japanese are deep into the lure of Fantasy Adventure. We've heard tales from good friend Marnie McBryde, who worked at Spencer Stuart in Japan, that it's possible to rent the most bizarre things there—going way beyond the expected office equipment and cars. How about being able to rent just the right golden retriever (handsome, solid) when you invite someone for a walk in a park? Or renting a family (probably more convivial than your own) when you're alone during the holidays? Even in America, we read in *Business Ethics* about a guy named Mike Correll, who, for "a fee that can run as high as $1,200 . . . will find busy executives friends to hang out with." It goes on to say that about 2,000 Atlanta *male* business executives have used the service. Women, apparently, have no trouble making their own friends.

Another Atlanta-based thrill that just barely qualifies as Fantasy Adventure involves an outfit called Sky Warriors. Everyday citizens (no flying experience necessary) can participate in real air-to-air dogfighting. You go up with a former fighter pilot in a military T-34A (or T-6) aircraft and fly combat maneuvers against a real opponent. The fantasy part is that the "machine gun" you fire is a laser "gun," so that any direct hits are simulated by billowing white smoke from the other plane's exhaust. The four-hour mission, including briefing, instructions, flight, debriefing, and a videotape, costs about $650. For us, these flying outfits fall under the same heart-stopping category as bungee jumping and hang gliding. Keep in mind that Fantasy Adventure does not have to be life-threatening: Check out the safety records first.

Remember, lo, those many years ago, when kids wanted to go away to camp ("sleepaway," as they say in New York) to learn to swim, sail, and make lariats. Now the summer vacation of choice for the junior high set might be the real Fantasy Adventure of Space Camp, run by NASA. There, participants experience weightlessness and what it would be like to land the Space Shuttle. NASA's camp is so popular that now astronaut-wannabe adults can join up as well.

Space holds a place dear to Fantasy Adventurers' hearts for its far-reachingness, its futuristic-ness. We even praise our Brain-Reserve staff to the skies with our term "the astronauts of Trends." *Star Trek*, the movie, has come back so many times that the *Enterprise* crew, instead of being sleek and dashing, all sort of putter around, paunchy and wise, while "Star Trek," the TV series, blankets the channels in its many guises and reruns. The Sci-Fi Channel has replugged all those vintage Buck Rogers shows, the ones that have Buck sitting stiffly in a studio, looking down on a cardboard mockup of a spire-y "Future Metropolis." The Discovery Channel covers the more serious stuff, programs on the galaxies, black holes, and whether dinosaurs were exterminated by an errant meteor.

What's also of never-ending interest "out there" are those little green guys, the aliens. SMA, a skateboard company, believes that alien contact is imminent and we should get ready to communicate. It publishes a newsletter that issues statements like this: "The time is at hand. . . . Open your minds. Let new ideas take precedence over all. For the past and its ideas are in the past and the future is a time for drastic change. Those not willing to strive for the new will be lost with the old." The people at SMA have created a promotional video titled *Debunker*, which reflects their belief that our government is keeping UFO sightings (and landings) a secret.

Numerous talk/tabloid shows on television agree, routinely gathering groups of people who've had "close encounters." A popular class on UFO studies, at the University of North Dakota, is taught by a professor who claims to have made "contact." The scary side to all this alien adventuring? Already there are "Alien Support Groups," overflowing with people who swear they've been abducted and sexually abused by outer-space visitors.

Somewhere between heaven and earth, there's cyberspace. One of the richest veins of the Fantasy Adventure trend these days is encased within the intricate circuitry of the mighty microchip. Drifting through cyberspace, we can stretch our horizons as never before. Sampling files of celebrity recipes; assuming the role of professional movie reviewer on an entertainment bulletin board; and entering the Flirts Nook, posing as a thirty-year-old carpenter named Mike from Milwaukee.

By influencing our fantasy lives, cyberspace can change our real lives. We've heard about a Boston publishing executive who had downloaded from the Internet a photo of a secluded beach in Bali and posted it over his desk. One year later, he replaced it with an actual photo of that perfect beach. He'd gone there on his honeymoon and made the dream real. Consider it a Click. "The moment I saw that image on my PC screen, I knew someday I'd have to go there."

BrainReserve's Creative Director Janet Siroto admits to being mesmerized by the computer game SimCity 2000, in which you build an imaginary city from scratch. You design the apartment buildings, shopping complexes, highways and byways; budget for education, police, and fire departments; deal with sanitation strikes and riots in the park. "I thought about majoring in urban planning in college," she explained. "In a controlled, stress-free form, SimCity lets me live out the career that I let fall by the wayside."

Another wildly popular computer game that has reached cult status is Doom and its follow-ups, Doom II and Doom Gunn. The three programmers who founded id Software are all under 30. Next, Doom movies, books, virtual arcades . . . and more gloom and Doom. On the downside, they've created such indelible demons and Death match tournaments that Doomers of all ages have reported actual perception changes. Walls shift as they walk, shadows turn into monsters. They have strong feelings of obsession and sometimes paranoia. This is just the start of the "cyberpsychotic." Will it spawn a new field of therapy? New medications? Instead of worrying about drugs, you have to worry about coming back from your cybertrip.

For a lighter trip into the-light-of-fantasy, there's the CD-ROM game Myst. This surreal adventure maroons its players on a deserted, Twin Peaks-ish island, testing their Sherlock Holmesian detective skills as they meander through forests, over footbridges, and into basement chambers. One Yale professor who makes thrice-weekly visits to Myst told us, "I don't know who's more fascinated by it, me or my 4-year-old daughter. She's completely transfixed by the images every time I boot it up." Said an artist friend in Seattle, "The nights of losing sleep over my mortgage worries are over. Now I just stay up obsessing over Myst. There's something about the setup—me, alone on an island, trying to figure out what happened. My mind feels more focused, my instincts heightened, when I'm clicking around that imaginary world." All we can say is that it's a pleasure to have a video game that's not violent, not trigger-happy, not totally boy-oriented.

Listen to how Rand Miller, a preacher's son and the soft-spoken co-creator of Myst, described fabricating this environment. "Sometimes, after I had done something really cool, I would look at my creation and say, 'It *is* good.'" That was his

Click. Maybe not worded with the most hype you've ever heard, but a Click nonetheless. A feeling of all the pieces falling into place. The bigger picture to focus on is that Miller felt the Click when he made Myst and that hundreds of thousands of Myst players tap into the same Click when they log on to his visionary world.

From the brainstorming sessions we've been having with 18- to 24-year olds, we've learned that "realness" (we'd call it "ordinariness") is what's thrilling them. Being submerged in an idealized state of existence, sort of like the '30s movies, "Father Knows Best," or "Ozzie and Harriet." One young woman couldn't imagine anything more exciting than a trip along America's back roads, stopping to play miniature golf. Witness the success of MTV's "Real World" pseudo-cinema-verité series. There's nary a rock god or a supermodel to be found. Instead, seven regular folks are tossed together in a house and they film what happens. Entry-level job blues. Battles over refrigerator shelf space. Fumbling attempts at romance. High adventure or high drama, it's not.

For this same sweeter, softer generation, there's a flip side. Going from Playing It Safe to just Playing It. Not being a "drone" to "being in the zone." Listening to the techno-wizards counting the BPM (beats per minute) of Moby's hit, "Thousand," which at a thousand BPMs may be the fastest ever recorded. Being mentally whiplashed by the taboo-rock of Porno for Pyros or the nihilism of Trent Reznor of Nine Inch Nails, who rages, "I'd rather die than give you control" or Bec's "Loser," whose top-hit video sociopathically snarls, "I'm a loser, baby, why don't you kill me."

You might say, so what's new about musicians and drugs? We'd reply, "Attitude." There's an angry destruction going on. Drugs of all sorts are on the scene. Ecstasy for the Rave scene. Often followed by a snort of Special "K," originally a horse anesthetic. Crystal meth. Mushrooms. Heroin (aptly coded "poison" or "body bag") for the white-collar set. But enough said about the small sliver of the population that worships "sex, drugs, and rock 'n' roll." Back to the more prosaic side of Fantasy Adventure. The side that shows up in the stock market and in annual reports.

What does Fantasy Adventure do for the multibillion-dollar

fashion and accessory business? Browse through a catalog such as the J. Peterman Company's *Owners Manual.* Its owner started out with one product—a long canvas horseman's duster coat, advertised in places like the *New Yorker.* It Clicked into consumers' imaginations by offering items with tales to tell. A hat modeled after Hemingway's, a tugboat captain's sweater, a David Niven blazer, a Gatsby shirt. More, a woman's long skirt like the one worn in *Out of Africa,* a blouse like Bacall's, Garbo pants. The founder's philosophy is: "People want things that are hard to find. Things that have romance, but a factual romance about them. Clearly, people want things that make their lives the way they wish they were." Last year, the company pulled in $50 million in sales. That's Clicking through a Trend.

What's going on with regular shopping, day-to-day, face-to-face? Is there anything new now that the luster is off mall shopping and it's viewed as "boring"? One alternative has surfaced in Costa Mesa, California. That's the home of the Lab, a so-called "anti-mall," rustic and garage-like. Not a lineup of pizza palor, greeting card store, and deli, but twelve very '90s stores, including two vintage clothing stores and one bead shop, set around a central lounge with a pool table. Watch for copycats elsewhere.

What would make a superstore Click into Fantasy Adventure? It's a natural at Travelfest, the vacation wonderland in Austin, Texas. You can find every travel need from luggage to maps to inflatable pillows. Best aspect: You can computer-scroll through various destinations to find prices of hotels and airlines, even buy your tickets and get boarding passes right on the spot. You'll Click if you land in Times Square and open the world's largest music and entertainment store. The Virgin mega-store of 70,000 square feet, carrying 150,000 CDs and tapes, has Fantasy vision: a cafe with live performances, a four-screen movie theater, and a restaurant dedicated to sports called the Official All-Star Cafe.

Other good ideas for this Trend are the Incredible Universe stores opened by Tandy Corp. The one in Arlington, Texas, offers a visual blitz of 220,000 square feet (the size of three football fields) full of TV sets, VCRs, stereos, and camcorders, all on and running. Practically every major audio/video product sold in the United States is there for you to test and compare. Every shopper gets a membership card (also, very Egonomics) and salespeople are called "cast members." The cast member's job is not to "push" a product or to sell on commission, only to answer questions and facilitate sales. Each carries a hand-held computer that can call the warehouse when you've reached a decision, and the purchase is conveyor belted to the checkout counter in ninety seconds. High-tech, low-cost buying.

As much as Americans love their TV sets for home entertainment, when we want to go out for thrills and chills, we love our amusement parks. In 1993, we spent the equivalent of most nations' national debt on roller coasters and animated exhibits. As people become jaded about one kind of ride, another comes along that's higher, faster, has a gimmick. Disney's Magic Kingdom has a "snow"-topped mountain and a 120-ft. Summit Plummet, a free-fall water slide. Elitch Gardens in Denver has Twister II, a new twisting, turning wooden coaster that will make your hair stand on end. Houston has the Mayan Mindbender, an indoor thriller ride encased in a huge pyramid, in which you creep and zoom in the dimmest light, past scary things that glow in the dark (yikes!). In a softer vein, computer-savvy Sony is testing the concept of advanced Cyberparks. If the first prototype works in the Bay Area of San Francisco, Sony plans a national rollout, geared to urban adults. Sega, too, is developing its own version of Virtual Reality Parks. If fun, they'll all succeed through Fantasy Adventure.

In a Wildering frame of mind, Disney is building another theme park in Florida, with acres upon acres of real and pretend animals (such as unicorns)—plus the "good deed" of an endangered species preserve. A Click for everyone on earth. Disney also offers a sweet, low-tech, high-romance opportunity for adults: theme park weddings. To get married in Disney's kingdom, fairy-tale fashion, means wearing a bridal gown copied from the images of Minnie Mouse, Snow White, or the Little Mermaid. You can opt to whoosh down the aisle as Cinderella, complete with a horse-drawn carriage for arrival, chocolate slippers for dessert, and even uncomely stepsisters hired for the occasion.

We're also seeing opportunites for the future in finding new ways of bringing what was traditionally outside into the safety of inside. Think out-to-in. For instance, outdoor cafes have come in out of the rain to become the now-popular coffee houses. At the Rainforest Restaurant at the Mall of America in Minneapolis, it's possible to close your eyes and think that you're in the midst (mist?) of the Brazilian jungle. In Buena Park, California, there's a restaurant where you can feast like King Arthur, while knights in shining armor joust right in front of you in an indoor arena. In the movie *Pulp Fiction*, one of the most astonishing dinner scenes has two main characters dining in the back of a '50s convertible, in which the seats are turned around and facing a table. Even better, the 14,000-square-foot eatery-cum-entertainment center, the Harley-Davidson Cafe, offers the newest of special interactive effects that will be able to simulate the *vroom-m-m* of the motorcycle experience.

More on In-ing. One can ride the Big Waves at the world's largest indoor beach at SeaGaia, Japan. Wind-surf across a choppy indoor lake, right outside Paris. Rock-climb at any of the various mountain-wall sports facilities, without fear of rock slides or serious falls. Even ski down a synthetic slope, created within a shopping mall.

For kids in inner cities, even playgrounds have been moved indoors—a definite Click for the late '90s. Parents' fears are quieted at these urban play centers: No little darlings can wander off, no strangers can approach, no drugs can be sold. Down the street here in New York City, WonderCamp has mazes, electronic wonders, and a clubhouse with bounce-off-able walls in cheery primary colors. Across the country, almost 30 million kids have played at the chains of the more fitness-oriented Discovery Zones (315 places and growing like Topsy) and Gymborees (400-plus), as well as the startup company, Ali Oop Play Environments, with its soft purple mascot. Now, what about an imaginative Wonder-Camp for adults? Who wouldn't love to act out their inhibitions by socking, climbing, and rolling around on big, soft toys? A fun Cocoon.

How else can our craving for Fantasy Adventure be satisfied? The way to race our hearts can be achieved . . . through our stomachs. Track the record of salsa sales, for instance. By 1993, salsas (mild, medium, hot, or on-fire) pulled in $634 million, outselling old-fashioned ketchup. If you look back to ten or so years ago, in the northeastern states, the only place you could find a fajita was in a big-city Mexican restaurant. Yet once we had our taste buds inflamed by jalapeños, we craved the whole enchilada of south-of-the-border cuisine.

Actually, many of our most interesting supermarket selections make it to the shelves only after we've gotten used to their taste at inventive restaurants. Trendy today are "fusion foods," multi-cuisine combos made by smaller companies. By melding Mexican and Italian, Señor Felix's Gourmet Mexican Foods has come up with a Southwestern lasagna, with melted ricotta and mozzarella cheeses, tomato sauce, and salsa, between layers of tortillas instead of noodles. Other "odd" blends are pizza burritos, nacho-flavored bagels, smoked salmon and cream cheese pizza, Tex-Mex egg rolls, and Thai salsa.

Talking heightened taste: For the first time ever, the spicier, peppier taste of Dr Pepper has edged out Diet Pepsi as the fourth-ranked soft drink in America (according to *Beverage Digest*), after Coke Classic, Pepsi, and Diet Coke. It's not only the stranger, stronger tastes that are in demand now. Startling packaging can do it, too. Saratoga Springs's beverage Toga wraps itself up with racy comic-strip labels that have a plot change every six weeks (a panel of 18- to 25-year-olds helps create the storyline).

For anyone interested in global expansion based on Fantasy Adventure, it's fascinating to note some differences between countries. Iced tea took 100 years to catch on BIG here. Yet it's still practically unknown in most other parts of the world. Many times, what's humdrum in one place takes on an electric charge somewhere else. Remember the excitement when McDonald's came to Red Square? The French, once insular and ultra-chauvinistic, are finally facing a foreign onslaught. *Vive la différence.* Now that the unsinkable Eurotunnel is open from France to England, the unthinkable is happening. British staples—fish and chips, steak and kidney pie, Yorkshire pudding—are creeping onto sacred French menus. An assault is also coming from the south: *panini* bars, serving little warm Italian sandwiches with ham, cheese, tomato, etc. Why not bring *panini*s over here? A future Click.

For schoolkids in America, the sandwich is still king. Yet school cafeteria food is taking on a definite ethnic cast. However, most children haven't a clue that tacos, fried rice, or beef empanadas are not basic American fare. One Trend to watch: the ever-increasing mixup of breakfast and lunch foods. Pizza for breakfast, pancakes for lunch. Melted chocolate on white bread (a classic Mediterranean treat) for breakfast, waffles for lunch. And so on.

The common thread, then, of the Fantasy Adventure Trend? It allows us to escape the all-too-predictable. By shaking up those lingering "what-ifs," it pushes us toward taking the first step in changing the status quo. But after the "what-ifs," what's next? With heavy work boots selling 350 million pairs a year, how much heavier can footwear get for a casual stroll to the office? In answer, we might start wearing the lightest of shoes when we enter a home or office, so that we can enjoy a freer feeling, quite yoga-esque.

And with sales of four-wheel drives and light pickups outstripping sale of regular cars, don't you ever wonder how much bigger, longer, more cumbersome our driving vehicles can get? We predict that, in a flip, we'll be driving soon-to-be-designed smaller utility vehicles. Easier to maneuver and park. Not such a hard ride. Softer, cushioned.

We'll also see more return-to-elegance cars, similar to the Jaguar convertible. But why, we ask, can't there be modular cars? Completely adaptable, hardtop or convertible. Adding extra trunks for trips, a clear top for touring, a hydraulic lift to see over traffic. Maybe even a feature like the accordion-pleated center that some of the long, snaky buses have: with different "tails" to add, depending on your and your family's needs.

The Fantasy Adventure Trend is one of the easiest to Click into, to introduce something thrilling into an otherwise luke-warm atmosphere. For example, BrainReserve was once asked by Estée Lauder's Aramis to come up with a positioning for men's fragrances of the future. A key theme that emerged from our research was the escape through Fantasy Adventure. One of the favorite fantasies was Latin elegance and all of its connotations: flamenco guitar, the running of the bulls at Pamplona, machismo radiating from Antonio Banderas. Add in such utter romance as captured by the film *Don Juan de Marco* and its song by Bryan Adams, "Have You Ever Really Loved a Woman?" Aramis came out with Havana cologne with its sexy air of danger.

Those who have Clicked thanks to Fantasy Adventure say that the first step is the most vital step: the thrill of dipping one's toes into fresh new waters. You never know: What you might find, what information you could gather, with whom you might chat. After a Fantasy Adventure, you can ease your way forward in a completely spontaneous, intuitive way. That's the ideal state of mind for a Click.

CLICKING THROUGH PLEASURE REVENGE

Another season, another reason, for making whoopee.
—Gus Kahn

Life being what it is, one seeks revenge.
—Paul Gauguin

No more Goody Two-Shoes. The newly emerging Trend of Pleasure Revenge means we're fed up with self-deprivation in the sanctified name of Health and Correct Behavior. As consumers, we're ready, willing, and able to Click into the pursuit of pleasure. Not sweet and pure, but the dark side of pleasure, the underbelly of pleasure. We're boomeranging back to fun . . . with a vengeance.

This Trend is akin to indulging in a secret bacchanal that's suddenly not so secret. In fact, it's beginning to erupt, like the Kilauea volcano; its steamy molten-lava stream consuming everything timid in its path. We're smoking defiantly, tippling harder, stroking butter on our buns, parading in furs, *not* running, giving in to our every whim. Why the semi-destructive change? Because we tried being model-perfect and yet nothing in our lives got any better. Layoffs still happened, to our neighbors and then to us. Kids are still on drugs. So we're mad as hell . . . and we don't want to take heed anymore. Our halos have slipped.

After years of restraint, we're suddenly singing out, "Turn me loose; turn me loose, I say." But more important to Clickers is the much larger question: Are the freewheeling '80s back? Are we re-embracing the fast-lane twins of Glitz and Greed? The answer is about half and half—"yes" for glitz, "no" for greed. Although the quest for hyped-up glamour seems to be making a comeback, it's without the '80s "Dynasty"/"Dallas" *selfishness*. A residue of do-good-ism is, we hope, here to stay. So when we make a decision to be "bad," it's much more conscious. We're not trying to fool ourselves, it's just that we truly, deeply, clearly understand that our actions have consequences.

Fatalism definitely has played its hand in forming these live-and-let-live attitudes. We have come to realize that, even if we do everything right, *still* terrible things can happen. And it doesn't hinge on whether we ate an oat-bran muffin for breakfast. Since life isn't necessarily fair and just, we reason, it might make us feel better to have those delicious, beer-battered onion rings.

Isn't it interesting that after so many years of the #1 and #2 New Year's resolutions being "Stopping smoking" and "Losing weight" (personal health goals), we've now switched to the financial arena (more arm's length)—"Pledging to save" and "Paying off my MasterCard debt." So when we go off on a Pleasure Revenge, we're saying a sporadic goodbye to fat-free, a partial good riddance to low cholesterol (concern peaked in '90). And a resolute hello to sinful taste and instant gratification.

The number of Americans who say they're trying to avoid fats is slipping down, down, down, to now only about 50%. We're tired of tofu, tired of dietary warnings. We want tasty options; some artery-clogging, some not. Sales of Hebrew National hot dogs are up. Best-selling pizzas are homemade-big or microwave-plentiful or store-bought with double layers or stuffings of triple cheese and sausage. Fresh seafood sales are sluggish, but people are digging into deep-fried seafood platters that generally contain over 2,000 calories and hold twice the daily requirement of fat.

Farmer-sized breakfasts of bacon and eggs are back. Even the American Heart Association has upped its suggested consumption of whole eggs to four or more a week (there's less cholesterol in yolks than originally thought). The slimming-image cottage cheese sales are slowly heading downward, while cheddar cheese sales (thanks to taco toppings) are climbing. Butter sales have rebounded to levels of thirty years ago, up 10.4% in 1993, 7% in 1994. Lowered prices had some influence, but so did a damaging report by the Harvard School of Public Health that concluded that, contrary to earlier opinion, most margarines were no better for you than butter. At the release of this information on margarine's hydrogenated vegetable oils, the butter-deprived consumers felt ripped off. Their protests sent some brands' sales, such as Uni-lever's Promise, down by as much as 32% in a matter of weeks.

Our willpower is weakening by the moment. We Americans have an incredible sweet tooth. Presugared cereals are being spooned up by adults as well as children. We're buying cookies by the bagful and ice cream by the giant waffle cones, the pints, the half gallons. In fact, sales of Ben & Jerry's super-fatted ice creams have trebled over the last six years. For total hedonists, their Chocolate Chip Cookie Dough has everything delicious that one could ask for. While yogurts may still have an "aura of health," the latest offerings of super-premium frozen yogurts have all the rich-ness of their ice cream counterparts, from sticky swirls of marsh-mallow to crunchy slivers of almond.

And take a look at your supermarket shelves. Americans spent over $15 billion on snack foods in 1994. Even though pretzels have a basically healthy reputation due to their low saturated fat, they're not all that great if we consume them by the handfuls. One sour-dough hard pretzel alone (and who can eat just one?) has 90 calo-ries and 470 milligrams of sodium. Skinny triple-rings, stout ones, long ones, little needle-sized ones, salted or plain, even honey-mustard-and-onion-flavored are flying out of the stores. Plus one can always grab a pretzel from the street vendors in New York, who sell a Northeast regional variation of chunky warm pretzels, squig-gled with bright yellow mustard. Doritos are still America's favorite crunch, followed by every possible variation of potato chips (almost $5 billion in sales alone, including steak-flavored), tortilla chips ($3 billion), corn chips, and finally tasty multicolored veg-etable chips. What's peculiar is the regionality of eating salty snacks. Certain places in mid-country, Green Bay, Wisconsin, and Grand Rapids, Michigan, salt-down the most, with New York City coming in at the tail end, as consuming the least per capita.

We're even splashing down calorie-laden liquids. Quite sur-prisingly, non-diet sodas are enjoying new popularity (up $22 mil-lion this year) while diet sodas have seen a decline of over

$40 million. These figures have been boosted by Snapple and other flavored iced teas. Again, fuller, richer, sweeter taste is winning over a saving of calories.

It's as if we've faced and embraced the Devil at his own game (tempting us at every turn). A mixed green salad takes on a whole new profile when chunks of creamy blue cheese are between the leaves of lettuce. Mom's meat loaf simply tastes better with a smothering of gravy. That whole baked potato, which we know to be so healthy when plain, simply is more delectable with a triple dose of fat: melting pats of butter, a slathering of sour cream, and a sprinkling of bacon bits.

In the fast food arena, KFC's Skin-Free Crispy didn't fly while its newer Popcorn Chicken, dipped in batter and deep-fried, was the winner. Its new brand effort replays the chain's heritage of "fried." McDonald's tried hedging its bets, testing out a lower-fat burger called a "McLean" as well as a hefty half-pounder with cheese sauce, the "Mega Mac." Guess which one did better in this just-say-yes world? Even in ultra-health-conscious L.A., where everyone seems to exist on alfalfa sprouts and aerobics, the tally per day was 5 McLeans sold for every 300 Big Macs. No contest. Wendy's, too, has entered the heavyweight competition with its Big Bacon Classic, a virtual orgy of beef, bacon, cheese, and mayo.

There's no doubt about it. Elsie has hoofed her way back in again. When we at BrainReserve predicted in 1984 that beef was on its way back within a few years, people just gave us blank stares. First the red meat came back in small doses, sneaking in as beef-as-a-topping. But now, ten years later, we're more than satisfied with our prediction. Statistics show that beef sales, which had been steadily slipping for fifteen solid years in a row, have turned around mightily. Consumption is at a new high (almost 64 lbs. per person in 1994 vs. 15 lbs. for fish/shellfish), with all expectations that this trend will continue. The rate at which we're biting through burgers is almost frightening. The *New York Times* reported, "Hamburgers are ordered in restaurants more often than any other food: some 5.2 *billion* were eaten in the nation's restaurants this year." And that's not counting how many came off the charcoal grills. The other staggering news: "Serving 28 million customers a day, McDonald's has retained its title as the largest single source of food, and of beef, specifically, in the world." It's hard to wrap our minds around that.

And that's just part of the beef story. Beef jerky is America's fastest growing snack. Everywhere you look, there's a new meat market or restaurant. In Queens, New York, you can see a huge, block-long place called Western Beef, the Meat Supermarket, that has targeted the consumers' wants. In Greenwich Village, one of those Stetson-hatted Eastern cowboys, Allan Dell, started a hangout bar, Hogs & Heifers, along with an incredible BBQ sauce of the same name. Right on Trend. In fact, steakhouses are the hottest category in the restaurant field this year, up 19% in casual dining places, 16% in the upscale ones. Mentioned in the Forbes "200 Best Small Companies" list, the Lone Star Steakhouse and Saloon has $164 million in sales, with the explanation: "The higher the price, the more a diner revels in the ritual of self-reward." Pubby, clubby taverns are overshadowing the California cuisines, the Italian family-style restaurants. Bargain steakhouses are franchising, multiplying, expanding. The most popular common denominator of all these spots is a 24-ounce rib-eye steak, listed on the menu for about $10.95.

We born-again carnivores are not satisfied with the mere taste of beef, not satiated with little strips of meat. We're hearing ourselves order the thickest, tenderest, most heavily marbled (read, fattiest) cuts of prime sirloin, porterhouse, filet mignon. And on their way in are authentic Brazilian rotisserie restaurants called "rodizios," in which waiters make their way around the tables carrying spit-roasted meats on huge skewers. You, as the diner, can beckon the waiter to stop at your elbow and carve off substantial slices of beef, pork, lamb, and more beef—until you give the signal to stop. The New York area has at least three of the popular eateries already.

One difference today in the Trend of Pleasure Revenge is that the red-meat renaissance comes with an overlay of health awareness. We may be going for the sizzle, but we're limiting our forays to cattledom to no more than once a week. One group, calling themselves the Red Meat Club, meets to gorge themselves once a month; if a dozen of the members convene, they order a quarter of a steer, blue-rare, and have a jolly fine time by mooing and bellowing. That's all well and good for the hard-core gorger, but there are many others who find it hard to admit to a primal weakness for red meat. As a perfect example, we know of one New Yorker who, although she was an avowed vegetarian, used to sneak off to her neighborhood steak joint to gnaw furtively on a plateful of the largest, greasiest, most succulent beef ribs. We call this oxymoron "Meat-Eating Vegetarians." The most infamous of these faux vegetarians was, of course, Adolf Hitler, who supposedly strictly stuck to his lettuce and lentils with one fleshy exception: a weakness for pigs' knuckles. He had another deeply indulgent craving—he consumed about 2 pounds of chocolate a day.

Still in the "greasy" category, we wish some Clicker would join the Pleasure Revenge quest with a delicious import. Why not copy the Dutch/Belgian corner stands or sliver street stalls that sell the crispiest, crunchiest, deep-fried French fries. They're cut medium-thick, well salted, and sold in paper cornucopias. But the special treat comes in the myriad of sauces. We, as a country, show no imagination when it comes to a topping for fries. It's ketchup, catsup, or catchup. Those clever Low Countries let you slather on "Frite" sauce, which is a lemony, thin mayo; spicy chili sauce; "Piccalilli," a mustard/pickle relish; gloopy peanut sauce; and so on.

You can bet that while we're busy stuffing ourselves, we're no longer exercising like fanatics. "No pain, no gain," is a passé refrain. Talking a good game about health and fitness from the comfortable vantage point of a Barca-Lounger is at an epidemic state. Most of our days are spent either sitting or reclining, going from bed to car to desk to car to couch to bed. A full 60% of American adults admit that they are not exercising. And the number one excuse: no time. Even the word "exercise" has recently been replaced in the governmental lexicon. Yes, the President's Council on Physical Fitness now refers to workouts as the more benign "physical activity." In pure Pleasure Revenge terms, "exercise" smacks of leg lifts and heavy chest-heaving, while today a nice long walk qualifies as an adequate calorie-burner.

Home exercise equipment, still based on the Cocooning Trend and ever-wishful hopes, continues to sell well, but notice how many NordicTracks and exercycles are for sale in your weekly classifieds (although they do make handy extra clothes racks). Since Pleasure Revenge is still in its early stage, it's a good place to look for opportunities to Click into. Think about something softer, something less strenuous to replace the Stairmaster and treadmill. Could it be that home courses in massage training will become commonplace? New York has a chain of drop-in shops called the Great American Backrub that give an eight-and-a-half-minute massage for $7.95. Wouldn't this momentary pleasure work for the airlines? Or better yet, imagine how soothing a foot massage (reflexology) would be on those long trans-oceanic flights.

We're constantly looking for shortcuts. A good body without sweating. Being thin while indulging in food. Weight-loss centers, including Jenny Craig's 700 outlets, have suffered dramatic drops in revenue. We keep hoping that a miracle will happen to stop any weight gain. Now that researchers have identified the "obesity gene," there's a cure in the future. A pill combination, such as Pondimin and PhenAm, which are the old appetite suppressants, or maybe a patch, a puff of something that will cut our pigging out or process what we wolf down differently. Every time we see an article about a company like PepsiCo that is working on a diet drink that will suppress the appetite, we anticipate help-in-a-gulp.

Or maybe we have finally realized that, for now, most diets don't work, long-term. Fat thighs or love handles are mostly unalterable (except for the vacuuming-out of liposuction). And as Susan Powter says, we're ready to "Stop the Insanity." Then there's the word that the once-feared "yo-yo weight gain and loss" isn't really as harmful as first thought (or is it?). This newly published fact has temporarily given us permission to binge and be good, binge and be good. The National Center for Health Statistics has said that 33.5% of the adults in the United States are 20% or more over their desirable weight, while the *Prevention* magazine index set the numbers much higher, with 68% of us overweight.

Even the way we're viewing "fatness" is changing. In 1985, some 55% of those polled thought that overweight people were "unattractive." By 1993, the percentage who agreed with this had dropped to 35%. Two men's magazines, *Esquire Gentleman* and *L'Uomo Vogue*, recently had features on "attractive corpulence." One of the editors spoke of a heavy man's "touch of humor and power." Marlon Brando, as round as Humpty Dumpty, but as bedroom-eyed as ever (romantically wooing Faye Dunaway's character in the movie *Don Juan de Marco*) comes to mind as a perfect example. In Beijing, China, there's a restaurant called Fatty's that offers a 15% discount to men who weigh more than 207 lbs. and women who tip the scales at over 183 lbs. In the book *Consumed: Why Americans Love, Hate and Fear Food,* its author explained that the American consumer is a "health-conscious Dr. Jekyll when answering surveys, but a junk-food-loving Mr. Hyde when fork

comes to mouth." That, in a nutshell, is why the two trends, Pleasure Revenge and the upcoming health-oriented Being Alive can
happily coexist.

We've certainly Clicked into Pleasure Revenging when we
accept our weight gains. Ever heard of the May 5th Coalition? Not
an old Russian revolutionary group, but organizers of the International No Diet Day, "a day to renounce the tyranny of thinness, proclaim our freedom from the demands of the diet and fashion
industries and to celebrate the many shapes and sizes of the people
in our world." Miriam Berg, the coordinator, urges all of us to listen
to our bodies and feed them if they want to be fed. On May 5,
you're supposed to wear a light blue lapel ribbon, smash your
bathroom scale, and pig out! This is one small attempt to combat
the distorted image many of us have that we would be "happy" if
only we were "thinner." However, adult Americans on average
gained 2.1 lbs. in 1993. That's millions of pounds from sea to
shining sea. In fact, one-third of all American women have to buy
a size 14 or higher.

Food is not the only thing we're Pleasure Revenging in our
mouths. Like the drinkers during Prohibition, today's new Smoke
Rebels are huddling together to light up their cigarettes. Evidence points to the fact that the twenty-five-year decline in
cigarette smoking may be eroding. This lends support to an
aggressive new attitude, a kind of a self-righteous swagger. Smoking diehards are tired of being social pariahs; they're inching in
from the back doors, the loading docks, and the stoops.

The latest cigarette ads have stopped being apologetic; they're
figuratively blowing smoke rings into their opponents' faces. In a
double-page magazine spread from R.J. Reynolds, one side showed
a macho middle-aged guy, with a small caption that read, "Archie
Anderson is a Minnesotan, born and bred. In the past he tolerated
the attacks made against smokers. But now he wants to speak up."
The opposite page expressed his viewpoint. "I'm one of America's
45 million smokers. I'm not a moaner or a whiner. But I'm getting
fed up. I'd like to get the government off my back."

Clinton and his government, instead of waffling, have actually
decided to take a stronger stand, calling for a "war" against smoking. For the first time, cigarettes are being talked about as coming
under the product control of the FDA, even being considered as a
drug. Will this rigid approach work? Don't kids like to rebel against

being told something is "off-limits"? Will there be secret Cigarette Police? Pressure against smoking is also coming from other quarters. When you think of the major changes in American social behavior, the "criminalization of smoking" has to be one of the most significant. Ashtrays used to be one of the most popular gifts to newlyweds or new homeowners—now they're almost as archaic as silver calling-card trays. In fact, two models of Chryslers are the first cars in seventy years to be made without an ashtray.

The major thrust of the tobacco industry harps on choice and coexistence. A Philip Morris campaign quotes a Time/CNN poll in which 73% of respondents affirm that people should be able to choose whether to smoke. Choice means "I'll smoke where and when I want to, as long as it doesn't hurt others." Demographically and surprisingly, it's the college-educated adults, earning over $35,000 a year, who are pushing the numbers of cigarette sales up. Claiming to be "social smokers," not junkies, they are thoroughly enjoying under a pack per week. The banning of all smoking in any area where people congregate though might have pushed American "live and let live" freedom lovers too far. However, every time we go in and out of a building these days, it's not so nice to have to enter through a cloud of smoke.

Yet, somehow, for some grown-ups, a moderate approach to smoking seems to be working (but *not* for addictive personalities). For instance, I was once a serious smoker of about two packs a day who gave it up more than a decade ago. I stopped instantly after being rapidly injected with a multiple needle "gun" holding a magic potion of vitamins from France (developed by the late Dr. Pistor). For the last year or two, I've had a "planned smoke" every once in a while. And it goes no further. In fact, when I go on my next business trip to Europe, I've decided to smoke once or twice (up to ten cigarettes an evening) during my four days there. Knowing the taboos of smoking, but being able to keep it under control, makes it thrilling. It's a feeling of being "bad." Perfect Pleasure Revenge.

We keep thinking about this returning influx of "pleasure" smokers. Could it be that social puffing goes hand-in-hand with the new influx of coffee bars? Couldn't some tobacco company Click into this upscale market with a glamorous single-cigarette-only pack? Or duo or triple pack? American Tobacco is already testing a 10-cigarette pack, half the size of the regular one, under the marketing guise of appealing to a cost-conscious audience. But what about upscaling it with an evening design (like special after-dinner mints)? Or making fresher, healthier herbal cigarettes, wrapped in beautifully designed papers? Ones that slowly burn a pale tinted smoke? Wouldn't it be interesting to substitute some kind of aromatherapy inducer, instead of tobacco: creating cigarettes that could change your mood, curb your appetite, energize you.

Watch for all kinds of better-for-you innovations in the cigarette industry. Certain ones have been on the drawing board for years and are finally making it to market, such as those that hardly burn at all, thus avoiding the dangers of secondary smoke. Larger companies are backing small, startup firms to create niche brands. Moonlight Tobacco Co. (under RJR's wing) has spewed a significant number of customized brands, such as honey-toasted Sedona, the thicker-rolled Jumbo, and those stamped with a peace-symbol, Politix. These are forerunners of the first breaks in the huge cigarette monopolies—Clicking into the entrepreneurial spirit that's sweeping across the breadth of American industry.

Positive reinforcements about smoking are starting to sneak into the media. The *New York Times* quoted a 30-year-old who said, "I gave up everything else. I don't drink. I don't do drugs. But I still get pleasure from smoking. I like the taste, the comfort. You eat, you smoke. You have sex, you smoke. It kind of all goes together." Just as throaty movie stars, such as Lauren Bacall and Marlene Dietrich, once enhanced the image of inhaling, power figures, such as King Hussein of Jordan shown lighting the late Israeli Prime Minister Rabin's cigarette, will influence today's generation.

For those who don't inhale, there are small, dark, cigarette-sized Davidoff cigars in their elegant white box. Big, Winston Churchill–sized Cuban stogies have been banned here since 1962, but a thriving "cigar underground" has been clever about locating Montecristo A's, which cost $36 each and take a hundred days to blend, dry, and hand-roll. While lighting up, cigar smokers can sit back and leaf through a magazine all their own, called *Cigar Aficionado*, a bit of genius from publisher Marvin Shanken. Cigar sales in the first eight months of 1995 were up more than 28% over the same period of 1994 (total yearly cigar sales: $2.8 billion). In August 1995, an all-female "smoker" was held at Manhattan's Monkey Bar, and about 150 women paid $95 to attend the dinner, puffing vanilla-flavored cocktail cigars with their champagne, and larger ones (requiring versatility with a cigar cutter) along with coffee. Overheard were such comments as "Cigars don't pose a health risk" and "They're the lesser of potential vices."

The doctor's-little-helper against smoking, the nicotine patch, has slipped drastically in sales: From $500 million in its first year, 1992, to $225 million in 1993, to an estimated $150 million in 1994. Sales of the brand Nicoderm fell 34% in the first six months of 1994. Of course, when patches are over-the-counter instead of only by prescription, more people will slap them on their upper arms or chest and try them.

Now what about smoking the illegal stuff? Pot is America's biggest cash crop and stronger than ever (both more popular and packing more punch). Feelers are starting to go out about exploring the relative safety of marijuana and its medical value (overcoming the nausea of chemotherapy). It's possible that we will someday see pot being separated out from the other, really addictive drugs such as crack or heroin. Writers Steven B. Duke, professor of law at Yale, and Albert C. Gross, a lawyer from San Diego, have published a book, *America's Longest War: Rethinking Our Tragic Crusade Against Drugs.*

One premise is that certain drugs are not as deadly as cigarettes or alcohol and could be, should be, regulated wisely: no sales to minors, no consumption in public. It's tough to control. In a 1994 governmental survey of student usage, almost 40% of high school seniors had smoked marijuana and, more alarming, over 16% of 8th graders had already tried it. Although small in numbers, a full 2% of 12th graders admitted to smoking pot on a daily basis. There's even a headshop on the Internet, giving a listing and loving description about the different strains available.

The idea that "liquor is quicker" is absolute Pleasure Revenge. More of the population is drinking, even though total consumption is down. In other words, it's okay to have a social gulp or two, but no longer hotsy-totsy to get stinking drunk. Sales of imported French wines are up 20%, with red wine outselling white. Pricecutting wars on champagne are over and it's the luxury brands of bubbly that are being popped. In the field of hard liquor, there's a definite retro trend to suave clubs, piano bars, and sophisticated lounges, such as NYC's Monkey Bar and Temple Bar, or L.A.'s Dresden Lounge. No grunge, no Rap. We're seeing the return of the well-dressed "lounge lizard" and haunting torch songs. After all, what could be better than the honey tones of Ella Fitzgerald singing "Autumn Leaves" or "Stormy Weather"? Our Trend director, Ash DeLorenzo, recently confessed (while playing one of our favorite games: "What Would I Do, If I Could Do Anything in the World?") that he would love to open a '30s-style piano bar. "It would be highly stylized in red, black, and chrome, and I would call it Knife." We predict someday he'll be Clicking and tickling the keyboard with his own version of Mack, the . . .

And finally, something else that we predicted in *The Popcorn Report*, the Return of the Cocktail. Especially the martini. Not just the eyedropper of vermouth in a V-shaped glass of vodka or gin, but new '90s variations. Catering to the palate of a younger generation, these martinis are sweeter rather than drier. In response, such places as the Four Seasons Hotel on Manhattan's great 57th Street have devised a martini-only menu. Shakers of peachy Bellini martinis, strawberry Metropolis martinis, crème de menthe Candy Cane martinis, and cranberry Cosmopolitan martinis.

With occasional drinking comes occasional hangovers. We've all heard of "hair of the dog," chewy bread, and vitamin B, but new (and untried by us), from David Outerbridge's book *The Hangover Handbook*, is cabbage. Outerbridge says there's something in this heady vegetable that acts to soak up the acid from your liver and helps normalize your system. So bring home the cole slaw.

It's hard to grasp, but remember a few short years back when coffee drinking was considered "injurious" to your health and coffee sales were sinking faster than the *Titanic*. People were switching in droves to decaf or giving up the dark brew entirely. Coffee substitutes, made of a blend of grains, were being touted as "good for your health." One such impostor is Postum, a concoction of bran, wheat, molasses, and corn, which has actually been around for 100 years; another is chicory-flavored Kaffee Roma. The Dutch have a delicious ersatz coffee called Bambu that is a health-food staple there. It looked, pre–Pleasure Revenge, as if the end to a good strong cup of java was near.

When BrainReserve was working with Maxwell House about fifteen years ago, on an assignment to reposition coffee from a "rite of passage" drink to a "contemporary experience," we suggested starting a chain of coffee bars. They responded, "Not us—we don't want to get into real estate." But we saw coffee bars as filling the void left by the demise of the corner soda fountain and as a safe alternative (yet with a jolt) to the corner bar. Enter the Click of Starbucks, with its amazing growth from kiosks in Seattle to more than 630 stores and a $200 million business, so far. And New World, the Coffee Beanery, Gloria Jean's Coffee Bean (franchised in 200 malls), Timothy's, Brothers Gourmet, Coopers Coffee, among the crowd. Even Chock Full o' Nuts has come back, along with its addictive cream cheese and date-nut bread sandwiches. In three short years, this country has gone from under 300 dark, dusty, leftover Beatnik-y coffee houses to almost 6,000 European-style places now, with a figure of 10,000 projected by 1999. These numbers are still small, compared to the proliferation in a coffee-bar country, such as Italy, which has about 200,000 for a much smaller population.

We're still in the experimental stage: testing our taste buds on Peruvian chanchamayo beans, and demitasses of Indian monsooned Malabar, and freshly brewed cups of indulgent white chocolate mudslides. We even saw a coffee flavor that takes the cake at the best deli in the world, Andel's, in Roslyn, New York—Apple Crumb Cake Coffee Beans. This is truly Pleasure Revenge merged into Small Indulgences. Is it the craving for the security of Mom Food? When sitting around the kitchen table in simpler days meant having a steaming cup of coffee in a familiar chipped mug and discussing the business of the day? The return of kaffeeklatsch.

One personal aside: on Saturday nights, my local Starbucks (66th St. and Third Ave. in NYC) looks like the '90s version of the teen-scene soda shoppe. But as Starbucks gets bigger and more popular, its service staff seems to get younger in contrast to the nearby New World with its smoother, more European flair. The last time I made a quick run into the New World coffee bar for an iced cappuccino, the sharp-eyed counterperson (John) spotted my little black and white Japanese Chin dog, Miyake, through the mesh siding of her zipped-up carrying case and offered the panting pet an ice cube. In contrast, a similar sighting happened at a Starbucks and the service guy stuck to the letter of the law (no animals in food places) and told me he wouldn't even give me a fast coffee-to-go unless I first took the dog outside and left her tied up (where she would have lasted a "New York minute"). Sure. (Late-breaking note: The personnel at Starbucks have gotten more mellow.)

Yet, undeniably, the aromatic brew is in its early Click mode.

There's time to join in, with handmade coffee mugs, etc. Even the most mainstream signpost of Americana, McDonald's, is testing having espresso machines on premises. Only time will tell whether having the satisfaction of a good cup of coffee to sip slowly will make customers hang around, turning the fast-fooderies into convivial salons. Or will customers down a shot of speedy espresso while standing up at the coffee bar? It's interesting that we still shudder with daringness when ordering the deep, syrupy dose of caffeine in an espresso. Yet, according to a short mention in *Longevity* magazine, the caffeine level comes from the amount of time the brewing water is in contact with the grounds. Hence, the very concentrated espresso in its smaller cup comes out with less of a kick than regular Joe in a cup. And one other thing about coffee, the Food and Drug Administration has bestowed its blessing, saying that there are no serious health risks from drinking three cups per day.

What if coffee did more than deliver a jolt? What if a cup could offer time-released energy and a promise of weight loss? With no jitters? There's a bioengineered product called Thermo-Coffee that claims to have one-third the caffeine as well as a trace mineral called chromium that supposedly works miracles. The company, Life Services Network of Neptune, New Jersey, also makes a zero-fat creamer with added protein. The Japanese have devised a vehicle for getting your wake-up call of caffeine without going through the brewing process. Real coffee chewing gum. If it's possible to capture the aroma, it's not a bad idea for America's on-the-go mornings. Are you listening/reading—McDonald's, Coca-Cola, Starbucks, 7-Eleven, Wrigley's, Life Savers?

Alongside the coffee bar per block, next could be the bun shop. First in line, the Seattle-based (again) chain of almost 300 Cinnabon bakeries, selling enormous, fresh, aromatic cinnamon rolls with icing, weighing in at 810 calories each. They also have their own blend of coffee, Rubymoon. Well, what about a franchise of sticky bun shops, simply called Sticky's? Or Baba's, serving variations of Baba au Rhum? Or strudel shops, with strudel logs stuffed with everything from raisins 'n nuts to seafood? Or Danish pastry places, specializing in prune, poppyseed, and those spread-out, flaky bear claws. And everything topped with thick Devon cream or its Turkish equivalent, the artery-clogging *kaymuk*.

More Pleasure Revenge. Another dying industry that's struggling to reposition itself is fur. How is that consummate symbol of luxe, the fur coat, faring? It's a showdown between the anti-fur People for the Ethical Treatment of Animals and "no one can tell me what to do" individuals. PETA has on its side a slew of celebrity sympathizers and a fantastic media campaign. Unclothed super-models holding only a sign saying, "We'd rather go naked than wear fur" captures our attention. The "Fur Hurts" posters have gotten under *our* skin. It's what we call a kind of "MTV-Activism": Make it fast, make it fun. These tactics have helped along the decisions of such major designers as Ralph Lauren, Calvin Klein, and Donna Karan to forgo their fur licenses. But master fur designer of all, Karl Lagerfeld, is still creating fur fantasies for Fendi and Maximilian. He's the main target now. Let's see if he'll fold.

One problem with PETA is that its policies tend to go *fur*ther than most of us want to embrace. It extends its protests against *all* animal usage by humans. That includes leather, wool, silk, shearling, suede, down, honey, horse races, and so on. Still, our consciences have been irrevocably twinged. To wear a fur coat is to be defiant. When Aretha Franklin tossed on her mink on the bitter cold day of Clinton's inauguration, she was pelted with an icestorm of negativity. Actually, a harsh winter is the answer to a furrier's prayer. When the wind-chill factor hits a minus-something, the deep freeze tends to throw us back to some Flintstone instinct—when man and woman survived by wrapping their bodies in downy fur. But of course, that was pre-Thinsulate.

In answer to the tough critics, the fur buyer's response is to get defensive. "Mink is farm-raised, just like chickens." Or, "When these animals get overpopulated, they'll overrun their habitats . . . or starve . . . or have to be poisoned." The fence-straddlers are compromising by wearing reversibles, cloth on the outside, the fur hidden discreetly within. And given this country's anti-"being-pushed-around" mood, it's possible that PETA's belligerent tactics could backfire. In a recent Prodigy poll of over 35,000 people, a clear majority of 60% said they didn't see anything wrong with wearing fur. Pundit and fervent Pleasure Revenger Fran Lebowitz said in an interview with writer Stephen Drucker in *Mirabella*: "These are the two biggest crimes you can commit in this country. Smoking while wearing a fur coat." She happily commits both criminal acts.

According to the furrier trade publications, the rebound

back to fur has begun. Carla Fendi, happy about her company's sales, was reveling, "Fake fur is over." Fur sales figures are up for the second year in a row, although not nearly back to the late '80s heyday, when coats were cheap and considered a sign of success. Whatever the media hype, pro or con, the industry is not history. Selling fur is still a billion-dollar business.

How else are consumers protesting being "good," being safe, being politically correct? By sitting in the sun again. The beaches are jammed at high noon, and many sun-worshipers, tired of counting their SPFs, have actually gone back to using those silvery sun reflectors to bronze their faces. Tanning salons and tanning machines are more popular than ever. A fit and handsome guy named Chuck Holmes in San Francisco has a deluxe tanning pod right in his home. When asked, "Isn't that dangerous?" he drawled, "Hell, living is dangerous." How Pleasure Revenge is that? And let's consider the heightened interest in erotica. Adult-themed XXX videos, such as those from the successful Falcon Studios, have gotten slick and story-lined in the best of filmmaking traditions. There are clever New Age sex toys that the timid can boldly order from catalogs such as *Xandria*. It's not a coincidence that both *Time* magazine and *U.S. News & World Report* came up with the same cover story, "Sex in America." *Mademoiselle* joined in the exposé with its cover line, "Sin Is In and It's OK." *Penthouse* magazine logged over 800,000 visits on its first day on the Internet. And on the World Wide Web *Playboy* is not only zinging out stories *and* pictures of its Playmates of the Month, but it's put out a call requesting that women 18 and up e-mail their exact measurements and send along electronic photos of themselves, wearing a bikini—or less. Today, we've all gotten so blasé that no one even blinks at gender-jumper RuPaul or at the drag-queen "waitresses" at Lucky Cheng's in New York's East Village.

Finding the lowest possible cultural denominator is also a form of Pleasure Revenging. Watching daytime "confess" shows. Reading the *National Enquirer*. Caring about the private lives of Prince Charles and Princess Di. Renting Sly Stallone movies. Reading trashy novels. Going out of your way to get a free *Pocahontas* drinking cup when you buy a burger—and using it. Gossiping, on the phone, on the Internet, or over the back fence. Not using your brain. It's what we read on a pillow or a T-shirt: "Tired of being depressed? Pop a Prozac. Be happy."

The final question concerning Pleasure Revenge is, of course, "How long will this last?" I often say that it's only going to get crazier, until a cure for AIDS is found. But what is the definition of "crazy"? Take this mini-quiz: By the year 2020, will such things as eating red meat, smoking cigarettes, or stopping in for a Happy Hour be:

1. Considered dangerous and closely monitored.
2. Totally banned by law.
3. Still going full swing.

Only time will tell. For now, the devil-be-damned way we feel about indulging ourselves today goes hand-in-hand with the mini-surge of economic recovery, feeling blessed that recent recessions didn't turn into deep-down dark and dismal depressions. Pleasure Revenge is a feeling of reward for all we've suffered.

As the cynical Dorothy Parker wrote in her four-line poem, "The Flaw in Paganism":

Drink and dance and laugh and lie,
Love the reeling midnight through.
For tomorrow we shall die!
(But, alas, we never do.)

Clicking into Pleasure Revenge is an overriding obsession, both of a feeling-deprived younger generation and of an aging population. For once, the generations are bonded together by a common theme, expressed by our four-line "poem," a '90s "Reason for Paganism":

Eat, drink and be merry.
For the future is uncertain.
Don't wait until tomorrow,
Click today.

SMALL CHALLENGES

CLICKING THROUGH SMALL INDULGENCES

As for the largest-hearted of us,
what is the word we write most often
in our chequebooks?—"self."
—E. PHILPOTTS

I f we live it up in Pleasure Revenge because we believe that "Living well is the best Revenge," then how do we Small Indulge? Isn't a steak and a glass of wine a petite, small, teeny-tiny indulgence? Again, technically yes, but there's a difference. In Pleasure Revenge, there's an anger, a distinct decision to go ahead and be naughty, a vengefulness. Small Indulgences just happens to be a sweeter, softer Trend; it's more about thinking highly enough about yourself to treat yourself well.

To some, it might be a bottle of Veuve Clicquot champagne; for others, a spray of Yves St. Laurent's Champagne eau de cologne. The width and breadth of the Small Indulgence Trend rises and falls with the economy. When the money was growing and flowing in the last decade, an indulgence may have been splurging for the BMW convertible, instead of the sedan. But when money tightened up in the recession, the notion of an affordable luxury, a "reward," was pared down to a bouquet of tulips or fresh raspberries at $6.99 for a small box. When we were frustrated, it was a macadamia-nut chocolate chip cookie.

It all boils down to some deep sense of deprivation. We grew up thinking that "quality of life" was something that automatically improved from generation to generation to generation. Then, without warning, the implicit promise that we would do materially better than our parents was broken, smashed, tossed onto the garbage heap. And not only didn't we have as much job security or make as much money as our folks, but a few other "givens" were shaky: that our skills would stay marketable, that Social Security payouts would always be available, that business meals would stay reimbursable, that college payments would be manageable, and that life's ethics would be ethical.

Can you blame us for jumping into Small Indulgences feet first? It's an age-old method of getting an emotional fix (When the Going Gets Tough, the Tough Go Shopping). We're sad and we're mad (is this why discretionary income is called mad money?). And we feel entitled to some ego gratification, and most definitely to some oral gratification—for one of the easiest ways to Indulge is with our mouths open.

Food. What we look for in Small Indulgences are higher-quality things to eat; you can't Indulge on familiar everyday food, nor can you get much of a psychic soul-lift on "junk" food. Certain foodstuffs are so intrinsically excellent or made with such care that we're willing to overpay for the best. For example, we are Small Indulgencing when we choose two perfect, platter-sized Portobello mushrooms instead of a bagful of ordinary small white toadstools. When we forgo the Mazola and take home that little bottle of truffle-infused olive oil in order to drizzle a few precious droplets into our pasta or rice dishes.

When you think Small Indulgences, think about a container of fresh-squeezed blood orange juice. A box of plump purple figs, tart kumquats, donut peaches (a trendy mutant fruit). Thick white asparagus, the kind the Belgians serve with blackened butter. Artichoke paste (how many thistled leaves had to be scraped, how many hearts had to be broken, for one jar?). Bags of chocolate-dipped Tuscan biscotti. And how about $7.50 for porridge? McCann's award-winning whole grain Irish oatmeal is unbelievably good (tastes nutty) and doing unbelievably well.

For a little double trouble, Häagen-Dazs has introduced

sophisticated Ice Cream Cordials (for after dinner) in rich almondy Amaretto di Saronno and Bailey's Original Irish Cream flavors. Godiva, also, has made a full-circle transition from deluxe chocolates to premium ice creams and now to a velvety-smooth chocolate cordial (great over ice cream). The 20-something crowd goes for the gold, bar-ordering a Swiss liqueur called Goldschlager Cinnamon Schnapps. The bottled drink looks like one of those glass snow globes that you shake up, only the liquid has real gold flakes (edible) floating through it.

With premium flavored coffees so "trendy" now, what about teas? Celestial Seasonings opened the market for both specialty and "cutesy" teas. Now we're completely used to Cranberry Orange, Passion Fruit, Moroccan Mint, and the more exotic blends of Macadamia Nut and Coconut Rum Creme Tea. New York's Takashimaya is one of the most original in making tea a Small Indulgence. Besides brown rice paper bags of tea, it offers polished wooden tea scoops and sugarcane swizzle-stick stirrers. In a Swedish market, we saw general store–like shelves with long cylinders containing different varieties of tea leaves, so that you could dip into one or more and blend your choice of teas yourself. One of the teas looked almost like potpourri or granola. Called Tropical Beach, it had little chunks of dried pineapple, mango, papaya, orange rind, hibiscus, and coriander. Delicious.

Breads have suddenly risen into the hot property zone of consumer spending. No matter how bad (Wonder) or good (Pepperidge Farm's Oatmeal) supermarket bread can be, the prepackaged loaves can't hold a crunch to fresh-baked breads. At New York's Ecce Panis, an incredibly earthy bakery, it's hard to choose between warm, crusty focaccias, topped with sun-dried tomatoes; chewy bread braids, interlaced with onions, anchovies, and olives; and rustic round peasant breads, made fresh every day.

Maybe it's the charming influence of all the books by (now Hamptons-local) Peter Mayle on living in a 200-year-old stone farmhouse in Provence, but there's something very French-village going on in the bread business. Americans in big cities have been seen on their way home with long baguettes tucked under their arms. A company called Gerald Henry's Classic Breads of the

World is trying to get a close second to the fresh-baked taste into national distribution by blast-freezing breads and creating a network of local store delivery. The four choices, so far, are old-world-style Seven Grain, a French Sourdough Boule (round), an Italian Semolina, and a Raisin Pecan Sourdough, all preservative-free.

In a supermarket in Denmark, we were surprised to see packaged bagels for sale. Once a New York/L.A./Miami Jewish specialty, the plain ones have now made it as an international staple. But why haven't the bakers Clicked into offering the full Bagel Shop range: sesame, garlic, onion, poppyseed, the new green-tinted spinach, and the most-popular "everything" bagel, so perfect with a *schmear* of low-fat vegetable cream cheese?

If we like our breadstuffs fresh, we like our donuts even fresher. At a nearby East Hampton place, Dreesen's Market, the donut-making machine is right in the window, and has been spewing out perfect little dough rounds into boiling-hot oil for years. All day long, customers line up for a cup of coffee and one, two, or a small bag of six of those plain, sugar, or cinnamon treats. Owner Rudy DeSanti, after hearing his particular donuts being praised to the skies, saw the Click. He's decided to roll out the irresistible fresh-donut concept, enabling more and more people to Small Indulge. Dreesen's Famous Donut Mix is being distributed to stores in Manchester, Connecticut, and Wilmington, North Carolina. As an adorable (and memorable) promotion, Rudy made up little bags holding his card and a dozen little round Cheerios, calling them "Donut Seeds."

Seems like a lot of people have more dollars (than donuts) to blow. In late 1994, caviar sales were at a record high. What used to be a rare luxury is getting more commonplace (it's not quite so expensive anymore). Beluga, sevruga, ossetra—people are really able to tell the difference and are ordering their favorite. At Soho's Gourmet Garage, a lofty discount food outlet, all sizes and kinds of caviar are big sellers. Same at Zabar's, the food emporium on New York's West Side. At Christmastime, Zabar's engages in a famous price war with Macy's Cellar, and the limos line up for bargains in "black pearls."

Sometimes when one is feeling shaky or stressed out, a short stint of travel can qualify as a larky Small Indulgence, such as a three-day trip to unwind at Canyon Ranch in the Berkshires. Or a theater/museum fix in any major metropolis can feel like a "reward-thyself" happening. If you go to a place for an overnight stay, the Small Indulgence hotel should be someplace small. Nothing with elevator banks or long hallways.

Small chic hotels are finally coming into American cities and coming up to the standards of London's The Draycott or Paris's L'Hotel. Once scarce in New York City because of pricey property values, there's a growing choice of townhouse charmers or human-scaled boutique-hotels, such as the Inn at Irving Place, the Franklin, Morgans, the Shoreham, the Wales (by designer John Barman), and the Mansfield. San Francisco has the Sherman House and the Nob Hill Lambourne (where, instead of a good-night chocolate bonbon, guests get some healthy antioxidant tablets, along with an enigmatic saying, such as "No pillow is as soft as a clear conscience"). Other such hotels are the Cambridge Club in Denver, the Townsend in Detroit, Nicollet Island Inn in Minneapolis, La Colombe D'Or in Houston, Seven Gables Inn in St. Louis, and so on. People are attracted by the extras and the comforting sense that, more than a name in the computer, you're a real live, valued customer.

When looking at the sudden popularity of small hotels, we realized it fits into a separate part of Small Indulgences, a mini-phenomenon that we are calling Zending or the Zen of Spending. It's about paring back and stripping down, about selectively choosing smaller, more soulfully satisfying things. For overnight accommodations, this distills down to no glitz, no big front desk, no fancy uniforms, no silver-domed room service, hold the fruit basket and just give me a soft bed in a pretty room where I can read a book from the 18th century.

Yet . . . there are moments when we crave (we rant and rave for) something small, but something smart, sensuous, statusy, and overpriced. We're into retro-buying the luxuries at a snappy pace. Cashmere mufflers and socks, Barry Kieselstein-Cord keychains (or even better, 20K gold crocodile pins), Lalique glassware, Dunhill sweaters, Gucci shoes, Hermès silk ties and scarves (at $225 each, up 24% in sales). Both Lys and I have been carrying (lugging?) our daily wares for the past two years in all-purpose, lightweight black Prada backpacks (an elitist $470 each, but after the snap on mine recently broke for the fourth time, I replaced it, at the suggestion of Gap Design Chief, Lisa Schultz, with a terrific ultra-functional Gap one, $28). Yet status shopping, although on its way to revving up to '80s intensity, has changed for the mid- to late-'90s sensibilities. It's more understated, less show-offy. Things have to be built to last, finely crafted, have an integrity of their own.

Fortune magazine labeled this "decadent utility," explaining in more detail that "status now resides in enduring value and utility." The writer of the article called BrainReserve to get my Trend-slant on the subject. Among my answers was this very Small Indulgence–oriented view: "People want real quality products with a history and an ethical heritage. But they don't want LV stamped all over something." These days, we prefer the long-lasting craftsmanship of Louis Vuitton luggage and handbags, only in the new solid primary colors—greens, blues, reds, and yellows—instead of those familiar stamped golden LV initials (so often knocked off) on the field of muddy brown. Vuitton's plain leather, black attaché cases, at a pricey $1,660 each, have seen a 31% increase in sales in the first six months of 1994.

We've been saying that in this age of laptops with unseen chips and built-in obsolescence, there's bound to be a swing back to some old-fashioned tangible things. Such as fountain pens— that you have to fill with ink, that smudge all over your fingers, that sometimes even stain your shirts—with the hands-on allure of building sandcastles. Unbelievably, fountain pens costing in excess of $50 are the fastest growing area of the writing instrument market. Top-of-the-line Mont Blancs, Dunhills, and Cartiers sold about $300 million worth in the 1993–1994 sales year. Mont Blanc has opened its own boutique where some of its limited-edition pens, such as ones named after Ernest Hemingway and Agatha Christie, are Clicking as collector's items, increasing in price as the years go by. The whole category of upper-crust pens is not just for graduation and "Today I am a man" presents. They're Small Indulgences, purchased to bring out the poet in us. And they last (at least) a lifetime.

Being Trend-savvy can mean taking on new twists. One smart road for a marketer to ride is to down-scale, rethink, or rework big-ticket items into a Small Indulgence. A Ferrari heated towel rack? Range Rover night-vision binoculars? A mahogany ChrisCraft canoe? Porsche or BMW sleekly designed flatware? A Steinway perfectly pitched clock-radio? Consider this: You may not be able to walk into one of the Bulgari shops around the world to acquire a signature gold watch with the name written around the face ($14,500). But you might be more inclined to buy one of their own Bulgari Swatch-like, pigskin-banded black-face watches for $320 (that is, if you can possibly locate one; they all sold out in a week). Or find a way to purchase their new, ice-cool green unisex fragrance, Bulgari Eau Parfumee, at $185 for the giant, but unadorned bottle.

Focus on the word "small" in Small Indulgences. Things seem to be getting tinier and tinier. Nano-trains that actually run around nano-tracks. Small-format compact discs. A palm-sized Marantz 4-inch color TV, including AM/FM radio. RCA's frying-pan-sized compact dish antenna/satellite receiver that will hardly be noticeable on your roof. The Compaq Contura Aero 4/33C laptop (on which this book was written) with its built-in M&M-Peanut-sized mouse.

Books are shrinking, too. Regular hardcovers the size of paperbacks. The Running Press started its sprightly Miniature Editions in 1989, after noticing the sales of fat little foreign-language dictionaries. Now there are sixty titles of these handy stocking stuffers or little thank-yous, with their own miniature bookplates and bookshelves for collectors. You can leaf through *The Little Book of Magic Tricks, Bible Stories, Quotable Women, Audubon's Birds* and, quite appropriately, *Thumbelina*.

For the 70 million soap opera addicts, it's possible to get a small fix with the teensy new magazines appropriately, amusingly, named *Soap Dish*. The idea for them came from Lauren Canno-Tabach, who was such a devoted follower of "All My Children" that she and her pal, Frank Nowicki, would call each other up every day and discuss what had happened to the characters and their convoluted plot lines. And they lamented that the existing magazines covering the soaps never had enough about their favorite show. So Lauren and her husband, Joshua, remedied this by publishing a slew of micro-monthlies, each one focused on just one soap, starting with "All My Children." In it, there's a wealth of star profiles, gossip, birthdays, all for 99 cents. There's also one for "Another World" and "As the World Turns" and "Guiding Light" and "Melrose Place" and "Beverly Hills 90210," and so on. And for daily dish, you can call 900-454-DISH, 24 hours a day.

Speaking of small things, sales of baby clothes have doubled dramatically in the past few years, especially in the areas of undies, T-shirts, and sleepwear. Indulgent grandparents, prime big spenders, should like the news that Ralph Lauren is now designing small. Polo shirt rompers, cable-knit baby sweaters, infant-sized sweatshirts and coveralls. What's next, a milder Polo Sport to dab behind little ears? Who's next to capitalize on the success of Baby Gap? Baby Calvins (only definitely non-provocative)? Baby Chanel? Baby Bean?

Fragrances provide a good excuse to Small Indulge. The perfume bottle has regained the complicated and regal place it had in the past. There's Lagerfeld's Sun, Moon and Stars in its intricate orb. True Love by Elizabeth Arden, an old-fashioned romantic look, with entwined gold wedding bands on top. But none is as spiffy as an antique Baccarat bulldog atop an early 20th-century perfume called Toujours Fidele by D'Orsay. Why doesn't someone copy the best of the past in perfumery for a Click? In today's modern, multifunctional vein, there's an interesting concept that's captured by Demeter's Atmosphere. You can spritz the multipurpose scents, which come in lavender, cedar, orange, or geranium, anywhere you so desire—on your pulse points, onto your musty beach towel, into your odorific tennis sneakers, or just into the air as a bathroom or car freshener.

Flower power is definitely part of the Small Indulgences Trend. Whether it's one long-stemmed red rose on your desk or a Teleflora bouquet sent to your Mom, fresh flowers are one more example of something that used to signify an "event" and now is routine. Today it's a no-big-deal treat to pick up a pot of forced paperwhites in midwinter while you're out buying your bunch of bananas and low-fat milk. You can order mums or miniature rose bushes, birds-of-paradise or bonsai trees (Lys has to be one of the first non-gardeners to keep a St. Nick gift of a stunted evergreen alive and flourishing), by phone or computer online shopping 24 hours a day. Think back to the time when only horticulturists or people with green thumbs ever tried to raise such a rarefied tropical plant as an orchid in their living rooms. Now phalaenopsis orchids are as commonplace in the home as fuzzy purple violets.

The flower business represents a major Click that is still growing (again, no pun). The 800-Flowers company, for instance, reported an increase of revenues in 1994, up 50% to $200 million.

Americans are also barking up the tree of Small Indulging on their pets. Everyone's going gaga over the new pet super-stores, giant emporiums of 10,000 square feet or more, that are catering to the $15-billion-a-year pet business. A Click. Basics, such as dog food and kitty litter, cost less there (by bulk) than in your local supermarket. These pet stops are following the same concept as Home Depot—stocking everything you could possibly need from aquarium gravel to gerbil feed to Santa suits to pet tartar-control toothpaste. And these superstore chains provide what we call Shopping as Entertainment. There are contests with photo ops for you and your Snookums. Customers are encouraged to shop with their pets, making it a breeding ground for "getting to know you" conversation stops and long-leash playtimes.

Dog food sales alone are a $900-million-a-year business in the United States. People spend $210 per year on toys (actual dried pig's ears, at $2 each, are our doggies' faves, our least faves—yuck) and grooming for their dogs; $75 a year on extras for their cats. But there are plenty of Small Indulgences to lavish on your pet. Perhaps your indoor, declawed cat would like a taste and a view of the wild? You can leave her home by day, safely fixated on *Super Kitty Video,* in which one hour of chirping birds, scurrying mice, and scrambling squirrels should whet her selective appetite.

In *The Popcorn Report,* we extended an idea that was just on the cusp of happening: "Indulging at Discount." Buying cheap, but buying well. It's Clicked because it feels so good, a sort of patting oneself on the back for being clever. There was always the classic, bratty part of Indulging that said, "I want it and I want it now," which is now being overridden by the part that says, "Gee, I know what I want and I know where to get it at a better price."

There's something so satisfying in being able to combine quality *cum* convenience. Saving a few bucks and buying enough (in quantity) to satiate your impulses at such stores as Cheap Sam's and Price-Costco. Our sometimes-quirky friend Ayse, filling out a biographical questionnaire for a proposed presidential appointment, when asked to name her club affiliations, was *so-oo* conscientious, she actually listed the Price Club. Going to one of their giant stores provides a shopping experience that's still so exciting that Lys and I have both spent many a Trend-scouting hour there. These places remain surprising to the uninitiated, because although huge, they are not filled with shoddy products. Though they're void of the haute-aura of plush rugs, seductive lighting, and solicitous sales help, they offer tons of upscaling products on the acres of shelves, from Armani eyeglass frames to hardcover best-sellers to more sun-dried tomatoes in one jar than you could ever consume in your lifetime. The overkill on food sampling also helps cajole people into buying impulse treats.

With discretionary income in the United States for the 46 million people ages 18–29 figured at a high of $150 billion, and with that of adults age 55 and over expected to be almost double that in the next few years, we're talking about a substantial Small Indulgence market. Of course, all affluent households have extra money, but so do one in five of the least affluent households. We are walking around with jingles of pocket change— and compelling reasons to spend it. With the fear of high unemployment, the constant threat of an always-risky stock market, and even talk about yet another recession (sh-h-h), the Trend of Small Indulgences shows no signs of abating. It's like a protective net beneath the high-wire of our anxieties. A soother for our psyches.

Even if this country's bumpy course smooths out in the near

future, the idea, the fantasia that we're *entitled* as human beings to small thrills and chills has carved out a unique niche in the nation's economy. If you have a Small Business, it will pay to concentrate on a way to tap into Small Indulgences. It's a guaranteed Click.

Tulip looking out at David's Lane.

CLICKING THROUGH ANCHORING

When the anchors that faith has cast
Are dragging in the gale,
I am quietly holding fast,
To the things that cannot fail.
—W. GLADDEN, 1836–1918

The New Frontier of the '90s is an inner one.
—PEGGY NOONAN, BUSH SPEECHWRITER

The bad news is that our society is adrift, but the good news is that it's still afloat. Even though we have been getting tossed about like flotsam and jetsam on the sea of life, we are managing to renew our spirits by grabbing on to a line of hope. We like to think of this lifeline as our "anchor." Our safety, our salvation. What keeps our beliefs steady. It's our *route* to a snug harbor and our *root* for support. After a decade or two of materialism and meanness, we're looking for simpler answers. Yes, we're saying, "You can take away outer layers—my job, my wallet, my car, but you can't squash my inner spirit." Like that old Italian motto, "*l'ultima che si perde 'e la speranza*". . . the last thing we lose is hope.

This new Trend about the inner spirit is called Anchoring. The most important part, the core of Anchoring, is taking comfort in what was safe and secure from the past in order to get ready for the future. Looking for the meaning of Life, seeking the answers to the Big Questions. Why now, and not at any other point in our recent history? you may wonder. Because collectively, we're digging deep into our memory, searching for some leap of faith, some link of primal instinct, to help us cut through the daily chaos, or maybe to prepare us for the Big 2000. What a cause for celebration . . . and concern. A new year, a new decade, a new century, a new millennium.

Even though things don't change by markers of time, we superstitiously heed the turning points (if you have a major problem on Dec. 31 at 11:59 P.M., it doesn't go away on Jan. 1). Yet contemplating the year 2000 is triply awesome. All those fat round zeroes. The coming of the Third Millennium. The last one was fifty generations ago, the year 1000, when time moved at the speed of an oxcart. Now, only a few years away, we're bracing ourselves for the unexpected. We're tiptoeing toward the unknown. Will there be more natural disasters? Are the worldwide typhoons, the tornadoes, the floods, the earthquakes, the volcanic eruptions some kind of negative sign from God? Will the New Age dawn with its promise of universal love? Will another Messiah show his face? Her face? Will the enlightened ones stay at the Millennium Hotel and use Millennium shampoo?

Spirituality is at the very heart and soul of the Anchoring Trend. Think about this spiritual seeking as a very focused quest. There was something intangible we lost that's now again found. Amazing Grace? Being Anchored also means taking part in a grander scheme. You know that when you're moored in some warm and cozy spot, you can scan the stars, in hopes of finding some solace in a higher power. As the poet Tennyson once penned, "Cast all your cares on God; that *anchor* holds."

How near and dear to Anchoring is the Jungian idea that the sea holds the collective memory (and future) of all mankind. It's not only that the waves of the ocean are soothing to us, but that the water is symbolic of everything spiritual. The mysterious depths help us to be "whole" again with our ancient past. This could explain the basic urge that all of us who live near the ocean have: We drive to the beach and just sit there, staring at its vastness. (Or, for those who are landlocked, there's a 60-minute video called *Ocean Waves*.) This captivation, according to C. G. Jung, takes us back to the Flood, birthing, and baptisms.

Jung also theorized the way-out idea that the piercing songs of the whales and the dolphins might just be some kind of laser beams that are holding up the sky. In Japan, there's a video about "dolphin therapy" for stress reduction. A priest from the Kyoto Temple's Dolphin Ki Healing Center guides you as you view the videotape of dolphins swimming and making dolphin sounds. Couple this with the wonderful old recording of the *Songs of the Humpbacked Whales* and you might find spiritual nourishment. To take this communication further, to Click into Anchoring, we might have to make it an earthly priority to stop polluting our waters, clean up the ocean of all its garbage, and, of course, Free Willy.

Maybe we're so interested in our personal salvation because we're fast approaching the final salvation of Planet Earth. Teetering on the cusp of 2000 is something none of us has ever faced before (unless there are some time travelers reading this book). It's the beginning of real Star Trek time. In the few remaining years of the '90s, we can expect our emotions to ricochet from giddiness to worry, from elation to doubt—as we formulate ways to anchor and ground ourselves. For all its newness, we may experience a profound sense of belonging, an eerie feeling that we and our ancestors have trod these paths before.

It's as if we're in one gigantic group therapy session, eternally wondering, "What does this all mean?"

It's not surprising that we're turning to some form of religion for the answers. Years ago, in *The Popcorn Report*, we predicted (page 8) this coming: "This decade will see a full turn from fast-track living to a return to home and self-protection. We'll experience a new morality, new religions . . . "

Today, church attendance is soaring. People are going to services in record numbers. In a *U.S. News & World Report* poll, 60% said that they attend a church or synagogue regularly, with half saying that they get there weekly. In this land of believers, 96% think there is a God. Down in the Deep South, the religious are active doers: Some 82% of the populace said they had prayed in the past week, while 47% of them had opened up the Good Book to read—whether born-agains or re-lapsed agains. We're seeing more adult confirmations and bar/bas mitzvahs. Will we see a related resurgence of nuns, priests, ministers, rabbis, and cantors (a Career Click)? Besides performing the still-sacred ceremony of marriage, clerics have new extra work performing the latest in trendiness: divorce rituals. Couples (presumably the ones still speaking to each other) join together in front of a minister or rabbi to remember the good times in the relationship and to forgive hurting each other.

Mega-churches (about 400) with mega-congregations sometimes have to rent the nearest stadiums to hold the thousands of the faithful on an Easter Sunday morn. Some have large-screen TVs to show the follow-the-bouncing-ball lyrics to the new "pop" versions of the hymns. Or the services include rock bands and skilled dancers and skits. To attract even more parishioners, many ministers have been hiring professional stand-up comedians to crack up the audience with their cleaned-up jokes. And sermons have loosened up, often filled with more practical advice than Scripture lessons. Critics of these non-traditional ways may fear that this is the McDonald-izing of religion, but isn't it closer to the communality of the early churches, when the whole populace turned up from the countryside, and children and dogs played ball in the nave?

After all, a relationship with the Divine may be the ultimate expression of Anchoring. The pinnacle Click. Who could have predicted that the pope would attract 400,000 teenagers to an outdoor festival when His Holiness was in Colorado? Or that, as an author, John Paul II would have a global best-seller, *Crossing the Threshold of Hope*? Or that years after American Catholics had successfully banished Latin from their services, the very same parishioners would be snapping up a double CD of the pope reciting the rosary in that ancient language? Or that the pope would be a major marketer, so much so that for his 1995 visit to the East Coast, twenty-three official papal products were blessed and hawked?

This is certainly a new age, when those thought to be in direct contact with God avail themselves of the most modern technologies to spread the word. In fact, televised religion has tapped into an intimate connection with the public. Evangelists are burning up the cable channels. The Faith & Values Channel runs 24 hours a day, reaching at least 20 million households. Charlton Heston stars in a series of Bible videos, filmed in the Holy Land (only how did they redo the Passion scenes?). We've witnessed thousands of Hasidic Jews who stationed themselves outside a New York hospital, waiting for their 92-year-old rebbe to give them a sign that he was the Messiah. A major difference from the days of Christ: these Lubavitcher Jews wore beepers, all the quicker to signal the Word to one another. (Update: Now that the rebbe has passed on, his gravesite is covered with thousands of messages *and* faxes.) Anyway, why should people in 1995 have to worship in the same fashion as people did fifty years ago?

Christian music has gone mainstream too, with sales of $1 billion in 1994. Religious bookstores selling CDs are being included in *Billboard*'s Top 10 List tracking system. Warner Bros. and Sony have launched substantial Christian music divisions. And what MTV did for rock, the Z music channel will do for Christian devotional singing. There's also a small but devoted audience for the newly digitalized CDs that Lys collects of the legendary cantors. They have been remade from some historic recordings that were hidden and managed to survive World War II, giving us a chance to hear the lulling and lyrical tenor voices of the "Caruso of Cantors" Josef Rosenblatt and Gershon Sirota, who perished in the Warsaw Ghetto.

Real "soul" music seems to be a good way to Click into Anchoring. Isn't it truly amazing that *Chant*, a collection of Gregorian hymns (again, in Latin) sung by the cloistered Benedictine monks of Santo Domingo de Silos, could have, would have, ever in this rap 'n' roll lifetime, topped the music charts. In a mere nine months, almost 3 million copies were sold. Its follow-up, *Chant Noel*, turned into a Christmas classic. The fad started in Europe and quickly caught on here. There are a slew of me-toos: *Chill to the Chant, Beyond Chant, Quietude,* and *Old Roman Chant.* Their eternal soothingness almost qualifies them as the "elevator music of the '90s." Several steps up is the soaring revival of Rachmaninoff's *Vespers,* fifteen chants of the centuries-old Russian church.

The music we're listening to is akin to the books we're buying. The operative word here is "buying," not necessarily "reading" (did you ever think that if you put a book by your bed, you'd somehow absorb it by osmosis?). We wish we had a dollar for every time we've heard someone piously say, "By the way, I've just finished *The Celestine Prophecy,* and it changed my life." This book is one of many spiritual uplifters that are continuing their strong hold on the best-seller list. The prophecy hearkens back to an ancient Peruvian manuscript that reveals nine key insights into life itself. Its mission is to move us along from the material world to a spiritual one. James Redfield, the author, paints a picture of a Utopian future in which we might be paid for brainwork instead of brawnwork. His most delightful foresight: if you can heighten your spiritual energy enough, you can become invisible. Will we all be able to float past one other, creating mischief, undetected?

The same folks are reading *Jesus CEO: Using Ancient Wisdom for Visionary Leadership,* by Laurie Beth Jones, based on the motivational skills used by Christ in his relationships. That's a tough act to follow. Another big hit, selling in the millions, is Betty J. Eadie's

Embraced by the Light, a tale about her 1975 experience of "passing on" while having an operation and returning five hours later with the secrets of Jesus. Similarly, there's *Saved by the Light,* by Dannion Brinkley, who tells his dramatic story of being struck by lightning, shown a "cathedral of knowledge" of future events, then revived in a morgue. That the *Light* books are reportedly true and today-based make them less cosmic and crystal-y than *The Celestine Prophecy.* Near-death experiences, to an aging Baby Boomer population, are compelling because they let us mere mortals peek into the bright light-at-the-end-of-the-tunnel of eternity.

It's not just the big publishing companies that are bringing spiritual messages to help readers Anchor. Originally self-published, Marlo Morgan's *Mutant Message Down Under,* about a spiritual trek with the aborigines in Australia, sold over 350,000 copies before HarperCollins picked it up. Similar story for the mini-bible of homespun wisdom, *Meditations for Women Who Do Too Much.* This thick little volume first sold around 1 million copies through desktop publishing, then went on to a commercial venture, offering daily spiritual thoughts on serenity to nurture all those overstressed, 99 Lives women workaholics. Similarly, a pair of outputs from a small press are *Simplify Your Life* and *Inner Simplicity,* both by Elaine St. James, which collectively give 200 simple formulas for reducing the clutter in our lives and focusing on what really matters. Backing up these books on the balance of work vs. family, a recent study out of the Wharton School has just concluded that those of us who place more emphasis on a good family life actually end up earning higher wages than those with less regard for family values.

Today's spiritual revival is as much about Buddha, Allah, Brahma, higher powers, and self-discovery as it is about the Old and New Testament God. More than the monks are chanting "Om Mani Padme Hum" over and over and over. This particular mantra slows down the pace and makes one feel calm. In *SPIN* magazine, singer Courtney Love of the band Hole made this stunning claim about her late husband, Kurt Cobain, "I know he never would have killed himself if I just kept up with my chanting."

A spirited woman named Cyndee Irvine, mother of twins (Jory and Jeremy), after a horrible divorce started her own catering company. For one of her first jobs, she was hired for a party of 200 on the 14,000-foot summit of Mauna Kea, serving "chocolate, oxygen, water, and tea sandwiches." Even closer to God is her second business venture, called Latitude 20: Beads and Botanicals, which makes sandalwood prayer beads (*malas* in Hawaiian) for Buddhist priests and sandalwood rosaries for Catholic orders. Very on-Trend, namely S.O.S. (Save Our Society), part of the company's profits are plowed back into reforestation of the island's sandalwood trees.

Not every culture is thrilled about the sharing or borrowing of its deeply religious rites. Native Americans are organizing in protest those New Agers who are usurping the Indian rituals of shamans, sipakus, and sweat lodges. Dream catchers, rain sticks, and ceremonial pipes have been commercialized to the point that they're being sold in gift stores next to Donald Duck lamps. One of the American Indian targets is the Church of Gaia, named after a Greek earth goddess, which blends Indian rituals with ecology.

To create a holiday celebration that African-Americans can truly call their own, the concept of Kwanzaa was developed almost twenty-five years ago. Coming around the same time as the hustle and bustle of Christmas and Chanukah, Kwanzaa is a family festival lasting seven days, during which close groups gather to feast and light candles dedicated to a different guiding principle. One is "Ujaama," a Swahili word for cooperative economics. In a small-business expo held in New York during 1994, over 300 participants came to show off Kwanzaa holiday products, African sculpture and fabrics, and depictions of Nia Umoja, the counterpart to Santa Claus.

And, according to Helen Tworkov, editor of *Tricycle*, a trendy Buddhist review with up to 150,000 readers, America is on the verge of a breakthrough in Buddha-dharma, a flowering of the wisdom that has enlightened zillions of souls around the world. This quarterly reports on everything from Virtual Reality to "Awakening with Prozac," and even covers such a regular guy as Phil Jackson, coach of the Chicago Bulls, who has been meshing Zen principles with his work life (let's take it as a good sign that the Bulls have won three consecutive NBA championships). And thanks to certain celebrity meditators such as Richard Gere, Oliver Stone, Ellen Burstyn, and Tina Turner, the remote purity of the followers of the Dalai Lama is now part of the *People* magazine pulp. Not druggy or flaky, many of the American Buddhist set, including a few Rockefellers, are social and powerful.

We've watched other signs of Zen Buddhism's popular infiltration. Director Bernardo Bertolucci made a $35 million film, *Little Buddha*, about an enlightened youngster. Lys's last birthday dinner was at one of the elegant Zen Palate restaurants, at Union Square in NYC. The very upscale New Age shop Felissimo stocks

Zen gardening tools, natural linens, jot-a-good-thought books, candles, tea sets, and Yanni CDs.

Perhaps you can find the road to Nirvana with some of the newer ways to tap into Buddhism. You can listen to the badmouthed rap group the Beastie Boys, with their rap song "Bo-dhisattva Vow," celebrating the inner joys of meditation. While relaxing, you can be absentmindedly combing one of those desktop-sized Zen gardens, containing sand and rocks, with a small wooden rake to make peaceful, wavelike swirls. Or you can read that fat volume of *The Little Zen Companion*. Or the "pithy ponderings" of *Zen to Go* by Jon Winokur. Some of the sayings in this book are self-explicable and very Clickable: "Zen is simply a voice crying, 'Wake up! Wake up!'" "Zen does not teach, it points." And "Zen is like looking for the spectacles that are sitting on your nose."

When performance artist Laurie Anderson went on a trekking trip in the Himalayas to find a sky-high lake where clues to the next Dalai Lama's name are mysteriously supposed to show up on the water's surface, she fell dangerously ill from altitude sickness. Because she ran a high fever for five days, had hallucinations and a splitting headache, she was sent back down in a body bag, by donkey, with a guide and an American mountain climber. This near-death experience in Tibet freed her to write her album *Bright Red*. One song, "Freefall," was dedicated to the mountaineer who helped her and is about losing one's sense of direction when drowning in an ocean. Another song, "Tightrope," looks at the symbolism of a tightrope as connected to mortality. Laurie sees it not only as a family bloodline, but also as a lifeline connected to someone else. A spiritual anchor and security when exploring the meaning of life.

The search for life's Anchor simply can't be viewed as weird anymore. It's gone from California fringe to national mainstream. It's a must for filling the void that so many are feeling. Humbly speaking, we should all be paying attention to this and thinking about the benefits of taking a daily meditation break. Bring this concept to your office, if it's not already there. Condé Nast, the magazine group owning *Vogue, Glamour, GQ, Gourmet*, and *Vanity Fair*, offers its employees a midday *t'ai chi* break. Talk about inspiring collective kinship. Talk about radiating energy.

For all those who can't find a quiet place even in their own backyard (who can, now that there's always some modern machine either ringing, singing, whining, belching, or buzzing?), there are many serene hideouts around the country. In California, there's the Soto Zen Buddhist monastery, Tassajara; the tough Ashram, Marin County's Spirit Rock Meditation Center; and the 160-acre Zen Mountain Center in the San Jacinto Mountains—and in upstate New York there's Zen Mountain Monastery. All are places where you can meditate to your mind's content.

One of the biggest draws of these centers is the offering of total silence. At the Insight Meditation Society in Barre, Massachusetts, you can go for three- or ten-day retreats, for six weeks or three months of silence. No talking, no distractions. Just a concentration on living every moment to the fullest in the present. After such a stretch of outer and inner peacefulness, your breathing gets better, your mind is more focused and alert. It's restorative to your body and its problems. Supposedly, chronic pain is reduced, insomnia fades away, fertility is enhanced. You can keep this bliss going by saying a mantra (a simple word, phrase, or sound) once or twice a day for ten minutes or so. Keep it different from the anxiety-ridden yuppie mantra: Get ahead, get ahead, get ahead.

These havens are not necessarily all Zen-based. There's the more traditional cloister, the Abbey of Gethsemane, near Louisville, Kentucky. And Wainwright House in Rye, New York, which caters to midlife transitions, where you can go to "feel the wisdom of your future self." And Wisdom House in Litchfield, Connecticut, which is set up as a religious sanctuary with an emphasis on feminism and the arts, where you can retreat to deepen your faith. In the snooty suburban haunt of Darien, Connecticut, the Catholic Sisters of Saint Brigitta have set up the Vikingsborg Guest House as a "B&B" for the world-weary. Even in London, you'll have a chance to unwind in the ultra-hip Life Centre, housed in an old church building, which has a staff of holistic therapists doing hands-on stuff from shiatsu to food allergies to yoga.

Just how middle-of-the-road can Anchoring get? Middle enough to bet that a new theme park will have an intrinsic attraction to the masses. In the works is Maharishi Veda Land, a billion-dollar theme park near Niagara Falls, created by magician Doug Henning with the Maharishi Mahesh Yogi. The attractions will be a cross between magic illusion and high tech. For the first time, the entertainment will be woven around enlightenment and knowledge, so that the Mountain of Immortality, for instance, will cleverly teach visitors about issues of preventive medicine. Instead of heaps of junk food, the park will be offering the best of veggie burgers and dogs.

Yes, yes, yoga is Clicking. Literally meaning "unity" in Sanskrit, yoga also has the same root as the English word "yoke," which carries the double connotation of "to unite" as well as "to place under discipline." This 4,000-year-old "discipline" of mind and body health is knocking the gym socks off aerobics. Frantic exercising seems too close to real life. With yoga, you get to leave the everyday world and focus inward. Its quiet intensity increases your flexibility, improves your concentration (great for golf games), and strengthens unused muscle groups. Just in our office neighborhood alone, there are a plethora of yoga centers: Yoga Zone, Urban Yoga Workout, Iyengar Yoga, Astanga Power Yoga, and Sivenanda Yoga Vedanta Center. Watch for the rapid growth of centers for yoga, spreading as fast as coffee bars across the continent. There's already an 800 number to find a class in your area (800-359-YOGA).

If you can't find a practitioner, you can always join in on yoga TV on PBS or buy yoga videos, such as *Jane Fonda's Yoga Exercise Workout* or the magnetic *Buns of Steel Yoga*. According to a recent survey, yoga now is being practiced by 4 million Americans, double the number who practiced yoga in 1991. Isn't this a market just waiting to be leveraged? Just as golfers and schoolkids need special clothes, why aren't there yoga/meditating outfits with plenty of give so that the pants don't stretch out at the knees? These soul shops could also offer meditation pillows and collapsible benches for all-day sittings.

Yoga limberness can be incorporated into another realm of mind/body unity: Tantric sex. In ancient Hindu Tantra practices, sexual union is a sacrament, when both partners achieve a state of oneness with each other and the universe. The physicality goes like this: through controlled breathing and body positioning, you can expand your orgasmic energy to flow through your entire being. Ecstasy, supposedly for hours and hours. To help you achieve the alignment of spiritual harmony involved in Higher Sex, there are books, magazines, courses, catalogs. In *Ecstasy Through Tantra*, Dr. Jonn Mumford suggests that "one possible translation of the Sanskrit prefix *tan* is 'expand,' while *tra* means 'liberate'; . . . a colloquial translation of Tantra would be 'mind-blowing.'"

But if you don't have the patience to master the techniques (or are a prude), or just can't sit still for even regular yoga, you can always try prayer-walking. As Linus Mundy, author of the book

Prayer-Walking, put it, it's "a stroll with your soul." Saying a prayer as you walk is apparently very good at relieving stress. Whether you step lively with your favorite passage or just a simple "Thy will be done," it serves to elevate your thoughts and well as speed up your circulation.

At BrainReserve, we first started to identify some of these inwardly focused Trend indicators as belonging to a group we called the Mystical Tribe. Stores in Manhattan such as Enchantments and Star Magic do a brisk business in goddess candles, harmony balls, wave machines, old-fashioned kaleidoscopes, and astrology decoders. Many small towns have shops specializing in crystals, geodes, and mystic ambers. Top jewelry designers have taken a mystical lead, from Byzantine and Maltese crosses to Robert Lee Morris's talisman necklaces. What about Sanskrit bracelets?

The call to mysticism has been backed up by several popular polls. One 1994 *Self* magazine survey showed that 84% of respondents said they believed that "a higher power listens to and answers prayers," 76% believed in miracles, 63% in life after death, 55% in ESP, 51% in Satan, and 46% in out-of-body experiences, and 39% reported they had "personally experienced or witnessed a miracle." Pertaining to being a "witness" to a miraculous happening, the readers' stories ranged from "My father-in-law was diagnosed with terminal cancer. It totally disappeared in six months," to "My mother passed away when I was 6. I got a visit from her at age 10, when I was very sick. I got a rare opportunity to tell her how much she was missed."

Such once-strange, now seemingly normal tales were repeated daily on NBC's daytime show "The Other Side," which aired right after "The Today Show" and probed "the other side of everyday living." How did the producers find such fantastic fodder for the imagination? During a show on channeling, one woman confessed to being able to hear John Lennon's voice. She was obviously finely tuned in to the music world: she also was in contact with Wolfgang Amadeus Mozart. Speaking of making connections with the past, one of the eeriest musical experiences we've heard in a long time is a CD, *The Sinking of the Titanic*, by Gavin Bryars (Point Music 446–061–2). Bryars writes, "The initial starting point for the piece was the reported fact of the band having played an Episcopal hymn in the final moments." According to a survivor, "The last I saw of the band when I was floating out in the sea with my lifebelt on, it was still on the deck playing 'Autumn.' How they ever did I cannot imagine." The composer goes on to speculate, "It would appear that the musicians continued to play even as the water enveloped them . . . on a poetic level, the music, once generated in water, would continue to reverberate . . . and descend with the ship to the ocean bed and remain there, repeating itself over and over." Listening to it, along with echoes of the voices, is like being Anchored to the bottom of the sea.

We crave people who can tell us who we really are (or who we really were). What we are meant to do. Is money or fame coming our way? Are we going to Click soon? An ancient Indian astrology called Jyotish, more sophisticated than "What is your Sun Sign?" according to Arpad Joo, can dispense practical as well as personal advice. Magicians, psychics, and palm readers are no longer considered "corny" at dinner parties or events. In certain restaurants, it's possible to get a reading over your arugula for $30. And for those who prefer to get their psychic fix at home, there's always Dionne Warwick's televised Psychic Friends Network. For a $3.95-a-minute phone call, you can get insights into your personal life. (One warning: A former employee blew the ethics whistle, claiming that phone callers were strung out on the line for twenty-two minutes, so that an average phone-in cost over $80. Put on your kitchen timer.)

For specific help in business, you can consult *Sphericles—The Business Oracle: Your Intuitive Guide to Enlightened Business Behavior,* by Joanne Black and Christine Roess. Sphericles are clear marbles with numbers, along with a guidebook explaining what the chosen numbers mean. To tap into your creative powers, you must reach into a velvet pouch for three marbles, then read what the book says about your choices. It supposedly works, "not because there is magic in them, but because there is magic in you." And even if you don't locate the perfect business solution, if you dip into the bag during a meeting, at least you can succeed in starting a lively creative dialogue. The advertising agency, Bates Worldwide, apparently thought so, ordering 1,000 copies as gifts.

Some of the more open-minded CEOs we know are consulting with spiritual guides to help them understand their business (it's a far cry from the arrow-straight execs, the Charles Revsons and Tom Watsons, who grew multibillion-dollar companies their own way). They hire people like Charles Nunn, who discovered over the course of his business career that he had "intuitive gifts" and that he could "read" people and situations in remarkably accurate ways. Now he's hired to go to board meetings, be introduced simply as a "consultant," and then, afterward, meet with the chairman to reveal what he "senses" is really going on. He's sort of a witch doctor and headhunter rolled into one.

If "intuitive consulting" isn't your thing, maybe "archetypal analysis" is. This involves a myth expert who analyzes the management styles and personalities of your executive team. Follow this. You can actually find out what archetypes (magicians, warriors, discoverers, travelers, etc.) are active in the company and what journeys different people in the company are on. Who cares? you think. Well, a senior management team with a lot of warriors may do well against the competition, while too many warriors on one board may end up in constant squabbles. A traveler who is deskbound may not be a happy camper, and so on.

And these days, when someone ends a meeting with the words, "Let me sleep on it," it may mean more than meets the shut-eye. Some people are studying or even manipulating their dreams as a source of knowledge, inspiration, or personal direction. In the past year, two serious books have been published revealing a literary dreamlife: *My Education: A Book of Dreams* by William Burroughs, and *A World of My Own: A Dream Diary* by Graham Greene. Descartes was said to have formed his main Rational philosophy during a dream. Authors such as William Styron and Isabel Allende have found their story plots in dreams. Even scientist Albert Einstein told of dreaming about the theory of relativity as a young teen. Dream workshops are springing up all over the world. The Pacifica Institute in California offers a degree in dreamwork. The Discovery Channel ran a five-part series entitled "The Inner World of Dreams." And the humanly progressive Swedish government recently agreed to fund dream studies as part of its national health plan.

If you have the slightest doubt about the swelling surge of Anchoring, look at the flutter of angels who have come calling. Earth angels, teen angels, dream angels, sheltering angels, lusty angels, trusty angels, even fallen angels. *Time* magazine's cover story, "The New Age of Angels," cited its poll indicating that 69% of Americans believe angels exist and 46% believe they each have an individual guardian angel. Some 20 million viewers tuned in to the NBC special, "Angels: The Mysterious Messengers." These downy-winged creatures have supposedly been given the power to bring us sacred little handwritten notes from God, plus they can wrap us in the glow of unconditional love and protection.

Our Dutch painter friend Gerti Bierenbroodspot has had a major exhibition with an oversized catalog for which Lys wrote the introduction, naming it *Angeli: A Celestial Renaissance*. In it, she penned:

> Hark, the heavenly angels are here. Divine messengers on gossamer wings; dream travelers with cosmic wanderlust; astral bodies of light, radiating an aura of majestical Renaissance. Angels tread lightly with echoless footsteps, their silence haunted by blasts of unheard trumpets. We are attracted to angels intuitively (like moths to a flame), transporting us beyond the realms of logic, experience or common sense, opening us up to strange new dimensions, tickling strange new thoughts in our everyday minds.

Bookwise, among the many best-sellers, there are *Where Angels Walk* by Joan W. Anderson, *A Book of Angels* by Sophy Burnham (in its thirty-sixth printing), *Answers from Angels* by Terry Lynn Taylor, *Inspired by Angels* by Sinda Jordan, and *The Angels and Us* by Mortimer Adler. Most revolve around recalling dramatic non-human encounters or astounding angel-assisted rescues. For those who feel they have angel tendencies, there's a handy reference book, the *Handbook for Aspiring Angels*.

Actually, these fine-feathered friends are a big business. But it's the angels of the cherubic kind (pink, plump, and playful) that have truly Clicked, replacing friendly pigs and mooing cows as the popular fronts on greeting cards, kitchen magnets, and soap dish holders. There are more than fifty angel-only stores in the United States and Canada, angel-specific mail-order catalogs selling such angel paraphernalia as heavenly pillows, wall plaques, fine china, even Angel perfume by Thierry Mugler in a star-topped atomizer. Most of these depictions are as close to angels as angel food cake—light, airy, and excessively sweet. You can try to follow popular angelic goings-on by subscribing to an angel newsletter called *Angel Watch* or the bimonthly magazine *Angel Times*. A newspaper columnist aptly termed this angelic obsession "Angels R Us." A good use of angels comes from toy company Heaven on Earth, based in Washington, D.C., which makes soft, cuddly guardian angel dolls and Blessed Bears. Founded by Gerry McClure, the concerned firm donates 10% of pretax profits to help needy children globally, sending donations to Bosnian and Chinese orphanages and to the Children's Emergency Medical Fund here.

On the more serious side, the Broadway hit *Angels in America, Parts I and II*, featured a heavy-winged golden creature who swooped down from the rafters to offer heartfelt but cryptic advice on the salvation of the world and hallelujahs. But still, most of the angels you see these days are way far afield from the sword-bearing figures of yore, with avenging hearts and terrible swift swords. Today's angelic kinds are positioned as guides to point us to the path, a kind of spiritual nanny. They don't smite, nor do they storm. Theologians have suggested that these angels offer people who've been disenchanted with strictly traditional religion a safe new bridge to God. For angels are the ultimate in ecumenism, appearing in the Koran and the Cabala, Islam and Zoroastrianism.

Our prediction: If angels are everywhere, can devils be far behind? The flip-side of good: evil. Fiery red Satan, the Prince of Darkness, and his horned tribe. "I had a halo but it slipped." Or as the Cowboy Junkies sing, "Misguided angel hanging over me . . . so like Lucifer." Aren't you curious to know, now that Jeffrey Dahmer has been executed, did he go straight to Hell? The Hannibal Lecters and serial killers. Haven't Americans always glorified the outlaw (Jesse James), the gangster (*The Godfather*, the Dapper Don), the vigilante (Bernard Goetz)? Imprisoned killer Charles Manson has released an album, *Commemoration*, on White Devil Records. Actually, a woman we know, Rosemary Rogers (not the romance novelist), who has a day job running a jingle house for commercials, has been writing a book with co-author Sean Kelly that has this new Anchoring hook: *Who in Hell?*, a Who's Who of the denizens down below. A "good Catholic girl," Rosemary first co-wrote *Saints Preserve Us*, about the saintly guys who influenced her childhood.

Interview with the Vampire, both Anne Rice's novel and even more, the unscary movie, served its purpose in inspiring an awareness of Vampire Chic. In an imitation of the vampire hero Lestat (his ever-continuing story is detailed in the 1995 best-seller *Memnoch the Devil: The Vampire Chronicles*), men are donning Dracula black cloaks, high-necked and wrap-tied white poet's shirts, and brocade vests. All the better to comb the back alleys of sensual fantasies. The newer beauty-looks for women are pale of face with dark-rimmed eyes and blood-red lips. Will we be drawing faint blue veins on our skin next, to imitate the living dead? Satanic cults are thriving, with their ritual slayings (more than just chickens). Paganism and witchcraft are being openly practiced. Wicca, goddess worshipers, are led by self-declared witches. Gone are the days of being burned at the stake.

To protect our homes and guide us along a mystical way, many of us are creating our own altars in some corner of the house. One room can be dedicated to solitude, filled with tranquillity. An aviary or aquarium would be nice. Or it can be a small space where you display your special or sacred objects. Blessed waters, a sand bottle, seeds from your favorite plant, a pyramid, a statue of a saint. Unlike an altar at church, you can change it at whim. Little shrines are also being built as an outpouring of emotion when there's a tragic death. When River Phoenix OD'd outside the Viper Room in L.A., fans left flowers, notes, and little mementos of affection. Here in East Hampton, after an 18-year-old was killed when a deer crashed into her car, strangers spontaneously pinned straw crosses and bouquets on the nearby telephone pole.

And then there's the Twilight Zone aspect of Anchoring. A longing to step into a time machine, take a Quantum Leap and step out into a far simpler time. Retro-time. The *Back to the Future* movie and its time-travel sequels captured the essence of this era-crossed adventurous spirit. So does the underground cult book *Time and Again,* by Jack Finney, which was published in 1970; yet sales are stronger than ever. It's your basic story of leaving late 20th-century life and re-entering in January 1882. No cars, no planes, no computers, no AIDS, no flip-the-channel wars and starvation nations on TV.

Fashion can Click into Anchoring or retro-timing, too. If it's done right. A very tuned-in design team from Arnhem in the Netherlands captivates customers with the sheer magic and erotic joy expressed in their clothes. Geert de Rooji and Hans Demoed named their company, The People of the Labyrinths, and the two men run it exactly the way they want. They produce only as much as they can hand-print in their workshop, but the gossamer silks and soft leathers with their signature scrawlings of golden messages, looking like opulent 16th-century creations, are in demand worldwide. Every six months the poetry shifts, incorporating such themes as Lava to Angels to Reverie to their favorite, Taurus. When the whim hits them, they may accept a commission to custom design. Recently, Hans related the story about "a pregnant woman who requested a special bedcovering on which she could birth her child." They concocted one with "symbolism capturing strong things in life: eagles, lions, hands, crowns, old references such as Ice Age and Meditation and new references such as DNA." Prices are high for our dollar, but each piece is a work of art.

The 1909 Co. has put out a vintage clothing catalog that has closely copied original turn-of-the-century clothing and accessories. In it, romantic frocks and velvet opera capes are draped on dressmaker dummies. The photographs are sepia-toned. Guess they struck the right consumer chord. When the 1994 edition was sent out, the company did 50% of its 1993 sales in just the first week.

Do you know who your great-grandparents or great-great-grandparents were and where they came from? The American Genealogical Society reports that record numbers of people are trying to retrace their roots. In fact, genealogy is listed as the third most popular hobby in America. More than preparing a pedigree, it Anchors you in your family history. Oliver Wendell Holmes said it this way, "Every man is an omnibus in which his ancestors ride." Computer helpers make the backtracking easier: Family Ties for Windows or DOS and the super-duper Family Tree Maker Deluxe CD-ROM. To show how a little genealogical digging can help, take the example of the "Kmart Sisters." Katie Couric on NBC's "Today Show" told the incredible story of two women who worked at the Kmart in Port Huron, Michigan, and didn't know they were related. Until one woman's daughter did some sleuthing on the Prodigy genealogy bulletin board and pieced together bits of information about the family name, Vanderpool. It seems that these half-sisters, one who worked at the bakery, another at the deli, had actually become friends and took lunch breaks together. The older sister, Jeanette, given up for adoption as an infant and raised as an only child, suddenly had a big happy family.

Family ties matter. Since everything from liberal voting patterns to adultery is now thought to be genetic, you can create your own "genogram" or behavior tree to be aware of characteristics that show up generation after generation. Books such as *How Healthy Is Your Family Tree?* or *Voices in Your Blood: Discovering Identity Through Family History* will explain how. You might want to create your own oral/visual history. Camcorder it or just audiotape as many members of your family as you can. Ask when your Great-Aunt Dot had her elevator accident or how Grandfather Floyd, a small-town guy, won the hand of the beautiful, worldly Suzanne. If your family is nonverbal or shy, egg them on with something fun, such as a Monopoly-like board game called LifeStories: A Family

Game. Pore over old photographs, collect family recipes, describe family heirlooms, read out letters from the past. Try to find out the way they hugged, the way they coped, the way they communicated. Patterns that shaped you. Before it's too late.

This history-taking could actually be a good profession for someone. Or it could be a service offered at, say, Price Club. The personalized tape could be put together with footage of the times: a shot of immigrants coming to Ellis Island or of farmers raising a barn. For the future, there could be Virtual Genealogy. Your children or grandchildren could see/hear your hopes and dreams in context—and be interactive with you. Wisdom could be dispensed at different times of their lives. Real guardian angel-ism.

Hand-in-hand with family trees, family crests have come back again. On baseball caps and fax paper as well as on Tiffany rings and blazer pockets. Or in heritage books, listing all the other people in the United States with your particular name. How clubby, how clanny. Plus it really doesn't matter if you ever had a family crest in the old country. You can merely make one up to be imaginative, artsy-craftsy, or just plain funny. Isn't the family golden retriever just as regal as a feudal lion or a unicorn? You can have a pen, if you're a writer, a toque if you're the chef. It's possible to consult a florigrapher, such as Nan Keenan of Ligonier, Pennsylvania, who can tell you what flower your name is associated with— or the floral symbol of your particular profession. Anything to help you identify yourself. Anything to help you Click.

So many people have been inspired to make pilgrimages to find their ancestors' graves. Will the practice of making tombstone rubbings become more popular? Or in the case of the 6 million lost in the Holocaust, it has to be enough to try to locate the family villages or any records. In the very brilliant film *Schindler's List,* Steven Spielberg accomplished the impossible. He allowed us to be able to sit through the horrors without breaking down. The litany of the lists of names, the names, the names, served as a chant to remind us to fight forgetfulness. Elie Wiesel, author, Nobel Prize winner, and concentration camp survivor, tells us over and over, "Never forget." The U.S. Holocaust Memorial Museum in Washington, D.C., also Anchors that unspeakable epoch and hopes that its reminders will keep the past present. More than 2 million visitors bought tickets for it in its first year. We tread through in tears, choked for air in its actual boxcar, sick in our hearts from its recorded testimonies. Fighting forgetfulness appears in other guises, from the finely chiseled Vietnam Memorial to the sad, storytelling patches that are sewn together in the AIDS Quilt. Memories can Anchor us.

Whatever it is that Clicks into a deep meaning for your life one thing is evident: We're at the start of a Great Awakening. A time of spiritual upheaval and religious revival. A time to dig into the core principles of the past to provide some sort of Anchoring for the unknown ahead. What's different about this Awakening is that there's very little agreement on who or what God is, what constitutes worship, and what this ritualistic outpouring means for the future direction of our civilization. After the soul-free '80s, we're busy trying to put passion and meaning back into our everyday lives, to find the old values—faith, hope, and charity. We're looking for the essence of ourselves—our lost souls.

There's a melting-pot-ism on the fast lane to enlightenment. A sampling of spirituality, like a soup du jour. A little this-a, a little that-a. An early Russian Orthodox chant to dine by. A rooftop "wizard" to shield our homes from lightning. Ghosts, maybe. Reincarnation, definitely. A fear that we're in Sodom and Gomorrah Revisited. Repent! Another chance, the ultimate Click.

And all those we've talked to, in the last few years, seem to define their karma and ground themselves by following one Golden Rule: What Goes Around, Comes Around. If that's not Anchoring, what is?

CLICKING THROUGH EGONOMICS

The greatest magnifying glasses in the world are a man's own eyes
when they look upon his own person.
-ALEXANDER POPE

Every Trend has a life of its own, and Egonomics is in its prime. Me, myself, and I are the driving forces behind Egonomics. "Me" wants customization; "myself" is a name, not a number; and "I" demand personal service. If you Click into the Trend of Egonomics, it's one of the most effective ways to reach customers, by appealing to their individuality, the singular part of them that says, "There is no one out there quite like me."

Egonomics is everywhere we turn and look. Even where I literally sit down. My chrome yellow Mustang with its "Popcrn" vanity plates (by the time this book is done, my new vanity plates will say "Clicking") comes with a driver's seat that can be adjusted three ways so the seat contours differently to different body shapes. That's Egonomics—thinking about a person's comfort as well as design. And the everywhereness of Egonomics can also be reflected by our personalized hair colors. In Lys's case, a blue streak (pun here—talks a blue streak, writes a blue streak) and in mine, a combination of Mustang yellow and fuchsia. This touch of whimsical identification (which lasts about four weeks) is painted on by the very artistic Louis Licari at his salon, where we tell him to "Just add it to our *natural* colors." We've been blond (Lys) and red (me) so long, we don't know the difference. In another example of Egonomics, which is about anti-identification, Lys painstakingly cuts the outside labels off (or inks them out) of her running shoes, her walking shoes, her T-shirts, her duffel suitcases. This anti-logo attitude signifies a real desire to be yourself. Interestingly, in Europe and here, there's a new brand of shoes that is selling very well, simply called, "No Name." Would you want to cut this label off?

Egonomics is the integration of, the Clicking of, business and personal life. Americans have gradually been getting used to a 24-hour day. Between 7-Elevens and diners and 24-hour supermarkets, it's been possible to feed your late-night hunger pangs with a burger or a pint of Cherry Garcia. But now we have Kinko's, the chain of 24-hour copy shops, to run off multiples of reports finished by the burning light of midnight oil. By never closing, Kinko's conforms to your schedule, you don't have to conform to theirs. Egonomics drives The Body Shop when it takes your order for your favorite peppermint foot lotion and refills it through the mail, according to a timetable that you personally set.

Egonomics says no niche is too small. If you can Click with one segment of the population, but Click solidly, you'll make it happen. After being asked to speak at a CEO Forum (for YPOers—Young Presidents Organization—who've reached the age of 49) in Berlin, we were constantly amazed at how many of them made their fame and fortune on little widgets and necessary wadgets. For a clearer sense of Clicking into this Trend, it's about making thinner dental floss for people with tightly spaced teeth. It's about the old sporting goods company, Everlast's, smartly deciding that it could expand on the traditional black and red boxing gloves and come out with a choice of a pastel glove for women. Egonomics is also about self-expression. Hallmark's Personalize It! line of greeting cards lets you customize your cards (instead of just Mom or Son, you can imprint their nicknames). American Greetings' Create-a-Card has set up computers in drugstores and airports to let you soar as your own art department.

If you want your customer to feel personally targeted, an 800-number will definitely help. Everyone from mutual funds to Clairol haircoloring has had contact operators or Help lines, but now even the fashion field is getting into the we'll-be-there-for-you act. L'Eggs, the stocking people, has launched a new line of pantyhose with an 800-number so that its answering lines can guide women through the complicated maze of finding the perfect size.

Speaking of sizes, the Institute for Standards Research has finally decided to look anew at women's body types and update body measurements (sounds very forensic). It's long overdue, since the last national survey was in the '30s. It'll be collecting data from at least 10,000 women from ages 18–55, with an ethnic and geographical balance. Lots of questions can be answered. Are women thinner, fatter, taller, better built than they were? What does a size 2 look like? A size 12? A size 2X?

The laws of Egonomics say personal touch is everything. Trying to be in touch is Judi Roaman of J. Roaman in East Hampton, a double storefront of DKNY clothes, one for women, a separate one for men. Same name, different location—she also has a DKNY/women's store in Aspen. In both places, Judi keeps a record (both written and mental) of her good customers, their sizes and color preferences, and what they've purchased at her stores. Then she lets them know when something new comes in that they may like (or may need to extend a "look"). Her go-the-extra-mile service works the other way around, too. If someone walks into one of her small stores looking for a specific DKNY jacket, sweater, or sweatpants, and she doesn't have it (or it's sold out), Judi whips into action, calls around to DKNY boutiques in nearby metropolitan department stores. She has to order at retail on the customers' charges, but she makes sure that they get exactly what they want. Can you glean a lesson from this? Do you know any other store owner whose business would Click if he/she did this?

Other examples of customer service are Egonomically positive in that they can help turn an ebbing business around. For instance, a British chain of retail establishments, the Burton Group, came to BrainReserve after reading our ideas in *The Popcorn Report*. Their CEO, John Hoerner, and Chief Executive, Stuart Rose, inquired about having us reposition one of their divisions, Dorothy Perkins, which has a total of 564 women's and girls' stores in the U.K. After interviewing hundreds of women there and drawing on our research (both TrendBank and TalentBank) here, we made our recommendation about what women ideally want from their clothing store.

The strategy for Dorothy Perkins was called "Bonds & Bridges," meaning the stores had to become "consumer-responsive" by creating closer ties with the customer. For example, we suggested that they stay open longer to catch the newer commuter group of working women, open up their display windows, and relocate their cash registers from the backs of the stores. But the biggest contribution, related to the strong pull of Egonomics, was to advise them to log all purchases on computer, so that in a future selling season, if a mix-and-match blouse, skirt, jacket, or accessory came in, they could call up the customer and either invite her to come in or even send the item to her home. This concept came in part from a premise long-held at BrainReserve: There should be no difference in service between an upper-crust store and an everyday one. Everyone wants the same amount of attention. If you can deliver it, you can get a customer for life.

The potential of Dorothy Perkins in the Burton Group blossomed under this new connectiveness. We'd like to think that BrainReserve can share a part of the glad tidings (*Wall Street Journal*, 5/19/95) that their pretax profits for six months (ending 3/95) went up 91%. One of its directors explained that "the company is just starting to reap the rewards of a business strategy to re-establish better-quality brands and entice customers to come back in."

The shift in direction to brand-name stores, such as Speedo, Reebok, and Nike, is a mid-'90s marketing phenomenon—Clicking into a combination of company and consumer needs. Although the products are sold also in traditional department and large discount stores, the smaller, free-standing, single retail outlets offer distinct benefits. Manufacturers get the chance to show off their entire product lines and say how they're displayed. Customers get more concentrated service and faster selection.

Another trick of Egonomics is going off the well-trodden path to tantalize a new audience. It's a known fact that the 18- to 35-year-old market has been avoiding malls of late, as well as department stores. The clever answer: Go where they go. Calvin Klein introduced his new unisex fragrance, CK One, in the Tower Record stores throughout the country. What will be next? Selling low-fat yogurt at sporting goods stores? Backpacks at coffee bars? You get the picture.

By following the tenets of Egonomics, even the bigger guys

do better if they focus on personal attention. Barnes & Noble, for example, launched 231 stores and superstores with its we-care-about-you attitude. You are encouraged to browse, actually hang around for as long as you like, settling into comfortable couches and chairs for a quick read before you buy—or not buy. There's even a coffee bar, to order a cappuccino, to congregate, to chat about the last Bruce Chatwin book or latest best-seller. As mentioned in "Clanning," singles like bookstores because they're a cozy place to meet like-minded people (mega-stores, in fact, are popping up on many a magazine's "Best Places to Meet a Mate" lists, along with weddings and health clubs). Young parents especially like these bookstores for their early Thursday night story-hours, when you're urged to bring your kids (even wearing PJ's) and listen as someone reads aloud from the Babar books.

One of the reasons Barnes & Noble Clicks (revenues up $250 million last year) is that the personal touch isn't something the marketing department dreamed up, saying one day, "Hey, let's be nice guys." Instead, the Click comes from the top. Years ago, while in college, the now-Chairman of the Board/President/CEO Leonard Riggio was steered into an engineering program because of his high math scores. But while he was working at his part-time job at the NYU bookstore, he felt the Click. Len liked the activity of a bookstore; he enjoyed helping people find the right book. "I felt connected, becoming part of a whole." Following this, he dropped out of engineering and took business classes, then dropped out of school and just read. Eventually, he was able to follow his heart and bought Barnes & Noble in 1971. It was one store then (more toys than books) on Fifth Ave. and 18th St. in Manhattan, and he still keeps his office on top of the store to keep his pulse on Egonomics. We like that.

The correct practice of Egonomics enables a company to turn a problem into a profit. Case in point: One time last year on a trip via San Francisco to Hawaii, I decided to pack in one of those sleek black suitcases-on-wheels made by Tutto from Ham-macher-Schlemmer in New York. We use them on all BrainReserve business trips because they're so easy to pull. Unfortunately, en route, the zipper split, disastrously beyond safety-pin repair. My lucky break was that the luggage company happened to be head-quartered right there in San Francisco. Although it was on a weekend, Susan Lee of Tutto personally hand-delivered a new pullman bag to my friends' house on Jackson Street. That's how a negative turns into a positive. Tutto won a customer's loyalty.

The friendly principles of Egonomics can be applied to the most technical of products. When a customer perceives a product line as cold, sterile, and almost inhuman, you need to go all out and prove them wrong. Apple Computer certainly has shown us that high-tech doesn't have to be cold-tech and that the me-oriented microchip can be man's (and woman's) new best friend. The epitome of Apple Egonomics in action is their advertisement that inquires, "What do you have on your PowerBook?" On one side of the page, there was avant-garde author Tama Janowitz, holding her laptop and a list of what's in it, including "Journal of My Deams, Gingerbread Recipes, Possible Character Names for Future Novels." Facing her is ex-magazine editor Frances Lear, clutching her PowerBook and her special list: "Living Will, Exercise Schedule, Grandson's Photo." That ad stretches our imaginations about what a machine can do and what we can do with a machine. Apple Clicks in with its playful yet powerful message: You are master of your own technology.

In an attempt to make the computer more human and personable, a CD-ROM has come out called "Handwritten Fonts." Three hundred computer types have been selected that resemble human handwriting. Great for thank-you letters. For an extra $45, you can send a writing sample and have "My Font" custom designed.

More personalized hard-goods. With so much of our time spent slouched over a wheel, not only my Mustang, but much of the automotive industry has finally Clicked into Egonomics. Lincoln Mercury suggests that—thanks to technology—you can now have an intimate relationship with your car. A new print ad for the Lincoln Continental slyly states, "It Knows Your Voice, Height, Even Your Weight. (But Don't Worry. It Also Knows How to Stay Quiet.)" The rest of the copy details how the Continental offers voice-activated phone dialing (just sing out a name). And how the suspension adjusts to your weight and whatever you're packing up for the trip (luggage, groceries, etc.), so the car stays level, the ride smooth.

Other car manufacturers seem to be stressing Egonomics rather than big motors or speedy starts. The Lexus ad asks, "For Centuries Man Has Adapted to His Environment. What about vice versa?" "Express your individuality," they say.

What could be more Egonomically correct than machines

that "read" your individual body parts. Someday they'll be able to read your body temperature and adjust any interior climate (car, office, home) to make you comfortable. We've come to know that, like DNA and fingerprints, a person's eyes or hands can be used as ready identification. Several government offices have Iris Recognition machines that scan your orbs (your peepers?) as a method of James Bond–ian ID. To speed up the logjam at customs, the U.S. Immigration and Naturalization Service has launched a pilot program called INSPass. This biometrics system records your handprint on an ATM-like card. Preselected travelers get to skip the lines at JFK or Newark airports by using the card in a machine and verifying ownership/identity by laying their hands on a scanner. If this becomes accepted worldwide, you'll never need a passport to cross a border again.

What an improvement over the behind-the-times system nowadays. After Lys had her passport stolen in London, she was given a temporary one for a year, and then told to start again anew. Although she'd had one since childhood, without the number, American passports are either not on computer or impossible to access. To complicate matters further, her original birth certificate's raised seal (a major requirement) had become flattened after all those years pressed in a Bible. It took two months of forms, fees, visits, and vexation, and our attorney, Bob Edmonds, to cut the red tape. So, we'll be among the first to applaud a hand-recognition system instead of the traditional passport. We'd rather high-five it, anytime. (Late-breaking news: Canon has developed an Optical Card, able to store a digital image, visa, permit, entry and exit records, and, yes, a fingerprint, voiceprint, signature, and retinal scan—making it immune to counterfeiting. Wishes do come true.)

Banks, too, should be looking into ATMs that will recognize a customer's handprint. Won't it be nice never ever again to have to carry ID cards that can be lost or stolen. Meanwhile, an interim step will be some form of plastic that will hold everything on microchips, from your medical history to insurance records and banking information. One aside: We recently recommended to a pharmaceutical company that it "hold" an individual's medical records for life. Or store the medical records of all prescription drug users in one central file. This could be cross-reffed so that no one would be taking a bad combination from different pharmacies—or if someone was taking a calcium-leacher drug, such as Prednisone, for years, he or she could be advised to take calcium supplements. Steady record keeping would be great so that no matter where you move, no matter what doctors you see, no matter what age you get to be, there will be one cohesive medical story on you. For instance, wouldn't it be smart to know how many times in your life you've been on steroids, antibiotics, and penicillin, and which drugs were most effective—or not. An even closer step is a patented credit card for seniors that cleverly has an added magnifying strip so that they can better sign on the bottom line.

Egonomics has gotten to the point at which we almost expect to be marketed to as individuals. It's natural to question and criticize places that don't take the time or make the effort to do so. Design should be democratic. Why, for instance, can't office chairs or movie and theater seats have the same technology as cars to accommodate different body types? Come to think of it, why aren't lecterns adjustable? Remember when then President Bush stood at a standard-sized wooden lectern and introduced the diminutive Queen Elizabeth in California a few years back? No one in the audience could see her face and she was immediately dubbed "the talking hat."

AT&T knows from experience what happens when you ignore a person's individuality vs. when you enhance it. Several years ago, it tried to take away its familiar calling card setup that tacked on a simple 4-digit PIN code to your home/biz phone number. It reissued cards with an endless stream of meaningless numbers that you couldn't possibly remember. To charge a call, you always had to have the card with you and take it out to read off the digits as you dialed. There was an immediate drop in usage. Then someone at AT&T woke up. They got the bright idea of bringing people back by going one better: letting customers customize the charge numbers themselves. Your card can spell out your pet's name (M-I-Y-A-K-E or T-U-L-I-P), a favorite team (O-H-I-O-S-T-A-T-E), a food craving (C-H-O-C-O-L-A-T-E) or a message (P-E-A-C-E or I-L-O-V-E-M-Y-M-O-M). Click: you'll never forget what you yourself chose.

Airlines have also jumped (landed?) on the Egonomics bandwagon (isn't it about time?). Today, instead of only inviting us to "Fly the Friendly Skies," a United Airlines ad tells first-class passengers about the new "option of designing your own flight experience."

You can choose a major meal or a light snack. Set the pace of dining. Pick times to nap. No more rigidity and uniformity. It used to
be that if you didn't eat at the moment the cart rolled through, the
food would vanish into thin air. Along the same lines, Swiss Air woos
first-classers with a pledge that "every minute you spend with us is
your time. To be spent precisely according to your wishes." That
includes a concierge at Zurich or Geneva to whisk you through
check-in, priority baggage handling, early boarding, and luggage
delivery to your home or hotel. On night flights, there's a dreamy
Dream Time Service that supplies a duvet, sheets, and pillows as you
catch some shut-eye. Wide awake? Watch your own personal video
monitor with a choice of more than thirty movies. Another airline
has computer games on the backs of seats, even in coach.

Virgin Atlantic Airways, founded by a creative British entrepreneur Richard Branson, offers a unique hands-on approach.
On select flights, in-flight beauty therapists can be booked to massage the kinks out of your neck and shoulders; or if trained in
reflexology, press the pressure points on your feet; or relax you
with the subtle guises of aromatherapy. It's even possible to get a
manicure (although not a change of polish—flammables are pro-
hibited). On the ground, first- and business-class passengers can
get a free cut, facial, manicure, and pedicure at the clubhouse in
Heathrow. With gambling legal above international waters, the
airline is trying to set up in-flight video gambling games. Sound
farfetched? Not for Virgin. This iconoclastic airline already has a
croupier at Heathrow airport, where passengers can gamble at a
blackjack table for frequent flier miles. Other savvy airports, too,
are trying to make layovers more Egonomically attractive. Our
HarperCollins editor, Cynthia Barrett, exercised and took a revital-
izing sauna and shower during a two-hour stop at the Singapore
airport.

All these amenities are great perks when things go right, but
airlines still haven't gotten into the Egonomics of what to do when
things go wrong. Case in point: When on an internal forty-five-
minute flight in Denmark, Lys and I tried to crane our necks to
watch our one consolidated overnight bag as the SAS check-in
woman lifted it by hand and deposited it through a door, instead
of putting it on the moving carrier. She acted as if we were crazy
Americans when we inquired, "Why?" "What?" and "Are you sure?"
and told us, "I guarantee it." Famous last words. When we arrived

at the small airport of Karup, the PA system was paging us to say that the bag didn't make it onto the flight (they found it sitting behind that door). The SAS rep there didn't help. After many excuses, he told us, "Okay, this was the last flight here, but we're going to try to send your suitcase to a place one hour away and drive it to your hotel by 2 A.M. But there's no way for you to check on this because we're closing up and I'm going home." So instead of getting a good night's sleep before giving a TrendView the next morning, we were up and waiting for the late arrival (it did come)—but we had nothing to change into for dinner, no night-clothes, no sundries. What could have been done Egonomically?

1. The airline could have a 24-hour tracking number.
2. It could offer a $50 stipend to buy toothbrushes, whatever.
3. The SAS rep could have offered to call us with up-to-date info on the later plane and the status of the driver. Just for reassurance and a feeling of being-in-this-together.
4. Or, why not fly the luggage on another earlier-landing air-line?

How is the entertainment industry handling the Me Quest? An Egonomics winning team is Blockbuster Video and IBM working together to develop a machine that lets consumers choose from zillions of songs to custom-create their own CDs. It's Time Warner being the first to release an interactive movie in which each member of the audience is given a hand-held device to vote on which way the action will go. Girl gets boy? Push "A." Kill the villain? Push "B." You could say this started with *The Rocky Horror Picture Show,* during which the audience would chant responsively along with the script. Custom movies are where Egonomics will expand into Hollywood economics. Interactive movies are where people will Click into the future. An idea: Take a favorite character home with you on CD-ROM to learn more about his or her life and adventures.

Newspaper companies are also experimenting with a wide range of custom-publishing projects. To meet the consumer on the consumer's terms. For daily papers, it's truly a matter of survival. Since 50% of future readers (18- to 24-year-olds) polled never pick up a paper, the obvious direction is online. It's a pretty safe bet that these reluctant readers are more likely to scan their computers for up-to-date information than to get ink on their hands. News companies also realize that this demographic group will be more likely to seek out what's going on if the news is segmented into what interests them.

In 1989, only 42 newspapers had started on electronic ventures, but today close to 3,000 are taking that route. *The New York Times*, for example, is published online every day. The "front page" is a screen of graphical icons (business, sports, entertainment). Readers click (and Click) onto the areas they want to read and skip those they have no interest in. One of the pluses of online news is finding out what's "behind the story." For real news buffs, it's possible to click and access in-depth information such as court records, press conference transcripts, maps, and photo files. The online "newspaper" becomes a veritable treasure trove of information.

The computer networks CompuServe and Prodigy already offer a service to gather news stories from papers all over the country on any topic you like—and then spoon-feed it to you in a newspaper format. Let's say you want the news of the day on herbal medicine, King Hussein of Jordan, and pro tennis. You'll not only get your chosen topics, but they'll be arranged on pages complete with headlines, sidebars, and even cartoons. Your very own Egonomics newspaper. A Time Warner interactive experiment, the News Exchange in Orlando, Florida, will provide news on demand—day or night. This will definitely change viewing habits and impact, because you'll be able to hop and jump from one program, one topic, to another—according to whim.

Personal self-expression gets to the very core of Egonomics. The thinking goes like this: In a world besieged by an information assault and an advertising avalanche, art may be the best way "I can connect with who I am." What finer place to project your own personal vision than on a canvas, with a chisel, or even on stage? Five years ago, it seemed as if everyone wanted to connect to the "child within." Now the talk is about getting in touch with the "artist within." And in the most futuristic way possible, there's a techno-leap forward to really getting "within": It's now possible to take an artist's hair strand (or blood or skin cell), extract the DNA, and mix it directly into the paint used for the signature. What a foolproof way to prevent forgeries. (No more fake Rembrandts, Vermeers, and the more recent ersatz Dalís, Chagalls.)

Art is no longer the exclusive province of the gifted (although being gifted sure helps). Adult education art classes are filled with novices, accountants trying to draw nudes and housewives learning to weld metal sculptures. Garages are being turned into studios. Local museums or community centers offer venues to sell or display your creations (another good source of "gallery" space is to approach a new business with empty walls). It just takes an attitude of "I can do that."

Pernod Liquors has paired up with Liquidtex to sponsor painting parties at New York City restaurants at which you can get that licorice-y drink, some paints, and a prestretched canvas with the instructions, "Express Yourself." Malibu Comics, the sixth largest comic book outfit, sees the possibility of commercial potential in home artists. They recently ran a "Create Your Own Hero" competition and invited comic book fans to draw and describe a new superhero. Currently, we're developing a Faith Popcorn, alias Trendar, animated look-alike to be a guide through the Internet, deliverer of seminars, star of a sitcom, a comedian. Like Lucy in Charlie Brown, the character never ages . . . and the wisecracks, we hope, stay wise.

Poetry has been undergoing a Renaissance. First thought: Maybe because it's so un-tech. You only need a pen, a clean sheet of paper, and an idea. Or on second thought: Maybe it's because President Clinton had the fantastic Maya Angelou read an original poem, "On the Pulse of the Morning," at his inauguration, bringing the concise beauty of a poem forward for the first time since JFK's invitation to Robert Frost. Or third: Maybe it's because today's most vocal poets, the rappers, often ring out, sing out, in rabbly rhymes.

On any given night at certain cafes and bookstores in New York, Chicago, New Orleans, or Phoenix, budding poets stand up and read their works (kind of the Comedy Clubs of the mid-'90s). They may even compete against one another in what's called a "slam." During slams, a panel of poetry judges rate the poet's work and performance on a scale of 1–10 while the audience cheers or jeers. Like the scores of an Olympic diving competition, slam ratings work on a decimal system, so a great poem might get a 9.6 while a bad one comes up a mere 2.8. What would Shakespeare's sonnets rate in a slam?

Former President Jimmy Carter studied poetry after his White House days and published a book, *Always a Reckoning*, of almost fifty concise, often homey, poems. Corporations (inevitably) have started picking up on this creative craze. There's a thick-ish book of office poems entitled *For a Living: The Poetry of Work*, which included some business execs' own inspirations. Levi Strauss has been featuring a poet in one of its campaigns. MTV is sponsoring poetry specials, featuring Maggie Estep, who's had her jagged lines recorded on Polygram records. And there's the over-a-million-selling poem book by Jenny Joseph, *When I Am an Old Woman, I Shall Wear Purple*, whose purple poetry lines have also shown up on greeting cards. This has obviously Clicked into the collective psyche of an aging population.

Literary agents and publishing houses are being flooded with unsolicited manuscripts. Particularly from lawyers, after the astounding success of lawyers-turned-novelists Scott Turow (*Presumed Innocent, Pleading Guilty*), Richard North Patterson (*Degree of Guilt*), and John Grisham (*The Firm, The Client, The Pelican Brief*). Best-seller Joseph Wambaugh (*Finnegan's Week*) was a cop. Michael Crichton (*A Case of Need*) was educated at Harvard Medical School and was a post-doctoral fellow at the Salk Institute. Robin Cook (*Coma*) was also a physician. And Tom Clancy (*Clear and Present Danger*) started out as an insurance salesman. Even though "everyone has to start somewhere," there are groundswells of people taking up novel-writing in hopes of getting their story sold. And Clicking. Our literary agent, Binky Urban at ICM, has contributed to the myth of "unknown gem discovered among the rubble." She was sent the opening 200 pages of an unfinished first manuscript from a 26-year-old video store clerk (who still lived at home with Mom and Dad), picked it up to read, liked it, and sold it for about half a million dollars. Or you can be like former ad exec Richard Paul Evans (*The Christmas Box*) who originally published himself, was picked up by Simon & Schuster, and ended up with the #1 book both on *The New York Times* hardcover and softcover lists.

It's the new American Dream. Telling your own story. Being heard. Having people pay attention. It goes beyond being on talk shows—anybody these days who weighs over 400 lbs. and cross-dresses can do that. Egonomics is all about self-definition. Self-awareness. Self-actualization. It's as if people are trying to sort through the gray haze, the very blur of their lives, to find the rainbow. Companies and individuals who Click into this concept and market to magnify a person's sense of self-worth (ego) will prosper.

Ergo, Egonomics.

CLICKING THROUGH FEMALETHINK

Women hold up half the sky.
—CHAIRMAN MAO

If we were the same, we wouldn't be different.
—ADAM HANFT

Women are different from men. Not inferior, not superior—just different.

Although it's been politically incorrect to say this over the past decade or so, men and women don't think the same way, don't communicate the same way, don't buy for the same reasons. That's the sum and substance of this Trend. And if you can Click into the new female-oriented positioning for products and services, you can Click into FemaleThink.

Understand that we're not saying you have to be a woman to FemaleThink. You just have to be awake, aware of the differences and learn how to handle people in different ways. At BrainReserve, an 88%-female company, we've named this phenomenon of being different, this newly identifiable Trend, FemaleThink. We've interviewed more than 1,000 men and women, asking them a simple question: "After living and/or working with a person of the opposite sex, would you say that person thinks significantly different than you do?" A whopping

99% of the respondents unhesitatingly answer, "yes."

In my seminar, TrendView, I use a restaurant scenario as an example. When a couple sit down at a table and the waiter introduces himself, "Hi, I'm Richard and when I'm not waiting here, I'm an actor in the soaps," the woman is fascinated. She wants to know what shows he's been on, whether she's actually seen him act, where he's studied, how many brothers and sisters he has. The man wants to know one thing, "When can we order dinner?" He's hungry and simply wants the transaction to take place. She's interested in creating a relationship. That's the essence of FemaleThink.

In her Pulitzer Prize–winning book *No Ordinary Time*, Doris Kearns Goodwin looks back to the time of World War II when women were first called upon to go onto the production lines. She relates a story about Eleanor Roosevelt visiting the plant where B-24 planes were being made. "Once again, Eleanor took special pleasure in hearing that women were 'doing a swell job, better than they expected.' Supervisors reported that women were more patient with detail, more capable of handling repetitive jobs without losing interest, more eager to learn, less prone to hide their greenness, more willing to ask directions and take instruction." Goodwin went on to quote a male executive at the company: "If I had my way now, I'd say 'to hell with the men. Give me women.'"

Every place that women go, they make connections—in cabs, in schools, in playgrounds, in supermarkets, in stores. Everything becomes a personal experience. For a business to Click into this bonding of FemaleThink, it needs to understand that *how* you sell to women can be as important as *what* you're selling. Women are looking for a relationship to be made before the sale that will continue to support the product/service afterward. This defines the way women will relate to the business world. Will engage that world. Will change that world.

We've gone through the Year of the Woman, the Decade of the Woman, but we believe we're approaching the Millennium of the Woman. We think that the next thousand years will be the time when women find their true strength and use it for real world good. A Singapore-born woman trader on Wall Street, Mei Ping Yang, a wizard with numbers, pointed out an interesting theory: All the dates in this past thousand years started off with the number 1, a MaleThink number, independent, direct, ego-concentrated, singular. But very soon, starting with the year 2000 and going on—2001, 2002, 2003, and so forth—the next thousand years will be leading off with the number 2. And "2" is definitely a more basically female number. Two: partnerships, familial teamwork, a balance of power, being relational, FemaleThink.

FemaleThink Is NewThink

It might be easier to understand FemaleThink by comparing it to what it's *not*. FemaleThink is not OldThink (which was the only way Old Business, Old Discussions, Old Ways of Looking at the World happened). FemaleThink is a whole NewThink. OldThink represents the past. FemaleThink/NewThink offers a future way of solving both business and relational problems. It's a Click on, a Click forward.

OLDTHINK	FEMALETHINK
Works through hierarchy	Uses teamwork (familial)
Needs to know answers	Wants to ask the right questions
Role-identity	Identity is divided in many roles
Single-minded	Multi-minded
Resists change	Seeks change
Goal-driven	Process-aware
To a destination	On a journey
Transaction-oriented: thinks in terms of getting from A to B to C in a direct line	Relationship-oriented: sees how A relates to C, how B relates to F, what B and D share in common

Upon studying this list, you will see that there are essential differences between the way men and women think and behave. After spending years trying to think OldThink, women realized that it was against their nature. And finally, science is backing up FemaleThink.

The Science of FemaleThink

We can hardly open up a newspaper, newsletter, or medical journal without reading about some new discovery about the perceptual and cognitive differences between men and women. Because of a technological breakthrough in imaging machines, scientists have been able to track our brain activity. And, no surprise, men and women process information differently. Because in those tests the part of the brain that was being activated actually "lit" up, making it possible to see that when sounding words, men used a tiny area in the left front of the brain and women used both the left and right sides. Does this account for women being more fluid in their thinking?

Another finding: Because of the development of various sections of the brain, women have greater sensory discrimination. Women not only are able to judge sad facial expressions better than men, but are able to do so with less effort. Also, the area of neuron activity in women's brains, when recalling sad events, is larger than men's. In other words, neuroscientists have simply proven what we've known all along. Women are more emotional. More observant. More sympathetic. Anne Moir and David Jessel, authors of *Brain Sex: The Real Difference Between Men and Women*, wrote that "women are probably 'hearing' much more than what the man himself thinks he is 'saying.'" Does this mean women make better therapists? Better salespeople?

A professor in Canada, Doreen Kimura, has been working on the very different ways men's and women's brains work on handling spatial relationships. Picture yourself figuring out directions from a map. Most likely, if you're a woman, you'll turn the map toward the direction you're facing. In other words, you, the car, and the map will all be heading the same way. (It's more personal.) For most men, however, the way the map is pointing means little or nothing. They see a destination as separate and apart from them—and find things by distance and linear direction. Apart from being ah-ha interesting, this gender differentiation has implications when designing such today things as computer games or tomorrow things as Virtual Reality gear.

Another little-known fact: Women can actually see better in the dark than men. How can we use this? Could we be better spies? Private eyes? A famous female writer, Anais Nin, captured the positive aspects of the way women see things and the way FemaleThink could possibly make some improvements in our lives: "We don't see things as they are. We see things as we are." Through a FemaleThink filter. *Vive la différence.*

In another fascinating study done this year, both men and women were asked to clear their minds of any thoughts. The results clearly showed a cultural distinction. Women's brains were found to be more active in a region where complex expression taking place, while men's brains showed higher levels of activity in the primitive zone where aggressiveness resides. This strongly suggests a fundamental difference in the response patterns between men and women. And weighs more heavily on the nature side of the nature vs. nurture theory.

Does this explain why little boys grab guns and fire trucks while little girls prefer to play with dolls? In the pre-FemaleThink past, when women felt the need to demonstrate resolve, Iron Margaret Thatcher's invasion of the Falkland Islands was pulled out as proof that a woman could be as tough as any man. (A client recently told us that she took testosterone shots to boost her aggressiveness. But now, in a medical reversal, it turns out that testosterone may *not* be the source of male growliness. The testy male hormone may, in fact, promote feelings of well-being.)

From a different angle, technology may be the way to alter our basic perceptions. Take the case of our friend and ex-client Carol Peters, who has delved into the "man's" field of higher technology. Carol was responsible for developing one of the world's most advanced graphic workstations, Iris Indigo for Silicon Graphics, but then left to start her own company, daVinci Time & Space. Its mission will be to develop interactive television programming that creates an environment to "learn" the child's interests and capacities, instead of the other way around. It's fun, yet complicated, and can be personalized to the child participant, based on how quickly he or she responds to the different cues. Very FemaleThink to have the human interests come before the technological drive.

"I'll only consider it a success if 50% of our viewers are girls," Carol told us. "We did focus groups to try to root out what appeals to little girls. It's hard not to stereotype what girls like vs. what boys like vs. what we were told. For instance, I've never found playing with model airplanes exciting, but maybe I was given the message that as a girl I shouldn't be interested in planes." Carol continued, "I hope my new programming will change the most basic boy-girl perceptions (how to interact, how to view the world). If we can mold a mind while it's young to be open, mission accomplished. By the time we grow up and work together, it's too late. As a woman in a company today, you can get passed over because you don't play golf or pee the same way. No matter how smart you are or how hard you work, you can still never fit the form. So it's time to change the form."

Don't Conform, Don't Reform—Just Transform

The way to try and reach these scientifically different species, women, is to market to their strengths. P.S.: That doesn't mean showing a woman with a tie around her neck and a briefcase in her hand.

Forgo trying to convince the world about relative sameness. Instead emphasize—and then capitalize on—how women differ. The sports arena has finally awakened to women. Hillerich & Bradsby, makers of the legendary Louisville Slugger baseball bats, are now Clicking with softball gloves and bats designed for women athletes. In welcome contrast to the pretend FemaleThink of years ago, the products are seriously competitive. Anne Flannery, manager of women's athletics at Spalding, said it perfectly, "The 'P' word today is performance, not pink." In an experiment of FemaleThink, the first 100%-female America's Cup yachting team was put together, to see how women would fare, cooperating as a well-oiled machine, against the traditional, highly competitive male sailors. Their America^3 boat, the *Mighty Mary*, showed that an all-woman crew could hold its own as true winners.

This is just the beginning. Watch for more areas in which the differences will be highlighted rather than smoothed over. One-A-Day Vitamins has just changed its positioning to "People Are Different," as the company markets a new line of vitamins created especially for men or for women, not for both. In a commercial to change the previously macho/pickup truck image of 7-Eleven, the company enlisted comedian Brett Butler of the hit TV series "Grace Under Fire." She walks around the convenience store, surprised to find her favorite bottled water and yogurt, finally asking: "Is this heaven or what? What, are women running 7-Elevens now?"

A sterling example of strong FemaleThink role-modeling is Beverly Harvard, the current Police Chief of Atlanta, who Clicked into the job by a mayoral appointment, mainly because of her brand of leadership: "by example and consensus." Her un-tough, un-paramilitary style allows police officers to fax her with any suggestions or complaints, skipping right over the usual chain of command. And then she acts on the recommendations.

The First Lady, Hillary Rodham Clinton, in a small meeting that I was asked to attend, along with about forty other New York professional women, urged the group to remember the power of storytelling. "Think of all the situations each of us finds ourselves in where telling a story could make people think. For instance, I once sat next to a woman who is a hotel housekeeper whose husband got very sick a few months ago. If it had not been for the Family Medical Leave Act, she could never have taken time off from her job to care for her dying husband. She became aware of the act because of dire necessity, but she said, 'Most of the people I work with have never heard of it.'" Ms. Clinton ended her point by saying, "Women who have a platform in business and the public sector need to assemble an audience and send out a larger message by becoming storytellers."

When we interviewed White House Deputy Assistant to the President Marsha Scott, a charming Arkansan, she delved even further into the positive way women can communicate. Marsha tries to bring a spiritual approach to her worldly position. "It's a big and powerful feeling to have everything lined up just right—to be connected in a larger sense to the world. Women develop networks, strengths of communication. It's all there, when we speak our own truths."

Linguistic scholar Deborah Tannen, who wrote *You Just Don't Understand—Women and Men in Conversation,* pointed out some of the salient differences in an interview in *People.* "Men use language to preserve their independence and maintain their position in a group . . . Women use language to create connections and intimacy." How can you use this insight to Click when you're trying to communicate what you do—or what your business does?

The Undervalued Role of Intuition in FemaleThink

Sometimes women's sense of intuition is referred to as a pejorative, a joke, illogical, crazy. "She relies on her instincts" sounds more like a liability than an asset. When we're asked, "Where's the proof?" we secretly smile. It's about acting on a hunch, instead of using deductive reasoning. Think of Angela Lansbury as Jessica Fletcher on "Murder She Wrote," when her eyes widen and her subconscious gathering of clues suddenly Clicks into place. While the police are still baffled, she alone has fingered the killer. Woman's intuition Clicks and triumphs, week after week.

This FemaleThink ability to "read between the lines, hear between the words," "understand the gestalt," to fuse tangibles with intangibles, to Click into the single right answer, can often mean the difference between success and failure. Between life and death.

Chalk it up as a sixth sense. A perfect example of super-sleuthing happened when internist Dr. Colette Spacavento looked at our dear friend Vivian Shapiro's lung X ray. When she noticed a tiny blur, she conferred with her husband, a pulmonary special-ist. He said, "It's nothing. Just a nipple shadow." But something kept nagging at her, even though she couldn't explain why. An inner voice told her not to ignore it, so she insisted on a CAT scan. The weird thing is that the shadow was just as he said. Noth-ing. But the in-depth scan revealed something else—a micro-scopic spot on Vivian's lung. Woman's intuition saved a life. The tiny cancerous tumor was removed, and because it was discovered so incredibly early, Vivian is thankfully fine.

If you ever observe a woman listening, it's almost as if she's waiting to hear the Click. Women scrutinize and scan the whole picture. Actually, what's going on is an assembling of visual cues, a reading of body language and facial expression, and a nose (olfac-tory perception is important) for news. FemLogic: Understand that if A equals B and B equals C, then A equals C, but that may change if it rains. Sound familiar? No, we're not all psychic. Just sensitively and intuitively tuned up to be tuned in. There are boundless opportunities to Click into the natural powers that women have developed over millions of years of evolution.

In fact, FemaleThinking will provide the necessary shift away from the hard and fast ways to project success. Standard IQ tests will be less important than EI—Emotional Intelligence, a touchy-feely term that covers a range of emotional stability including cooperation, controlling anger, personal charm, and resolve. Schools will be tuning in to the importance of emotions vs. grades. Valedictorians will be chosen not for their grade-point averages, but for a more well-rounded mix. More like Miss America. Congeniality, talent, service to the community—all will take on new weight.

FemaleThink: One of Our Great Resources

When John Gray wrote *Men Are from Mars, Women Are from Venus,* he made the point that women inhabit their own planet. A planet where we are paid only 72 cents on the male dollar (women constitute 75% of the world's poverty). A planet where there has been a corporate glass ceiling (although "cement ceiling" may have been more accurate). Where we've had a hard time finding adequate and affordable day care. Where we have been under-represented in government. Where our particular diseases have been under-included in medical surveys.

Hopefully, this planet is slowly revolving, evolving, changing for the better. Female consensus building (often seen as too "soft") and female sensitivity (often patronized) will be embraced as prized attributes in a successful business endeavor. The whole image of business will be altered; no longer seen as a war to be won by trouncing the competition, but viewed as a complicated mosaic to be developed, one relationship at a time. FemaleThink works because it's efficient, economical, and effective. It's a way of reaching out (and being reached), a leap into the future.

- No business will thrive without understanding Female-Think.
- No business will survive without speaking FemaleThink—without thinking FemaleThink.

The shift in outlook is subtle in some cases, powerful in others; some we'll slide into easily, others will take years to break through. One important point to clarify and overclarify: You don't have to be a female to FemaleThink. It's not gender specific; it just happens to come more naturally to most women. But whether you're a newly minted female college graduate or a 55-year-old male CEO, understanding FemaleThink will be key to Clicking—particularly in the business world (as well as helping some marriages)—during the coming decades.

Even when we think this "women in business" thing is seen as such "old news," we're reminded that there are still brick walls. For instance, look what happened at a very urbane dinner party. One summer night when I was chatting away with a group of twelve at Richard and Eileen Ekstract's New York apartment, my dinner partner—the owner of a multimillion-dollar, medium-sized company—blurted out-of-the-blue that he thought the idea that women were discriminated against in the workplace was over-stated. Impulsively, inevitably, recklessly, I bet him a cool $1,000 that at his company there wasn't a single woman within seven levels of his lofty perch as CEO. The entire table held their collective breaths. It was a risky wager—there was always a possibility of the token Human Resources Director. The executive mentally ran down his chain of command, and, slightly flustered, admitted, "You're right."

But maybe I had an unfair advantage. The odds were on my side. For I knew that:

- Only thirteen of the Fortune 500 have a woman among their top five highest paid executives.
- 97.4% of America's corporate heavies are men.
- 94% of the Fortune 500's board members are men.

Consider the following story as an example of the bafflement of OldThink language on a FemaleThink head. We know a female account executive at a pharmaceutical advertising agency who pulled in a $30-million piece of business for her firm. After the deal was signed, the head of the company stopped by her office for a congratulatory chat. With the idea of showing her how she fit into the company, he sat down and drew a picture of a box.

He said, as if talking to a child, "Here is a box. I'm in that box and our other key executives are in that box. Now, where would you place yourself?"

She smiled and pointed outside the lines of the box. He was delighted that she seemed to grasp what he was getting at. "Yes, yes," the CEO agreed. "You have been outside the box, but we would like you to come into the box with us." He wanted her to join the insular "boys' club" that had been running the company. Instead she left and took the business with her.

Moral of the story: FemaleThink breaks the box. Erases the box. Dissolves the walls of the box. Doesn't even consider the existence of a box. (Women think more about the inclusiveness of a circle, never ending, constantly in movement.)

What is the cost of this "boxing in" of women? At best, some stay and grumble, but most make their plans to leave as soon as they can find the opportunity. Our guess is that at least 20% of women working for large companies will leave and start something of their own (whenever I say this at a corporate seminar, I see lots of knowing smiles and nods).

How many countless times over the years have we heard the refrain of a woman in a traditional corporate job complain, "There's got to be a better way." Now the lament is more action-oriented, crooning, "I'll do it my way." And that way for more than 7.7 million women is to start their own businesses (according to the latest figures from the National Foundation for Women Business Owners), employing 15.5 million people and generating nearly $1.4 trillion in sales. And women are starting companies at twice the rate of men. Imagine that. Twice the rate.

And where do you go if you don't fit? You go home. You stay home. You start a business at home. Some 18% of all working women are running businesses from home—and that number is mega-growing.

We could make endless lists of entrepreneurial women (myself included) who had an idea and started a business on their kitchen table. Even Lys's small mail-order company for the anti-wrinkle product, Hollywood Wings, was started by three women at home, including Mary Roebling, the first woman to head a major U.S. bank and to be Treasurer of this country (she signed the greenbacks). Although the reasons for Clicking into FemaleThink might vary, the passion exhibited by nearly every female entrepreneur we interviewed was extraordinary. And many cared as much about sharing as about making money.

For Gayle Martz, a flight attendant with TWA, the Click came after her fiancé died unexpectedly. Feeling lonely when she became stranded in Korea on a long layover, she wished that she could have taken along Sherpa, her Lhasa Apso puppy, for company. Her answer: to design a perfect travel bag, which would persuade more of the major airlines to loosen their regulations, and one that would encourage people to bring their pets with them whenever they traveled. She tried to think of everything, both for the pet's comfort and for the airlines' rules. Her soft-sided carrier slips under the plane's seat; has side and top zippers for access, mesh vents for ventilation, a handy pocket for toys, treats, brushes, and a long shoulder strap and short handles for carrying ease. Everyone who saw her handsome prototype wanted one. Working out of her one-bedroom apartment, with little startup capital except for $5,000 borrowed from her mother, she launched Sherpa's Pet Trading Company. After a successful national rollout, Gayle exchanged her overcrowded apartment for more space in the same building, where she and Sherpa still work at home.

Gun Denhart, CEO and Chairman of the children's clothing catalog company Hanna Andersson, also started her $44-million company in her Portland home. For the very first catalog in 1983, she and her husband, Tom, laboriously cut and glued one-inch-square fabric swatches into 75,000 catalogs and ended up grossing $53,000 in six months. She pioneered a clever concept called "Hannadowns," by which customers can return their child's out-grown clothing for a 20% credit toward their next purchase. The returned clothes are then given to charity (that's the passion part). Each month, more than 3,000 articles of clothing are recycled—and customer loyalty to the "company that cares" is guaranteed. A win-win (that's the FemaleThink).

Our close associate Kate Newlin, who specializes in a new kind of public relations that she calls Reputation Management (RepMgt), first started her firm at home. Today she handles a roster of clients that includes one futurist (me), the legendary opera singer Jessye Norman, and such leading national brands as Foster Grant sunglasses. Her office now occupies an entire floor in a building on Madison Avenue, plus she's expanding nationally by having three co-workers use her original work-at-home model in San Francisco, Washington, D.C., and Rochester, New York.

In a reverse move, Karin Dubinsky, a smart corporate strategist, started her firm in a small office, but after it grew larger, she moved it into her newly purchased townhouse. She believes the change to a home-based environment has made her thinking less corporate, more familial, more FemaleThink—and more successful. Adding to the integrated work/personal picture, she gets to spend much more time with her adopted baby boy, Jack Rose, who stays nearby in the nursery working on strategies for his stuffed animal menagerie while his mom solves the problems of corporate America.

Women-owned businesses are diversifying beyond retailing and service, into manufacturing, construction, agriculture. In fact, women-owned business in transportation/communication, wholesale trade, and finance/insurance/real estate grew at twice the rate of these industries as a whole. There's a visionary commercial from AT&T that shows a woman sitting on a park bench, looking at an empty field. She says to the man sitting near her, "See that? That's where I'm going to start my business." He asks, "What about all those little things you need to know like financing, creating business plans?" As she talks about how AT&T's Resources for New Business has made things easier, a building starts going up on the site and is completed before our eyes. Very inspiring. Think about how many fax machines, computers, and software programs would be going into that building. How many support systems this business would require, how many services it would generate. There are so many Female-Think opportunities out there for someone to Click into. Are you ready?

Who Out There Has Clicked into FemaleThinking?

Although understanding FemaleThink could give anyone in business or in marketing a well-leveraged access to millions of consumers, very few of the major sectors have wooed women.

Surprisingly, Saturn, the car, with its "no-dicker sticker" policy and its advertising that treats women respectfully, intelligently, is one hard-goods manufacturer that has studied the female market. The whole idea of no-haggle pricing is supposed to cure the male-biased world of car shopping. In a shocking Chicago study of general car buying, white women were quoted prices $142 more than white men and black women were quoted prices $875 more than white men for an identical car. How unfair is that?

Our BrainReserve research showed that the Saturn dealership was the only one of fourteen we visited that voluntarily popped the hood for a female prospect. It was the one where the salesperson offered to help calculate the monthly carrying costs and suggested that a woman customer should go out on a test drive. It was the only one that had a comfortable place to sit and mull things over with a cup of coffee or soda. And it was the only one with a "day care corner" where female browsers could temporarily park their youngsters. In addition, the people at that dealership went out of their way to congratulate and hover over a female purchaser who had stopped in to pick up her new car. Something different is happening at Saturn: maybe because of their name, they, too, understand what it is like to be from another planet.

After interviewing a total of 500 women for one of our automotive clients, we found out that women, if given a choice, would really prefer to buy from home. That would eliminate the experience that all our "undercover shoppers" reported—salesmen who look over the shoulder of any woman and address all their comments to the man. In our own personal experience, one day, throwing caution to the winds and checking out a certain German status car, Lys and I learned what it must be like to be Caspers—as completely invisible as friendly ghosts. Not one salesman approached us during our twenty- minute Mercedes showroom visit, even though we did everything from peering intently at the window price lists to blatantly kicking the tires.

This experience seems all the more insane when we read in *Working Woman* magazine that women write the checks and sign the leases for 50% of all new cars sold in the United States—that's a $67-billion segment. By the year 2000, the numbers of female car purchasers will rise to 60% (one writer figures that U.S. women are actually as big a market as the rapidly industrializing Chinese). Couple that with the fact that women influence between 80% and 85% of all new car purchases, and you begin to grasp the cost of ignoring women. Going beyond cars—according to the IRS (and they should know), of individuals with assets over $500,000, 40% are women.

Other areas of the hard sell in dire need of FemaleThink are the appliance discount stores. When you go into stores such as P.C. Richard or the Wiz in our area, you need nerves of steel. Slick salesmen, intent only on making a sale, try to talk you into a model *they* want to sell, not caring what *you* want to buy.

Wouldn't it be better to have a woman salesperson:

• Who knows how to bake a cake, melt a square of chocolate, and roast a 28-lbs. turkey talk to you about a new oven?
• Who will be honest if this/that item is the very latest model or an older one for a good price?
• Who doesn't try to sign you up for the world's longest extended service warranty, which provides nothing more than an easier drop-off point for repairs?

Ditto for refrigerators, microwaves, televisions, VCRs, stereos, cameras, computers. A print ad for NEC CD-ROMs sums up this feeling of anti-hustle: It shows a serious-looking woman with the caption, "Don't lie to me." One surprising ally of women in business today is technology. We might have had trouble programming our old VCRs but we know how to log onto the online Women's WIRE (Worldwide Information Resource Exchange). Harriet Rubin, an executive editor at Doubleday (and as we've said before, our last book's editor), expressed this opinion in *Inc.* magazine, "Technology doesn't get enough credit for being the feminist's friend. Technology has killed hierarchy. When you get into companies that have e-mail systems, you don't have to be the loudest man or the biggest braggart. It flattens gender differences."

Who Else Is FemaleThinking?

The Body Shop is. Naturally, its founder and leader, Anita Roddick, would know how to FemaleThink. When you buy something from The Body Shop, you know that you're also supporting struggling people in villages all over the world. In a "Trade, Not Aid" program, The Body Shop helps these villagers become part of the global economy, by training them in necessary skills and buying from them such indigenous ingredients as dyes, plants, fruits, herbs, and spices.

BrainReserve is helping Chesebrough-Pond's apply a FemaleThink perspective to its marketing platform for the late 1990s–early 2000s. What will motivate women, we think, is a concept we identified as Female Realism. The term indicates that women will want to deal with companies that directly recognize the reality of their lives. Instead of fast talk, women will be looking for companies that communicate with candor. In Chesebrough's new campaign for its double-whammy face cream, Prevent and Correct, the name simply describes what it does—without the overlay of "alluring" French or mysterious biochemical "break-throughs." Its introductory ad is a Herb Ritts photograph showing a woman holding her face in her hands. No glamorous models, no overpromises. This concept came about under the guidance of the French chairman of Chesebrough-Pond's, Patrick Choel, along with Natalie Danysh (who balances her FemaleThink worklife with the reality of raising four children between the ages of 3 weeks and 9 years) and Mike Indursky. In its unadulterated honesty, this whole new direction for a "beauty" product is a style we call Female Realism, marketing that Clicks.

Who Has Not Clicked into FemaleThinking?

For years we've been saying that major soap companies could be undone if a female-run company decided to market a detergent. Its president would come forward in its commercials and begin discussing the ins and outs of stains. Her knowledge would be coming from real-life experience. How many EVPs at the big companies now have ever washed a crib sheet? A pair of toddler's socks? A silk blouse? How many CEOs have? How many Chairmen? Our hypothetical company—let's name it WASH (Women Are Stain Haters)—would give a percentage of its proceeds to starting or supporting childcare centers. WASH would also distribute information on marital counseling and child-rearing, and even offer an abuse hotline. It would donate some profits to the much-needed area of female medicine. And spend some of its dollars feeding low-income households that have children. That's our idea of a Female Thought-Out packaged goods company. It's a wasted opportunity that no major marketer has Clicked into this idea yet, although we never stop trying to spread the word.

At best, we've managed to jangle the nerves of more than a few corporate executives. When we suggested this FemaleThink approach to one major soap and detergent conglomerate, its main reason for a firm "no" came from the OldThink perspective: "We're not running a social institution, we're running a business." It missed the point entirely. To succeed today, businesses need to be run more like social institutions, and social institutions need to be run more like businesses. And the truth is that from a FemaleThink perspective, a woman's brand loyalty could be guaranteed by a caring/sharing platform. Women definitely like to know that they're contributing to a company that has what we call Corporate Soul. That some of the profits go toward helping women and children. It would quickly show that women don't buy simply from coupons and jingles. That giving back has more value, believe it or not, than "buy one, get one free."

Same goes for a definitely female-only business, tampons. Wouldn't it be a good idea for a personal products company to get involved, issuing gender-/age-specific health information—for teens, post-pregnancy, the onset of menopause (along the same lines as pet food companies have been doing with their simple brochures on every stage of an animal's life). We were thinking that it could be under the umbrella of a coaching-type of relationship, called Sistering. Information on a wide range of relevant topics such as raging hormones, breast cancer, having a baby, or whatever, could be passed on through package inserts, home gatherings, telephone chat lines, or even Sistering sessions online. The tampon covers could also have encouraging FemaleThink info printed on them (don't laugh), such as the top twenty female-run companies and their earnings . . . or even the work of female artists, the way Absolut Vodka used fine paintings to educate, inspire, and reflect well on its product.

At BrainReserve, we were generating some ideas to link up not-for-profit groups with marketing organizations to create new business opportunities, going beyond the long-established Girl Scout cookies. How about NOW tampons. Or Rainbow Coalition Cosmetics (similar to The Body Shop, but concentrating on low-income pockets here in America—inner cities, some Indian reservations, depleted-resource communities). Or Gay Men's Health Crisis Shaving Cream. Or recycled Sierra Club paper plates and cups. American Cancer Society Herb-Veg Teas. American Heart Association jumpropes, free weights, steppers. When the products reflect some of the standards we live by, that's Female-Think.

What Does FemaleThink Look Like in Action?

When a woman starts a company, there's a shift in the bottom line. Financially, it is still (and always will be) simply about survival and, we hope, about success. But the underlying theme for having your own company is more about enjoying life quality, proving oneself, and doing good. BrainReserve is set up that way. There's a feeling of one big happy family (usually). The FemaleThink economy is a two-way street: We want to work with companies with a mission we agree with, and we want to work for companies whose values we share.

Sally Helgesen, in her book *The Female Advantage—Women's Ways of Leadership*, described an "ecology of leadership." Whereas men have a big-picture orientation that is more economic, "women's view of the big picture . . . encompasses a vision of society—they relate decisions to their larger effect upon the role of the family, the American educational system, the environment, even world peace."

FemaleThink government, then, should look different. Consider the strategy of Washingtonian Ellen Malcolm and her brainchild: EMILY's List. EMILY stands for Early Money Is Like Yeast: It makes the dough rise. In the 1994 election, 34,000 EMILY's List members contributed $8.2 million to women's campaigns. It brilliantly tapped a new market, asking mainly women members to pledge at least $100 to two recommended Democratic candidates. When Ellen began in 1985, there were only twelve Democratic women in the House of Representatives, and none in the Senate. Around for five national elections, EMILY's List helped elect thirty-three Representatives and five Senators. The long-term goal: Changing the face of power. Making the government reflect more closely the makeup of the population base. The theory behind this is that the more women there are in politics, the more emphasis there will be on child care, sensitive welfare reform, better health care. So-called women's issues. But aren't they ultimately human issues?

This strong sense of "We Can Do Anything"—even elect a

female president (if the energy were harnessed properly)—radiates when a group of concerned women get together. At a Valentine's Day luncheon that both Lys and I were invited to, given by TV-news reporter Judy Licht, we were astounded by the power of the working women there. Billed as an annual event for "Ladies Who Don't Lunch," the group included television anchorwomen Lynn White, Magee Hickey, and the New York City mayor's wife, Donna Hanover Giuliani; writers Nora Ephron, Erica Jong, Barbara Goldsmith Perry, and Gael Greene; Manhattan borough president Ruth Messinger; photographer Jill Kreicentz; fashion people Frances Grill of the Click Agency (you can guess why we like this) and designer Joan Vass, and her PR powerhouse daughter, Sara Vass; among others. The amazing FemaleThinkness of it was that Judy went around the room, generously introducing each of the sixty or so guests by name and by lists of accomplishments (no notes). Everyone felt terrific to be in the spotlight. And the recitation made us all aware of the enormity of the female talent in the room.

FemaleThink philanthropy looks different, too. When Carole Isenberg, Hollywood screenwriter and producer (*The Color Purple*), paired with Lynda Guber, they started a nonprofit organization called Education First, whose goal was to send educational messages into the community through the media. "Media is an incredible tool," attested Carole. They're running public service campaigns with such stars as Richard Dreyfuss, as well as subtly weaving "stay in school" messages into sitcoms and movies.

Carole's own company, Big Light Films, concentrates on ideas to inspire people. "Film is like a tarot deck," she said in our interview. "It's quite metaphysical." Breaking into film used to be incredibly hard for women. In an effort to pay back her good fortune, Carole often takes on female interns and teaches them the ropes. "We have a responsibility to help each other."

In New York, there's a unique helping hand called the Women's Resource Center, which is a nonprofit organization geared to helping solve any problems a woman could have. As its brochure explains, "We have information on everything—from getting your home tested for lead paint to getting your blood tested for HIV. From childcare to eldercare. From birth control to financial planning. In short, we're ready to tackle any issue of interest to women." All this good stuff is free and nonpartisan, backed by a paying membership that gets a newsletter and access to their files and database. A model to copy in your hometown?

Barbie Is Gaining—But It's Still Ken's World

While FemaleThink is making inroads, some women are increasingly frustrated at the bias that still persists across all job categories, at the blue-, pink-, and white-collar levels.

Anna Quindlen, the Pulitzer Prize–winning writer, in a magazine interview talked about connecting to "the anger" on her daughter's second birthday. In a beautifully written column, she described her daughter as "ready to leap into the world, as though life were chicken soup and she a delighted noodle." But Quindlen reported that she "made me see fresh this two-tiered world, a world that, despite all our nonsense about post-feminism, continues to offer less respect and less opportunity for women than it does for men. My friends and I have learned to live with it, but my little girl deserves better. She has given me my anger back, and I intend to use it well."

Is it anger or self-assuredness that's bringing women to the pistol range? According to the National Rifle Association, young girls are the fastest growing group learning to shoot, with 70% of the basic pistol course students being female. Pack that in with the statistic that 20 million women own a gun and 42 million have access to one.

The anger is showing up in and out of the courtroom. More women are pressing claims against sexual harassment on the job. Or in the military. A man can stare, but not leer. Leer, but not be a leech. Walk, but not stalk. The rule of thumb that you can pass along to a borderline sexist is "Would you say that to a male co-worker?"

Anger creates stress. And one of the least wimpy ways to reduce high anxiety is to join forces in a support group. One such group is the Burned Out Businesswomen's Association of Kansas City. According to *The New York Times Magazine*, forty or more members meet once a month to produce a direct-mail campaign that is sent to the highest level of executives and professional organizations. Trust us, these letters aren't sugar-coated. An example that was mailed to bigwigs in the medical field: "Women are too busy to wait a half-hour for the doctor and another 30 minutes in the exam room. If we are forced to wait in the offices of gynecologists, don't give us magazines that deal with the latest recipes; we want periodicals we can sink our teeth into."

Speaking of anger points, the relative neglect of women by the medical community over the years is another incendiary topic. As women smacked their heads on the glass ceiling in corporate America, it didn't do much good to turn to doctors to heal those concussions. Consider these statistics. The Physician's Health Study, done in 1988, came to the significant conclusion that taking an aspirin a day might reduce the risk of heart disease. The study tracked 22,000 men—and no women—even though heart disease is the number one killer of women. A Harvard School of Public Health Study, probing the possible connection between caffeine and heart disease, studied over 45,000 men—and again, not one woman. It took a feisty and dedicated female attorney, Terry McGovern, and her HIV Law Project to challenge the U.S. government and to make a change in the Centers for Disease Control's definition of AIDS, so that it would also embrace symptoms found in females. Terry's efforts have provided health benefits, education, and inclusion in research trials for previously discriminated-against infected women.

The NIH (National Institutes of Health) is trying to make amends in the field of women's health research by conducting a $600 million study, The Women's Health Initiative. The plan is to gather a large database on 160,000 women, according to one of the project's former advisory board members, Liz Karlin, M.D., director of the Women's Medical Center in Madison, Wisconsin. It's a start, but far from perfect. Preliminarily, they forgot or chose not to include questions relating to any political hot-buttons. There was nothing about abortions or sexual orientation, areas that will be statistically important in any long-range survey. Plus, the directors of the hormone therapy arm of study were both men, "one who bragged he was not a feminist."

Back to Mirror-Shiny Floors: FemaleThinkLash

We're also picking up backlash elements aimed against women. Clearly, there are those who want women to stick to more traditional roles: to stop working, start having babies earlier, go back to being homemakers. "I Love Lucy" and "I Remember Mama" instead of "Murphy Brown."

Publicity machines have started to hype the message that women can't possibly have it all. In a *USA Today* story, the reporter gathered some recent indicators. A 1994 *Barron's* headline prophesied, "Working Women: Goin' Home." The cover story, complete with a photo of an apron-clad Mom bearing a home-baked pie, forecast a "return to the 50s." The *Detroit News* concluded, "Superwoman has had enough." The *Wall Street Journal* suggested, "Young women may trade jobs for marriage."

While the headlines may abound, the facts just don't follow. As the Bureau of Labor Statistics reported, "It is difficult to find any evidence that women might be leaving the labor force in large numbers to take up homemaker roles." The minimal dip in female employment that gets bandied about actually falls within the under-25 age group—and the evidence suggests that these young adults are simply staying in school longer. According to the American Council of Education, the number of Ph.D. candidates rose 6% in the decade between 1982 and 1992, with the heftiest increase among women: 28.8%.

One factor that has been driving some women home is the high cost of adequate daycare. Millions of kids are left in the hands of strangers. If the care is bad, the experience threatens to harm the child's emotional and intellectual growth. No small matter. In a recent survey, the outcome wasn't very promising. Only one in seven circumstances of childcare were termed "very good." Statistically, the level was highest if the daycare was on-site at the office or supplemented by government funding. A support system started in Boston, Children First, provides "backup" childcare for times when your own nanny or caretaker can't make it. Now in four sites in New York, Children First can take up to forty kids at each place, from ages 3 months to 12 years, where they are watched over by staff of seven. Companies buy yearly subscriptions for their employees. Click.

At one of our BrainJams, someone came up with the Click concept of a modular childcare center, including construction, play area, cafeteria, toys, recruiting and interviewing, insurance, everything. The model could be dropped into place anywhere— off and running in no time. Another FemaleThink solution that our group worked on would be if a company such as Disney (maybe with Microsoft) would open a chain of "day-care-tainment centers" across America. Sort of a "Y of the '90s." What parent wouldn't trust a child there? If something like this could happen, it would be a Click heard around the world.

How Do You Click If You're a Woman?

Go with what you know. Women have a better chance of launching an original and brilliant concept that speaks mainly to women than any other group. Target into a segmented or niche market. For instance, if you're Latino, consider the untapped potential of the 27 million Latinos living in the United States—and the 200 million in Latin America. Just figure out what would appeal to you, and study your competition. If no one is doing anything remotely similar, make sure you know why. Compare your ideas to the TrendBank, and if they're synergistic with four or five of them, then you may be the next big-shot female entrepreneur.

Create a small office off your kitchen and begin. We've got a good chance of success in starting a small business because of the hours we're used to putting in. Women have always viewed the workday not as 8 or 10 hours long, but as a 24-hour cycle. We're used to going to a job, picking up the kids after school, helping them with homework, reading a report while dinner's cooking, getting back down to work when dinner's over, trying to get some sleep, waking up if the baby's crying, getting the kids off to school, working again, and so on. Hillary Clinton summed up the steely aspect of FemaleThink: "for many women, it's an act of courage to get through the day."

You get the picture. We believe this is going to be the work pattern of the very late '90s. Only we'll be doing it to move our companies ahead. A typical FemaleThink-run company understands that you have to open at convenient times for your customers . . . or even go to their homes to make a sale or explain a product. Don't be surprised if the success of the venture gets a husband or significant other to join up. There's a lot of sex appeal in running your own show.

Crow about your ideas. You know the old adage about "giving credit where credit is due." We would change it to "taking credit where credit is due." Know your worth. Many studies show that when a woman thinks of a great idea, the men in the room attribute it to the man to her left or right (if they attribute it at all). Women, on the other hand, support, credit, and compliment any idea given. One of our common faults, however, is that we apologize too much (on the job, in conversation). Mumbling "I'm sorry" when there's no need. Giving indirect directions. The problem we call "share/share": sharing the blame (when it belongs to others) or overly sharing the credit, or even worse, denying any credit (when some of it clearly should be yours). Neither bodes well for doing well.

There's a new movement being tested to try to build up confidence in young girls at a tender age. Controlled all-female environments are being looked at to see how emerging egos might flourish if you remove the pressure of being mocked or being overrun by young boys. Some schools in California and Virginia have started girls-only math, science, and computer classes to try to erase gender-bias. A new magazine, *New Moon*, offers an alternative to the usual fashion/makeup/how-to-talk-to-boys articles. Started by a set of parents in Duluth, Minnesota, with their twin daughters in mind, *New Moon* covers serious stuff: voting age, cyberspace, support groups if a parent has cancer. Then there's Jane's Brain, the Prodigy chitchat line for girls 12–19, which, when first blueprinted, banned boys in order to give girls a chance to flourish. Now, as a real-world experiment, 10 young guys have been invited to join 3,500 of the opposite sex.

The Fe/Male Click

Because separatism isn't the long-term answer, men and women have to Click together. To find a way to shift the balance in the way we all live and work. Boosting women up does not require putting men down. We have to get rid of the stereotypical female-hoodwinking, Dumb Man imagery. And we have to be conscious of turning from the more familiar macho emphasis on *winning* to a warmer, friendlier emphasis on *value*.

Instead of a battle of the sexes, men vs. women, today's split is really OldThink vs. FemaleThink. At the wedding of our friends Laura Saver and Blas Candau, the performing woman judge read

"Lucy Stone's Marriage Protest," written in 1855, which pledged not to "sanction the present laws or customs of marriage as confer upon a husband an injurious and unnatural superiority." Female-Think goes far beyond the battle for equality to follow a quest for the recognition of differences. In the brotherly Trend of Mancipation, we more closely examine the men who are right now immersed in creative, out-of-the-box thinking. During my interview with Gloria Steinem for *Interview* magazine, she mentioned, "Yes, I've met a few men who also think in a connected, nonhierarchical way. . . . If we explore human potential instead of restrictions, it's a whole different ball game. Then, one day, some teacher will be standing in front of a classroom trying to convince kids that people once thought that the amount of melanin in one's skin dictated intelligence, or that our genitals controlled our brains, and the kids will be saying, 'Oh, give me a break.'"

The end result of this FemaleThink Trend for both men and women is that people and companies in *every* category can be responsible, caring, and sensitive to their place in the larger universe. Can move from a transactional level to a deeper relationship with everyone from their casual contacts and customers to their closest family circle.

FemaleThink: YOU DON'T HAVE TO BE A WOMAN TO SEE ITS FUTURE.

APPLYING FEMALETHINK

A NEW MARKET FOR METLIFE

A life lesson that I learned from my grandparents, local shopkeepers, was that the first place one should look for new business was near home. If you can't develop new customers through friends and family, next best is to scan the neighborhood. That's why, one day, when my sister Mechele Flaum (President of BrainReserve) and I were having a new business meeting, we decided to revisit this family philosophy. Coincidentally, we had just finished a project for the Burton Group in the U.K., where we were hired to reposition Dorothy Perkins, a chain of 563 department stores. It was a terrific assignment, but after a year of traveling back and forth to England for research and meetings, quite frankly, we were all exhausted.

So Mechele suggested, "Wouldn't it be nice to get an assignment right here in New York City?"

And I said, "What about looking right here? Literally, right here." (At that time, our offices occupied the 28th floor of the MetLife Tower on 23rd and Madison.)

She answered, "Geographically perfect."

A little later that same week, we had already arranged a luncheon meeting with the people upstairs, Ted Athanassiades, President and COO, and Harry P. Kamen, Chairman and CEO of MetLife, one of the most innovative insurance companies around. Although we knew that the company was already actively involved with national women's groups, we came prepared with what we felt was an important question, based on information culled from our FemaleThink Trend: "How many female entrepreneurs do you sell to?"

Their reply was that even though they had formed a Small Business Center, they hadn't collected data in a way that would let them identify how many of their customers were women. We countered with an ambitious proposal: "Let us look at female small business owners and work with MetLife to position itself to help these women realize their potential, and we bet it'll represent a $1 billion business for MetLife." It worked. We got the assignment, along with the chance to be shepherded by a real future thinker, Jim Valentino, Senior VP at MetLife. The irony of this project was that by the last page of our final presentation, we had shown how and why, if they were to create a FemaleThink division, the target number of a billion-dollar revenue stream (originally only an enthusiastic guess on our part) was actually a real possibility—and accomplishable within the time frame of five short years.

BrainReserve based its conclusions on several other Trends, beyond FemaleThink, that supported our premise.

- Icon Toppling: Many people, and especially women, no longer want to buy from large, anonymous companies. "Clicking Through Icon Toppling" explains why "Big Business" is faltering.
- Clanning: The PLU (People Like Us) Trend indicates that women would like to be in the business loop with other women.
- Cashing Out: Quite a few of the small, female-run businesses are at-home operations and very computer-oriented. Onlineness plays a part in our recommendations.
- Egonomics: The customization Trend suggests retailoring many of MetLife's existing products to fit the female entrepreneur and her needs.

- Cocooning: Because women are spending so much time at home, we created a selling plan to take place in the living room, among the safety of friends.
- Vigilante Consumer: To not raise the antennae of the ever-watchful consumer about the possible conflict-of-interest inherent in commission-based sales, we devised a new approach to selling products and services, based on education and trust.
- 99 Lives: A reminder that the female entrepreneur is not *just* a female entrepreneur, but also juggles the roles of wife, daughter, mother, caregiver, homemaker. We believe that after she learns to trust MetLife with her business insurance, there is a likelihood that a businesswoman would turn to the same company to protect her home and family.
- S.O.S.: Ethics and education are the backbone of our concept. Ethically, MetLife had the opportunity to help women have a better future, while educationally, it would be teaching women what men have learned by male bonding in business schools and boardrooms.

Here was our concept for MetLife. After questioning hundreds of female entrepreneurs, interviewing about fifty MetLife executives, and brainstorming internally and with our Brain-Reserve TalentBank members, we arrived at a premise that we felt could build on an emerging strength in the insurance business. Simply transform the "insurance" agent into a "success" agent.

We had heard from so many women (just like me) who had started their own businesses, in spite of a serious lack of organizational know-how. It would have been a terrific help to have had a *mentor*—someone wiser and more experienced—to guide them in figuring out what kind of bookkeeping/payroll system to set up, what kind of telephone/computer system to purchase, and what kind of people to hire.

We confirmed with MetLife that this female market was being undervalued and underserved, and, therefore, they were under-purchasing financial services. And the first company to really demonstrate deep levels of concern would be in position to gain market share and loyalty.

We also looked at the price of ignoring this market. Most probably, some of MetLife's competitors would someday soon be looking at the same opportunities and grappling with the same issues. The fringe benefit was that this move could most probably boost MetLife's overall strength in the insurance and financial service arena, since once women are won, they tend to spread the word.

Our main idea was to create a program that responded specifically to the needs of the female entrepreneur. Its working title is "FemaleThInc." and its mission is to mentor the female entrepreneur to her successful financial future. The directive and acronym we devised for this effort was "GetREALER." *R*each out to Female Small Business Owners (FSBOs). *E*ncourage them. *A*nalyze their needs. *L*isten to their concerns. *E*ducate them. *R*espond. A real business opportunity. Helping to make it possible is Judy Weiss, Senior Vice President, of their Small Business Center (800-METLIFE), whose experience makes her the perfect person to lead this exciting and revolutionary initiative.

The "success" agents would be known as "MetMentors." The concept of mentoring was developed from more than 10,000 BrainReserve interviews in which women talked about wanting to do business only with companies they can trust. Clearly, MetLife could benefit from offering an entirely different level of service: mentoring support in lieu of traditional selling.

Here's one woman's typical response: "I am what you'd call an insurance illiterate. The language is always so complicated and confusing. I still haven't found anyone who can sit down and explain the finer details to me."

In essence, women who are running small businesses could be helped by a female-supportive sales force who would offer women information and advice on insurance and other products. This sales force could be compensated by a different standard— not by the monetary amount of the policy they sell, but by measuring how much they grow their clients' businesses.

There is also an opportunity for MetLife to create new insurance and financial products for female businesses or else "female-frame" their existing ones. Our research showed that there are six general areas of concern to the female entrepreneur that need to be addressed:

1. Nurturing/growing the business.
2. Multiple obligations to family/business (home/office umbrella).

3. Stress of too much work/too little time.
4. Fear of running out of resources in later life.
5. Lack of access to capital.
6. Desire for individual attention to problems.

By understanding and using the Trends, it's possible to focus a corporate strategy that will meet real market needs. Since MetLife now has the detailed research to better address the female business owners' concerns, it can chart a course to help them achieve their life's dreams.

The post-Click from this assignment: One recent weekend, Mechele and I decided to work on redefining BrainReserve's mission statement. After much trial and error, we came up with a brief motto that best captured what we are trying to do, to "Lift Ourselves and Others into the Best Possible Future." More than that, we wanted to try to specifically help lift other women into their best future. I'm proud of this—and I'm proud of MetLife.

CLICKING THROUGH MANCIPATION

Macho does not prove mucho.
—ZSA ZSA GABOR

M ancipation" is a new word we coined for a Trend that is just starting to take wing. It means the emancipation of men or the flipside of FemaleThink. It's a way to give a name and identification to the New Male. The '90s man. Unshackled from the bondages of macho-ism. Liberated from being distant, disconnected, remote, unromantic, analytical, forever Strictly Business. Released from always, always, having to be the strong shoulder to lean on.

What a free-feeling Click.

Think about the message being sent by the cartoon from a recent women's magazine that showed side-by-side rest rooms with the signs: "Evil Oppressors" and "Victims." It may have produced a chuckle once, but it seems more sad than funny now. Just as FemaleThink frees women to run things their way, Mancipation lets men become free to be. Lighter, more sentimental, willing to try things "men" don't do. And the examples of Mancipation may push men to be who they've never been.

Or back to where they partially were. Once upon a time in history, the male was unabashedly the preener, the peacock, the fop. Powdered wigs and beauty marks. Warriors in the past, from Alexander the Great to the ferocious samurai in Japan, were first schooled in the finer arts and poetry, then graduated to swords. In her book *The Natural History of the Senses*, Diane Ackerman relates how "ancient he-men were heavily perfumed. In a way, strong scents widened their presence, extended their territory." (An interesting way to think about fragrance, as a power enhancer.) In 400 B.C., Cretan athletes anointed themselves with aromatic oils before the games, with particular kinds picked for different body parts (a Click for a perfumer today?): mint on the arms; thyme for the knees; cinnamon, rose, or palm oil for the jaws and chest; almond oil for the hands and feet; marjoram for the hair and eyebrows. The book goes on to point out all the early masculine habits. Egyptian men would be bedecked with garlands of flowers and perfume at dinner parties. Flower petals would be strewn for them to crush underfoot. Roman gladiators (as well as ordinary citizens) also rubbed on a variety of scented lotions, pre-chosen for the various pulse points. Jasmine, orange water, musk, lavender—"a tapestry of aromas." Napoleon went on his warring campaigns wearing rose or violet lotions under his gloves (revealing his sensual nature).

It's only since the Industrial Revolution when men trudged off to the factories that the feminine side of life was given solely to women.

The Mancipation male wants to be more attractive again. There's no news in the fact that women splash on men's fragrances, but it's a new oddity that it's happening vice-versa. To be fair, what has prompted this cross-spraying is the marketing success of the decade, "unisex" fragrances. Top honors go to CK, providing equal fragrance from the equal underwear people. The Gap has joined the unisex arena with its line of bath and beauty Gap Scents, with the outdoorsy and friendly names of Grass, Earth, Day, Heaven, and Dream.

Here is the future, Mancipation-wise. The softer ways of behaving will prevail over the harder edge. Men will feel no embarrassment about crying big fat tears . . . admitting for all to read, as top-of-the-charts songwriter and singer Babyface has, "I try to cry when I write." Nor will males squirm when it comes time to baby their babies. Instead, they'll welcome these raw displays of emotion. Take, for example, the Johnson & Johnson Baby Shampoo commercial that shows a big, burly, man-hand cradling a small infant's head, and mentions something about how short a time before the start of ballet lessons and when boys come knocking at the door. Then it cuts to a shot of that father tenderly shampooing his newborn daughter's hair. Sweet Mancipation. Or the Lands' End print ad that shows one adult-sized and one kid-sized turtleneck, simply saying for a nice change "Like father, like daughter."

The passing of the Family Leave Act plays into this Mancipation happening. How has it worked since the summer of 1993 when all companies with more than fifty employees (including part-timers) were required to give twelve weeks' unpaid but job-guaranteed leave for birthing, adoption, family illness? Not brilliantly, yet. Right off the bat, the football player David Williams was fined $100,000 by the Houston Oilers for being at the birth of his first child instead of playing the game. In one survey, a full 40% of employers were found not complying with the law. Another query found that when workers took such leave, the majority of them had problems, such as being replaced or asked to shorten the time off.

The biggest obstacle is that few workers can afford to lose three months' salary. An article in the *Boston Globe* described what happened at the relatively small Millipore Corp. in Bedford, Massachusetts, which offered four weeks of *paid* leave. Then the numbers jumped to about half the takers being men, with forty-five men requesting paternity leave. Even though the Family Leave Act is far from perfect, it's a start. The bottom line is that if, God forbid, you need time off, it's comforting to know you have a job to come back to. It will take a few years to change actions to be in synch with the more Mancipated attitudes. But there are all kinds of reassuring statistics. The Families and Work Institute in New York found that 80% of the men it interviewed wanted a stronger role in childrearing than their own Dads had. And 57% of the men at Du Pont, up from 37% five years ago, would like more flexibility in their work schedules so they can hang out with their wives and kids.

Add this to the phenomenon of full-time House Dads. There are over 3.5 million men who stay home now while their wives go to work. It's out of choice. Being a homebody for a man, just as for a woman, doesn't necessarily mean whiling the days away vacuuming and watching the soaps. No one knows this better than those men who've started businesses or who create at home. For example, John Stegeman, who started and runs a politico-satirical wristwatch company, White House Watch, out of his home, while wife, Linda, charts the future of voice mail as VP of Marketing for Octel Communications.

Any man who was sweet and not overly dominant was classically misunderstood. Those traits were viewed as a weakness, not a strength. In a *Mirabella* magazine interview, Estée Lauder talked about the sacrifices she had to make as the prime breadwinner forty or more years ago. She said, "My husband, Joe, was the dearest man in the world, but I was moving further and faster than he, and frankly, I didn't know how to be Mrs. Joseph Lauder and Estée Lauder at the same time. Remember, there was no such thing as feminism then, no rules to help a strong women live with a much-loved but gentler man."

Contrast that story with the premise of Mancipation. Joe could stay at home now and Estée could be more comfortable with her more intense drive. There's such overall good news in this "life flex." Neither of the sexes is stuck in a rigid box (see the box story, page 168). Men and women are partnering each other economically. In an interview in *The New York Times*, Gloria Steinem talked about a future project, writing a book with a working title "Men Are Mothers, Too," about "the need for men to be parents." Steinem said, "I mean, we've proven that women can do what men did, professionally. But we haven't convinced ourselves, or them, that men can do what women have done."

It's akin to what Susan Sontag once penned: "What is most beautiful in virile men is something feminine; what is beautiful in feminine women is something masculine."

Not everyone is pleased by this. There was a throwback opinion in an article that announced, "Men Whose Wives Work Earn Less." The writer tried to prove a point that working women sap husbands of earning power. In this view, men who don't devote all their waking hours to their jobs simply are not as successful, because they don't accomplish as much as their driven colleagues.

That's anti-Mancipation, and as dated as a Davy Crockett hat.

For the Mancipation Trend is growing and spreading into the mainstream of American businesshood. In a marriage announcement in *The New York Times*, the bridegroom, Joseph Baumer, 27, a securities trader at J.P. Morgan, was very offhand about his future plans. "He talks about family life as excitedly as some men talk about hanging out at bars with models. 'I'm a trader, a job I picked partly because the day is over at 4 P.M.,' he said. 'I plan to be home at 5 with my kids.'"

This notion of making a career out of fatherhood is fading as an oddity. Help is also coming from a surge of peripheral networks. A newsletter, *At-Home Dad*, was started by Peter Baylies of North Andover, Massachusetts. There's a support group in Atlanta called Dad-to-Dad (a good idea for many communities). And there's even a comic strip, "Adam," that features a man with three kids and no outside job.

Eric Jonsson, 37, is on the threshold of being an at-home Dad. He had been working at a large construction company, obtaining financial backing for their projects, while his wife earned her living as a mutual funds manager. The couple made a decision, with the blessing of their pastor, that Eric would be the one to stay at home and take care of their upcoming baby. His mother has expressed some concern about "maintaining the balance" in their relationship, but Eric is not worried about that. His main strain is the same as that of any educated woman when faced with hours of warming bottles and washing babies: how to keep current/be interesting and stay a part of the larger world. He's come up with an entrepreneurial solution, to start an at-home business locating small companies with big potential for investors. When Eric was asked if the couple has considered a time when they both would be working in the outside business world, he laughingly said no. That they don't believe in what they call the "Rent-a-Mom" situation. "If you're going to have kids," Eric Jonsson added, "then you should make them your life's work."

One novel way of spending more time with your kids while you hold down a full-time job comes from Richard Fairbank, the CEO of Capital One Financial Corporation in Virginia. Before his children were even in kindergarten, he and his wife decided to shift the young ones' sleep schedules, so that they could stay up later. The children were put to bed at midnight or 12:30 A.M., and awakened late in the morning, so that when Rich returned home after a day at the office, the family would have hours to be together, shopping at all-night stores and having fun. When the children went to preschool, he and his wife found an afternoon program so they could stay on shifted hours. Now his sons are 10 and 13 and his daughters are 7 and 6 months. "I'm somewhat fanatical about being with them," he said. "I so dearly love my family, despite having a demanding, exciting job. They really give meaning to my life. It's easy to get immersed in work; the pressure is so great, but you need to pull up, get perspective, and spend more time on the things that mean the most. Otherwise, you are *mortgaging your future.*"

To keep this commitment, Rich made up some guidelines to live by:

1. "Exploit the flexibility of your job, whenever possible." Since he often has to travel or work late hours, he takes advantage of any downtime that comes along.
2. "Force yourself to stick to reasonable hours." Rich shared his belief that "work is like your closet—even if you have twice as much closet space, you still fill up every inch. Work expands to fill the time allotted. So if you mobilize your resources effectively, you can get the same quality of work done."
3. "Work on time-creation." You have to be clever to carve out quality time together. Use your idle hours to do things that would otherwise interfere with your family life.
4. "Restructure your activity profile." Instead of taking up something solitary and adult-oriented, Rich made a family activity out of canoeing and now golf. He's also taken up his kids' favorite sports, soccer and hockey, so that he can play with them.
5. "Make your home kid-friendly." "The basement of our house is like a sports facility, and it's an open house for other kids. And we temporarily put in a basketball hoop when we were remodeling our sunroom. It just stayed there and the furniture never got moved back in." That's a Mancipated man who puts his family first.

Mike Lorelli, President of the Americas, for Tambrands, Inc., just completed a book called *Traveling Again, Dad*—a self-help guide for families who have to live with the fact that Daddy (or Mommy) is often on the road for business. The book gives needed advice on how to turn such crises as missing important events (Little League games and dance recitals) into deeper ways of communicating.

We're seeing more of the Mancipation Trend being incorporated into the office arena of big-business types and tycoons. Witness Wolfgang Schmitt, CEO of one of this country's most smoothly run companies, Rubbermaid. His secret? He tries to apply the rules of nature to his work. Inspiration comes from being lucky enough to live on an eighteen-acre arboretum where he can watch the intricate harmony of 3,000 varieties of trees, a lake, and two streams. From this, he figured out a system of new-product entrepreneurial teams, much like the leaf system of a plant.

Nothing abrasive, no mano-a-mano combat references in Wolf's management style. He listens to unlikely voices: children and his own intuition. An eclectic thinker, he's looked into strange places for new product ideas, from food storage innovations of the ancient Egyptians to a toy based on his son's interest in farm machines. It's unusual for the top manager to be so hands-on with the details, the creative ideas. But it works. Rubbermaid was voted one of "America's most admired corporations," in a *Fortune* magazine survey.

In an interview with Leslie Wexner, chairman of The Limited, Inc., a leading specialty retailer, we found some real Mancipated attitudes, if not actions. In reverse of what everyone has been talking about in the past few years, listening to the inner child as an adult, Les listened to the inner adult as a child. He couldn't wait to be in charge. "I wanted to be my own boss." "When I was 5," Wexner reminisced, "I taught myself to draw in perspective. I figured out that the furthest place was the smallest by looking down highways and along the lines of telephone poles. Now I have a library of about 3,000 books on architecture and city planning. I would have wanted to be Howard Roark [architect from Ayn Rand's novel *The Fountainhead*]. But my father insisted that I go to business school instead."

Wexner's relationship with his father was the foundation of his outlook. "My whole childhood can be explained by the movie *The Chosen*. It's about a father and two boys. One young man is very smart and curious, but it's the other, the younger one, who gets all the affection and love. At the end, the father tells the older boy, 'Because you were a special child, I made a tough decision not to do all the things a father wants to do. I had to deal with you in silence because you had the innate ability to be creative and figure things out yourself. If I held and cuddled you,

you never would have reached your full potential.' I watch that movie about once a year and always cry. And now I have a little boy who's named after my father, Harry. I hug him and kiss him and wonder what he is going to grow up to be. I get up thirty minutes early every day to have breakfast with Harry. He sits in his high chair and I make him laugh. I just hope that I'm smart enough to understand where his natural inclinations are, to accentuate the positive and not force my ideas on him. I would also hope that if I sense that he needed more affection to mature fully or if he needed more silence or whatever, I could provide that right balance."

The concept of balance is Wexner's definition of Clicking. "I believe people need a balance in their lives between personal and career. There's also a balance that goes to community responsibility. We have a moral obligation to use our God-given gifts for the benefit of society." When his philanthropist mentor, Max Fisher, related how he retired at Wexner's age to go into community service, he struck a chord, partially. Wexner thought about the concept of retiring, and realized how much he likes what he does. "It's not work, but fun. I counsel people all the time and say that if you spend 40, 50, 60, 70 hours a week doing something that is not fun, go out and find something that is." On his late-in-life marriage, Wexner is candid. "I had never found anyone who I wanted to share my life with or whose life I wanted to share. But Abigail was quite different. She's the best person I've ever met."

Another name in Big Business who is surprisingly Mancipated and Trend-wise is Jim Morgan, president of Philip Morris. He credits his mentor, Jack Landry, with teaching him the "power of intuitive thinking and the freedom to let oneself go." Recently he let himself go on a ten-day trip through the American West in a big-rigged truck, sharing the cab with another business pal. "We had these incredible long stretches where neither of us talked while we were riding down the road, which was okay because I had time to figure out that I was in control over my own schedule again—for the first time in forty years."

"The second thing that was different was that I only had to think about five minutes ahead. In fact, we didn't even know what roads we were going to take, where we'd stop to eat or sleep. In the morning, the first place we saw that had four trucks in front of it is where we'd pull in for breakfast. I had the most unbelievable breakfasts I'd ever had in my life—a stack of flapjacks, a couple of eggs and bacon, grapefruit juice, and a cup of coffee, all for $2.89. Because I was so open and unscheduled, I got to meet fantastic people—our consumers—for some real talk. In Shell, Wyoming, about four miles west of the Bighorn Mountains, we stopped for gas at a general store called Dirty Annie's and I started a conversation with a man who turned out to be one of the original aeronautical engineers who worked on building the very first Boeing 727. He told me this incredible story about flying on that same plane's last flight to the Boeing Hall of Fame in Seattle. He asked me what I did and I told him I was just driving this truck across the country. He said, 'Sounds like fun,' and I answered. 'Yeah, it's great fun.' I didn't know his name and he didn't know mine. That's real freedom." We call that free-to-be-your-real-male-self: Mancipation.

When we first saw the DreamWorks trio of Steven Spielberg, David Geffen, and Jeffrey Katzenberg, we thought, "Where's the suit?" It's unusual for three creative guys to get together without a pin-striped heavy in the mix—that old, wiser banker-type lurking in the background to make sure that things are kept on track. But this is exactly what Mancipation in business is all about. An acknowledgment that it's all right to have fun while you work. That's the Click, to enjoy what you do. Another sign of Mancipation in this group came when details of the new media group leaked out. It seems that Spielberg gave his wife, Kate Capshaw, veto power over the deal. And she only flashed the green light after Katzenberg (closest to an Organizational Man) vowed that Steven would still have plenty of home-time to spend with Kate and the kids.

We'd all agree that there's a long stretch between doing business and the question, "What's your sign?" That much-poked-fun-at opening line from the Flower Power days is no joke to entrepreneur Henry Weingarten. A professional astrologer for 28 years, Henry has successfully merged the softer world of clairvoyancy into the tough, fast world of the international stock markets. His astro-economic mutual fund uses the basic tenets of astrology as an analysis tool for managing customer's investment moneys. Before starting the Astrologers Fund (motto: "Naturally a Stellar Performance"), he had the slightly wacky honor of being the first "Executive Astrological Analyst" for a New York–based commodity firm.

Henry predicted the coming of the Tokyo market crash of 1990 and the onset of the Gulf War as well as the *very day* the Dow Jones Industrial Average broke 3,000 and the *very day* gold broke 400.

If the old way of doing business is regimented and hierarchical, then the colorful, freewheeling offices of the advertising agency Chiat/Day are a shining example of a Mancipation business. There are no outward symbols of power. No titles on the doors, just captions on the walls. No big cushy offices with polished wood desks that gleam with brass pulls and locked drawers. No one in this quirky place, not even a top exec, has an assigned office or even a desk to call his or her own (although you can sign up for a room by the hour or day). Nor does anyone have a computer that belongs to only one user. The so-called Virtual Office in lower Manhattan, designed by Gaetano Pesce and Jay Chiat, has a pair of giant red lips, behind which is a "store" that dispenses daily computers and telephones for the roll-around workstations. For those inevitable personal items, there are employee lockers that are highly stylized to look like native sculptings. It goes without saying that no one has to punch a time clock. On the contrary, Chiat/Day has become a successful model of flex hours, and some of the staff works part-time at home. We think that this kind of "employee empowerment," acknowledging that responsible individuals should be able to decide "what needs to be done" and "how long it will take," will become more prevalent in the business arena. Everything about it Clicks into future change.

What about the way men are looking at themselves these Mancipated days? We've certainly come a long long way from the days when a book titled *Real Men Don't Eat Quiche* could be written. Real men are primping, nipping, and tucking in record numbers. The no-frills men's magazine *Men's Health* has a very healthy 1.2 million circulation. It covers all the basics about health and fitness, plus gives advice on how to have great sex and lose weight faster. American males are spending more than $55 million annually on skin care products, up from $25 million a few years ago. The number of men going under the knife for plastic surgery has increased a radical 200%, including liposuction to suck away that extra flab. Men also account for more than 40% of all check-ins at major health spas, such as Tucson, Arizona's Canyon Ranch.

The other concern, besides a paunchy belly, is baldness and

related hair problems. Getting hair plugs, once an esoteric operation, is considered normal now. Sales of a product made for coarse horse hair, called Mane 'n' Tail, took off at a gallop after ex-quarterback Terry Bradshaw mentioned on television that the equine shampoo and conditioner was making hairs grow atop his shiny pate. Men might want their hair as thick as Secretariat's mane, but to carry the horse analogy further, they're not interested in having the gray coloring of the latest super-colt, Holy Bull (for trivia buffs, only 1% of the equine population is gray). Human males are drowning out the gray strands at home with openly and suddenly aggressively advertised products such as Just for Men, which also has a line extension targeted just for the harder-to-cover, but telltale aging signs of graying beards, moustaches, and sideburns. And you should see the action at Louis Licari's Color Group in New York. Men used to sneak in wearing dark glasses (as if they were frequenting a brothel) and hide in the back room or upstairs, out-of-sight. Now the majority of males casually sit in any available chairs and have their youthful hair color subtly restored, in full view of all.

The downside of all this self-focus: Up to 1 million men are now suffering from those eating disorders that were considered young women's diseases. Anorexia nervosa and bulimia among young men is getting more widespread each year.

That's because men, like generations of women before them, have started to believe that their sex appeal is more contingent on their looks than on their bank accounts. In the old days, portliness and a pot belly signaled affluence. It was proof that a man did not have to sweat to earn. Look at the male movie stars of the '30s, '40s, and '50s. When the handsome-faced hero took off his shirt, his body was often flabby around the waist, his arms and chest undelineated. We don't even realize how much we take sculpted pecs and rippling arm and leg muscles for granted now.

Now women swoon at the sight of male bodies. The permission to ogle started with Chippendale's and its "take-it-off, take-it-all-off" striptease evenings for hen parties. It went on to the graphic posters for Calvin Klein briefs (lumps, bumps, and all). Then the Diet Coke commercial from mid-'94 Clicked in and reinforced the okay-ness of it all. In its now-infamous shots, a klatsch of female office workers stop work and rush to the window each day at the appointed hour to catch sight of a hunky construction worker pulling off his shirt and gulping a soda. Link this with the advent of male frontal nudity in the movies. From Harvey Keitel in *The Piano* to Sylvester Stallone in *The Specialist*. It's rumored that if you don't blink, you could catch a peek at Robert De Niro, completely naked, as he was playing the part of Frankenstein.

This interest in "beefcake" has made some men even more conscious about broadening their shoulders and whittling their waists. In a further show of vanity, men have taken to razor-blading off the Levi's patch that tells the size of their jeans. To cinch those inches, men are going on furtive quests for special corsets. Belly Buster Contouring Gel, at $30 a pop, is sought after for its promise to "melt fat cells." For the man's answer to the Wonderbra, Super Shaper Buns Briefs will add rounded bulk to a flat bottom, plus they come with the optional snap-in "front endowment pad." It means that in these days of Mancipation, men have achieved the rank of sex objects.

But Mancipation isn't only about the heftier Grunt Set. As a role model for softer times, we have the once-flinty Clint Eastwood trading in his monosyllables for the very talky, poetic, "Let me help you get dinner ready" character, Robert Kinkaid, in *The Bridges of Madison County*. Wearing sandals instead of cowboy boots. In fact, we're seeing more and more men with an androgynous look, wearing their hair long and flowing, their ears pierced with multiple earrings, their clothes narrow, their feet lifted in high-heel boots, their bodies tight, but not so muscle-bound. Unlike years ago, this type of dressing is very unselfconscious. All kinds of men, from truckers to contractors to accountants, are affecting this "pretty" look. A Click that will only get stronger over the next years.

Ordinary Joes are starting to wear skirts, too. We're not talking about "drag" or the "cross-dressing" of *To Wong Foo; The Crying Game; Priscilla, Queen of the Desert;* or *Mrs. Doubtfire*, or of Mama J of "On Our Own." And it's beyond the bagpipe brigades . . . or the desert world where men have a falcon on their wrists and a caftan flapping around their ankles. We're talking fashionable men in sarongs and kilts. Donna Karan showed a long wrap skirt on her male runway models who didn't look any more gender-different than men who knot a bath towel or beach towel around their waists. Movie star Jaye Davidson was beamed worldwide as he accepted his Oscar for Best Supporting Actor wearing a peau de soie sarong. In Japan, it's a real fad among teenage boys to dress up in skirts, according to a story in the *Mainichi Daily News*. Tokyo stores such as Milk Boys and Super Lovers supply the clothes for the "fem boys." One 19-year-old was quoted as saying, "I don't care if people say that I look like a girl. I love it, and I'm expressing myself that way."

It's often been expressed that if a man and woman could change places for a time, we'd be more sensitive to each other's problems and be able to figure out what is real and what is stereotypical. Maybe we're just tired of the game of "them" against "us," and are bent on blurring the boundaries. Looking for the answer to the eternal question: "Why are they *like that?*" we can try to be *like that* to find out. *Ladies' Home Journal* actually conducted an experiment whereby a man and a woman changed places. The magazine's blurb copy ran like this: "Have You Ever Wondered What It Would Be Like to Live as a Man? Or Wished Your Husband Could Walk in Your Heels—For Just a Little While? One Couple Carried Off a Role-Switch—With Surprising Results."

After *LHJ* arranged for a makeover, complete with haircuts, leg shaving, professional makeup, and padded body suits, the transformed mid-thirties couple went out in the world as gender opposites. At the end of the experiment, they shared their findings. Mainly, women smile more than men, show more expression, and are more animated talkers; while men have an easier time getting dressed and have more confidence. The real woman in the article concluded that the best thing about being a man "was the sense of being able to take up space. I didn't have to sit with my arms crossed and my legs together."

What will happen to a person's space when we cross our roles? *Glamour* magazine once wrote up a device that allowed men to experience breast-feeding. It looked rather like a saddlebag that draped around a man's neck, with its two pouches full of milk formula. The invention didn't seem to galvanize American fathers at the time, but it wouldn't be surprising if, as Mancipation gains steam, this handy provider were to Click in the late '90s.

Why shouldn't men want to nurture their offspring?

In fact, *Discover* magazine had an article written by a new father, Jared Diamond, which went further than "milkbags" and actually explored the possibility of being able to nurse his twin sons. He first found out that other mammals, such as male domesticated goats, sometimes spontaneously grow udders and lactate.

He also learned about the milk-bearing male Malaysian fruit bat. As Diamond went on to point out, men have the anatomic equipment, which is activated in extreme cases, such as near-starvation in prisoner-of-war camps. If it's possible then for men to do it, he muses, why can't he? With a shot of hormones and manual stimulation (he cited cases in which adoptive mothers begin producing milk after putting the infant at their breast), involved fathers may be unbuttoning their shirts and breast-feeding in the future. Then they, too, will share the experience of having to get back into shape after weaning.

The movie *Junior* gave everyone a good time by taking the very masculine hulk Arnold Schwarzenegger and creating an incredible story about a male pregnancy. There's already a product on the market that lets men approximate the experience of what the bulk, weight, and awkwardness of being pregnant feels like. Called Empathy Belly, it's a weighted canvas vest that comes pre-shaped with a large, extended belly, full breasts, and everything but the craving for pickles.

The *New York Times Sunday Magazine*, tuning in to the intrigue surrounding this new male fantasy, ran a highly speculative article pushing the limits on the topic, entitled "How to Get a Man Pregnant" by Dick Teresi. The writer suggested that the technology needed to make a man pregnant has been around for a decade. The still medically risky procedure would go like this: in vitro fertilization of an egg; embryo inserted into the male abdominal cavity; an attachment to the fatty tissue; hormone shots; gestation; *voilá*, delivery via C-section. (He failed to mention, "Cross your fingers.") Quoted is one of the pioneers of in vitro fertilization, L. Shettles, who still believes it will be accomplished someday, "What's good for the goose is good for the gander."

The press is not the only place this discussion is appearing. A young radiologist we know has been intrigued with the even more radical what-if: figuring out whether two people of the same sex could ever have a biological child together. "For instance, if it happened to take place between two women, it's a given that the baby could only be a girl, since there wouldn't be any Y chromosome in the mix."

Nudity and sex may be in the spotlight, but there's a new shyness surfacing in the Mancipation trend. The right-of-passage from boyhood to manhood is being delayed, the bragging put off until later. Keeping your virginity is turning into a badge of pride. A survey on sex in America shows that the percentage of 20-year-old men who've never done "it" is greater today. On the streets, these guys are called "Chase," short for "chastity," and, for the most part, get respect, and chiding, for their integrity. In fact, an organized movement called True Love Waits has supposedly signed up thousands of young kids who have pledged to keep sexually pure until marriage. This is a new Click for Teens (could this be the start of a shift away from the enormous number of unwanted pregnancies?). Carefree is seen as careless; abstinence, equated with strength of character.

How do you market to a Mancipated male? Things will Click if you catch these chrysalis characters just as they emerge. Any product or service that panders to a kinder, gentler, but still strong man. That emphasizes that a man's man can also be a woman's man, can also be a child's man. It's all kept in balance. Men like being the ones who hold open the door, and women like it that way. But that does not preclude today's men from going grocery shopping and rustling up dinner. There are gaps for more and more beauty products that work for men. For instance, if so many Dads are caretaking their infants, shouldn't there be lotions to make masculine hands softer? Or changing tables that come in adjustable heights to accommodate a taller man? And what about catering to the look of being more flamboyant, more fashionable. Beyond products, we need a change in outlook. Each and every print ad, each and every daytime/nighttime television show and its commercials needs to be scrutinized for an anti-Mancipation slant. For instance, why are all household products being targeted to women if so many men are working at home?

Mancipation isn't a "movement." It acknowledges that every man is different and unique, and doesn't move in a pack. Mancipation is more of a forward attitude that welcomes individuality and self-worth. It calls for a closing of the book on old ideas of postponing living until after retirement. A gradual end to clichés that "men always . . ." That men only shake hands, but that men don't hug and men don't kiss. That men can't remember to buy birthday presents or anniversary cards. Forget it. The Mancipated man can do anything. And can Click while doing it.

CLICKING THROUGH 99 LIVES

Anxiety is like sand in an oyster;
a few grains produce a pearl, too many, kill.
—OLD SAYING

If you are too busy to laugh, you are too busy.
—NEW SAYING

The highly charged 99 Lives Trend, once careening at full speed ahead, has settled down into a less frightening and more manageable mode. The idea that we have too little time, too many responsibilities, and not enough of ourselves to spread around is now a given. For millions of Americans, the feeling of being overscheduled, overcommitted, and always-on-the-run is a fundamental part of our high-tech life. How many times have you heard the lament, "I wish I could clone myself." Or the excuse, "I just can't be in two places at one time."

What's new and 99 Lives–ish about today is how we're coping with what sociologists are calling our "time-compressed lifestyles." These days, no one blinks twice at the beep-beep-beep of pocket databank organizers or stares at people who walk down the street barking orders into pocket phones. In France, flashy little big-city phones are now so amazingly affordable that there's a danger that phones will soon become evolutionary appendages to ears. At BrainReserve, we're all completely addicted to those two-minute

Voice It recorders, the size of credit cards, for fast meeting recaps or reminders, before we lose a thought. The contents can be turned into a memo—before you can say, "Click."

We've gotten used to double-duty stores: Laundromats that sell videos and supermarkets with ATMs on their walls. If we live in urbania, we've come to expect junk mail menus from every takeout joint in the neighborhood, based on the assumption that, as busy city folk, we don't have the time—or the inclination—to cook. If we do, we clip magazine recipes that promise multiple meals in 20 minutes (or under) with few ingredients. At the TrendView seminar, one of the biggest laughs comes when we flash a cartoon picturing a kid watching his Mom putting something into the microwave and complaining, "2 minutes? I thought you said it was instant."

We live in a land of multiple images, fragmented in at least 99 ways. But . . . if you can do something, make something, or license something that will stand out in this hall of mirrors, it can definitely Click. If you can somehow tap into the fast lane of products and services geared to the Trend of 99 Lives, you will definitely Click. It's that clear-cut.

One way is to think up hassle-free helpers, extra hands, services that will unburden our overly cluttered lives. Type-A personalities respond particularly well to this concept. For instance, a weekend spent in Deer Valley, Utah, at tabletop magnate Audrey Friedman's "ski-in, ski-out" house, opened our eyes to a Clickably ingenious service business for second-home owners. A central outfit does everything for you—without hassle, at a fixed hourly rate. People come in and Polaroid every corner of your house so that when the cleaning staff finishes, everything is put back in the right place. Details, details. Even your bed pillows are arranged exactly as you like them. They've interviewed you about your particular preferred brand names, so when they do the shopping, they buy your favorite honey mustard and not the grainy kind. They handle repairs and wait for deliveries. And before guests arrive, they get tickets for the local symphony and line up the pampering experts—scheduling massage therapists, an aerobics instructor, even an Indian trail guide for a mountain hike. That leaves the host and her guests uninterrupted time to exchange ideas and life plans. A true Clicking luxury.

Another small example of this helping-hand concept is the

Elephant Secretary, a 24-hour service that remembers all your important birthdays, anniversaries, and holidays, and selects and sends out cards in *your own* handwriting. Cold and callous? Maybe, but unlike you, its main focus is never forgetting. Or you can un-99 your life with the Turtle, a green robotic solar lawn mower from Sweden that crawls around on its own and cuts your lawn. The key here is the unspoken promise: It works . . . while you do something else.

In the coming years, 99 Lives will still be on an upturn, marked by a steady acceleration. We'll continue to rely on (and ever demand) things that save us time, keep us terminally in touch and overconnected. Time is measured not in minutes, but in nanoseconds. A coveted watch in Europe and Japan is the German-made Junghaus, the most accurate timepiece on the market. It's guaranteed to lose no more than one second in a million years. And if it does? Will someone be around to fix it or replace it?

Madison Ave. is a good gauge of how entrenched we are in this accelerated-life Trend. Advertisers like to remind us that they know just how busy we are. A TV clip announces, "You have such precious little time you even pay someone else to smell the roses." Whirlpool sympathetically suggests, "If only you could duplicate yourself." The print ad features seven photos of a mother and her daily tasks. In one shot, she's holding her baby; in others, lugging bags of groceries, walking the dog, stirring and cooking, on the phone. You get the picture. A routine nonstop day. Clicked into 99 Lives. Another tactic is to get one more thing "off your mind." The prescription birth control product Depo-Provera now comes in an injection form, with the enticement: "Introducing Birth Control You Think About Just 4 Times a Year."

There are other signs that 99 Lives continues to flourish—particularly on the road. Lately, drive-throughs have become the biggest source of sales for many of the major fast-food chains, showing a recent 24% increase. At McDonald's, for example, customers in cars pulling up to order Egg McMuffins or Big Macs and fries account for an amazing 60% of total purchases. Anyone starting a restaurant should know that now one meal in ten is eaten in the car. And it's not just the van-with-kids crowd who are eating in their cars. As Willie Nelson sings, America is "on the road again."

Wouldn't it be nice if someday you could fax a fast-food place (or a restaurant) ahead, order, pay by credit card, and have the food ready when you arrive? Expensive but already here is a tracking feature that lets you scan for oncoming gas stations, rest rooms, and such. Even further along is a system written up in *Business Week* magazine that turns a "car's computer into a restaurant guide on wheels." By analyzing your past eating patterns (what restaurants you've gone to before, when, why, and with whom), the "smart" program, designed by Ray E. Eberts of Purdue University, can accurately predict where you'd like to eat at any given moment. Next? We'd like a guide to concerts, dances, movies, other happenings.

Every time Lys has to fill up her hefty gray Ford Explorer, she invents new ways to speed up the long, boring process of standing there and hand-squeezing 20 gallons of gas into the tank. Thinking "Until we go electric, why can't some advances be made?" Playing the "what-if" game. For instance, what if you pulled up, pressed buttons for octane/amount, and an automated nozzle reached out to quickly pressure-pump the gas into your car? Or what if the car's tank opening was underneath and fed in from the ground? You should also be able to slip your credit card (or debit card) into a slot on your dashboard to pay for the gallons used. Of course, an entertaining way of passing the time has been devised at a gas station in L.A. The owners installed mini-TVs right into its pumps, originally set to the O. J. trial, so that customers could watch while they gassed up.

Several states are looking now at ways to make life in the car easier and faster. New York City has set up a midtown office called License X-press that promises to renew your driver's license in no more than eight minutes. Some places are trying out new automated tollbooths (so we don't have to dig deep in our pockets and purses for change). These booths have devices that "read" your oncoming car, then deduct the toll from your prepaid account. In Houston, the City Traffic Center has started a program to transmit information via television monitor to the larger office buildings to let the workers know how and where to avoid tie-ups at rush hour—before they leave the premises. That's an improvement over the Long Island Expressway (affectionately known as the "world's longest parking lot"), which tells you in big letters that you are *in* a "traffic delay." Or puts out miles of orange lane-blocking cones when not one single soul is working on the road.

In an interview with Diane Sawyer, she talked about her antidote for being stuck in a car. "I like to keep a book of poetry in my
purse for traffic jams." And went on: "If I could be granted one
wish, it would be to figure out one of the big problems of the '90s
for two-career families—time. No one has the time anymore for
extended conversations. My husband (Mike Nichols) and I get in
the car just to be able to finish sentences. I'd also wish for the
return of spontaneity. I dream of being able to call someone and
say, 'Hey, it's one o'clock on a Friday afternoon. Let's go to the
movies, have a margarita, and talk about life.'" Sounds good to me.

So many people have to deal with spending hours per day sitting in traffic. If you ever write out a timed activities chart for your
day, you'd be surprised at how long just the mundane things take.
Project that timetable out to a year—or ten years—and you'll
really be shocked. A daily shower could mean a quarter of one of
your waking hours gone. Add ten minutes or so to blow-dry your
hair. Watching television—it's the number one time-burner in
America, with video and computer games coming in a close second. Another way for 99 Lives people to save time would be to
call your doctor/hair stylist/mechanic/*fill in blank* to make sure
your appointment is still on schedule. You can literally save one or
two hours of waiting time if any one of those is running late.

Do you know that it takes five minutes to fully, leisurely
smoke a cigarette—with or without making O-rings. That means
pack-a-day smokers are putting around one and a half hours into
dragging on their cigs. Impatient smokers who get a quick fix,
then snuff out those cigarettes after a few puffs, will be able feel
less guilty about the waste. Phillip Morris has been looking at an
idea for a shorter cigarette (Marlboro Express) for time-pressed
smokers. Cravers, relax. The basic idea is to deliver the same
amount of nicotine and tar in a foreshortened cigarette. For the
smoking-age-MTV-audience, the tobacco company could name
this tough little one "Butthead."

In a way, technology isn't always an advance. Often we rush to
embrace without considering all the consequences. In fact, certain
"advances" seem to recomplicate certain tasks. Take voice mail systems. It's true that we can call in from anywhere 24 hours a day,
and pick up dozens of long and private messages. Or, broadcast a
message to 30 people. But it's one more responsibility added to
our overburdened shoulders. Remember when you strolled into

your office and were handed a packet of little white message blanks that told you who and when to call someone back? You could look at them at your leisure or shuffle through them, prioritizing the messages as you cradled the phone on your shoulder. So is voice mail any better than a receptionist? Or a receptionist combined with an answering machine?

What about other machines? Where we once used to wait in a bank line for a teller, now we wait in a bank line for an ATM. Is air travel any less pressured now that we have pre-issued boarding passes? Are first-run movie lines any faster now that we can call 777-FILM for showtimes and even tickets? Or use the even more tech-y MovieLink for your PC or TV screen, whereby you can watch the movie preview before ordering tickets? Or are the A&P supermarket lines any shorter now that there are scanners at every checkout? No, no, no. There have been various attempts to make time seem to move faster; in *The Popcorn Report*, we mentioned the experimental Checkout Channel. Ted Turner's idea of putting TV monitors near supermarket cash registers to entertain the customers stuck on slow lines was short-lived. Seems that people felt bombarded by the television barrage. Maybe it's too tempting to scrutinize the other people in line and see what they're buying. Or maybe to sneak a peek at the headlines on the tabloids, "300-lb. Monkey Weds."

One ray of hope: In Holland, the over-600-store Albert Heijn supermarket chain is giving out small scanners to each shopper at the entrance to one of its stores. Then, as each item is selected, it can be scanned and totaled, so customers can swiftly pay up at checkout. And if you couple this technology with a debit or the computer-chipped smart card that could be inserted at the end of shopping, what an improvement this could be. (AT&T's Smart Card is already being used on Delta Air Lines shuttle flights to reserve/buy a ticket, get a receipt, receive a boarding pass.)

Some of the technology that accompanies 99 Lives can be looked at as a Click into time control. Multi-tasking products excel. Sanyo has introduced a sport cassette player that comes with a built-in pedometer and calorie counter, so you can listen to Salt-N-Pepa as you watch the meter showing how you burn up the track and burn up the fat. Not to be beaten, Sony's new Walkman can come with a stopwatch and a timer, and some even have mini-telescopes. Microsoft has a deal in the works with Timex to develop a wrist computer, so that you'll always be ready to be a TechnoPreneur. Timex's Data-Link watch gives you the option of transferring your datebook from your PC into your watch, without any cables ($100). Another innovation on your arm, Casio's Wrist Remote not only tells you that it's time to watch your favorite TV show, but also lets you control your television set and VCR from something that can't slip behind your couch cushions.

And move over, Dick Tracy, the phone watch is just about here. With the newly developed Telewatch, you can ring your home number, buzz another intercom, and tick off the minutes with its standard wristwatch, but this promising unit can only make calls within 300 feet of the base station. Seiko has another version: a worldwide paging wristwatch that displays text messages. You'll be able to glance down and see stock quotes, sports scores, winning bids, and "Call Home."

High tech is macho tech. How many meetings have you been in when someone's beeper goes off and everyone automatically reaches for his/her belt? Some are even wearing two or three beepers at once. You can be tethered to your job, your spouse, and your mom, wherever you may roam. Or as the rock song repeats, "You can run, but you can't hide." *The New York Times* calls this connection obsession "Beeper Bondage." According to the Personal Communications Industry Assn., 11,000 pocket pagers are activated each day, so that by 1997, there will be an excess of 33 million pagers beeping or vibrating on the belt.

But these gadgets have become part of our daily living—helping us connect in all sorts of ordinary and even some bizarre ways. Once, radio talk show host Howard Stern was on the air when a man from the Bronx called in on his cellular phone to inform everyone that he was teetering on a span of the George Washington Bridge while contemplating a fatal jump. That portable phone turned into a busy instrument. Stern and a few of the radio listeners had words of encouragement to help him relax and not do anything rash. Some of the responding police officers got on the line to say a few words to the audience. Several passing drivers stopped to offer their assistance and to chat with Stern. Carrying a cellular phone to participate in a "group-therapy-session" suicide is taking 99 Lives to the max.

It's true, too, that when you get hooked up to a fax machine, you get hooked on faxing. It's faster to scribble a note than get involved in a phone call. It's clearer to mark an "X" on a map of your town than to give someone lengthy directions to your house. It's more accurate to order several catalog items by fax than to repeat everything to an 800 operator. It's more fun to fax a roughly drawn heart and a flower than to say something mushy. And it's a lot quicker and cheaper internationally to fax a letter than to mail (Lys faxes everything from birthday cards to condolence letters to hand-sketched village maps and her signature bear drawings).

Yet as popular as fax machines are, it's surprising how few service individuals use them. Wouldn't a plumber Click over his or her competition with a home fax? It would be a "leg up" for many reasons. Since you can never reach your plumber by phone, nor can you ever easily explain exactly where the leaky pipe is, it would be less stressful to fax about your problem. Helpful for the plumber, too, who could set off with written instructions and the right tools. A dandy shop-by-fax idea comes from a beauty counter at Barney's in New York. The concept is called Clinique to Go, and its appeal is based on speed. You merely fax in an order, and a messenger will be sent out to deliver your beauty supplies the very same day.

Big-business-wise, a recent Gallup Poll has found that sending faxes accounts for an astounding 36% of the telephone bills of the Fortune 500 companies. Will this fall off when belt-tightening execs realize that a one-page e-mail message costs less than a fax, less than a postage stamp? Meanwhile the Electronic Messaging Assn. estimates that the number of e-mail senders will leap by 50% this year to a very well-connected 60 million participants. Another alphabet-designated invention comes from Bell Atlantic, called T-Mail. This 99 Lives product lets you send one message—by phone—to many people at once. When the personal or business recipients pick up their phone receivers, they'll hear a stutter-dial tone that tells them there's a message being stored for them in Bell's network. The sender can also easily check on who has collected the message and who has not.

More and more clever ways to Click into home computers are being devised every day. The figures support this business/home link. About 38% of U.S. households now have a PC, and the numbers are multiplying faster than bunnies. America Online and Shoppers Express have joined forces to provide interactive home grocery and pharmacy delivery services. Banking and bill paying by home computers are getting commonplace. Tele-medicine is teetering on the edge of a virtual explosion—with networks (there's no such thing as small-town medicine anymore) linking doctors, patients, nursing homes, even prisons. Hollywood is getting instant feedback on movies via Prodigy. Artists are painting on computer, dancers and choreographers are working out their movements, musicians are composing online. And now Echo online is soothing psyches and creating positive, although passive, interactions by offering group therapy with a board-certified social worker shrink, for about $100 a month. These real-life dramas could feed into America Online's cybersoap, "Parallel Lives."

As millions of us embrace these outward manifestations of 99 Lives, there's a distinct undercurrent of Trend backlash. For many, this backlash means taking a breather from the assault of information that bombards us daily. Don't you ever get plain annoyed (or feel like screaming) at the endless intrusions of Call Waiting or car phones or Fed Ex delivery people knocking at your door—at the right place at the wrong time. The arrival of still another magazine, newsletter, or catalog can make us want to light an information bonfire. The communications avalanche is getting to us all.

We feel a craving for downtime, private time—unbuzzed, unbothered, unbewildered time. But finding peace of mind isn't easy when you can be reached 24 hours, day and night, night and day. In my little 750-square-foot rose-covered cottage in the country, I was assigned the old phone number of Sears as my second line. It rang all the time, asking me questions about store hours or particulars about stoves, refrigerators, vacuums, and lawn mowers (this was a good lesson for me on how much people want to know). These inquiries, coupled with about nine telemarketing calls per day (am I on *every* list?), can turn a relaxing weekend into a nightmare. One interruption gimmick to end these phone calls quickly is a Call Waiting imitator, Gotta Go. This gadget emits a tone exactly like a phone company one, only it's under your control.

The bigger question for today is: Why do we feel compelled to answer every call? In those delectable '30s black-and-white movies, you always heard Cary Grant murmur charmingly, "Let it ring, will you?" when he was too busy being a flirt to be bothered with a phone. Except for a handful of people—doctors, emergency gas crews, stockbrokers, and pregnant women—most calls are miss-able. Or call later–able.

The next "must-have" appliance for your home, your car, and your 99 Lives will probably be a noise neutralizer. Imagine being able to blot out the ear-splitting din of leaf blowers, twig shredders, power mowers, chain saws, hedge trimmers, electric generators, low-flying jets, cement trucks, car alarms, vacuum cleaners, washing machines, clothes dryers, etc. The microchip technology exists that can compute the pattern of the offending sound waves, then duplicate the direct opposite pattern, which cancels out from 50% to 95% of the irritating noise. The principle of yin and yang miraculously reduces loud sounds to a quiet hum. The airline JAL passes out noise-canceling headphones on some flights to enhance the movie experience. Small companies in Stamford, Connecticut, and Phoenix, Arizona, are working on developing lightweight headsets for consumers. The best part about "active noise reduction" is that, unlike stuffing your ears with cotton or plugs, it allows you still to hear conversation, music, or a ringing telephone and just blank out the nerve-jangling blasts of modern living.

You can also figure that there's a 99 Lives backlash when the classifieds have "sell" ads placed by people finally weaning themselves from their television sets. Or putting time constrictions on viewing hours. It's a badge of courage to be able to say, "I don't have a television in my bedroom" or "in my weekend house" or "where I go on vacations." "Television used to be relaxing," said one acquaintance. "Now it requires a response." He went on to complain about "blowing $1.50 a night on calling Yes or No answers into 'Hard Copy.'" More tension. Who would have ever predicted that multiple millions of listeners would care enough to pay to cast a vote about Miss America's swimsuit contest?

There's a backlash in our midst when friends who've always prided themselves on being well-informed now shrug and say, "I can't read [see, hear, view] everything." The overriding feeling is, "Enough already. Turn off the assault." Staying informed takes too much energy.

If we are going to keep our sanity, the key challenges in the next years will be how to manage information and how to manage communications tools. We're already seeing consultant companies with names like Internet Navigators and Network Buddies that are starting to Click into helping steer us along the information superhighway. The best of the new Line Consultants will not only help you make connections, but will also give guidelines to help you switch off and go back to normal "offline" life. We're calling that necessary new assistance DeTeching, turning off your machines. During a recent AT&T assignment, one of our Talent-Bankers said, "Just teach me to take a detour off that super-road."

By the way, even in the vastness of computerland, not everyone is happy with the umbrella superhighway term. Even Microsoft's Bill Gates reputedly doesn't think that "highway" is an accurate description, because it implies that everyone is rushing in the same direction. Instead of a straight-line highway image, why not think of the network as being made up of more complex diagrams and directional veers: multi-cursal mazes, connect-the-dots, cross-currents, winding pathways, concentric circles, and pentagrams. In a way, the highway of the future promises to alter our society more radically than what happened when the automobile replaced the horse. The Info-bahn will profoundly change so many of our familiar institutions: the library, the bank, the movie theater, the shopping center, and the office.

Some people are TechnoObsessed. Our previous book editor, the very smart Harriet Rubin, stayed up half the night connecting on The WELL. It's not unusual to run up thousands of dollars in monthly online calls. There are some college kids who don't want to shut off their computers and leave their campuses at Spring Break (ugh, the boring old sun and sandy beaches of Ft. Lauderdale) because they're "mudding," or exploring Multi-Dimension Realities (MUDs). The day is around the corner when there'll be a recovery program to wean people offline. "Hi, I'm Bob. I'm a computer-holic."

Where we live on Long Island, there's a club for cranky old - fashioned people who solemnly pledge to hang up on voice mail, avoid faxes, and never utter the dreaded word "interface." They believe that if any computer should catch a virus, no one should seek a cure. This group of curmudgeons calls itself the Lead Pencil Club (a self-described "pothole on the information superhighway"). One of its leaders fired off an editorial to the local paper complaining that American culture had gone

"Gizmo Gaga." The writer, Bill Henderson, overwhelmingly favors "the lead pencil—simple, erasable, light, portable, and responding immediately to the greatest computer of all, the mind." He fears that unless something is done, we'll all be facing a cold and lonely future. "We won't write letters to friends because we won't have any friends—just electronic images approximating faces on screens. 'Handshake' and 'hug' will become anachronisms."

In the same spirit, some individual companies are trying to help their world slow down. From planning employee meditation breaks to *t'ai chi* exercise groups to merely doodling. A California company encourages everyone on staff to take a deep breath when a phone rings and to answer it casually on the third ring instead of compulsively on the first. We've heard of another laid-back place that has instituted a companywide Quiet Time. Every workday, between the hours of 10 and 11 A.M., all phones are turned off and messages routed to voice mail. The fax and copy machines are unplugged. Quiet Time has become the most productive time of the day. There's even an anti-tech resort in Hawaii where you can rest through your vacation without being called, faxed, or newspapered. It's possible to Click into a Big Idea because your thoughts aren't jangled by the constant noise of communications machines.

The next big Click lesson to mull over might be: It's not how long you work but how well you work. For living proof that a slower pace and higher concentration can be more valuable to Clicking than frantic longer hours, take note of one of America's movers and shakers in the business world. Powerful billionaire John Malone, who became President and CEO of Telecommunications Inc. at the tender age of 32, garnered vast control and wealth on his own terms. He works only five hours a day and goes home to eat lunch with his wife. Professionally nicknamed the ruthless "Darth Vader" of communications, he has miraculously managed to keep his private world private.

The quest for a respite from 99 Lives reminds us of being back in kindergarten when the teacher tells the class to put their heads on their desks and rest after cookies and milk. Or a Grownup Recess. It's also similar to the search for the dreamy solitude that Thoreau found on Walden Pond: "A cabin on a pond a mile away from your nearest neighbor." One way to find a moment of peace is to do something totally different from your routine. To jolt you off your treadmill. For instance, Peter Roaman, a New York textile executive, recharges by playing the bass fiddle in a small band called the Cool Jerks, whose motto is "Legends in Our Spare Time."

Even though it's possible for many of us to drop out momentarily, unplug, or set our own limits, others have harder 99 Lives. Filling the fractured hours isn't all fun and games. Today over 7 million Americans are holding down two jobs to make ends meet. Most of those multiple-job holders are married, and for the first time, there are statistically as many women as men in this category.

99 Lives is also about multiple roles. As living past the age of 100 becomes more commonplace, odds increase that you'll be forced into being your parents' (or even your grandparents') caretaker. When you really think about it, our concept of "family" today is really only half a century old. It wasn't until after World War II when housing became affordable (Levittown was a major model for the spread of suburbia) and jobs became mobile that families became so spread apart. Maybe we're experiencing the return of multigenerational living—a more natural state for socially interactive human beings. We're also seeing more "boomerang" kids, grown children who've packed up and moved out when accepted at a distant college or have even gotten married, only to swing around and move right back into their old rooms. Many cartoons and sitcoms mention this national phenomenon, trying to find the humor in the never-quite-empty nest.

Rebellion against all our 99 Lives often leads to imperfectionism. The white-glove type of housekeeper who suddenly rebels and overlooks that dustball in the corner. The workaholic who starts playing hooky. The control freak who learns to delegate. What's the future in store for 99 Lives? Finding ways to impose a speed limit on one's life. Or, if not, understanding the boundaries.

In a brainstorming session, we tried to find ideas for cutting out some of the frustration points and making things generally nicer. A few results:

- To save us time, why can't more stores pick up and deliver with ease?

- Why don't dentists/doctors/vets start office hours at 6 A.M. on some days? End at 10 P.M. on some nights? Why can't there be all-night nonemergency medical help (get a flu shot at 2 A.M.)? Or 24-hour department stores, florist shops, garden centers? Why don't medium-priced hair salons start cutting and perming at 6:30 A.M.—the higher-priced ones do this for special customers?

- To abolish waiting in lines, how about honesty-is-the-best-policy stores where you have pre-established credit, take things on approval, and pay for them later?

- To avoid being kept waiting at a restaurant for an NPP (Non-Punctual Person), we'd develop a vibrating beeper system to nudge the slowpoke along (nothing as serious as a cattle prod!). Or an arm-tickler device. Or create a portable message center to soothe the person who's stuck waiting.

- Along the same lines, another question: how to make restaurants more user-friendly? Have a buzzer to summon the waiter, or to tell him or her not to disturb you. Start a system of pre-ordering, pre-paying. Computerized seating that will show you, upon request, the floor plan of the restaurant and an up-to-the-minute indication of which tables are available (no more maitre d' abuse). A car service to take you there and bring you home, extra helpful if you've had a glass or two of wine.

- Another time-saving wish for someone to invent: a closet that constantly fresh-air cleans the clothes inside.

- On the same subject of clothes, a big-city business hotel could really Click with travelers if it provided an emergency borrowing center for missing/ripped/soiled apparel.

- We've already found the perfect solution for easy-packing for the day or evening while traveling (or staying at home). Our favorite designer, Issey Miyake (and the namesake of my dog, Sissey Miyake), makes intensely pleated silky (actually 100% polyester) clothes that weigh only a few ounces, take one minute to put on and one minute to step out of. Not only that, most of his designs can be hand-washed and rolled up into a tight ball to dry into chic permanent crinkles. As we like to quip, "They're great for traveling—they don't wrinkle."

- We'd also like a device that records all our phone calls

automatically and stores them in an easily accessed archive. Would be useful in disputes, to remember detailed instructions or directions, or to re-listen to a chummy chat with someone no longer around.

- It would be wonderful to Click into slowing down with a meditation phone service. Maybe called MantraPhone or TeleTrance. Also, for those of us who are insecure, what about being able to connect with a positive-affirmation phone number: Dial-a-Compliment. Whenever you feel insecure and need a little reassurance, you'd call up to hear simple praises, such as "That was a brilliant idea you just had. You're a genius." Click.

The TimeLine as we head toward the year 2000 is accelerating. And spinning slightly out of control. Anything that anyone can do to simplify our lives, to help us maintain a steady course, to lessen the stress, will be a success.

Our goal for 99 Lives? To cut the craziness in half and get back down to 49½ kinder, gentler, happier Lives. But realistically, we're saying that anyone who can make it possible to keep up with our impossible 99 Lives world will Click—Big Time.

CLICKING THROUGH CASHING OUT

All I wanna do is have some fun,
I've got a feeling I'm not the only one.
—SHERYL CROW, #1 SONG, 1994

The essence of the American dream of today: no boss, no red tape, no climbing or clawing your way to the top. Working the hours you want, working with the clients you choose. Nirvana, no. It's Cashing Out, the low-keyed Trend that recognizes that quality of life is more important than the title on the door. That you'll be happier in the long run if you like what you're doing—rather than do what you're doing just for the paycheck. Or because you've been educated to do it. And why not relook at what you're doing with the bulk of your day? With merging and purging, downsizing, and our favorite euphemism of all, rightsizing, many of the best and the brightest in big business are—or should be—leaving to do their own thing.

It doesn't matter whether you've handed in your resignation or were forced to leave, as long as you come up smiling. Cashing Out is not about Dropping Out or Copping Out. We've even thought of changing the name of this Trend to Opting Out. Out of boring jobs, out of bad neighborhoods, out of a deplorable school system, and, most of all, out of a corporate mindset that doesn't appreciate mavericks, that doesn't applaud loyalty, and that has no demonstrable will to help us to survive.

In the '80s, when we first coined the term "Cashing Out" at BrainReserve, it centered on, as we said in *The Popcorn Report,* "some fast-track, hard-driver—maybe a Wall Streeter or a corporate executive—who suddenly (it seems) leaves his briefcase in the Out-box and resurfaces, making goat cheese in Vermont. Or running a small New Hampshire newspaper. Or a dude ranch in Montana. Or an environmental action group ten blocks from his old office. Or a classical guitar lover's newsletter ten steps from his bed."

Today, Cashing Out certainly embodies this same idea, but the Trend has evolved to an even greater level. For many reasons. First off, we have even less trust in the corporate life. And less drive to wear the old gray flannel suit. Other successful entrepreneurs have made great role models. We're less scared to take a chance. Also, advances in technology have made it easier to create a home office, put together a professional-looking newsletter on a laptop, contact people by broadcasting a fax.

If you've done your homework, selected a dream so strong that the thought of not doing it makes you really unhappy—then you're ready to go. One Casher Outer, Steve Bromberg, said he figured out it was time to work at home when the *New York Post* had its third or fourth management shift. Steve felt he'd do better helping his wife, Linda Kallman, grow her public relations practice and would rather be editing her corporate newsletters than the *Post*'s sports news. Besides, Steve figured, in the event it didn't work out, he would have had a year spending more time with their kids (a benefit he never dreamed of having when he was younger). Timewise, he figured he could bounce back into the corporate world at his same level, with fewer than two years given to the experiment.

In the book *Entrepreneurs Are Made, Not Born,* Lloyd Shefsky, the author, pointed out that in the typical entrepreneur mindset, risk is conceived of differently. The worst case means going back to the corporate world, while the best case means living the part of your life designated as "work" being happy and content off on your own. Shefsky mentions one study that shows that even though entrepreneurs may work long hours and get very little sleep, when asked, the self-starters say they get a fuller night's sleep than when they worked for others. Talk about fulfilling your dreams.

All over the world, the corporate system is caving in and smaller businesses are taking over as the chosen place of employment. *Inc.* magazine reports the five-year growth rate of the top one hundred small businesses "approaches the incomprehensible." The most shocking change is coming about in Japan, where previously, the culture dictated one job for life. In a recent research study, more than 50% of Japanese workers in traditional salaried jobs said they would consider walking out the door to either switch laterally or start up their own businesses, if possible.

In *PowerShift*, Alvin Toffler tells us we're moving away "from an economy of monoliths . . . The small business entrepreneur is the new hero (and often heroine) of the economy." He sees an "economy built of boutiques, rather than behemoths (though some of the boutiques remain in the belly of the behemoth)," referring to those small firms that stay in a "power-mosaic" arrangement with bigger ones. A good example would be all the small bioengineering labs that have been partially acquired by the large pharmaceutical companies. Likewise, the startup computer component firms aligned with Microsoft, Apple, IBM. Toffler goes on to talk about a new breed of people whom he calls "business commandos." These fast hitters know how to build businesses on their own terms and work by a whole new set of rules. If, as Toffler believes, "the power of the market is down-shifting into smaller businesses where opportunities seem much more unlimited," it means that it will become commonplace for every person to Cash Out at least once during the course of his/her business life.

We're seeing more and more evidence of those who Cash Out and follow their hearts (more about that in "Careers and Clicking"), such as Margery and Larry Nathanson, parents of Erica, an Assistant Project Director at BrainReserve, who made their exit from the advertising and design worlds to successfully pursue what had been their hobby. They opened Grass Roots Garden in SoHo, doing plantscaping for interiors and terraces. Also qualifying for this category would be Michael Jordan, the Bulls' basketball superstar who took time off from his team and megabucks contract to do what he loved, play pro baseball (even though not as well).

The Cashing Out bug bit Richard Dittmar while he was working at GTE as a computer technician. Since he spent his spare time bicycle racing as part of the U.S. Cycling Federation, he knew all about taking bikes apart quickly and efficiently. So, without leaving his job, Dittmar went to bike repair school, then started a service-oriented home business in Tampa, FL, called Bike Ambulance, where he picked up bicycles in need of repair and delivered them in his van. He cultivated new customers by placing fliers on every bike he laid his eyes on, especially targeting the bike racks at the nearby college campus. When the business looked promising, Dittmar quit his computer job to concentrate on his passion. Now he's not only doing fixing, but he's also selling bikes. His next enterprise: Using his fleet of mountain bikes, he's started working with the local Weight Watchers groups offering trail-riding as exercise; and advertising nationally and through surrounding hotels about his 3-day, long-distance "bike road trips." In an interview with the *Tampa Tribune*, Dittmar said, "It's everybody's dream to have their own business, especially something they love so much. I'm living that dream."

Doctors and lawyers, as well as corporate types, are ardent about Cashing Out. Dr. Hy Lerner gave up a career as an epidemiologist to open Baldwin Hill Bakery in Massachusetts. His medical-knowledge approach: to sell thick, chewy stone-ground whole-grain breads that are good for your health. We've also heard about an orthopedic surgeon from Florida who traded in his rubber operating gloves for boxing gloves. At one point, Dr. Harold Reitman's record of eight wins and two losses actually made him the International Boxing Council's twelfth-ranked heavyweight. Kerpow! A Click punch.

There's even a magazine based on the idea of reprioritizing your life, called *Simple Living*. Its Cashed Out editor, Janet Luhrs, has a law degree but chooses to spread the word about consuming less and enjoying life more. In fact, this lifestyle has a movement attached to it: Voluntary Simplicity.

Cashing Out businesses don't have to stay small. Take Geerlings & Wade, a personal wine service, founded by two former accountants in Boston. Huib Geerlings, a Dutchman working here, decided in 1987 that there must be more to life than calculating taxes for the IRS and getting through the crush of every April 15. So Huib merged his two loves, wines and computers, and with partner Phillip D. Wade created a wine-by-mail service. Today, their business, based in Canton, Massachusetts, has a twelve-state reach and revenues of $3.2 million, as reported by the *New York Times*. It's been favorably called the "L.L. Bean of Wine." Their specialty is simplifying the buying process for unsure wine buyers who don't know a shiraz cabernet from a Chianti. They send out a newsletter explaining a focused selection of good-value wines, highlighting their personal preferences. Customers can call 800-782-WINE to order, with free delivery, at about 30% below retail prices. (One picky complaint: when Lys inquired a few years ago about ordering, she was put on their mailing list as *Mr.* Marigold—not female-sensitive?). Yet these two partners seem to have Clicked into what today's new ventures strive to deliver— value, convenience, information, service that's a cut above, and high-quality products. After all, why Cash Out and just be the same-old, same-old?

The wine business seems to hold a particular attraction for Cashing Out. It provides a certain romance, a sense of travel and adventure, a conviviality and pleasure. The lure of wines certainly acted as a magnet for our friend Colleen May, who up until recently worked in the heart of Manhattan for Inflight Duty Free Shops, Inc., a large and successful worldwide organization that employs around 500 people. At a certain point, Colleen decided she wanted to do something more entrepreneurial, more hands-on, and left to be the majority owner of Intervine, Inc., a Napa, California, company that buys wine from around the world and sells it to airlines. A business that she knows well—and does well. And Intervine has a very manageable total of five employees.

Cashing Out to the Cocoon

People are coming home these days in droves—and staying home to start a successful business. Early retirees are not even considering looking for another job back behind the corporate desk. There's also the new wave we mentioned before, in which 20- and 30-year-olds, the kids of fairly well-to-do Boomers, have their minds set on starting out entrepreneurially. They're what we call "Earlypreneurials"—people between 25 and 35 who are confident about taking the risk of being self-employed. In many cases, this group is being led by young women whose moms had personal experience in hitting the glass ceiling and have warned their daughters of the futility of banging their heads against a corporate wall.

Look at a restaurant in Greenlawn, Long Island, with the unusual name of Me and Mom. It's owned by a mother/daughter team, both runaways from corporate America. There's also Best Friends Cocoa, started by two female friends in Massachusetts who took their favorite recipe for cocoa and managed to sell it to restaurants along the East Coast. Or Gooseberry Patch, a mailorder catalog of inexpensive country nostalgia items, which was developed by two friends. It reads like a chummy newsletter, offering cookie cutters and cinnamon-scented candles (the #1 bestselling home scent; gingerbread is #2), and now has $4 million in yearly sales and up to 75 employees for the holiday rush.

A propelling reason to work out of the home or in your own business is the lack of high-quality child care. And it's too expensive to hire a competent nanny. On average, 80% of a working mom's paycheck now goes to child care and the support of the kids. Increasingly as parents grow discouraged with public education, more mothers will be opting to stay home to teach their children, taking a hiatus from the workplace. While percentages are still small, it was reported in *Barron's* that "the two paycheck family is on the decline; the traditional one paycheck family is now the fastest growing household unit." In BrainReserve jargon, we refer to them as SITCOMS, Single Income, Two Children, Oppressive Mortgage.

Are we seeing a new badge of "having it all"? A new power symbol? The family who can afford to have Mom (or sometimes Dad) extend maternity leave into a few years' time. This Cashed Out Mom is definitely not a carbon copy of the earlier stay-at-home housewife. No, even the "house executive" of today stays close to her nest with '90s savvy: a computer, a fax, and a good job evaluation in her file. How we'll see this market evolving—what it can mean for a new surge of home-grown businesses and services—may be the central power of Cashing Out as the turn of the millennium goes into the 2000s.

Even when you examine the sheer numbers of Cashing Out Cocooners today, it's quite amazing. More than 15% of the U.S. workforce work for themselves. The vast majority are running single-person businesses out of their homes. Marilyn Ross of Communication Creativity Inc., who publishes books on small businesses, makes a distinction between those part-time $20,000-and-under-entrepreneurs, people in vocations like crafts and repairs, and those $60,000-and-up professionals, who are probably using technology to run their companies.

However, we think that the statistics for the nontech businesses may be low and inaccurate, due to the enormous amount of bartering that goes on. Part-time home business owners might be trading goods for services (or any combination) and actually be doing better than the numbers forecast. Who can keep track of an exchange such as "I'll prune your bushes into topiaries if you paint a mural in my kitchen." The give-and-take business of bartering is even getting organized. Networks of small companies, Barter Basics and Barter Advantage in Manhattan, publish newsletters and take a small cut. Isn't it a particularly Cashing Out phenomenon to seize an opportunity to make a small business out of helping out small businesses? Bartering can be seen as something other than a tax dodge—the exchange can be reported to the IRS as equivalent dollars and taken as a legitimate business expense.

At BrainReserve, we refer to the split in entrepreneurs by technological skill sets as the Tech-Knows and the Tech-Nots. Both groups are simultaneously driving the Cashing Out Trend to greater and greater popularity. The latter group, the Tech-Nots, feel they are offering what's lacking in the corporate world: hard-to-find service and personal attention—whether it be in home repair, beauty services, pet maintenance, etc. The Tech-Knows have set up businesses using the latest in technological support, whether it's installing cable TV or answering beeper calls on how to install Windows 95. A great many workers are in demand to supply the computer-based know-how that we don't know how to do for ourselves. Importantly, for the first time in history, there is now a new "universal" communication tool: the computer. A few of us may not yet, or may not ever, want to learn it, but to compensate for our lack of know-how, others have to be hired to make up for that deficit. BrainReserve foresees a window of time in which big earnings will be paid by the Tech-Nots to the Tech-Knows for their in-depth assistance in overcoming this technological gap. And it's well worth the effort, for on average, the self-employed person who uses a PC makes $70,000 versus $42,000 for nonusers. A program that can really help out the home business person is LegalPoint, which offers more than seventy-five basic business contracts and documents, from non-competes to partnership agreements to purchase orders. Handy.

Telecommuters have Cashed Into a global village where you commute to your job electronically—but not physically. And it's not just computer nerds, programmers, and data processors who are benefiting from telecommuting. We're seeing more and more lawyers, real estate brokers, stockbrokers, and such who are working out of their homes. It's estimated that almost one-third of the adult workforce is putting in some part of its working hours while at home, either full- or part-time.

The advancements in home office supplies have helped this move. Staples, the office superstore, is now a $2-billion business, and according to their buyers' profiles, 25% of their customers have a family member in a home business. Kwik-Kopy has more than 1,000 locations; Sir Speedy, almost as many. Then there's Kinko's and Copies Now, all convenient and competent. It's possible to sound as if you have an office setup with such techno-help as the digital answering system called Friday. It comes with eight mailboxes, transfers calls, gives out private messages to callers, beeps your pager. At under $350, it's a lot cheaper than hiring a receptionist. Even less expensive is Cobra, a cordless state-of-the-art system with four mailboxes. Catalogs, such as Reliable Home-Office, out of Ottawa, Illinois, can set you up in business in a flash, even if you're a hundred miles from nowhere.

A possible business to support these computer users at home would be a specialized insurance company. It could have a "Loaner Rider" to provide you with "loaners" by the day, if your computer, printer, phone, fax, or copier breaks down. Plus, you could be insured for any loss of documents in the event of a computer crash. And an expert could be phone-connected with you to help reconstruct your files. The company could even offer home/mobile or even virtual office insurance for your equipment and your documents when you're at home or traveling that would come out to be less expensive than most homeowners' home office or car insurance. Another benefit to the entrepreneur's insurance package could be something as wide-reaching as "other professional" liability—which can cover you if your lawyer, accountant, or financial consultant happens to make a mistake that you'll end up being responsible for.

The ClickPoint is that home-based business owners are a huge market of potential customers that represent $401 billion in yearly revenues. Companies from Avon to AT&T, Panasonic to Pizza Hut want to reach out to that growing pool of entrepreneurs and their disposable capital. At BrainReserve, we've been helping our Fortune 500 clients get a clearer picture of the entrepreneurs who will be making up the future consumer arena. Targeting the Small Office/Home Office (SOHO) types isn't quite as easy as targeting other distinct market segments. Some home workers are reluctant to alert the phone company about the nature of their business, in order to avoid the startup costs of higher deposits required and business-line charges. Apartment dwellers might not want landlords or co-op boards to know they are running home-based businesses. Same with house renters or owners, with strict landlords, neighbors, or zoning boards.

The Home Office Association of America (HOAA) was formed in 1994 in response to the needs of this massive workforce. For its $35 yearly dues (telephone: 800-809-4622), members can access numerous services, including group discounts on health insurance and package delivery. HOAA has a monthly newsletter, *Home Office Connections*, and a firm in Washington, D.C., that lobbies for home office tax deductions. Another way for an individual or a marketer to connect to semi-clandestine home businesses is by attending or sponsoring seminars with a particular field of interest. There's the old-fashioned direct route of networking through customers, associates, and friends, or even setting out a referral book for people to write down names of others to contact. Local bookstores, libraries, and the Chamber of Commerce may be rich sources of helpful information.

This SOHO marketplace is going to grow to be even bigger over the next ten years. It'll be what makes the Trend of Cashing Out similar to Cocooning. It's no surprise to us that *Fortune* reported in an article entitled "Kissing Off Corporate America" (February 1995) about how many business school grads, the very ones who went for an advanced degree to learn how to run corporate USA, are taking a different route now. *Fortune* said that "as recently as 1990, a quarter of Columbia University's new MBAs joined large manufacturers: last year only 13% did so." Stanford's grads were similarly disenchanted about going corporate. In '89, 70% went to work for big companies; five years later, the numbers dropped to 50%. Plus, many of the ones that have signed up have plans to "make big money for a few years and then find a small company to buy . . . "

Working for yourself has always had the additional benefit of letting you dress the way you like (except for client meetings). One recent change in corporate dress codes has come about almost totally from employee pressure. Most companies allow casual dressing on Fridays and more often during the summer months. Liz Claiborne even calls its casual shirt line Friday Wear. Now a total of 77% of American employees are estimated to be wearing more easygoing clothes for work. Contributing to this casualization is the replacement of so many face-to-face meetings with fax, modem, e-mail, and conference calls. The biggest shock came when IBM, paragon of dark suits, white shirts, subdued ties for men (and a similar conservative code for women), announced a relaxation of its dress uniform. Even Big Blue had succumbed to a barrage of internal surveys asking for permission to dress down. (Question is, what will local thrift shops do with all those white shirts?)

When one of our corporate clients first went casual, there was some confusion and a fair amount of misguided outfits. Finally, a senior person sent out a good-natured memo that said, "If you wear it to the beach or to change the oil in your car, don't wear it to work." That immediately eliminated any cabana shirts and shorts, for those who were in doubt. Our guess is, as Cashing Out sweeps across the country, the jacket may become identified with important events only, like meeting with the Big Boss, award events, formal signings, and weddings. The necktie is already getting obsolete, giving way to turtlenecks, banded collars, or open-collared shirts.

Comfort is the password. Or you can always go half dressed/half comfortable. When my sister, Mechele Flaum, as President of BrainReserve, went on a national nightly news show recently, talking about Cashing Out and other Trends, she was amused by the way the anchorwoman was dressed. Television viewers saw her only from the waist up, looking very buttoned up and professional in a silk blouse and blazer. But hidden below her desk, she was wearing a favorite pair of old faded jeans. The interviewer explained that since she was out of camera range, why shouldn't she be comfortable? That's her way of Cashing Out at the workplace.

Actually, blue jeans sales, which had been in a slump for a few years, went back up to over $400 million in 1993. And in a recent study for a men's fragrance, 82% of the men interviewed said they'd rather be wearing jeans than a suit. We have to remember that the most startling change in dress comes in the big-city corporate operations across the country. It's always been more relaxed in small and medium offices in the American Southwest; and in places like Dallas or Santa Fe or Vail, boots and Stetsons have long been considered a badge of success.

Cashing Out to the Country

Interestingly, to a vast majority Cashing Out is strongly connected to packing up lock, stock, and barrel and moving to the country. Away from the hot-asphalt streets and smog-filled cities and back toward all things green and natural. Being able to say "Good morning" to the butcher, the baker, the Fed Ex driver. In *Country Home* magazine, readers were asked to chose their ideal home: a Beverly Hills mansion, a four-bedroom Tudor in the suburbs, a sleek designer loft in Manhattan, or a country farmhouse on a few acres with a pond. More than 50% chose the farmhouse. So it was no surprise to read in *EDK Forecast* that in a recent study querying American women about where they would like to live, if money were no object, only a paltry 8% said they would be happy to be ensconced in a city setting. There's a definite Country Nostalgia. Perhaps this is part of the reason that both the book and the movie *The Bridges of Madison County*, the sentimental romance set in an Iowa farmhouse, struck such an incredible communal chord. It was pure Cashing Out fantasy.

We're following the country pipe dream with the cars we've been buying. What the four-wheel drives (Jeep Grand Cherokee, Explorer, Jimmy, Land Rover) were to the early '90s, the newer, pretend-I'm-a-country-roader wheels are pickup trucks. Preferably in red. Only they're not as bouncy and jouncy these days. GMC's Sierra announces its "refined road manners" with "vibration-eating" suspension "smothers road shock," yet its "commanding view of the road" makes Sierra decidedly "un-car-like."

However, nothing can out-"rugged" the Hummer for Cashing Out Souls. It's advertised as the "Most Serious 4x4 on Earth," and goes on with unadulterated Cash Out–speak: "In an environment where only the strong survive, some species refuse to be compromised by a world of glass and concrete. For them, freedom is the ultimate privilege. The highest premium. So, go ahead. Move. Run. Drive a Hummer. And find out what freedom feels like." The $70,000 vehicle, a civilian version of the Desert Storm hero, is made of aircraft aluminum, and can climb cliffs, creep up sand dunes, jump from boulder to boulder. Inside is a plaque with the only instructions, "Deflate tires when fording rivers." That's Tough with a capital "T." We have two in our neighborhood: a red convertible and a dark green tank, and if we predict this one correctly, plenty more will be on the way. You have to see one to believe it. It moves like a magnificent turtle—wide, low, flat, invincible.

Country is spreading into all areas of our lives. It's especially strong if you're not living on the farm and fall into the category of being one of those city pretenders. As mentioned in *New York* magazine, you can decorate your downtown dwellings with weathered barn siding, washed painted chests, old oaken buckets, hand-sewn quilts, and carved rooster statues. Put folk art on the walls. Probably the fastest growing movement in contemporary art is Outsider Art, done by people "outside" the so-called normal loop: indigents, handicapped, ex-cons, and other naïve, non-trained artists. A common thread seems to be little, if any, schooling. Some of the names are William Hawkins, Mamie Deschillie, Jimmy Sudduth, Mose Tolliver, and the Reverend Finster, who related, "The Lord spoke and said: 'Give up the repair of lawn mowers . . . give up the preaching of sermons; Paint my pictures' and that's what I done." (From the *Encyclopedia of 20th Century American Folk Art and Artists*, by Chuck and Jan Rosenak.)

To complete the outdoorsy feeling, you can cook your meals on a portable BBQ for your fireplace (it urges you to "Bring the Great Outdoors Indoors"), balcony, or stoop. Called Hearty Chef, it takes little space with its fold-up legs. Major appliance manufacturers, such as GE, are also offering commercial-type stoves with built-in grills, so that you can get those burned-in charcoal marks across your chicken cutlets, just as if you're at home on the range.

What about the fashion of dressing as if you've Cashed Out to the slow lane? The current rage for hip young urbanites: Carhartt worker's overalls, the ones with the loop on the side to hang a hammer on. Dress like a country carpenter even if you live in the heart of the city. With this very blue-collar look go hiking boots for crossing the wall-to-wall carpets or heavy work boots to go to the coffee shop. Reportedly the top look at the Las Vegas shoe show this year was desert sandals with wide straps and tread soles.

Country music, a sure sign of Cashing Out, is twanging more than ever. Just turn on your radio. There are more than 3,000 all-country stations today. And at least 2 or 3 on cable television where you can hear the harmonious, true-blue songs and hypnotically watch couples two-stepping around in circles. Deep in the heart of London, the staid Brits are getting away from their usual reserve and going line dancing. It's the fad to slip into 501s, tie on a bandanna, and prance around in high-heeled cowboy boots while doing the Tush-Tush, a shake-your-hips country strut—even though Piccadilly Square is a far, far distance from Nashville, as the white doves fly.

Job-wise, what could be more in keeping with the freedom not to work in a stuffy office—or more positively, to work in a bucolic setting—than all those who have Cashed Out to complete the "I wish"-ness of opening a country inn. What's different now is that it's not just middle managers but the really high-powered corporate types who are trying it. An article in the *New York Times* mentioned William Schreyer, former chairman of Merrill Lynch, who purchased an inn in State College, Pennsylvania, to add "a little extra spice to life," and Robert Minuchin, former Goldman Sachs partner, who owns the Mayflower Inn in Washington, Connecticut, with his entrepreneur wife. Actually, you can pick any inn and it's a good bet that the innkeepers are happily into their second career.

We read a true story in *New Age Journal* that exemplified the C-L-I-C-K. Doug Self told about using Shakti Gawain's book, *Creative Visualization*, to try to find a way to change his life (**Courage**). After doing the exercises, he became convinced that he and his ad-exec partner should go to Hawaii, look for land, and become flower farmers (**Letting Go**). Even though he thought it was "the wackiest thing I could have come up with," his visualization work gave him five specifics about the land: two acres, near the ocean, fertile soil, good growing climate, great neighborhood. They flew to Maui and knew after a day of looking that they'd found (Insight) their dreamland, overlooking Waipio Bay. But, alas, someone else had already sealed a deal on the land. On their last sad night there, not only did they find out the name of the owner: the author Shakti Gawain (small world, big coincidence), but that evening, the phone rang with the shocking news that the planned purchaser had just been killed.

Doug and Guy got the land they'd envisioned for their flower farm and settled in to till the soil (Commitment). It wasn't all a dream come true. When their short-term debt overwhelmed the bank's long-term trust in their business, the partners quickly turned a glassed-in meditation and yoga space into a bed-and-breakfast (Know-how). Doug explained that "by sharing the land, we were able to stay here—and this also allowed us to bring the special energy of the place to others." A Click.

Ranching is another daydream category. Kim and Sue Fowler closed their small construction firm in San Diego and opted for a life in Oregon, where they began Skyline Bison Ranch and raised herds of buffalo. Very low-maintenance animals, buffalo are becoming popular with the American consumer, because their meat is lower in fat. After the initial investments, it's even possible to turn a profit as a bison rancher. But the main reason to go into the herding business is far simpler: It's open skies, open minds.

But for a new profession that's closer to our hearts, you could always Cash Out and write a book. Or start a publishing house. Or a newsletter, such as *Plain*, a plain-talking monthly from a few Amish editors that is attracting new followers because of its Cashing Out philosophy about living simply and sensibly without modern interruptions. With all the computer programs geared to desktop publishing and a wee bit of imagination, it's easy to find some quiet spot and just begin to write. We've noticed that there's a trend toward entrepreneurial business books indulging in extra-long titles, such as *When Friday Isn't Payday: A Complete Guide to Starting, Running—and Surviving in—a Very Small Business* by Randy W. Kirk, as well as another mouthful, *The Ultimate No B.S., No Holds Barred, Kick Butt, Take No Prisoners, and Make Tons of Money Business Success Book* by Dan Kennedy. Or if you decide not to write anything yourself, but just publish others, the first thing you should think of is a clever name, such as Upstart Publishing of Dover, New Hampshire, or Ten Speed Press in Berkeley, California. We're sure you'll be inundated with plenty of manuscripts.

And in keeping with this return to the simple life, honest values, and trustworthiness is the experiment that Citibank has initiated for small businesses, its new "character loan" program. Loans of up to $50,000, the seed money needed for many a Cashing Out dream, are being granted on your branch manager's assessment of your character. Already $10 million has been lent to 460 "good character" companies, and so far only two of the loans, totaling $30,000, are in default.

One thing you can be sure of, masses of us are looking for a slice of life that's easier, happier, more straightforward, and full of personal satisfaction. Wheeler-dealer-ism is out. In the reality of Cashing Out, even though you may become more shackled with loans and work obligations than you were as a nine-to-fiver, the difference is that you're doing it for yourself. As John Donne quilled, lo, so many years ago, "Be thine own palace, or the world's thy jail."

The Click into Cashing Out just takes the courage of your convictions.

CLICKING THROUGH BEING ALIVE

Hope I die before I get old.
—PETE TOWNSHEND

There have been two revelations in my life:
The first was bebop, the second was homeopathy.
—DIZZY GILLESPIE

When we wrote *The Popcorn Report*, we'd been tracking the Staying Alive trend for more than eight years. This trend was about an aging population looking for longevity. It had to do with eating right, exercising correctly, even meditating to the right Om, just to hang on a few more years. The sands have shifted right under our feet from Staying Alive (we wanted to stretch the time before meeting with our maker) to Being Alive. Instead of mere longevity, we're interested in enhancing the current quality of our life. Adding to the present value of our lives . . . right now.

Where before we were saying, "I don't want to die. Keep me alive at all costs," we're now feeling "survival" isn't enough. The more important word is "quality." Quality of life. It sounds so rich, so balanced, so . . . healthy. If we can't feel like ourselves, it's time to check out. Maybe we're influenced by the very sensible country of the Netherlands, which has had the very sensible euthanasia law on the books for a few years now—and it works as a humanitarian exit visa.

(Astrologically interesting, it's been observed that a person is more likely to die during the week of his or her birthday than at any other time. Birthdays are key markers, arriving as symbolic deadlines, with one gender difference: Men are more likely to die right before the date and women right after.)

We think that much of this new focus on present quality of life is happening because we simply don't trust the future. The "iffiness" of the environment, the economy, the politics, the plagues, and pestilences have shaken our confidence that there may be no "there" or "then." No future ahead. No guarantees that we'll be toasting the millennium. Or as someone put it recently, "Life is too short to drink bad wine."

We're always trying to see the brighter side of things, singing "Don't Worry, Be Happy," or more recently, from *The Lion King*, "Hakuna Matata, It Means No Worries for the Rest of Your Days," but it's getting tougher to stay buoyant:

- When the incidence of skin cancer has doubled since 1970.
- When strains of bacteria that were conquered fifty years ago have mutated and developed resistance to our medicines.
- When you add new problems: Chronic Fatigue Syndrome, Lyme disease, Attention Deficit Disorder, and Carpal Tunnel Syndrome.
- When everyday stress is at an all-time high.

Being Alive isn't easy these days. Even when we think that we're making the most informed of healthy choices, we're not. We worry about what we're told. And we worry about what we're not told. We eat fruits and vegetables instead of sweets, only to discover years later that our oranges and bananas have been zapped with lethal pesticides. We move to the country for less stress and clean air, only to learn that a nearby landfill is leaking radiation. We thought that the word "plague" was something from the Middle Ages, only to find that our friends are being felled by a deadly infectious virus that is sweeping the globe.

Food Schizophrenia

It's no wonder that we're frightened and confused about everything. Even what we eat is filled with lies. Innocently, we grab a low-fat blueberry muffin every morning from the corner deli (thinking we're being good), only to find out months later that, according to lab tests, our big, healthy muffin contains 1,000 calories.

Soon after that comes an even worse betrayal: That medium-sized container of popcorn we gobble up even before the movie starts has more saturated fat than a cheeseburger *and* bacon n eggs. And remember what was once an old standby for brunch, Eggs Benedict? It's about as welcome on the menu now as a garlic braid at a banquet for vampires.

According to *The New York Times*, guessing how much fat is in a slice of our favorite junk food relates directly to how much fat is in our cells. When customers at various pizzerias were questioned: How many calories and how much fat are in that pizza slice, no one knew. Funny thing is that the answers were uncannily related to body weight. Fatter people thought a slice had 120 calories with 4–5 grams of fat while thinner people calculated 1,000 calories and 10 grams of fat. All were wrong. The analysis from NYC's Famous Original Ray's: One slice is 577 calories with 21 fat grams. That's a-lotta.

As we mentioned before in "Pleasure Revenge," we're both "health conscious" and "junk food loving" at the same time. Michelle Stacey, in her book, *Consumed: Why Americans Love, Hate and Fear Food* explains it this way: "Americans eat badly for a lot of reasons—indifference, belief in their own immortality, habit and upbringing, or simply a botched attempt to eat well. Add them all up and the result is a nation that sits down to doughnuts and Diet Coke." At the food stores in LAX, 2 million donuts and 1 million pizza slices were sold last year—compared to only 84,000 salads.

We'd like to add another reason/excuse for not-the-best eating habits—information confusion. For instance, 2% milk is labeled "low-fat," which is supposed to mean under 3 grams of fat in an 8 oz. serving. But did you know that 2% milk actually has 5 grams, compared to 8 grams for whole milk, 2 to 3 grams for 1% milk, and half a gram for skim milk? Pretty confusing.

Can we have it both ways? *The Wall Street Journal* reports that marketers of snacks and sweets are in the process of adding vitamins and minerals to their products. All in the quest of calling them more healthful. But will anyone be fooled by zinc-fortified or B12-injected Twinkies? Former football hero Franco Harris, for example, is leveraging his Super Bowl reputation in his position as president of Pittsburgh-based Super Bakery, Inc., selling "Super Donuts" to schools and nursing homes. The recipe still retains all the fat and sugar, but tosses in a blend of fourteen vitamins, minerals, and proteins. "We don't just sell a donut, we sell nutrition," Harris claims. Hmm.

On the other hand, a Gallup Poll has indicated that most of us have been restricting the intake of fat and cholesterol; that 67% of us report cutting back on food purchased, based on fat content alone; and that we're conscious of trans-fatty acids. As long as it *says* low-fat, we seem to be happy.

Look at the success of Nabisco's SnackWells. This group of reduced-fat cookies and crackers is even a bigger seller than the former gold standard, Oreos. In a zippy year and a half, they've had sales of $400 million. Number one cookie: the vanilla cream sandwich. Procter & Gamble's fat substitute, olestra, has been passed finally by the F.D.A. after a 20-year study—on the very last day of P&G's patent.

We're finding that a new, integrated vision of health will be emerging, embracing a concept of wellness. We'll be eating foods that will foster the total package of physical, emotional, spiritual, and mental health. Aren't we already drinking certain beverages with this in mind: coffee for energy, herbal tea to calm us down, isotonics (Gatorade, sports drinks) for stamina? Food could be used in the same way, fruit chips, rich in sun-vitamins, or ultra-thin waffles and pancakes with pure-fruit fillings for breakfasts on the go.

What else will be Clicking next? Will it be possible to achieve a combo of low-low? Low-fat and low-cal duos. (Now it's one or the other. If it's low-fat, check out the high-high calorie content or sodium ratio.) More likely, the next health breakthrough will be a shot that dissolves fat cells, like the one being tested in England on pigs (real oinks) and sheep. Or one that fools the chemical balance of the appetite.

What's New on the Horizon?

Here's a Click: Watch the liquor industry turn around and go right through the roof again if a patch were available that made you instantly sober—or kept you at a reasonably safe one- or two-drink high (a light buzz) all evening long—and completely eliminated the morning-after blues.

Door-to-door wellness calls may bring the more unusual, more natural healing techniques out of the spa/practitioners' offices and into the home. Already a Japanese company, Nikken, is creating a U.S. sales network for its Magnetic Field Therapy products. In a technique similar to acupuncture (only without needles), rubberized magnets are placed on your skin. By generating heat and energy, they promise to help in the healing of aches and pains. The same company also makes magnetized shoe inserts, mattress pads, and pillows, all de-stressers.

Magnetic field disks may well be the antidote to today's electronic overload. For future health Clicks, little magnetizers could be slipped into lots of things. Phones, headsets, massagers. Headbands to combat migraines. A bracelet for arthritis. An ankle bracelet for gout. Chairs and car seats for back pain. Set into your home's or office's doorjambs (any place you pass through at least once a day) for overall good health.

Add these to the growing list of things we can do to take care of ourselves. To take the control back from the medical profession, into our own competent hands. (As proof-positive of our self-diagnosing mania, the bulky *Physicians' Desk Reference*, the doctor's guidebook, reports increased sales to ordinary consumers.)

Tough Choices About Ourselves

What if we were all given a personal chart of our DNA to hang on the fridge door? The recent breaking of the very basic code is creating new insights and new nightmares. As the science of genetic testing progresses, beyond facing our own life/death decisions, we're faced with making choices for future progeny. What are the chances of beating the odds—of not having a faulty gene (or combination) that predisposes us to a catastrophic illness? Since more and more specific genes are being identified that relate to specific diseases, ethical questions that never existed before are being raised. We're looking through a high-powered microscope at molecular biology with all its possibilities and paradoxes.

Let's play a future game of Ethical Dilemma. Should infants be tested for a genetic predisposition to Alzheimer's, cancer, obesity, diabetes? If found, what should be done with this deadly information? How will insurance companies handle the newly found methods of predicting upcoming illnesses? Will genetic status be considered a preexisting condition? How should we deal with the embryonic field of behavioral genetics, with its search for alcoholism, depression, fits of rage, adultery, the gay gene?

Will there be more instances of Kevork-icidal (Kevorkian/ suicidal) conundrums? How would you decide, what would help you make the right choices? For instance, it is now known that 1% of a certain group of Jewish women have been dealt a gene that can result in either breast or ovarian cancer. Should those in the targeted group grit their teeth and undergo operations to remove the threatened organs? What about pretesting fetuses? Would you selectively abort if you knew your unborn carried the gene for some to-come disease? Or some socially unwanted behavior? Weigh these potential dilemmas:

- You're pregnant and a horrible disease is expected to show up in, say, your baby's fourth year. Four precious years, but too short for a full life. What do you do?
- What if you find out the disease is slated to show up by age 70? And degenerate into a terrifyingly painful ending? Then what?
- How would you handle it if there was only an 80% chance of the problem manifesting itself at all? 48%? 30%? 20%?

Welcome to the next century's sleepless nights.

With the concept of breakthroughs comes the good with the bad, the comfortable with the scary. For instance, needle injections may soon become obsolete. No more being lunged at with long, pointed hypodermics. We can expect the painless delivery of drugs via a gas-fueled "pen" that fires the right dosage into the skin at three times the speed of sound. We've heard about a vitamin B12 gel named ENER-B that cleverly goes into the bloodstream from a tiny dab in the nose. Why shouldn't other medications be administered this way?

Maybe we've seen too much of the hand scanner from the doctor's operating techniques from *Star Trek*, Captain's Log, Stardate 41209, but the same old X-ray machines of Earthdate, late 20th century, seem hopelessly slow and complicated. How long do we have to wait before laser light, sonic vibrations, or digital imaging will be able to detect microscopic tumors or weakened blood vessels?

Someday soon, operations will take place right in our own homes with Virtual Surgery. A Rent-a-Robotic arm will follow the real surgeon's instructions or arm movements via computer. In virtuality, the operating doctor will think he/she is working on real flesh-and-blood while the actual patient will feel as if a top surgeon is right in the room. A win-win.

EarthHealth: Low-Tech Healing.

We may not trust the test tube, but we still have some trust in nature. People in our country are finally beginning to do what cultures all over the world have done for eons: medicate themselves naturally. Remember, herbs are an important source of primary health care for 2.5 to 3 billion people in the developing world. It's interesting to note that aspirin, digitalis, and morphine were all folk remedies long before they were "discovered" by modern medicine.

Some 42% of British physicians have started to put their trust in and routinely make referrals to homeopathic physicians. One-third of family physicians in France prescribe homeopathic remedies, as do more than 20% of German physicians. Even here in the United States, Dr. Andrew Weil, botanist-turned-M.D., says, "For every single prescription that I write for pharmaceutical drugs, I probably give out 40 or 50 for herbal remedies." Sure enough, sales of homeopathic remedies increased 50% between 1989 and 1992. There's even an American Holistic Veterinary Medical Association, which is exploring the use of such alternative treatments as herbal therapy and homeopathy in treating cat and dog patients. We watched a local chiropractor give an arthritic, almost-paralyzed Dalmatian a massage and manipulation treatment—and Parsons got up on his feet and frisked away.

One of the first Clickers into homeopathy was Edward Bach, a physician who worked in Britain in the early 1900s. Sometimes he would walk through the countryside, work himself into emotional states, and then taste various plants and petals, noting their effect on his mood. He went a step further and packaged these natural remedies. And so was born Bach Flower Remedies, now marketed in the United States. The business has hit its stride now and has doubled every year for the past ten years.

In a triple whammy, Rainbow Light Nutritional Systems, partnered by Tom O'Leary and Linda Kahler, from beautiful downtown Santa Cruz, has managed to combine the good-health benefits of herb, vitamin, and food therapies. Their 3-Way Stress System offers not only the more usual B vitamins and minerals, but also herbs such as valerian and kava kava, for natural calming and therapeutic effects. Rainbow Light also has an Advanced Nutritional System, a daily supplement full of potent herbal extracts, that draws on the best of the world's vital traditions: Ayurvedic for balance and longevity (using gotu kola and gymnema sylvestre); Chinese for digestion and detoxifying (ginseng, sausserea, reishi), and European herbalism (ginkgo for mental vigor). Although these herbal helpers sound strange now, someday soon they might roll off your tongue the way aspirin and benzocaine do today.

As homeopathic medicines become more accepted by the common folk, we're bound to see these remedies dispensed through neighborhood vending machines—or delivered door-to-door. It'll be a good day when bee pollen and crushed violet petals are passed out instead of tranquilizers. How about prescribing nasturtiums to make one more loving (less expensive than a shrink)? Honeysuckle wards off feelings of homesickness. Elm is good for self-assurance. Maybe a mélange of wildflowers for mega-energy and crushed essence of crabapples for confidence. Not to worry: They are nontoxic and not habit-forming.

The basic types of herbal supplements, such as garlic and ginseng, have increased 46% in sales in the last year (now at $82 million). In fact, the potent powers of a head of garlic are being taken so seriously that New York Hospital has opened a Garlic Information Center with its own Garlic Hotline and Garlic Research Network (all this is good for Listerine sales). In the Glendale Galleria in Southern California, a huge mall near central Los Angeles, there's a single-focused garlic store that sells only-garlic and everything-garlic: oils, condiments (such as garlic salsa), cookbooks, wreaths, foods, roasters.

For those who want in-depth knowledge of herbal medicine, there's a CD-ROM program called the Herbalist, which provides more than you could ever imagine on the subject, from homeopathy's uses to classification of all medicinal plants. We hear that ever-changing Madonna is spending a good deal of time at her computer, monitoring and analyzing every aspect of her nutritional intake. Could she be getting her aerobicized body ready for a baby? A clone?

Speaking of herbs, the biggest tragedy in hacking down the rain forests, chopping everything in sight for land development and industrial pollution everywhere, is the destruction of trees and plants that may have been the natural source for potential cures. Yes, nature's drugstore really holds powerful potions. Look at:

- Rosy periwinkle: This is a Madagascan plant from which scientists have developed the most effective cure yet for Hodgkin's disease, upping the survival rate for kids with leukemia by 60%.
- Calophyllum lanigerum: A Malaysian tree was found to yield a chemical compound that seems to work against an AZT-resistant strain of the AIDS virus. However, when researchers returned to gather more samples, all the trees had already been razed by loggers.
- Aspidia: After watching chimpanzees chomp on it to relieve stomach problems, researchers discovered that aspidia not only killed nasty parasites, but also slowed the growth of cancerous tumors.

These plants could save our lives—if we don't kill them first. Only the tiniest percentage of the world's plants (some say as little as 1%) have been tested for their medical potential. In *Tales of a Shaman's Apprentice,* ethnobotanist Mark J. Plotkin, Ph.D. (a cousin?), tells hair-raising stories of searching for new medicines in the Amazon rain forest.

In the South Pacific, the locals have been imbibing the medicinal drink of the kava for hundreds of years. Now coming to health food stores here, this bitter-tasting liquid reportedly helps ease headache pain, relaxes muscles, and makes you feel kind of peaceful and floaty. A National Cancer Institute study indicates that ordinary green tea could possibly reduce the incidence of cancer of the esophagus. Pfizer, the pharmaceutical giant, and the New York Botanical Garden have undertaken a $25-million, three-year program to collect/study plants from all over the United States. They're looking under every rock and cranny for possible sources of new medicinal agents.

The magic mushroom, Kombucha, is a slimy white fungus that reportedly works wonders for every ailment, including indigestion, high blood pressure, acne, and prostate problems. Clairol can't be too happy about these mushrooms' ability to restore gray hair to its former color. The vim-and-vigor fungus has up to 3 million devotees already. We got our health mushroom from Alyce Khasday of Kombucha Magic Mushroom Farms (tel/fax: 212-249-4463). She and her partners started out growing the baby mushrooms in their apartments before moving to a six-story warehouse venture. They distribute "mother" Kombuchas that can reproduce themselves in ten days (used to make fermented tea), as well as their preparations, Kombucha Tonic and Pooch and Kitty Power Punch. Mushroom fever is hot and spreading like yeast on a warm day.

Healthful Helpful Smells

We're still at the infant stage of sensory understanding. We will see new findings and new awareness in the area of aromatherapy. The scent from a mixed bouquet of flowers may hasten learning skills, helping you solve problems faster. Aroma persuasion has been around for a while. An insider real estate trick is that the homey smell of baking bread in the oven will sell a house faster. Take a whiff, a sniff, of vanilla or jasmine. Both are stress-lessening fragrances. One New York hospital has actually been releasing a vanilla fragrance under a patient's nose to help relax the person before performing an MRI scan. Lavender oil, with its mild sedative powers, is being seriously tested as a drug replacement to treat insomnia in older people.

The wildest take on food scents comes from a mention in the *Times* magazine about a study done by Dr. Alan R. Hirsch, director of the Smell and Taste Treatment and Research Foundation in Chicago. He has found out that the powerful combination of pumpkin pie and lavender increases blood flow to the penis, causing erections. Other exciting flavors? Licorice and donut. The center's conclusion is that these experiments may help with impotence or in deprogramming sex offenders.

One day, Lys and I took her old Explorer (it was making a funny noise) to the Georgica Getty station in East Hampton. One mechanic there, Anthony Alfieri, while looking under the hood, pulled out the oil stick, put it to his nose, and inhaled. Never having seen any mechanic make this particular move, we asked him what he was doing. Essentially he was sniffing out the situation: He said if gas or antifreeze mixed with the oil, there'd be a strawberry smell and a good indication of a leak somewhere. Next, he tested the transmission fluid to see if it smelled burnt. There are some problems you can smell before you see. (That's why dogs and cats are always alerting their owners to fire.)

Probably the oldest technique around for rejuvenation through fragrance happens with the addition of one more ingredient: hot water. Soaking in an aromatic bath has been an age-old spa treatment as well as blissful home therapy. Every culture has some variation on the aquatic theme, communally or singly: Roman thermal baths, Turkish hammans, Finnish rock saunas, Japanese hot tubs, Mexican sulfur springs, Russian steam rooms, American Jacuzzi whirlpools.

Way-Out "Alternatives" Are Going Mainstream

We think the "traditional" world is ready to Click on to what we've known, or at least have suspected, for a time: that holistic medicine really works.

Insurance

Even Mutual of Omaha, the nation's largest provider of health insurance for individuals, announced it would reimburse patients participating in a preventive program that combines diet, medication, exercise, and support groups to reverse heart disease. It's only a matter of time before all alternative treatments—acupuncture, biofeedback, TM, hydro-relaxation, craniosacral therapy, reflexology, all chiropractic adjustments—will be reimbursable. And why shouldn't Oscillococcinum for the flu, Metagenics HP8 for sore throat, Boiron's Arnica Montana for trauma, and the whole spectrum of vitamins be covered?

At our local health food store, Second Nature, owned by Lisa and Cliff Blinderman, a steady seller is CoQ-10, which counters and controls the achy, debilitating effects of non-curable Lyme disease. Also, since it's thought that HIV-positive men who took a multivitamin were one-third less likely to develop full-blown AIDS, why wouldn't insurance companies be interested in them? Consumer spending on unconventional routes is estimated at over $14 billion a year, and yet 75% of those expenses are not reimbursable by our health plans.

Government

Is Congress getting more progressive? This arm of government recently passed a bill that allows general health claims for vitamins. When an industry reaches $4 billion, that indicates it's already home-approved, and now it's FDA-approved as well. Even the National Institutes of Health has an Office of Alternative Medicine, which has pumped millions into investigating nontraditional medical treatment options, ranging from massage to prayer intervention. The office points out that Americans spend $10.8 billion annually on alternative medicine, and it's their job to help us determine what works and what doesn't.

Stores

Of the fifty-three major drugstore chains, including Kmart, Payless, Walgreen's, and Thrifty, almost half now carry some homeopathic products. Five years ago? Only two or three sparsely stocked these products. Even your local supermarket is expanding its shelf space with plenty of good-for-you naturals. This futuristic concept of medicating yourself through what you eat is what we are calling Foodaceuticals.

It's not only the exotic plants from the far reaches of some remote edge of the world that can help you in Being Alive. Did you know that mangos may inhibit the spread of the herpes virus? A bunch of bananas may prevent ulcers. Onion juice may lessen the wheezing of asthma. Tofu could possibly work against the development of prostate cancer. And now that you do know, are you a believer? And if you're a believer, will you observe?

Have you noticed that most of these natural wellness providers come from Things to Eat That Are Not Meat? According to *Vegetarian Times*, 14 million Americans consider themselves vegetarians (or part-time vegetarians), double from ten years ago. Even more interesting is the number of young kids who've decided that they'd rather be eating lentils and rice than hot dogs and Steak-Ums. Linda McCartney, in her vegetarian cookbook *Home Cooking*, explained why she, Paul, and family stopped eating meat. She had figured out the amount of land (about 2.5 acres), or cleared rain forest, that it takes for cattle to graze on to produce 1,600 hamburgers (probably about one day's worth in one McDonald's). "This makes the true cost of a hamburger to be half a metric ton of rainforest . . ." Environmentally, medically, and morally expensive.

There's a new organization at work, the Vegetarian Education Network, trying to spread the word and pressure the educational system (esp. grammar schools) into offering vegetarian meals. In a Danish department store emporium, we saw shoppers grabbing up a product called Selleribof, celery burgers that are 34% celery with onions, rice, potatoes, bread crumbs, and spices (also, carrot burgers). TGI Friday's, the restaurant chain, sold 750,000 Garden Burgers in 1994. Even the big, beefy Hard Rock Cafe does a big business in them. Boca burgers, whose main ingredient is soy, were the winner of *The New York Times* Tofu Burger contest. In just four months, over 6,000 of these flavorful patties were served in the White House. Bambi and Cinderella have forsaken meat too. At both Disneyland and Disney World, the veg-and-grain-y Nature's Burgers, are selling around 7,500 per week.

Boosting Your Brain Power

A presidential proclamation declared that the 1990s is the Decade of the Brain. Evidence has finally made the connection that the brain should be treated like a muscle: The more you flex it, the bigger it grows. The brain's ability to change and adapt well into old age is encouraging to the Being Alive Trend. It shows that old dogs *can* learn new tricks.

Since centenarians (more than 50,000 now) are among the fastest growing segments of our population, it's worth a look at what's going on (see "Clicking Through Down-Aging" for more on this). It's definitely a survival of the fittest. If you get through your 80s without a life-threatening illness, it's been said that there's a good chance you'll make it to 100. But the point is to be not just alive and kicking, but alive and *thinking*. On a television segment, we saw a clip about a man named Sidney Amber who was born on Jan. 26, 1886, when Grover Cleveland was President. He had started a new job when he was 104, as a maitre d' at a San Francisco restaurant, where he was meeting and greeting customers on his feet for more than four hours at a stretch. If he asks people to guess his age today, they come up with, "75," "82," and not 110. His secret, besides stimulating work, is that he has ingested three tablespoons of Worcestershire sauce every night for the past 90 years. Thank you, Lea & Perrins.

For years now, doctors have been studying a group of retired Minnesota nuns, many of whom have the distinction of living well beyond the age of 100. The research shows that those nuns who have earned college degrees and who teach and actively use their minds live longer than those who do only manual work. The ones who continue brain-teasing with crossword puzzles, reading, or card playing have significantly lower rates of dementia and Alzheimer's.

There are other ways to stay alert. Chinese ginseng is said to boost the powers of concentration and memory. L-tyrosine converts into mental stimulants known as neurotransmitters, which means in layman's lingo, if you need to be sharp, say before a meeting or a test, you should gobble up a plateful of high-protein food: fish, skinless chicken, tofu. The gingko supposedly spurs short-term memory (very helpful if you're one of the millions who misplace keys, glasses, and, the most aggravating, the TV remote). Piracetam, a central nervous system stimulant, is reported to unclog the flow of data between the brain's hemispheres. Available in Europe now, it's one of those things that certain in-the-know travelers are smuggling back. Hydergine, an extract from the fungus that grows on rye, is believed to increase blood supply to the brain and is already being used here to treat memory problems in the elderly.

Some drugs can also cool you out. Inderal works on stage fright: It blocks the receptor site for adrenaline, on the assumption that being less anxious can make you more intelligent. Another, DMAE, supposedly works by raising the production of a chemical that delivers messages to the brain. Vasopressin, which now comes only by prescription, is secreted naturally by the pituitary gland. Advocates claim this drug can help your brain imprint new information.

Many centenarians grow into old age gracefully, attributing their longevity to maintaining a low level of brain stress. To reduce everyday tension, these simple stress-buster exercises are perfect for Being Alive. Hysterical! Grab two fingers of one hand with the other; hold a deep breath, and release fingers as you exhale. To calm yourself down even further, try breathing in ten or twelve times through your left nostril only. Or, even more pleasurable, just dig into a dinner of simple pasta, or a baked potato with red sauce. This combination will stimulate the brain into producing serotonin, a mood-relaxing chemical. Don't laugh. These easy remedies can help you cope and, hence, live longer.

Don't forget, too, that having a pet, a panting little beast to pet and take care of, can also add on years. Although the benefits of sending foster pets over to nursing homes has been well-documented, how often does that happen? No wonder there is such a hue and cry every time some urban landlord issues a no-pet apartment policy. It's medically negative. The breed of Lys's rare dog, Tulip, a pushed-in-nose English Toy Spaniel, which bonds to one person only, even breathes in tandem with her owner. In contrast, her other two dogs, the more independent Japanese Chin sisters named I-Say-So and I-Can-Do, snore, spit, and sneeze in their own separate rhythms.

Tulip.

There are so many unexplored ways of keeping the mind fit and at its peak. Better brainpower will definitely become the decade's next challenge, the next frontier.

HealthShrink: What's on Your Mind

Are we, as a society, so hopelessly depressed? Doesn't it seem as if there's more talk about raising our moods than about raising our children? Three new antidepressants are coming on the market this year alone. It costs less to have three solid months of drug therapy than one week of intensive analysis. With Herr Freud somewhat out of favor these days, deep/daily psychoanalysis is already an endangered species.

Today's latest technology is helping out shrink/patient communications in this quixotic world. Videophones are making it possible to have continual therapy, even if the patient can't physically get to the office chair or couch. What a boon to anyone who has a far-off commute, lives in a remote area, or is seriously ill or disabled. One question occurs to us: Are you more candid on camera?

And we can't skip over the unprecedented acceptance of Prozac. Almost 1 million new pill poppers per month. In five years, we've become, as the book says, a Prozac nation. Almost everybody we speak to is either "on it" or has a friend who is currently taking it. Some with real problems, real bouts of depression or flare-up rages that need smoothing out. We know someone whose level was upped to control her nail biting; another whose jealous and co-dependent husband became a sweet lamb; and another nutso dog who should be on it to control an obsessive fixation with shadows. But there are too many others, who are experiencing one of life's minor setbacks (say, the breakup of a stormy three-year relationship) and who should be allowed to feel the pain and work through their emotions. Not be numbed to life. It was said that the pithy writer Dorothy Parker had a cynical view of the world. And if she had been put on Prozac? No poetry.

Ancient Remedies Work Better

Chinese medicine differs from Western medicine because the Chinese pinpoint "health" rather than "disease" (ever since living in Shanghai, I've believed this approach). People there not only go to the doctor when sick, but they also keep going when they're well—to balance their bodies in harmony with nature. How fundamentally different is this from Western medicine, which focuses on finding a magic bullet to shoot the problem. Kill the disease— even if it kills the patient. Just think about chemotherapy. Chinese medicine says it is more important to support the body's natural-killer immune cells, and leave the body's vital growth mechanisms intact.

In many parts of Asia, the Chinese communities go to health restaurants where certain foods are consumed for wellness. *Wall Street Journal* reporter M. Brauchli described one such establishment in Hong Kong, the always-crowded Yat Chau Health Restaurant. There, "the restaurant's thoughtful host listens sympathetically and jots things down on an order pad. But unlike your conventional maitre d', Mr. Wong doesn't recommend dishes, he *prescribes* them. Have swollen glands? Try chicken and sea-horse stew. Feeling dizzy? Perhaps some fried rice with wolfberries." It's all quite exotic, and, one may say, repulsive to Western tastes. At Singapore's Imperial Herbal Restaurant, some of the well-prepared dishes are "stir-fried, wine-soaked scorpion, sans stinger, on prawn toast" (about $3.50 each); "stewed fruit-bat, at about $20"; and a "bitter-sweet wine of ginseng and deer penis." As the manager there, Doris Ho, explains, "An apple a day can keep the doctor away. So can a bunch of ants." We might not go quite as far as wolfing down a scorpion crunch, but watch out, Burger King—some of this might Click.

In still another example of an older, wiser Chinese medicine, acupuncture is in its infancy here. Yet when you meet people who have firsthand (first-needle?) experience with a good acupuncturist, you will hear rhapsodic stories of its miracle cures. Whether it concerns the vanishing-before-our-eyes of the redness, swelling, and sharp pain of a herpes virus or the freeing up of a spasmodic hand, this artful science has the ability to pinpoint (pun!) solutions that Western medicine can't touch. A poignant example occurred when Lys's mother, Virginia, suddenly found herself wincing in sheer agony (and she's not a wincer) whenever she walked or stood up. Her Florida physician diagnosed a problem with her year-old hip replacement and recommended a second operation with another long, bedridden recovery period and sessions of physical therapy. On our advice, she gingerly went *three times* to Long Island licensed acupuncturists Bobbie Aqua and Mikal Gohring, and came away symptom-free, operation-free.

Think of the time and money saved. And the quality of life added to Being Alive. Click.

This Oriental technique is now being tried out for the treatment of drug addiction, according to Dr. Michael Smith at Lincoln Hospital in the Bronx. Patients say they prefer acupuncture to going on methadone. A good-news side effect: It was found that acupuncture also made patients more cooperative and more inclined to continue drug counseling.

Another alternative science we'll be hearing more of is called Naturopathy. Naturopathic physicians are thought of as the "generalists" of alternative medicine. That's because they're quite eclectic, combining clinical nutrition, herbal medicine, homeopathy, behavior techniques, manipulation, and physiotherapy, as well as a combination of Oriental and Ayurvedic medicine. The point of this is to bolster the immune system with natural remedies, to make changes in diet and lifestyle—all to help the body heal itself. A far cry from quackery, naturopaths are intensely trained and actually receive about ten times more training in clinical nutrition than regular Western M.D.s.

We believe that a good Click would be the startup of Dr. Nature Clinics, an organized nationwide group of doctors who would create wellness through nutrition, stress reduction, energy balancing, and meditation—the smart new medicine of the late '90s.

SourceSmart

Under the category of NearFuture HealthWatch, we're going to be increasingly interested in identifying what particular cow our milk container comes from. There's an upcoming new field of passive vaccines. We are already producing hyper-immune milk, yogurt, and cheese from cows vaccinated against human diseases. The animals pass along the antibodies for human consumption— so it's like taking a passive vaccine.

We're seeing the start of the switch-the-benefit game. Besides storing antibodies, chickens/eggs are being used to pass along the benefits of the fatty acid Omega 3. Although Omega 3, which helps prevent heart disease, is found naturally in such oily fish as salmon and bluefish, Americans just don't eat enough of the oily fish to take advantage of it. A biologist from Omegatech came up with this solution: letting chickens feed on an algae-source of the nutrient so that when you dine on either chicken or eggs, you get a dose of heart strengthener. What do you think will be the next benefit transplant? Anti-cancer? Anti-aging?

There's already a residue of negativity coming from the overuse of antibiotics and other unknowns in cows and farm animals. To combat this, both Land O'Lakes and Marigold Foods (no relation), two major milk suppliers, are launching brands certified to be free of any genetically engineered hormones.

We at BrainReserve are calling this new behavior Source-Smart, which will inspire a new generation of consumer detectives who will demand full product disclosure as their given right. A galloping mistrust is making us anxious about what we're eating and where it's all coming from. In a recent brainstorming session, a new Click was discussed. Wouldn't it be comforting if you could own shares in a few farms in your area, so that you could actually check out the growing/living conditions of your family's meals: from vegetables to dairy to meat.

Another Click idea: what about a chain of SourceSmart restaurants that could serve all-organic, no pesticidal, low-fat meals created by the top chefs. Even though this may end up being expensive, it would be the eco-experience of your life. (This is probably as close to the Chinese experience of better-health dining as we reasonably can get in the near future.)

As the SourceSmart consumers are busy SmartDining, they might desire something safe but delicious to drink. Too many wines are saturated with sulfites and anti-fungal sprays from the grape-growing fields. There's a wine store in Amsterdam that is owned by two men trained in the science of wine toxicology. The store sells only pretested bottles, guaranteed pure. Why not bring the concept here?

A further Click idea: SourcesMart. A chain of supermarkets in which the origin and composition of *everything* is disclosed.

It's Not Only What You Take In, but How You Work Out

Exercise may not be the be-all and end-all of our lives, but it helps. Although researchers are squabbling about whether we need intense exercise 3–5 times a week, or whether light exercise every day is just as beneficial, we tend to agree with those who advocate more than the daily effort of dusting and vacuuming. So did Stanford University when it conducted a study that concludes that runners have lower death rates and fewer joint symptoms and take fewer medications than nonrunners.

There are about 12,000 health clubs in the United States with a total of 18.2 million members in 1993—up 10 percent from 1992. But we're doing different things while working up a sweat. The hottest?

- Spinning. The sleek stationary cycle, modeled after a real racing bike, has a Virtual Reality feature. At over $7,000 a bike, it's being purchased slowly, but unlike other exercycles, it's anything but boring. Spinners can choose road conditions, locale, and atmosphere. Ready for a hairpin turn on the Swiss Alps in a rainstorm?
- Gravity training. No music, no mirrors, no walls. Just unforgiving angles. Speed is not the point—it's technique, technique, technique.
- Obstacle courses. Crawl-through tunnels, monkey bars, ropes to climb, and other mixes of exercises. The exhilaration comes from the sheer exhaustion. The closest thing to an adult playground (Being Alive Trend-secting with Down-Aging).

New Age Fountain of Youth

Our waters, the elixir of life, are contaminated. That's fact. Still, the latest statistics from the EPA are shocking. During 1993–1994, some 53 million Americans drank substandard water, causing 400,000 known cases of illness and almost 1,000 deaths. How much those numbers will go up if the 1972 Clean Water Act is diluted (no pun), no one can even guess. Now, 1 in 5 of us drinks tap water that has poisonous lead, radiation, herbicides, or even feces in it. Recently, an entire residential area of East Hampton had its underground source of well water polluted by an undiscovered cocaine operation. It may take millions of dollars to clean up—not to mention the millions in property values lost.

Our fear of contamination makes it acceptable to pay $1.40 for a bottle of Evian. And makes us interested in every new pledge of purity—from Gap Water to Maxfield's of L.A. haute-couture clear liquid. (Next? Pepsi and Coke waters.)

Newest gush: spring water for Fido or Fluffy. After all, if we shouldn't be drinking tap water, why should our pets? When Gordon Matz, BrainReserve's computer mentor, moved into a new home, his chocolate Labrador puppy named Boulder became very ill. After scores of tests, nothing could be found as the cause of his vomiting and listlessness. But the simple act of putting the pooch on bottled Naya water stopped his symptoms. He became puppy-ish and playful again. Eventually, the culprit was found: harmful bacteria in the house's water system.

Florence Fabricant, a writer for *The New York Times*, reported that in a telephone survey of almost 2,000 pet owners, about 40% of them had serious concerns about putting out a bowl of tap water. To the rescue: the Original Pet Drink Company of Ft. Lauderdale, which makes liter bottles of beef-flavored Thirsty Dog and fish-tasting Thirsty Cat, slightly carbonated, enhanced with vitamins ($1.79 each). Yes, the FDA has approved it and, for those concerned, it's kosher.

We believe that all this interest in water is the late-'90s version of the Fountain of Youth. Living longer, healthier. Without fear of slugs and glugs and microscopic bad things floating in the very basis of our life chain. This suggests a new Click: water springing forth from the most indisputably pristine place on earth (if there is one left) and bottled under sanitized, regulated laboratory conditions—at even twice the price of Evian.

Disease: It's a Tough Way to Learn to Appreciate Each Well Day

Americans may be living longer than ever—life expectancy is 75.8 years right now—but AIDS is now the leading cause of deaths in America for those between the ages of 25 and 44. The disease has spawned its own subculture, with the traveling AIDS Quilt; New York's God's Love We Deliver and San Francisco's Continuum, serving hot meals to the homebound; AMFAR, researching the cure; Gay Men's Health Crisis, hot-lining and caring for children as part of its $30 million budget; and even a magazine named *POZ*.

Other "new" nefarious diseases are adding strange words to our vocabularies and a creepy feeling about casual contact. Biohazards. Level 4. The first new strain of measles in 1,000 years. Around here, folks are suddenly scared to sweep out their attics, cellars, garages, or toolsheds. There's a new death-dispenser, Hantavirus, making its sinister rounds; you can get it from inhaling the dried droppings/urine/saliva of white-footed mice. It felled two strapping young men from high fevers in two short days. Still another new danger, a malaria-like, microscopic parasite called babesia, contracted from the same little deer tick that causes Lyme disease, has claimed seven lives in New York. Will we have to garden, stroll on the beach, and walk in the fresh air encased in protective space suits?

Uneasily, we're building up to a phobic interest in bugs and viruses, evidenced by *The Hot Zone*, by Richard Preston. Besides cautiously buying condoms for sex, hygienic paper for toilet seats, and a treated kitchen cutting board that nullifies salmonella, we can even protect ourselves when calling home with Steri-Phone Shield from Healthy Calls. After researchers isolated 1,800 counts of "bad" bacteria on a randomly selected pay phone in New York, this well-meaning shield was devised to snap onto any standard phone.

Just as we have reasoned that "the wilderness is safer than civilization" (*The Popcorn Report*), these days it seems that even the sickest of us is safer at home than in any hospital. As Ralph Nader wrote to George McGovern (August 22, 1994), "According to the Harvard researchers, more Americans are annually killed in hospitals by malpractice than the combined fatalities from motor vehicle crashes, arson and homicides and that toll does NOT include the human losses in the Medicaid mills, clinics and physicians offices."

We're feeling vulnerable—and we're not wrong. But we're also feeling hopeful—and we're not wrong.

At the bottom of all the mysteries, all the unknowns, is the knowledge that the whole trend of Being Alive is transforming by the day. There are so many places where you, your family, or your company can glean ideas from this wellness Trend. Everywhere you go, everything you see, can be wrapped around the world of holistic practices, scientific breakthroughs, unthought-of curative uses for herbs, minerals, scents, foods affecting the body and the mind. Whether it's a Big Idea of starting something important on your 92nd birthday or as small as stocking new healthy drinks on the "not-only-coffee" wagon at work, Being Alive is ripe for exploring, set for Clicking.

We believe that pathfinders in the new ways of Health and Nutrition will be a sure Click for the late '90s. Are you ready?

DOWN-AGING

CLICKING THROUGH DOWN-AGING

We don't stop having fun when we're old;
we're old when we stop having fun.
—SAYING

To me, old age is always fifteen years older than I am.
—BERNARD BARUCH

I f you want to understand the Down-Aging Trend in a flash, just hang out at any ice cream counter and watch people order. We saw a strange, old, disheveled man with a long gray beard transform into a 12-year-old boy when he ordered a mocha almond fudge cone, grinned sheepishly, and asked for it to be dipped in chocolate sprinkles. His eyes lit up. His jaw muscles relaxed. His worries fell away. Everyone becomes a kid again when ordering ice cream. Just say those two words, "chocolate sprinkles." It's impossible to mouth them like a cranky grown-up.

In a culture in which 60 feels like 45 and 50 feels like 35, the reality about how we live, love, work, and play at a certain age is amazingly different from what we imagined or expected. The childish taunt, "Act your age, not your shoe size," has no meaning anymore, because acting your shoe size can be more fun. And acting funny, foolish, giggly, and silly is a great release from the stress of serious adulthood. Think about the last time you really laughed. Not a snicker, not an amused sigh, but a deep belly-laugh kind of laugh. Like the way you guffawed through the movie *Home Alone*. Or the reason the simplistic charm of *Forrest Gump* appealed to so many as the Tom Hanks's character earnestly said, "Stupid is as stupid does."

Down-Aging is all about throwing out the rules and constraints that dictate how we should behave by certain points in our lives. At BrainReserve, we try hard to remember that "should" is one of those words we should try hard to forget. "Should" is about other people's expectations. "Should" is about being static, resisting change, Un-Clicking.

Today we have 80-year-old marathon runners. Seniors who are sexually active and proud, experimenting with tickler condoms and lubricating creams. There are daytime talk shows featuring 62-year-old women who marry men in their 20s and second-family fathers who sire at 70-plus. School bells are ringing for the more than 2 million students over age 35 enrolled in college. Some 8.2% of these are age 55 or older. One friend of ours, Mary Nealon, at 40-ish, is just starting the long haul of going into the medical field. It makes perfect sense: to be a new practitioner at 50, knowing all the latest advances, yet having the life experience for sounder decisions. Another woman named Colette whom we met told us about her struggle to find a school that would "take a chance" and admit her. In her early 60s, she felt a calling to become a rabbi. Logic said, "It takes six years to complete rabbinical studies and that makes her too old." Clicking says, "It's never too late. Older is wiser and wiser is what a rabbi should be." Reconstructionist Rabbinical College in Wyncote, Pennsylvania, agreed.

And what about high-tech mothering? Now that science has advanced as far as giving women the capability of giving birth after menopause, what does this do to our concept of age? Oldest on record, an Italian woman who bore a son through in vitro fertilization (IVF) at the very grandmotherly age of 62. And there are the so-called elder-mothers (and elder-dads), encouraged by the acceptance in China for adoptive parents to be well over the age of 40—and even single. Before this book is published, Lys will have journeyed to Shanghai, China, and returned with her adopted orphan daughter. When questioned by an acquaintance about the advisability of adopting so late in life, Lys quipped sarcastically, "I might be the only one buying Pampers and Depends at the same time." As long as you have the energy and good health, the desire to be nurturing doesn't go away. (We should probably add money to the availability list, since the new figures from the USDA say the projected cost for parents who have a modest income of $32,000 a year is an estimated $231,000 to bring up baby to age 18.)

But for those desiring artificial insemination (shouldn't this name be changed? It's not really so "artificial," but pretty "actual," too), you can go so far as browsing through lists to read about the attributes of the sperm or egg donors. Do you want Genius? Green eyes? Creative? Next steps: baby-making choices from mail-order catalogs? Home Shopping Network? Internet? And just put it on your credit card.

The trend of Down-Aging isn't something limited to people old enough to receive a subscription to *Modern Maturity*. You can Down-Age at any age. For the pierced and dreadlocked set, there's a bar/cafe in New York's East Village called BabyLand that is decorated to look like a nursery. There are toy telephones, rocking horses, and wooden blocks to play with. You can sit on crib sofas and order malts, floats, and apple pie, or move to the bar and try the specialty drink, Mother's Milk, a Kahlua-laced concoction in, what else, a baby bottle.

Like a jack-in-the-box, this return-to-childhood theme keeps popping up. Madonna started a fashion look by posing in pink and pigtails, as the innocently seductive Lolita. Designer Anna Sui pushed it further with her spring 1994 collection of baby-doll dresses, anklets, and Mary Janes. Now we're seeing slews of fashion ads for grown women showing little, plaid pleated skirts or schoolgirl jumpers along with rubber-cap sneaks. This may be Down-Aging taken to the max, but it's not without its share of protests.

If wearing prepubescent clothing isn't your thing, you may Down-Age by wearing comic reminders of that aw-shucks time— your youth. There's no distinction in themes between the T-shirt sold for kiddies or those made to stretch across flabby love handles. You can throw yourself into the licensing craze, as a purchaser or a vendor; it's up to an astonishing $98-billion business worldwide. Ted Turner has been pushing his personal favorite: Yogi Bear. There's the newcomer from jolly olde England, BBC's Mr. Blobby, an eggplant-shaped character who chants "blobby,

blobby, blobby" over and over again. Dr. Seuss's *Cat in the Hat,* Casper the Friendly Ghost, Betty Boop, Batman, and the Muppets are still going strong. Kermit, the spokesfrog, is a major imprint. What's really interesting to a Click watcher is that the average age of these characters is around 50 years. That shows the incredible staying power of a cartoon figure.

Character retail stores are proliferating and doing well. Disney has more than 250 of its exclusive stores and Warner Bros. Studio has 80, selling everything from cartoon-y caps to mugs to posters. It's reported that 80% of sales are to adults for adults. You can get Pepe Le Pew oven mitts and athletic socks announcing, "I Tawt I Taw a Puddy Tat!" And these things can run into big bucks. For $450, you can walk off with a sequined bustier of Tweety or for ten times that, a desk-sized bronze sculpture of Road Runner. Read any exciting comic books lately? It isn't only those freckled-faced 10-year-olds who are plunking down their allowance. As any comic book salesperson can tell you, close to half of all comic books are bought by men over the age of 25.

Sports are a clear window into Down-Aging. Go to any gym and see what mileage the over-60 set is tracking on the treadmills. We have grandfolks who are cross-country skiers, tri-athletes, or winter-seal swimmers, in better shape than their grandkids. It's estimated that the largest numbers of exercise walkers (not *on* walkers) are over 65. Organizations such as ElderTreks and Backroads (800-GO-ACTIVE) have sprung up to sponsor camping trips, bicycle tours, and snowmobiling or climbing groups for people over age 55. A televised documentary, *Height of Courage,* chronicled the feat of Norman Vaughn, who, at age 89, climbed an icy 10,302-foot mountain in Antarctica—with an artificial right knee and an unbendable right ankle. He was accompanied by his wife, 37 years his junior.

Warren River Expeditions in Idaho runs whitewater rafting trips for seniors only. Nike's ad quotes Beatrice Brophy, age 72, and Barbara Anderson, age 74, canoeists and guides in the Boundary Waters of Minnesota: "Some people look at you and think you should stop now, rest now, grow old now, gracefully. But if you live gracefully enough you don't have time to grow old. You have a canoe. And that canoe has a river. And that river does not end. You hike thirteen miles at the end of the day and that is how you rest." Two who Just Do It. Nice, Nike.

In the hot court of tennis, sports promoters are thrilled that fans are flocking to see the senior champions like John McEnroe, Bjorn Borg, Ivan Lendl, and Jimmy Connors on their Advanta Tour. It's been nicknamed the Charisma Tour because this group of older but better players actually has more magnetism, more "moxie" than the ones left in the seeded pro tournaments. Who will replace crowd-pleaser Martina Navratilova in the women's arena?

Where do retired basketball players go? At the pro basketball fantasy camp in Negril, Jamaica, called Swept Away, you get to compete against former Knicks and NBA All-Stars from the '70s and '80s. Coaches share their strategies; trainers and conditioning experts instruct you about caring for injuries and prolonging your dribbling days. You even get to take home a videotape of your game with the good old sports—to show to your hoop buddies back home. Your own personal *Hoop Dreams*.

Sports and Down-Aging make perfect partners, and more than one company know that the connection is a good way to sell active shoes. Keds, for example, has been running a two-pager that shows a black-and-white photo of two little girls superimposed over a four-color picture of two grown women. The headline reads, "Your childhood isn't lost, you just misplaced it." The copy goes on, "It's probably in a closet behind an old Concentration game or buried under a pile of mortgage payments somewhere. So dig it out, use it. Do something incredibly un-adult." Keds has Clicked perfectly into this stir-up-the-memories Trend.

Just mentioning the game of Concentration stirs up nostalgia. In this era of rapid hand-eye coordination video games, it's interesting that the laid-back board games—Scrabble, backgammon, chess—are enjoying a revival. And what about the sense of accomplishment and thrill of jigsaw puzzles? First finishing the borders, then filling in the center, all the way to finding the very last piece of the puzzle. They become obsessions (one of Lys's favorites). She compares doing a jigsaw puzzle to the challenge of writing: finding the right word and putting it in the right place—or to detective work in archaeology: such as locating the missing piece in an ancient text or shard of pottery.

Down-Aging also sells at the bookstore. With the fastest-growing group in America, according to the U.S. Census, now approaching their Big 5–0, and one-quarter of the population already over 50, people want to read about themselves. What issues to face about aging gracefully or aging begrudgingly.

There's the "mid-life memoir" *Fear of Fifty* by erotic *Fear of Flying* writer Erica Jong, who states, "Sex is not a matter of life and death anymore." Yet Jong adds somewhat encouragingly, "It's gentler, perhaps less intense and definitely better." Gloria Steinem at age 60, in her recent book, *Moving Beyond Words*, addresses the "hormones within" instead of the subject of her previous book, the "child within." Betty Friedan wrote her tome, *The Fountain of Age*, in an attempt to change society's negative image about getting older. She extols the benefits of being "older," equating it with growing "wiser." Other books, such as *Age Erasers for Men* and *Love and Sex After Sixty*, cover such recharging topics as how to look younger, feel younger, and become more vital.

Just starting out in Spring '96, a cable channel called Prime Life Network will specifically address issues of interest to the over-50 crowd. In the privacy of the home, we can all click in and out to watch the more-targeted shows *Gourmet Cooking* and *Our House*, instead of *Kidfest* and *The Muppets*.

But we have to give credit to Willard Scott for doing the most to make us aware of the ripest of old ages in his daily recitations of record birthdays. He not only shows photographs of the elderpeople, but shares their particular secrets for long life. Also in his enthusiasm for letting you know that Elsa still gardens and plays the banjo or that George still does carpentry and drinks moonshine, he's promoting positively that there *is* life after the first 100 years. The numbers of centenarians are expected to grow: In the next fifty years it's projected that there will be 2 million people in this country over the age of 100 (see "Clicking Through Being Alive" for more info). Think of it. What will it be like? How can you Click into marketing to this group? How will you Click if it's you that's trying to blow out those eight-and-a-half dozen candles?

Products that help us Down-Age our looks are intensifying as Baby Boomers get older. Clairol's original line, "Does she or doesn't she, only her hairdresser knows for sure," shows its age as OldThink. No one thinks twice about coloring her or his hair today. It's simply not a secret. Not a day goes by without some new elixir to buy/to try, a new number to call, a new doctor to see. In California, you can dial 800-BEAUTIFY for a free referral to a plastic surgeon. Facelifts are supposed to look more natural now that muscles are lifted as well as skin. Thanks to advances in the study of wound healing, you may soon go under the knife without the telltale scars. Doctors operating on a fetus right in the mother's womb discovered that when the *in utero* surgery was performed during the first five months of pregnancy, there was no noticeable scar tissue. Now work is being done to isolate the prenatal cellular compound that makes this miracle possible.

Collagen injections are popular for four- to six-month fix-its. So are electric shocks to energize and give a lift to tired skin cells. Next step after Retin-A: the youthening effects of skin-smoothing glycolic-acid creams. Avon's Anew sloughed off $70 million in sales in its first year. A patented emulsion called Hydron Care broke the record for TV shopping sales, luring more than $750,000 during a one-hour program. An anti-aging formula that every star from Marlene Dietrich to Cary Grant immersed in, from that famous Romanian clinic, is now available here, GH3 from Vita Industries. You can opt for a lympho-drainage massage that helps move internal waste materials toward the lymph nodes and then out of your system, thus improving skin tone. Christian Dior's new cellulite remedy, Svelte, is causing a stampede at cosmetic counters. One-year sales forecast: 500,000 bottles.

Specifically for men, there are voluntary-ejaculation training workshops where, based on ancient Tantric/Taoist beliefs, men are taught techniques for withholding during sex to promote a stronger, more youthful appearance. This is based on the age-old idea that having a climax weakens a man and, therefore, it was not smart to do "it" before any test of strength (hunting, battle, or big football game). Kind of an energy reservoir idea, but like the child's song, too often "they swam and swam right over the dam." Hollywood rumor mills are flooded with stories about certain male stars who are trying in vain to pursue this new beauty treatment. Difficult Down-Aging.

Trend watchers also look to language as a good gauge to target Down-Agers. "Before," when adults were adults and kids were kids, people talked differently at different times of their lives. Street language filtered down from music. Folks in their 60s did not say Daddy-O. During the jazz era, Cab Calloway introduced "cool" when he meant "fine." Others said "dynamite" when they thought something was "really fine." What's different now is that certain words, phrases, and gestures are cross-generational: hand-slapping, high-fives, "awesome," "No-o-o wa-y-y-y," and still the use of "cool." Rappers today have made up a whole new way of talking. From hip-hop, we've got double, even triple meanings of words thrown in our faces, but what will remain in our lexicon? "Bumpin" is good, as in the music was "bumpin." "Ultra" is even better. "Chill" is "relax"; "cold chillin" is totally "relaxed." And "ice," "dope," or "fly" are really "cool." "WZUP" is "Hi, how are you"; "holla holla" is "bye."

Terms such as "Mr.," "Mrs.," and even the newer "Ms." aren't used as much as they once were. They seem too stiff and formal for today. Also, no one wants to treat age as a reason for distancing. Take the example of our good friend Carl Levine, the fit and fashionable ex-czar of Bloomingdale's home furnishings (we used to call him Czarl). He's off on his own now, a licensing success with a company cleverly called CLCL, Carl Levine's Consulting and Licensing. Based on this, his grandchildren, Ashley and Adam, simply call him C.L. It's a way to Down-Age somebody. Many children call their parents casually by their first names. Even the terms "Aunt" and "Uncle" are falling by the wayside, as the generational "look" keeps closing. And my godchildren, Sean and Chad, have taken a shortcut and just refer to me as "God."

Part of this generational mix-up, or blending, has occurred because Mommies and Daddies dress like teens. Blame it on the Banana Republic? On Reebok? Years ago, older folks looked "old." They wore suits and hats and gloves, even in summer. Department stores divided women's fashion sections into clear-cut areas or even different floors: Misses, Junior Misses, etc. No one over the age of 16 wore dungarees, unless you were a rancher or a farmer. We can only wonder what's going to happen when all those followers of the current fashion of wearing baseball caps take them off. Will there be hair there?

Computer visual imaging is also mixing up our heads with "What Is" versus "What Was." Clearly, there's the aforementioned *Forrest Gump,* which clearly shows a movie star of today talking with, interacting with, film clips from the past, from JFK to LBJ. And what about the Gap ads that feature a young Andy Warhol, looking perfectly natural, wearing this season's khaki pants. The subtext of that ad states, "We are every age. Not our chronological age. We are how we see ourselves." Downright Down-Aging. Andy may have died, before his time, in that New York hospital, but his youthful image—thanks to the media—lives on. An extravagant commercial for Chanel No. 5 "morphs" or computer-generates a live model into a sexy, breathlessly singing Marilyn Monroe. Quite the attention-grabber.

Expect to see more and more of that nether world until we're all completely confused about who's dead or alive, young or old. Wait until we can interact with a young Marie Antoinette or a very distinguished Winston Churchill at 80. This immersion will extend to more serious therapeutic stuff, such as being able to go back into your childhood and confront your parents at a critical time (or to conquer fear of heights, of darkness). Right on the Virtual Reality Machine. Nothing is true and everything is true, age included. "What you see" will have to be "what is real."

Adding to the confusion is today's penchant for clinging to yesterday's big stars. And not replacing them with anyone as meaningful. *New York* magazine did a story on Paul Newman, the sexiest man, at 70. Who can challenge the sex appeal of 50s Tina Turner and her fabulous legs? The average age of the group on "60 Minutes" must now be mid-60s. Mick Jagger, now a grandfather, and the Rolling Stones are gathering no moss, continuing to go on sellout tours to promote one new CD after another. The *Star Trek* crew, pot-bellied and toupéed. Regis Philbin, over 60, without an inch of flab. Marlo Thomas, still portraying a very young mother. The Bionic Woman and the Six Million Dollar Man, playing bride and groom in the autumn of their years. We could go on and on. "The Rockford Files." Matlock. A grayer, even grumpier Colombo. So comforting. So Clicking into ratings.

Was it a master plan or just fortuitous timing on the part of Barbra Streisand (a Master Clicker), now age 53? She said it was fear of audiences that kept her off the circuit for twenty-seven years. Whatever, when she finally announced the first series of live concerts, they sold out in every city in mere minutes at $350 for a good seat. Also big sellers, those $25 official Barbra concert T-shirts and baseball caps, plus $60 men's ties with a collage of photos from her career. Big business in Down-Aging.

What does this tell you about appealing to your customer? About starting something—or returning to a passion—at a certain age? Down-Aging can be an inspirational Click.

The quintessential generation-blender now is Tony Bennett, who at age 69 has definitely been born again and is flying higher than ever. This crooner of decades past was taken in hand by his son, Danny, who's managing his renewed hot-shot career, following a well-thought-out, decade-long plan. What's so interesting is that this is classic marketing repositioning. To take something out of sync with today and make it Click. How did a smooth-singing square with gray hair, who wears white jackets and black bow ties, make it happen in a time of grunge and violent rap lyrics? Credit for Tony's turnabout, besides his son's management style and a general warm feeling about him in the world, came from a new willingness to change. To move out of his thirty-year rut. From his 1962 Grammy to his 1992 Grammy, he stayed fixed in his "I Left My Heart in San Francisco" lounge lizard mode. Then he decided to cut *Perfectly Frank*, an album of Sinatra's saloon classics, and it went gold. The next year, Tony made an album of the great Fred Astaire songs, *Steppin' Out*; an MTV appearance with new pals, the Red Hot Chili Peppers; and a video and special, "Unplugged," complete with duets with k.d. lang and Elvis Costello. Everything right. Old reliable becomes supercool. Tony Bennett has done what no one else has: Clicked into and merged what both parents and kids listen to.

Then there's Fun. Being able to giggle is part of the Down-Aging process. A group in La Jolla, California, has formed the University of Light Hearts, whose motto is "A day without laughter is a day wasted." At their once-a-month meeting, the so-called Laugh for Lunch Bunch goes over such stress-busting tricks as "Create and invent funny nicknames for your family" and "Find a silly toy—put it on your desk." The search for humor is why comedy clubs and their ilk get such attendance and guffaws. Ditto for the Comedy Channel with its terrific aimed-at-adults cartoons: *Dr. Katz* and *The Critic*. It's why we're reading all those books by stand-up comics (more like comedy routines on paper). Jerry Seinfeld's *SeinLanguage*; Tim Allen's *Don't Stand Too Close to a Naked Man*. It's why Stupid People Tricks make us giggle out loud. It accounts for the never-ending appeal of knock-knock jokes. Homer and his Simpson clan. Why we have stood in long lines to see the *Home Alone* series or even the dumbest *Dumb and Dumber*, without a kid in tow.

In focus groups pulled together for Blockbuster (mentioned in the very hot-wired magazine *Wired*), the adults canvassed talked about wanting someplace to go "to hang out with other adults, play high-tech games, and act like kids again." Out of that knowledge, Block Party was created—an amusement center where a 45-year-old can go for fun and games. And no one under 18 is admitted—without parents. So far the centers are in Albuquerque and Indianapolis. Bound to be a Big Kids Click.

You can also find a never-ending marketing niche for turning little kids' foods into special treats for big children. Pop-'em-in-your-mouth chicken nuggets or French toast sticks. Our office refrigerator has a jar of Milky Way chocolate and hazelnut spread to slather on morning muffins. Nabisco reports that 50% of all Life Savers buyers are grown-ups, and the company is aiming at the same numbers for chewy Gummi Savers. According to the National Confectioners' Assn., a whopping 54% of adults freely admit to eating candy or chewing gum within the past twenty-four hours of being questioned. A restaurant in New York has Clicked into the Down-Aging trend. Twins, owned by twins, offers double the pleasure, double the fun, even passes out Doublemint gum. It has a quirky mix of sophisticated food with a few inside jokes. Oysters on the half shell with twin sauces; "Pate" Duke platter (remember, Patty played look-alikes on television). Most desserts are serious, but then there's kiddy-fave Jell-O with Whipped Cream and Chocolate Fondue with Rice Krispies Treats.

Good old-fashioned "nostalgia" with its sweet longing has a major place in the Down-Aging trend, too. It seems that we're always wanting everything back that we used to have. The ad campaign for Levi's 501 jeans plays on this by stating, "Don't know why Levi's 501 jeans have stayed in style for 150 years. The first jeans. The last great mystery." Coca-Cola's ads include an old-fashioned bottle cap, perpetuating its classic image with the tagline, "Always Coca-Cola." One of the favorite presents given to me for my dog, Miyake, was a double-dog dish, set in a vinyl-topped elliptical stand, copied from a 50s diner look.

And speaking about another type of vinyl, music lovers are again requesting vinyl LPs. (Also, 45 RPMs are coming back.) Sales have increased this year from virtually nonexistent to an 80% rise. Pearl Jam's newest, *Vitalogy* made it to *Billboard*'s top charts, selling more than 35,000 copies. What was so remarkable about this? It was only pressed on vinyl. The single from it, "Spin the Black Circle," is an homage to the old technology, reminding us of what we used to do with records. Eddie Vedder sings, "See this needle ..." and "Pull it out of the paper sleeve." Mariah Carey's hit song, "Dream Lover," had intentionally-added needle scratches. Will flea markets be suddenly scoured for record players? It occurs to us that Sony's 100-disc CD changer is like today's jukebox. It can play for about four days straight. What will be the next revival? Royal typewriters?

The same toys you played with as a pup are making a steady comeback for this upcoming generation. Now they are called Classics. And they're consistently anti-technological. Erector sets are selling by the tens of thousands. Consider this the return to the school of activities that wants to "build up and break down." Radio-controlled cars, planes, and boats will be another way to thrill away your Down-Aging hours. Stamp collecting, too, lesser known as philately, has returned as a hobby. You can share your exotic favorites by sending Say It With Stamps cards, decorated with real canceled postage stamps that have been soaked off and applied to greeting cards.

Down-Aging playthings can benefit many generations. The remake of the 1933 Schwinn Classic Cruiser bicycle with its one gear, foot brake, and retro curves is appealing to younger kids (for its simplicity) as well as to Down-Agers (for its charm). Kathleen Matthews, of Working Woman TV, just told us what a Click it was for her to get yo-yos and marbles from the Nature Company for her two sons and a Madame Alexander doll for her daughter. "The doll is traditional and dressed beautifully, and exactly like one I played with when I was a little girl," she said nostalgically. For one-of-a-kind collector dolls (mainly more for moms than kids), doll artist Patricia Kochie of Southampton, New York, makes the most incredibly expressive "babies." Each one has a name and a distinct character, taking about three weeks to create out of oven-baked clay and carefully chosen fabrics. Demi Moore purchased one of her early creations, Kira. Maggie has the most intense, flame-red hair and an infant in her arms, while Angel is a blond vision, all in white with feathery wings. Who could choose?

Grease is back on Broadway. Woodstock '94, the revisiting of the muddy love-in, with Crosby, Stills, and Nash, Bob Dylan, and Joe Cocker, has come and gone. The ultra-wholesome Brady Bunch has transcended from little screen to big. And the cool, cool, coolness of the Beat Generation is once again attracting today's restless Clickers. Jack Kerouac's *On the Road*, published in

1957, is being reissued, becoming a Coppola movie and appearing on CD-ROM. At a certain stage of your life, you can look back and relate even better to Allen Ginsberg's poetry: "I saw the best minds of my generation destroyed by madness . . . angel-headed hipsters burning for the ancient heavenly connection to the starry dynamo in the machinery of night. Sounding nihilistic, but really about being introspective.

The Down-Aging Trend, like other liberation/venting forms of social behavior, can also have a morbid fascination attached to it. There are the black-humorous "Death" cigarettes, emblazoned with a skull and crossbones (inhale, anyone?). Similarly, there are Skeleteens, natural soft drinks, also with the skull-crossbone motif, in such unusual flavors as Brain Wash, Black Lemonade, and DOA. These herbal sodas are sold at Urban Outfitters, a chain of clothing stores run by our sailing friend Michael Schultz. Rumor has it that Brain Wash will turn your lips blue. Rebellion at any age.

Whatever the crisis-and-change mechanisms at work here, the underlying feeling is "there's got to be more." And this search for ever-more leads to Down-Aging. Not forgetting about your age or railing against your age, but tossing away the old ideas of what chronological age is.

For Down-Aging is fundamentally about changing expectations, dreams, desires, visions. It's about a constant state of growing, of saying "Yes" to life and all its possibilities. We like a certain ad seen on the subways in New York. It quotes George Eliot, who once wrote, "It's never too late to become what you might have been." Right on the Clicking target.

THINGS TO WORRY ABOUT NOW

(THAT YOU NEVER HAD TO WORRY ABOUT BEFORE)

I t's pretty tough these days, with new fright headlines popping up on every newspaper and solemn "did you know" Hard Copy-isms on the telly every night, scaring the wits out of the most secure of individuals. To Click, you can't dwell on this flurry of new worries. But . . . we decided to list them (do you have others?) in order to face our fears and face the music, or as one country-western song says, "We're doin' our best; hangin' in, hangin' out, hangin' on."

Here're ours:

- Airborne tuberculosis or meningitis in an airplane. And to think that we *used* to complain about the fear of catching a cold from a sneezing seat fellow.

- Radioactive waste in space, orbiting the Earth. How will we safely rocket past it, or have UFOs wing in?

- That flesh-eating strep-A bacteria.

- Droughts that last 220 years.

- Life-imitates-art. Copycat violence from movies, such as firebombing subway token booths, serial killings.

- Sunken nuclear subs that will someday leak plutonium.

- Being shot as you pass by an abortion clinic (or the White House).

- Developing a brain tumor from your cellular phone.

- Innocently opening a package in your home—*boom.*

- Getting sick and having your insurance company decide it's a pre-existing condition.

- David Letterman will be canceled (or won't be canceled).

- About 75% of chickens/eggs are contaminated with salmonella.

- Re-scourge of head lice on New York City schoolchildren.

- What do you drink on a hot summer's day? Growing parasites in public water systems. Possible penetration in the soft-drink industry. Contamination of iced teas.

- Old age of the Concordes (first flights, 1976); no new ones being made. An elitist fear.

- Return of yellow fever.

- Online stalking: pedophiles, con artists.

- Availability of genetic testing for cancer. How to handle bad news.

- Bacterial gum disease caused by kissing.

CLICKING THROUGH THE VIGILANTE CONSUMER

An ounce of action is worth a ton of theory.
—FRIEDRICH ENGELS

If you're not part of the steamroller, you're a part of the road.
—GREGORY RAWLINS

Ever watchful. That's the consumer of today. Sleeping with one eye open. No more wool pulled over those peepers. We're out to protect our interests, and pity the poor company or group that tries to pull a fast one on us. We're on our toes, in wakeful attention. It's not just the angry few who are protesting with raised fists (calling, e-mailing, faxing, picketing, marching). Vigilante Consumers are everywhere, the seeds of discontent planted in all of us.

Every time you've been angry at a corporation for making a profit at your personal expense and have taken the time to write a letter about it, you're a Vigilante Consumer. Every time you've decided not to make a purchase because you didn't like the company's policies, you're exercising your right as a Vigilante Consumer. Every time you've done something as simple as switched off a channel because you find a certain program too violent or offensive, you have switched into being a Vigilante Consumer.

The underlying theme here is a *lack of trust*. Vigilante Consumers are suspicious of corporate motives, corporate sales pitches, and corporate bigwigs. We're tired of being wooed by advertisements full of false promises. When we see that sticker announcing "New" or "New and Improved," we remain skeptical. "Who are you trying to kid?" we mutter to ourselves. "It's no more than a sneaky way of charging us more for less." (We've been watching the number of tissues in the same-sized Kleenex box shrink from 95 to 85 to 70 tissues.)

We, Vig. Cons., seek out substance over style. Truth over packaging. Answers, not press releases. Vigilante Consumers translate feelings into action and wallets into weapons. Shopping is war. The enemy is any entity that doesn't meet our needs. Vigilante Consumers know that there is strength in numbers. We're often fighting to preserve something that's dear to our hearts (family time, animal welfare) or promote a point of view (vegetarianism, free speech). When we, Vigilante Consumers, succeed, we Click.

Woe to the corporation or group who gets in the way of the Vigilante Consumer today. With high-tech "protest tools" at our fingertips, speed is on our side. Tens of thousands can send off our humble opinions by "fax zap" or by "flooding voice mail." For politicians, there's a downside to all this electronic wizardry. Since governmental forums are carried gavel-to-gavel on C-Span, the notions of "I'll think about it" or the even longer-ranged, "Let me sleep on it" have gone the way of the gramophone. Every remark, every response, every vote has to be made in a snap.

When the venerable U.S. House of Representatives tried to insert a seemingly sound provision into an education bill that would require all teachers to be certified in their particular subjects, no one ever anticipated the avalanche of protests. Overlooked was the fact that this amendment, as written, would also cover tutors (mainly parents) of the more than 700,000 children who are being schooled at home. In a flash, the Washington phone and fax lines were jammed with agitated home-school advocates. The message from the voters was so clear that the policy for certification was defeated by a resounding 421–1. That's high-speed Vigilantism at its most focused.

Vigilante Consumerism is part of growing up when third graders can e-mail the White House with any number of questions and complaints. You know it's shaking up corporate America when certain Fortune 500 companies (Lotus, for one) hire Special Chief Ethics Officers to handle a variety of delicate problems, such as sexual discrimination. You know it's part of family life when parents and kids actually agree on products with a moral track record.

Warrior Parents

The Vigilante Consumer Trend has given birth to a growing group we're calling Warrior Parents (a basic part of a positioning project for *Parents* magazine). They're not fighting for themselves, but for their children's future. We're seeing evidence that these Warrior Parents are tackling the singular issues of literacy, childhood immunization, nutrition, toys, television, and music, and coalescing the scatter-shot efforts into a national movement.

With more women in the workforce (almost 60%), motivated mothers are bringing their job experience into play, to shake up school boards, consumer product companies, and entertainment providers. Barney, the purple dinosaur, a $500-million-a-year-business, was originally created by a mother from Houston who was concerned about the overacceptance of aggressive toys for kids. One group of Warrior Parents, upset about the sexist messages in the computer chips of Talking Barbie and Talking Ken, made quiet, unannounced raids on toy stores, quickly opening the boxes on the shelves and switching the voice mechanisms in the dolls, so that Barbie would issue commands in a gruff, rough manner and Ken would coyly make luncheon dates. Of course, even when the upset buyers returned their purchases, another point about sexual stereotypes had been made.

Warrior Parents can also take an active role in any suspected drug problem. After actor Carroll O'Connor's son died of an overdose, he swore to avenge the senseless waste by pressing charges against the pusher who sold the lethal dosage. Actually, a simple envelope holds an easy testing method for detecting the presence of drugs. Without needing any samples of blood, urine, or hair, Barringer DrugAlert can give an extremely accurate reading just from picking up invisible traces of drugs on everyday objects, such as a desktop in your kid's room, the computer or phone, the steering wheel of the car, the handle of the school locker. There's a small "collection" cloth that you use to "dust" over the surface of a few things; and a sealable sample bag and ID number. You send these to the company and wait for a confidential lab report that, if positive, can even pinpoint what specific drugs are being used: traces of cocaine, heroin, methamphetamine, LSD, PCP, THC (marijuana, hashish), and derivatives of any of these, such as crack cocaine. Call 800-378-4942 for more information.

When a Warrior Parent gets directly involved, social problems become easier to deal with. An idea from Officer Mike Tracy: to alert parents to their children's misbehaviors, the police in East Hampton should videotape certain weekend activities. For example, a parent drops a carful of kids safely, innocently, at the movie theater . . . and as soon as the parent drives out of sight, the kids turn and reassemble at a nearby parking lot where they hang out, smoke, start fights, damage cars. The cops might also invite local parents to ride with them on Friday and Saturday nights to observe firsthand what trouble is brewing. A sound Click idea for anywhere in the country.

Vigilante Boycotts

There is such free-floating angst out there that a Seattle-based magazine called *Boycott Quarterly* has started to help direct your ire. It spells out the reasons you should actively join forces with up to 150 boycotts at any given time, including a protest against Disney for its English-only hiring policy. Another rile-upper, the *Bottom Line* newsletter, pokes and provokes with undercover information about how to secretly check out your accountant's competency, which is the dirtiest airline, how to get VIP treatment in hospitals, and so on.

Ralph Nader could be called the Father of modern-day Vigilante Consumerism, for showing America that having a big mouth can do a lot of good. He became a consumer hero when he announced to the auto companies, in a loud and clear voice, that the cars we were driving were *Unsafe at Any Speed*. That Nader book came out in 1965, in a aura and era of tumult: student protests, sit-ins, and the rising growth of the women's movement, gay liberation, and civil rights. Now, thirty years later, we're protesting everything in our paths, from mere bad service in a store to monumental moral decisions that go against our beliefs.

An example of a 1990s Vigilante Consumer is muck-raker Michael Moore. After taking on General Motors in his low-budget, highly scathing documentary *Roger & Me*, Moore was given an NBC summer news magazine series, "TV Nation." With his wild sense of audacity, he created outrageous segments showing that New York cabdrivers were more likely to pick up a man in a clown suit than a well-dressed black man; and offered a viewer call-in to pick the next country for the United States to invade. "I want people to be angry," says Moore. "I want them to get up and do something." On one show, Moore camped outside Ford Motors headquarters and prodded its CEO, Alex Trotman, to show on camera that he knew enough about his company's cars to do something as simple as change the oil in a Bronco. "Prove it," in front of our very eyes, is the name of the game.

Cars, cars, cars. We're all so dependent on our wheels that if a newly purchased car doesn't work, we really get mad. And get even. One highly visible Vigilante Consumers' revenge is to drive around town with a legible banner, "This is a lemon." No local dealer wants to deal with that reputation. Nice things happen every so often. A friend of ours, the globe-trotting director Tina Ball, who has a 1991 Honda, remembered reading about a recall the automotive maker had on its 1990 models, for a distributor problem. When her car's distributor failed, she wrote Honda with the model number and asked if it were possible that her car might have one of the problem parts and therefore be covered, since it was purchased extremely early in 1991. Honda apparently agreed, as it picked up the tab for her repair. Now, Honda has a customer for life.

When Lys's new Explorer had a quick recall, it was a painless fix, plus she was sent a follow-up letter with a special plaid blanket as a present for any inconvenience. One teeny complaint: It would be better to skip the Double-Speak (unTrendTalk). The *recall* was very ambiguously described, "Our records indicate that your Explorer was involved in a recent *field campaign*." It sounds like it went off to war.

It's hardly new news, but the Center for the Study of Services, a consumer group that studies repair shops, reports that dealers always score poorly on its customer surveys because of lousy service and high prices. Here's a verbatim report of a conversation that I recently had with a nameless manager whom I've dealt with before at Ford's New York repair place.

> Faith: "I'm desperate. My water hose is leaking and I need to drive out to a meeting in East Hampton."
> Ford man: "But we close for lunch from 12:30 to 1:30."
> Faith: "I'm not far. What if I can get there by 12:40?"
> Ford: "Don't you stop for lunch at your job?"
> Faith: "Not when a customer needs me."
> Ford: "Too bad. Maybe you should work for Ford."

Besides stubbornness and not-great service, there's an endless litany of horror stories: unnecessary repairs, using rebuilt parts instead of new, shoddy work, bills that are three times higher than the estimate.

One citizen action group that clearly shows the power of a Click is MADD, Mothers Against Drunk Driving. It has changed the way we go out at night. By applying both political pressure for tougher laws and social pressure for appointing a designated driver (now a part of everyone's party vocabulary), this group is a strong reason alcohol-related traffic deaths have dropped a third from what they were ten years ago. Limo companies are not only for the rich and famous, but for regular people who are hiring a car and driver for birthdays, anniversaries, big evenings on the town. A future notion we heard from a militant Vigilante Consumer: "There should be an instant way to tell if a driver has a bad record—for DWI or even speeding. What about an identifying mark on a license plate?" At a glance, you'd know to stay clear.

Next? Crusading consumers are going to turn their heads toward a just-starting-to-rumble movement for "usage" taxes. "Why should we pay for things we don't use," will be the hue and cry of disgruntled taxpayers. If you don't have any children, shouldn't you be entitled to pay a lesser share of public school taxes? People who drive a lot should ante up more for road repairs, even if more toll roads are instituted. Tax bills will come with a checklist of services wanted and used. No more garbage pickup. That's fine. No more mail delivery. Whatever you want.

If you're thinking of stopping the mailperson because of the ton of junk mail you receive, there's an easier way. You can join the 50,000 people a month who write to the Mail Preference Service, Box 9008, Farmingdale, NY 11735, to have their names taken off mailing lists for five years. It cuts down, but doesn't cut out. the reams of unsolicited catalogs, flyers, sale announcements, requests from every type of charity, and so on.

You can also ask for your name to be deleted from telephone lists (same address, different box, #9014). Unwanted telephone calls always come at unwanted times. Michael Jacobson, co-founder of the Center for the Study of Commercialism, a non-profit organization based in Washington, D.C., says, "People are angry about intrusive calls. I hope that people file so many lawsuits that telemarketers finally understand that a nuisance call at dinnertime is not the way to do business." In an episode of "Seinfeld," Jerry told a telemarketer, "I'm sorry, I'm having dinner right now. Why don't you give me your home number and I'll call you back later." We've tried it. The person starts sputtering and says indignantly, "*You* can't call *me* at home." Then, you answer, "Well, then don't call me." Click. See, it works.

Angry Consumers

One of the obvious characteristics of the '90s consumer: a high degree of impatience, almost at the boiling point. Ever look closely at people who wait in line at the movies, at the supermarket, at restaurants, at the post office? Don't you sometimes think that any minute some explosion is going to occur as a result of aggravated restlessness? Not necessarily violent, just maybe a severe temper tantrum from normally normal people who've just reached the end of their time limit for waiting.

Keeping customers occupied in line would soothe these savage souls. So why don't movie theaters sell popcorn to those in line? Why can't banks (especially when the ATM breaks down) or the post office have more windows open during peak hours? In our brand-new, extremely ugly local post office, although the actual building has tripled in size and the entrance lobby is spacious, the same two postal employees are on duty and the same two lines are always there.

A new area for getting your dander up is in cyberspace. When an Arizona lawyer and his lawyer wife had the audacity to advertise their services over the Internet, literally thousands responded in flaming outrage, even with death threats. It was a breach of "Netiquette" in the highest degree, and the offenders were banned, tossed out, exiled from the service. But that was mid-1994. The viability of sending a message, instantly, directly . . . and cheaply, out to millions puts increasing pressure on the purity of the systems. New "commercial-based" messages can sneak in if they're not quite so blunt, not quite so blatant, but couched in more cyberspacey terms. "Please help" works better than "Hire me." Or digital business can now go directly to the right place: the World Wide Web.

In another online incident, a self-styled Internet Vigilante deleted more than 150 messages sent by Michael Wolff, author of the *NetGuide* computer-help books. This unnamed watchdog used a hacker's program called Cancelmoose to boot out all offending messages, and then declared to the Internet community that Wolff's messages, which referred to his latest book, were really blatant ads that ran counter to the spirit of the Net.

Computers can also come to the virtual rescue. Take the case of Bill Knutson, a freelance technical writer, who was asked to take a drug test by Hewlett-Packard before he could start on his next home-office-based job for them. It was a new policy, he was told. He refused, on grounds of privacy, and didn't get hired. Chagrined, Bill logged onto the WELL to spill his frustrating experience. Almost immediately, someone suggested a boycott of HP. Some wrote letters of protest or looked for replacement opportunities for him. Bill's tale of protest fanned out from the smaller WELL to the entire Internet. Others have joined in to say no to drug testing—especially for freelancers. It sometimes pays, plus it's fun to complain in the "global community." Even *Spin*, the hippie-zippy music magazine, has launched an online service called Night Whine that gives computer jocks and jockesses a venue to beat their breasts, to nag and complain.

Here's a Click career for a Vigilante Cyberspacer: Fighting Crime. Sgt. Jim McMahon is one of the nation's top cybercops, combating the "bad guys" who are messing up on the information superhighway. From scanning the chat bulletin boards to catch child molesters preying on innocent young hackers to the more sophisticated nabbing of electronic thieves who crack security systems and bank accounts, McMahon and his counterparts in other local, state, and federal police departments are pioneers in this growing field. Like the more visible chop shops for cars, stolen computers are broken up into chips and hard drives to be fenced in the huge black market. Then it's back to solid, old-fashioned police sleuthing to go undercover and find the high-tech "perps."

There has to be some moral and ethical standard applied to the information superhighway. How do you control hate mail? The rantings and ravings of bigotry and revisionism? How do you prevent altered "facts" from being presented to young onliners as the gospel truth? And still another future area of concern in this relatively uncharted territory: get-rich schemes in cyberspace. The same investment scams in the outside world are popping up online, such as pyramid schemes and stock manipulations. Psst, wanna buy a well-built bridge?

Another area in which the Consumer Vigilante is making noise is Health. The members of the group at the Center for Science in the Public Interest think of themselves as "Food Cops." First came their exposés on the high fat and salt in typical Chinese and Italian restaurant fare. They were the ones to describe Fettucine Alfredo as "a heart attack on a plate." After that, they sounded the nutritional alarm against those buckets of greasy, salty, finger-lickin'-good popcorn at the movies, and, via public pressure, got many a movie theater to offer the air-popped variety.

Food Cops of another kind are fighting thinness rather than fighting fat. Boycott Anorexic Marketing, founded by Mary Baures in the Boston area, focuses on a struggle against the practice of featuring skeletal models in advertising. To wit: bad role models for teenage girls (see "Clicking Through Down-Aging"). Companies that use skin-and-bones young models are identified, and consumers are asked to boycott their products. Among the early targets are Diet Sprite for its underweight imagery and, of course, Calvin Klein for its jeans ads with the model all normal-sized women love to protest, Kate Moss. Whenever Kate Moss's billboards are around, people feel compelled to write cartoon balloons over her head, saying "Feed Me."

The female estrogen replacement drug Premarin is coming under fire as a prescription for cruelty. Celebrities, including Hayley Mills and Sarah Miles, the writer-poet Alice Walker; many doctors; as well as just-us-folks are calling for a boycott of the Wyeth-Ayers product, which is made from pregnant horses' urine. For efficient production, the mares are supposedly tied up, confined to tiny stalls, and constantly impregnated, and most of their foals are shipped off for slaughter. Horrible, horrible. Surely there must be a more humane way. (The same sentiments were being expressed by the hundred or so English demonstrators trying to stop a truck caravan from carrying week-old calves to destinations on the Continent, where lax laws permit inhumane treatment of animals for slaughter.)

Boycotts and protests often force people to find other creative ways of coping. Many solutions are found in nature. Case in point: Some menopausal women are switching to natural yam-based alternatives, swallowing a variety of Chinese herbs, and chowing on estrogen-rich foods, such as tofu, fruits, and berries. Similarly, ultra-sensitive readers of the *Vegetarian Times* who've raged against using goose or swan's down plucked from birds may be inspiring a whole new cash crop for farmers. Milkweed, wild and woolly, is being tested by the Natural Fibers Corp. of Ogallala, Nebraska, in combination with cotton, for pillows and comforters. The floaty, flossy-soft weed might also be used to make tissues and baby diapers, saving trees.

Something bugging us that we brought up in *The Popcorn Report* is just now being evaluated: drug labels. Why should America's aging population have to take out a magnifying glass to be able to decipher the dosage instructions on over-the-counter drugs? After growing consumer pressure, the FDA is rethinking its guidelines. Simplify, clarify. What about using pictographs, such as the warning triangle (a universal road sign), for instant recognition of danger. This would be a boon, not only for failing eyesight, but also for the large non–English-speaking portion of our population.

Regarding prescription drugs, even more important than reading the labels is being able to speak to someone knowledgeable. A pertinent Kmart advertisement addressed the concerned Vigilante Consumer, strongly suggesting the necessity of shopping around for a pharmacist. It said, "My pharmacist wasn't checking for drug interactions so I decided it was time to interact with another pharmacist." Kmart gave this frightening message: "Not talking can cost you. Did you know that 30% to 50% of prescriptions dispensed each year are taken incorrectly? And 11% of all hospital admissions are due to patients improperly taking their drugs." Kmart has a Click going here. Besides providing customers with a take-home computer printout of medication information, it also has an 800-number to call for answers.

Vigilante Consumers can be born out of tragedy. Maybe it's from watching too many episodes of television shows like "Chicago Hope," but you'd probably feel relatively calm if your loved one suffered chest pains when already in the safe haven of a modern hospital. That's what Myra Rosenbloom thought: that the experienced doctors with the Code Blue team would leap into action and make everything all right. But when her husband died in an Indiana hospital that had not one doctor on duty, she went on a quest to try to right that wrong. After investigating the laws, she found out that Indiana, as well as twenty other states, simply did not require hospitals to have doctors physically present 24 hours a day. Cost was the reason. But Rosenbloom kept pestering the politicians and even went on a six-day "sleep in" at the capitol until a form of her measure passed. Click for her. And for anybody in a hospital in the state of Indiana. Now, what about the other twenty states?

The concept of Vigilante Consumer is also being extended to cover the category of citizen's arrest. Or being a squealer, in a positive sense. There's a television campaign against domestic violence that shows a concerned couple in an apartment late at night, overhearing the most awful fight from the apartment above. Man abusively shouting, woman crying and begging, "Please, please don't hit me again." Then the downstairs ones shrug and give each other a what-can-we-do look and turn off the light. The message: Get involved; it's your problem, too.

Remember the couple on a cruise ship that videotaped the crew hurling bags of garbage overboard? They received a reward of $250,000 for their vigilance. Now the Center for Marine Conservation (202-429-5609) has created kits for passengers, explaining procedures for policing the seas. Called a Citizen's Report Form for Observed Marine Pollution, it lends a hand (and spying eyes) to the U.S. Coast Guard. Maybe we're drawn to sleuthing stories, because Lys and I both got our start reading Nancy Drew mysteries and have continued being amateur detectives, both in Trend-tracking and in our social lives.

Yes, it often takes ordinary citizens to Click into making changes in the system. In the music being marketed to the public (especially for tender young ears), a consumer outcry influenced

Michael Jackson into rerecording and deleting certain anti-Semitic lyrics on his latest CD. Time Warner has been feeling the heat about some of the obscene and offensive things promoted in "gangsta rap." (It helps that prominent politicians have spoken out in favor of censoring phrases that promote rape, torture, and murder.)

Another consumer group, named Food & Water, in Vermont, has taken up the banner against toxic pesticides in food production. Members feel that the federal government has really stopped short by allowing the use of carcinogenic pesticides if they pose only a "negligible risk" to human health. "No risk" has a healthier, longer-life sound to it than "negligible risk." F&W is collecting signatures on Declarations of Opposition to Negligible Risk—about 500,000 in all, and is backing this up with local Neighborhood Networks, for additional education and action. Think of all the other Vigilante Consumer causes that could model themselves after this well-thought-out campaign.

Some protests, however, are silly. Or nuisance-oriented. We're all for truth in advertising, but wonder what's going on when we read that a woman in Toronto had a fit when her pizza pie had fewer slices than the pizza chain's photo of it. Or that a woman in New Mexico who was slightly burned when she spilled her coffee at McDonald's was awarded $2.9 million because the jury decided that the coffee temperature was too hot. Although fast-fooderies serve coffee in a range up to 184 degrees (McDonald's ideal was 180 degrees), 154 degrees was chosen as "sippable." Sounds lukewarm to me.

Look at the narrow-niche groups. There's the long-named, small-focused group in Colorado, Safety for Women and Responsible Motherhood, which has 1,500 women banding together because they want to carry concealed handguns. And there's a network for kids who want to rally against things they don't particularly like in their schools. Formed to protest being forced to watch the commercials in the classroom on Channel One, Unplug sends out a video on how to effect change on such common complaints as school rules, textbooks that are too old or falling apart, yucky cafeteria food. Call 800-Unplug-1.

Because of the high hourly rates of certain lawyers, client pressure has forced a change in billing practices, down to six-minute segments instead of the usual increments of ten minutes of work. Wouldn't this have been a good thing for law firms themselves to have initiated? Lawyers should learn to woo, not only sue. For instance, there are some sharks who prey on widows in Florida, and get away with it because of loopholes in the state legal system. Since lawyers and their billing practices are the butt of so many jokes, anything positive that they can do would be good PR with Vigilante Consumers, who have voted lawyers the most distrusted of all professions. Sample anti-lawyer joke: "Why does medical research now use lawyers instead of rats in their experiments? Because there were some things rats wouldn't do."

The ClickLesson is that Consumer Relations will be the most important wedge of the pie for any business today and in the future. Single customer interactions have the most profound impact. You can think of company-to-consumer relationships like a courtship. If the customer isn't treated sweetly and respectfully, the door gets closed. And once a company is dumped, it's hard for it to get another date.

A perfect example of a sour courtship (or Vigilante Revenge to the max) exists between Starbucks and Jeremy Dorosin of Walnut Creek, California, who bought an espresso machine at his local coffeebar. After complaining of a malfunction, he was given a "loaner" by the store while his was being repaired (so far, so good). Liking the one on loan, Dorosin purchased a like-kind to give as a wedding gift. Something was also wrong with that machine. Consumer Dorosin felt that his inexpensive gift machine should be upgraded for all the trouble. When Starbucks balked, he took out four ads in regional *Wall Street Journals*, costing many thousands, which included his toll-free number. So far, 3,000 other disgruntled Starbucks consumers have called in with their stories, and the Vigilante Consumer has been interviewed by TV shows (including CNN), radio, and major newspapers. Starbucks has tried to right the wrong, sending two new machines, gifts, and apologies, but too late for Mr. Dorosin. He now wants them to take out a two-page ad in the national edition of the paper (they refused). Now he's asking the company, which is involved in community service, to open a center for runaway children in San Francisco.

When we spoke with Mr. Dorosin, he explained his tenacity. "With all the moral decay and level of dissatisfaction in this country, someone has to say, 'This has gone too far and I'm going to stick up for myself.'" He continued, "If we walk into a store which touts customer service as their highest standard, pay for that service and still not get it, how can we expect anybody to adhere to what is right vs. what is wrong?. . . At least, the runaway center could make a bad situation good. Even though I'm not getting any pleasure out of this, I'm going to follow it out and make it my life's mission to finish what I started." Good luck on ending this public relations nightmare. For many injured consumers, J. Dorosin is a V. Consumer hero.

Sometimes, an incident just doesn't make any sense. (Everybody has at least one favorite example of illogical, irrational retailing behavior.) Mine happened recently when I was running late for a business dinner and dashed into Barney's department store to replace my $14.50 black Lancôme mascara. "Here's a $20 bill," I said to the young woman behind the counter, "and before you go to get my change, can you take it out of the package, so that I can start to put it on." "No way," she replied, "Security prohibits me from giving you your purchase until the transaction is completed." "But why?" I persisted. "These are the rules," she answered. Not one to handle a refusal lightly (remember, my sign is Taurus, the Bull), I countered with, "But it's not as if there could be any problem with a credit card. I gave you cash." "Your cash could be counterfeit," was her retort. After a few more interchanges, I tried a more supportive, instructive approach, suggesting that she could get those rules changed by telling her supervisor that, in a cash transaction under $20, the rule didn't make sense. Even though I gave her my business card to follow up, I don't think my attempt at reasoning made a dent. So far, I haven't heard from Barney's, but it won't stop my Vigilante Consumerism.

The common Click thread between both of these stories is that just a small amount of basic common sense and a willingness to service your customer would have made all the difference between anger and appeasement. What ever happened to a spontaneous gesture to please, instead of a stubbornness to resist? That's the smart way to approach a Vigilante Consumer.

In fact, in business, you can easily deflect the wrath of a Vigilante Consumer (before an apology is needed) by being a Vigilante first. Anticipate problems. If you know that an integral part of your product isn't working up to snuff, think about sending out a replacement to a customer's home before a recall is forced upon you. Even if you are working out of an old, pre-code building, why not consider putting in a handicapped ramp even before you're required to by law? Look closely to see if you and your staff are treating all minority groups with equal kid gloves.

Look to Click down a new avenue of integrity. Start by being forthright and admitting your faults. The new "honesty is the best policy" ad campaign for Jaguar cars confronts their well-known past mechanical problems: "We've kept what you've loved. The rest is history." And trumpet your strengths. Look at what Stolichnaya Vodka did when it advertised in major newspapers: "Next week this ad will disappear in hope that hunger will too." The money from their ad budget was earmarked to be donated to the charity Citymeals-on-Wheels.

You, too, can Click on a small scale, by offering customers free coffee and homemade butter cookies. Or by only tacking on the most minimal surcharge for overnight shipping. Or, if you have a clothes store or cleaners, by connecting with a good nearby tailor who can make fast alterations. Or by having weekly drawings of special prizes with random winners among your customers. Or by giving a percentage of your profits to a local non-profit organization (target the recipient to make it relevant: for example, if you sell stuffed animals, give money to the zoo).

Now that such old-fashioned ideas as "town meetings" and "orphanages" are being discussed, you might want to pre-empt a Vigilante Consumer by harking back to the good old "suggestion box." Or a more modern version, via a 24-hour complaint line, by phone, fax, or computer online. To Click with your customer as well as your company, personally read every note carefully. Weigh the solution, to evaluate whether it is feasible.

And never, ever reply with a form letter. Or a recorded message. If you do, you'll face an even more entrenched Vigilante Consumer. Remember this: Anger is only one letter short of danger.

CLICKING THROUGH ICON TOPPLING

No man roots for Goliath.
—WILT CHAMBERLAIN

There are two ways of exerting one's strength:
One is pushing down, the other is pulling up.
—BOOKER T. WASHINGTON

One day we woke up and all our friends were divorced, going to ashrams instead of Club Med, acupuncturists instead of doctors. Ma Bell was dissolved. We were startled when Pan Am seemingly disappeared into thin air. America lost its arch-enemy, in films, counterspying, and real life, when the Soviet Union broke up and the Berlin Wall came tumbling down. Nobody believed in God anymore. Woody Allen wasn't simply shyly neurotic Woody Allen anymore. And Prince Charles, the future king of England, had actually confessed that he wanted to be a tampon.

Business as usual wasn't. American corporations, the major ones, were trembling under the surface. The broad generalizations of the past weren't working anymore. The most conservative of big businesses needed a shot of new ideas, new paradigms. When the most conservative of companies started searching for answers and came knocking on BrainReserve's door for Future Directions, that's when we had our first inkling that the by-the-books business world had turned upside down.

We call this shake-up, wake-up Trend Icon Toppling. The socioquake of the '90s.

Icon Toppling is transforming mainstream America and the world. Over and over, the pillars of society are being questioned and rejected. We just don't believe in doing the same things the same way anymore. Who or what can one trust if one loses trust in government, corporations, marriage, religion, education, medicine, advertising, retailing, heroes, one's own family?

We're no longer sheepish about following authority. Accepting the old rules. Buying name brands. The larger the entity, the more reason we're suspicious. Or envious or resentful. Ove Sorensen, Exec. VP of Marketing at R. J. Reynolds quoted an old Danish proverb, "There are reasons why trees don't grow to heaven." He interprets this to mean, "You can only get so big, then you top out." Advertising agencies, such as Saatchi & Saatchi, which had spent the '80s building up, have started to unravel. Even institutions that have been around for a long time can't bank on touting their heritage anymore (it makes us think, "They've been around long enough to become corrupt"). Remember, only a "T" stands between immortal and immoral.

Can you blame us for a lack of trust?

Icon Toppling means that all the things you assumed would be there tomorrow, aren't. As we write this, Icons are Toppling, Teetering, Crumbling, Wobbling, Waffling, and generally Falling Apart. And as they fall, so falls the belief system that held them there.

Some believe this mass distrust of "what is" crept up on us slowly. We watched people with 30-year careers be "let go" after the major corporations downsized into oblivion. And we thought they were merely "unlucky." Then we realized that the savings and loans were failing. And we thought that it was gross mismanagement. And top government officials of both parties were being jailed for breaking the same laws they were making: drugs, stealing, fraud, sex crimes. Waco burned; the World Trade Center and Oklahoma City were bombed; the Tokyo subway was gassed. Open anarchy and hatred spews over talk radio and the Internet. And then it dawned on us that something was wrong, radically wrong. We've turned into a nation of cynics, bullet-fast.

We Pledge Allegiance . . . to Icon Toppling

Remember when the cop on the beat was a friend? How do we reconcile this with all the videotapes and audiotapes of police beatings and brutalities, with startling LAPD disclosures of evidence tampering, with the gutter language and lying of Mark Fuhrman. With the fact that four police officers in New Orleans have been charged with murder within a year; and now a fifth, 23-year-old Officer Annette Frank, has been accused of killing a young Vietnamese brother and sister as well as another police officer (her ex-partner and a recent father). That whole sordid story is shocking.

While the notion of a Corrupt Culture pervades, the icon of Noble Cop falls.

In New York's 30th Precinct, which encompasses Harlem, a total of twenty-eight officers (about 25%) face criminal charges for drug dealing. As Jesse Jackson eloquently explained to Charlie Rose, "The youth have been drug running; the police have been drug dealing. When there is no distinction between cops and robbers . . . [we] discredit the entire judicial system, and we are very vulnerable."

Even the vast and unwieldy federal prison system, which has been around for a hundred years, is starting to topple. Smaller prisons, with more emphasis on being personal and individualized, are a growth business. On a televised segment, we saw inmates wearing bright orange jumpsuit uniforms, watching TV, and microwaving their own dinners—in privatized detention centers. The efficiently run facilities actually save taxpayers about 15% of what it costs to house criminals in standard prisons. The goal should be to develop other such institutions, cutting bureaucratic tape, but not lowering humane conditions.

Remember when the post office was a place where you could mail a letter and believe that "neither snow, nor rain, nor dark of night would stay the postman from his appointed rounds"? Tell that to the folks in Chicago who were told about the thousands of pounds of undelivered mail that was unearthed from where it had been tossed and left to rot in trailer trucks and under roadside culverts. Or to the 10,000 names on Vice President Al Gore's holiday mailing list who received their cards up to ten weeks late. Or to those waiting, waiting, waiting for the promised two-day delivery of Priority Mail (at our post office, the postal worker said the name should be changed to "Possibly, not Priority") or overnight local delivery of first-class mail.

In answer to the resulting slowness of delivery, lost letters, and long lines at the post office, we're relying on UPS-ing or Fed-Exing (both enable us to track our precious packages, especially overseas), faxing or e-mailing to get our messages over and out. This is our Icon Toppling way to register our personal stamp of disapproval with an antiquated system.

There's still a chance for improvement. The post office is inching toward being interactive—letting subscribers buy rolls of stamps (how about personalized, vanity ones: your own picture, your dog's, a company logo. Click, Click, Click) or allowing them to call for fast pickups. Or the P.O. could expand its services—becoming an information and tourist bureau, a mini-storage unit for documents, an IRS headquarters (after all, it's always been a place to pick up tax forms), and a Social Security office. Click.

One bureaucracy that's on its way to a user-friendly Click is Connecticut's Department of Motor Vehicles (*Business Week*, 5/1/95). A cost-cutting attempt has actually led to improved service. After closing eight branches, the DMV has obtained fifteen places—rent-free—in shopping malls. The mall developers saw it as a traffic-builder, and the consumer sees it as convenient. Many large companies are also paying the DMV to send clerks in mobile units to serve their employees on the premises. Other states are letting go of control: allowing car dealers to register the new cars they sell. Arizona has cut down on paperwork, offering one license valid until age 60—with no need for constant renewals. California and Virginia are experimenting with ATMs for ordering plates and renewing registrations. In Massachusetts, you can even pay for a speeding ticket by entering your credit card number over a touch-tone phone. This article mentioned other future plans: digital photo imaging on computer, so that you don't need to be rephotographed if your license is stolen or expired; an interactive cable channel where you could be taught and tested for the written part of the driver's exam. For all of us behind the wheel of a car, these clever innovations will result in the end of DMV torture. No more holding on a never-answered phone, no more standing until you're numb on long, snake lines. Everything the state agencies are doing works toward the dual goal: customer *and* worker satisfaction. It proves that it can be done if you Click-think the future of your industry.

Remember When Working Meant 9 to 5?

Not long ago, working for IBM meant you were True Blue, and you worked there until you pocketed the gold watch. Now, instead of being comforted by a security blanket, the 36,000 employees (the size of a whole town) terminated in 1994 alone are singing the . . . blues. And they're not the only ones.

Just scan these headlines:

- General Motors Plans Layoffs of 74,000 Workers Over Four Years
- Ford Announced 9,000 Layoffs, Ranging from One Week to Indefinitely
- Whirlpool Eliminates 3,200 Jobs, Closes Two Plants
- Eastman Kodak Cuts a Total of 9,800 Jobs
- Brown & Williamson Tobacco Eliminates 1,680 Jobs
- Mattel Restructures, Eliminates 1,000 Jobs
- Boeing Fires or Retires 51,000 Since 1989
- AT&T Offers Buyouts to 78,000 Managers, Half of Its Supervising Work Force

Dusk falls on Big Business: It's the nightmare the Fortune 500 hoped they could sweep through—or sleep through.

Icon Toppling has made us aware that corporate giants could turn into corporate monsters and turn on us at any time. When you add it all up, corporations announced a half million job cuts in 1994. More than 2 million of us have been downsized, right-sized, and re-engineered out of jobs since 1991. That's a lot of people.

A group of the workers at Grumman Aircraft were so angry at being let go as the company moved south that they recorded a song to the tune of "Homeward, Bound." Some of the bitter lyrics are:

I'm sitting in a subway station,
With no ticket or no destination.
I can't afford the subway fare,
I'm losing all my teeth and hair,
I have no cash, the cupboard's bare;
They threw me out, because they don't care.

I'm on the unemployment line,
So many people, so little time.

I hope to pay my Visa card;
They're gonna repossess my car;
And every interview I get,
Reminds me it's not over yet.

If I ever work again,
I'll play the game and pretend,
That my job means the most to me,
To hell with friends and family.
I'm stabbing backs and on my knees,
Cause Grumman's taught me all of these.

Trust is at an all-time low. Remember when you thought that you had "made it" when you were mailed an "invitation" to become a card-carrying member of American Express? Your Green Card was proof positive that your credit rating was sound. But people began to realize that this credit card, while convenient, was mostly a vehicle to make a larger percentage of money for the credit card company. What was AMEX really doing for the consumer? Or the small business owner? Many women were turned off and told others (see "Clicking Through FemaleThink" and read about the chain of cooperation that links female entrepreneurs). American Express's rather transparent attempt to woo back the woman card-holder came through advertising: first starring Anita Roddick, in an effort to rub off a piece of The Body Shop's genuine Corporate Soul. And second, by having Martha Stewart pitch the Optima True Grace card, showing her clipping other company's cards to line her swimming pool. But even the credible Anita Roddick and incredible Martha Stewart can't change the fact that the mystique has been broken, the Icon has been Toppled.

Looking into toppling famous logos, a young African-American designer, Charles Walker Jr., has created a Heritage line of clothing that he calls "Afrocentric Preppy." Feeling that the regular Ralph Lauren and Izod T-shirts do not reflect his feelings of cultural pride, Walker has made shirts with the quite pointed slogan, "We Don't Play Polo," and an original crest made up of a Masai shield, crossed Zulu spears, lions, a scarab (Egyptian symbol of rebirth), and an outline of the continent of Africa.

Even the worm had to turn for the successful Gaps on every block. The first evidence of backlash came from its core group of buyers—kids. On the Ellen Degeneres television show, comedian

Ellen dubs her squeaky-clean neighbors "Gaps." The Gap ad campaign of showing icons of past generations (or deceased icons) as coolsters aimed at too old an audience. Most MTV kids don't recognize, much less identify with Miles Davis or even Andy Warhol by sight. Perhaps this is why the latest research shows the seemingly invincible Gap slipping among teens. In a 1992 poll, 90% rated the Gap as "great;" now the "can do no wrong" rating has fallen to the mid–60s percentile.

Yet it was good to see the AIDS ribbons prominently displayed in the Gap's New York City windows, showing off its sponsorship of the AIDS Walk (millions of dollars were raised). This illustrates an example of what something big and anonymous can do to act smaller and more local. We could point to this as a given rule for how to help a chain store stay in the Click-zone and not Topple off the popularity cliff. Doing event-related actions is a way of tuning into a neighborhood audience. Of staying personal with walk-in customers. Of not getting lost in the maze of the sheer mechanics of being an organization. Of working together as a sum of parts and not one big, unmanageable whole.

Take the example of a recent advertisement for the Cable & Wireless Alliance, which boldly announced its concept: "The Corporation is dead. Long Live the Federation." The ad said, "The traditional, lumbering, top-heavy and multi-layered corporations of today cannot survive in the new chaotic marketplace ... And what do they [business advisers] predict in their place? Federations of smaller companies and groups free to move quickly and efficiently in an ever changing marketplace." This is the basis of the Cable & Wireless partnership—to put together a federation of more than fifty groups worldwide, forging the fifth largest telecommunications group in the world.

When you think about this, there's something savvy going on here that harkens back to the ancient concept of trade guilds. Where cooperation, not back-stabbing, reigns among like-interests. This theme fits the true definition of Clicking: seeking different ways of doing things, ways that came from the past to fit the future.

Beyond the Brady Bunch: The Toppled Family

The Nightmare is on Elm Street, too. What else can we expect in a nation minus so many mommies and daddies? The American parent has been absent, leaving the latchkey kid too often Home Alone—and lonely. When you count up the hours spent together, an average parent (in a two-parent household) ekes out only a total of seven hours per week with her/his children.

According to the *Los Angeles Times* (12/18/94), a full 60% of marriages end in divorce (that's three times the rate of 1960). The married time isn't long. Half of those marching down the aisle arm-in arm in 1995 will be skipping out and speaking through their lawyers by 2005. The number of households headed by single women has also tripled since 1960. And an unbelievable one-quarter of today's children are born out of wedlock. "Without a father" reflects that 80% of children don't see their dads on a steady basis within two years of divorce. There Topples the Icon of the Ideal Family.

But have advertisers caught on? Have sitcoms? "Roseanne," "Home Improvement," "Dave's World," "Married with Children," and "The Simpsons" are still portraying a 1950s family unit. More reflective of today's population are the New FamilyThink setups of "Grace Under Fire" (divorced mom and three kids); "Full House" (single father with three kids, two men as roommates); "Party of Five" (five siblings, no parents); "Seinfeld" (single friends); "Frasier" (single male living with father).

School Daze . . .

And nobody's minding the schools, either. The new reality is a generation of kids raising themselves on a combination of junk food, junk movies, and just plain junk. Former New York School Chancellor Cortines told *Newsday*, "Sometimes, I think we should be handing out medals for bravery instead of diplomas." My own cousin, Maureen Rosenkrantz, a teacher who has dedicated the past 30 years to kids, was pushed down a flight of stairs at Washington Irving High School recently, requiring 53 stitches on her face.

It's not just a problem in urban areas. Police are being sent to athletic events in almost 90% of schools. For children, there's daily anxiety generated by walking through metal detectors; witnessing slashings, stabbings, and shootings; and slinking around in fear of bully intimidation. The old three "Rs" of our schooldays have turned into three "Gs": Gangs, Guns, and Getting high.

Two key new directions are emerging out of the rubble of our public education Icon. Home/alternative schooling, now a reality for 1% of America's children, is part of a push for more safety and stronger family ties. And the privatization of schools (kudos to Chris Whittle for trying). Big Click opportunities here.

Remember when a college diploma was a passport for getting a job? Today, that piece of paper doesn't guarantee anything (except that you'll have a lovely parchment to frame). Some 30% of graduates between now and 2005 will "march straight into the ranks of the jobless," according to a recent study by the American Management Association. The college-degree-as-job-entry Icon has Toppled. A full 15% of law school grads were still out pounding the pavement six months after graduation. Remember when MBAs marched proudly out of business schools, panting to belong to the corporate world? Last year, according to *Fortune* magazine, at Stanford University, where once 70% of the Business School's Class of '89 joined large companies, now, by 1994, the numbers had declined to only half.

Also watch for a growth spurt in publicly traded, for-profit higher education colleges or grad schools, such as a still-small but growing one named DeVry, which now has thirteen campuses throughout the United States, and Keller Graduate School, which has spread to seventeen locations. Run on tight budgets with no fat (saving on everything from lower electricity bills, due to solar heating, to less fancy campuses), these accredited institutions charge almost half the tuition of a large state university and a third the tuition of a private school. Click.

That's Entertainment

Remember when our biggest thrill for a Saturday was a double feature? Or a doubleheader down at the ballpark? Where are the heroes we can still believe in? For the first time in five years, the approval rating for featuring celebrities in commercials has dropped to a very disinterested 24%, according to a Video Storyboard survey. Yet we (or advertising agencies) still keep looking for someone fresh and viable to be Our Hero. Unlike the past when the featured player was a tried-and-true face, an unprecedented seven of the top ten celebrity endorsers today are newcomers.

Is it any wonder that the Icon has Toppled? Watch any one of the over fifteen TV news magazines, including "20/20," "48 Hours," "Prime Time Live," and "Hard Copy," on the air, and ask yourself, "Is anything sacred?" The trash gets trashed. We don't know what to believe in, where to turn. We're jaded and disappointed. Four of these tabloid shows are on the top-rated lists. And *America's Talking*, a cable all-talk channel, has people spilling their secrets 24 hours a day. Are we trying to have our worst suspicions confirmed—S&M as the national pastime?

Why do we need so much coverage? Because Icon Toppling pulls in Nielsen ratings. We want the gossip, the dirt, the intrigue, yet we also want the truth. In an age of information overload, Icon Toppling is, without a doubt, the best entertainment going. Forget the formula thrillers and action-adventure films that Hollywood churns out like clockwork. With most movies, it's easy to predict who's going to win and who's going to lose. Real life doesn't follow a script. We stayed glued to the TV console because we really can't guess what will happen next. If smiling O. J. is a cold-blooded murderer, then could we be guilty too? That's what is so addictive. "Sonya Live" on CNN was right on when Sonya titled an early-in-the-media-circus talk show "Hooked on O. J."

Court TV, the ultimate insider's view into the judicial process has the same pull. It advertises itself with the tag line "Real Drama, No Scripts." As every Court TV fan knows, there's more to the network than serial killers. It's making names for some of its anchorpeople, such as Terry Moran of "Prime Time Justice." Court TV had the best analysis on Heidi Fleiss and what was in her little black book. Even President Clinton admitted that he'd sneak away from meetings to check up on how the Menendez brothers' cases were proceeding.

Remember When We Believed in Marcus Welby and Ben Casey?

Now it's "ER" and "Chicago Hope"—drama and trauma in the fast lane. A group of real-life doctors critiqued the cast doctors and declared that their procedures were medically correct (although others find them laughable). The lingo of the Emergency Room is creeping into our vocabulary. We know about stopping the spurt of blood, putting a tube in the throat for breathing, applying electric shocks to get the heart going, and, in dire straits, opening up the chest and massaging the heart.

The annual physical is dead, replaced by the periodic health examination. The path of doctoring is being directed by one primary care physician who may or may not know your name. Which explains why herbal medicines and alternative treatments are on the rise. According to Tom Rawls, editor of *Natural Health,* there are two types of people who turn to alternative medicine: "Those who did not have success with conventional medicine and those who are simply taking responsibility for their health . . . People are tired of being blindly led by traditional medical practice." (See "Clicking Through Being Alive.")

We Stopped Shopping, They Started Dropping

Remember when department stores were the most fun and most satisfying places to shop? What's missing from our landscape? A&S (after 112 years), Alexander's, B. Altman, Bonwit Teller, Gimbel's, Ohrbach's (the best of imported "collection" clothes), even the venerable I. Magnin's (everyone *tsked,* "The end of an era, the end of an era") and scores of others. In *The Popcorn Report,* we reviewed BrainReserve's 1985 prediction that department stores are the "dinosaurs of shopping" and that they could be replaced by catalogs and then by interactive TV. It's happening; no, it's happened.

One Master of the Dinosaurs came to us a few years back to try to find out why his chain of department stores was steadily losing customers. BrainReserve went into project-action: setting up a team, probing our TalentBank, doing scores of one-on-one interviews, and scanning the culture to come up with some answers. One major reason, we deduced, was that women simply did not have time to shop in a poorly laid-out, poorly staffed, and poorly stocked environment. Department stores can be eminently unfriendly, even hostile, with merchandise tethered to the walls on metal cords, to prevent customers from stealing. (Tip: If you're frustrated by being ignored by the sales help and want instant service, just yank one of those security binders apart. Bells and whistles go off and you'll get the immediate attention you deserve.)

Our department store client turned to me halfway through the BrainReserve presentation and said, "Honey . . . " (My own informal analysis shows that everyone who calls me "honey" goes into Chapter 11 within one year. He did.) "What would women do if they couldn't shop?"

That's how Icons Topple. By not seeing what's right in front of their eyes. His corporate setup hadn't noticed that things had changed. Women, like men, are time-stressed, busy juggling home, career, relationships, children, health/exercise, repairs life. No one finds it fun anymore to waste hours trying to buy one needed item. As a quick alternative, it's too easy to dash into a specialty store that has a concentration of focused merchandise or to dial up a catalog 800 number (or QVC line) at any hour of the day or night.

The supermarket is next. The men (mostly) who run them haven't realized yet that the women who regularly shop there— with two screaming hungry kids in the cart and a strict budget to adhere to—don't *really love* food shopping.

If Barry Diller's vision is right, we'll all soon be monitored by "Smart Agents," specialized computers that will know us so well that they'll constantly be our personal scanner for all kinds of relevant information from hundreds of databases. At our leisure, we can be informed about the day's events, as well as any products/services that our Smart Agent thinks might apply to us—online or at the front door. A major Click.

In God We Trust

Remember when church represented a sanctified space, a shelter of compassion? Now we seem to be Icon Toppling and redefining exactly what was meant by the concept of "the sins of the fathers."

In Australia, the pope's joyous visit was overshadowed by a child abuse scandal. Six Catholic clergymen and teachers were jailed, one for a term of 18 years, for the flagrant molestation of underage victims.

The Church manages to keep its secrets. However, it's been estimated that about $400 million has been quietly paid out in legal fees and settlements to cover sexual abuse lawsuits. In Chicago, there's even a support group called SNAP—Survivors Network of those Abused by Priests—which has compiled a list to warn parents about several hundred known-pedophile priests. These days, churches can't get full-coverage liability insurance anymore because of the risk. The policies are beginning to exclude any clauses covering minors and pastoral liability. This fear has spilled over to coaching and summer camps as well. New rules are the norm, stating: "A counselor must never be alone with a camper," or ". . . never tickle or wrestle with . . . "

Socioquake? The aftershocks of such clergy abuse are devastating for the culture, Catholic or not. But what's the good news?

Icon Toppling is about the failure of belief systems and institutions that have dominated our thinking and way of life for decades upon decades. But where there's failure, there is also opportunity. That's why, as much as Icon Toppling seems to be about tearing down, it's an opening for creating something new that works better—like a phoenix rising from the ashes. After devastation, remnants of our society still get another chance (did you see *Waterworld*?). The few good survivors fight off the last vestiges of evil and violence and start free from the mistakes of the freshly fallen civilization.

See the Click here? Find the Opportunities.

- Lost your belief in Big Business? Start your own small one, based on your expertise.
- Lost your belief in formal religion? Create your own brand of ritual through Zen, yoga, meditation, even chanting. Look into Anchoring and find yourself.
- Lost your belief in the traditional family? Gather your own extended families through Clanning ties or online connections.
- Lost your belief in leadership? Get political and make it a priority to get everyone to vote.
- Lost your belief in doctors? See "Clicking Through Being Alive."
- Lost your belief in the police? Read up on the Guardian Angels.
- Lost your belief in men? Find a Mancipated one.
- Lost your belief in people?

Click your life.

CLICKING THROUGH S.O.S. (SAVE OUR SOCIETY)

There's no hope, but I may be wrong.
—BUMPER STICKER

The alarms are sounding. They're going off in Idaho, in Brazil, in Belgium. Their shrill sound can be heard above the din in London, New York, Tokyo. They're jarring us out of our sleep, asking us, as Bob Marley did when he sang, "Get up. Stand up. Be heard." These alarms are a global wake-up call, telling us to do whatever we can to Save Our Society.

What are you going to do? Go back to sleep or get up? That's the question underlying the Trend of S.O.S., or Save Our Society, which BrainReserve identified ten years ago. It's a Trend that we'll be tracking for decades to come. S.O.S. means that nothing less than our survival is at stake.

When it comes to surviving—or preserving things—as we know it, what seemed unusual or heroic a while back now seems commonplace. People do care. No one wants the Discovery Channel and all its features on wildlife someday to be called the Nostalgia Channel. It looks like electric automobiles are finally becoming a reality—prodded along by state laws. General Motors has one model in test market that can do anything that its gas-burning counterpart can. Its expenses run about the same as those for a gasoline-fueled car, but the downside is that the power pack needs recharging every 70 miles or so. The Solectria Corporation of Wilmington, Mass., is already busy with the conversion of Geo Metros and Chevy S-10 pickups to electric power, but the privately owned company is planning a '97 production of an under-$20,000 electric car called the Sunrise with a 6-hour charge. The demand is there.

America is not the only country searching for gas alternatives. The Autobahn-connected German postal service is conducting a trial of electric vehicles powered by replaceable fuel packs. Cities like Amsterdam have tried to cut down on gasoline pollution (and the damage it does to the historic canal houses and their inhabitants) by starting to ban driving in its inner city and extolling its public transit trolley system. Even traffic-choked Athens has closed its center in a three-month trial, providing free mini-buses until its state-of-the-art metro system comes into service. If one person leaves a car at home, it can save the environment 9.1 lbs. of hydrocarbons, 62.5 lbs. of carbon monoxide, and 4.9 lbs. of nitrogen oxides. Highways and byways have tried to encourage less individual driving by creating smoother, faster HOV (high-occupancy vehicle) or car-pool lanes or reduced tolls for multipersoned cars.

We've put emission controls on our cars to help clean up the air, but what about the other kinds of gas motors? On summer weekends, there can be up to 50 million lawn mowers sending out clouds of pollution (the EPA estimates that mowers and blowers account for 20% of *all* air pollution). The noisy gas guzzlers do as much damage in a half hour as a car does in four to five hours. The easiest answer: To fit lawn mowers with $100 pollution controls that should be tax deductible.

We can safely say that in few short years recycling has now become a way of life. After a brief period of balking, we're separating out glass and cans. We tie up our newspapers and break down our cartons. Twine sales are soaring. So are prices for recycled newspapers. You can't walk into a major corporation or building these days without seeing the recycling label on garbage pails. Some communities are holding monthly garage sales at which citizens can swap or sell their discards. Supermarkets routinely offer reusable or recyclable shopping bags, instead of plastic. CDs, once a protest symbol of overpackaging, have been stripped of their enormous outer layer, although we think there is still too much going on for covering. Consumers will regularly ask for "no bag," to save the trees. Have you noticed how many people are sending faxes with small Post-its instead of cover pages? It's totally ingrained in our social consciousness that it's smart not to waste paper.

Still, we have to be more resourceful about reusing packaging. If someone gives you a boxed gift, try to pass along the box. Like musical chairs, the last person to end up with a battered box gets stuck with the task of crushing it and taking it out for recycling. The Japan Environmental Exchange (JEE), a volunteer group, makes a small but vital point by supplying little cards to foreign visitors to distribute on their shopping sprees, saying: "Please don't overwrap what I'm buying."

Esprit, the California-based clothing manufacturer, had set up an ecology committee that employees dubbed the "eco-police." To make everything more palatable, the committee had made a short film with humor, showing committee members prowling around the offices at night with flashlights, foraging through wastebaskets looking for "eco-crimes." It became such a popular feature that Esprit shows it to its vendors, clients, and friends. Spain has its own version of "enviro-cops," Seprona, a public watchdog association that sniffs out anyone who pollutes the land or seas, with an easy-to-remember dial, 091. A tough global "eco-patrol" that is on guard against big company misdeeds, such as leaking barrels of radioactive materials or illegal dumping, goes under the moniker of Earth Alarm and resides in concerned Amsterdam.

The greater, closer-to-the-ideal answer to Click into S.O.S. is to figure out how to cut back on creating waste. In our resort area of the Hamptons the population surge can be estimated by the garbage collection: it goes from 18 to 20 tons a day in winter to over 120 tons a day on peak weekends. There's something scary about walking around New York on Big Pickup Day. So many people, so much stuff. Mattresses leaning up against parking meters, three and four per street. Where can it possibly all go? Maybe there should be soft-drink dispensers in supermarkets, where we refill bottles of sodas, fruit juices, and drinking water. We need to concentrate on making more products that can last a lifetime. Or that can be easily repaired, recharged, reconstituted. One of the problems now is that the cost of repairs comes mighty close to replacement value. Whenever our appliances—TV, VCR, fax machine, even toaster oven—break, we feel justified to toss and buy a brand-new one with all the latest features.

In just a few years, we've gotten clever about recycling products. Clothing manufacturers are using the darndest things. Polyester fibers are being made out of plastic soda bottles that are sorted, sliced and diced, washed, heated, pelletized, and extruded. Malden Mills has used about 140 million recycled bottles in one year (about 15 large bottles per jacket) for its popular outerwear fleece fabric, the warm and cozy Polartec. Patagonia, which pledges 10% of total profits to environmental concerns, has its own beverage bottle fabric, Synchilla. The company has developed a "Coat of Many Colors" program that donates Synchilla jackets to needy children. So far, more than 6,000 jackets have been shipped to southern Chile alone. Still another recycled plastic is going into making hiking boots by NatureTex. Green bottles are being spun into fluff that's filling the Rising Star futons. Called Cloverfill, it's lightweight and doesn't bunch up.

Ever reliable, Evian. To make more space in the recycling bins for all those clear plastic Evian bottles, the French marketer has made a commitment gradually to change over to using a newly developed collapsible bottle. It squishes down into a small ball shape and will add endless amusement value for your kids.

Freddie Heineken, head of Heineken beer, has invented a different beer bottle for the Dutch Antilles, where many of the poor live in shanties and had been littering their beer bottles. The so-called World Bottle is squared off, unlike the usual green rounded one, so that it can be used as a glass building brick when emptied. Gives new meaning to the old song, "A Hundred Bottles of Beer on the Wall."

Waste not, want not. If you're through with using something, maybe there's someone out there who would like it. Now Levi Strauss has started a program of making paper out of paper-thin recycled jeans. Street scavengers in New York have been making new furniture out of recycled trash. Called the Lot/ek Design Studios, it offers "garbage" lamps and tables. Old tires are showing up as retreads on running shoes and handsome doormats at Zona in New York City and on writing books at Manhattan's Kate's Paperie.

Computer Friends of Portland, Oregon, has made available a universal system (for about $80) to recycle ink cartridges and ribbons for 23,000 printers and photocopy machines. After switching to a plain paper fax by Brother, Lys was appalled to see the size and waste of the carbon/plastic refill needed every few hundred pages. Since many of our modern machines are obsolete every twelve months or so, what do we do with them? Although we've read that many computer companies have "take-back" clauses in their purchase orders, we've never been personally told about the wheres and hows of it. IBM does it in Europe, for a nominal fee. Is there a green Recovery (or better yet, a Disassembly) center in your neighborhood?

If you can't save shelf-fuls, then concentrate on the small things. Americans toss out a zillion batteries of the AA, C, D, and 9-volt types, all filled with leakable mercury, lead, lithium, cadmium, zinc, and other minerals. Why can't it be mandatory to use solar rechargeables only? Every little bit and bristle helps. A German company, Monte-Bianco, has even come up with a method of putting new bristles on old toothbrushes, so if you like the handle, you never have to throw it out. We've seen toothbrushes with fancy plastic handles, filled like "shake-up-a-snowstorm" balls, holding sparkles or little teeny shells or stars, also with replaceable head sections.

Instead of Styrofoam pellets, there's a protective packaging fill called Eco-foam by American Excelsior that is composed of 95% starch and a small amount of organic polymer. It simply dissolves in water or on your compost pile. Or environmental groups are pushing the use of popcorn for packing and protecting breakables. Popcorn, besides being delicious, is biodegradable and can be composted later on. One of the busy mail-order companies, Williams-Sonoma, explains why it has decided to stick with Styrofoam in a "Dear Customer" letter that is sent out with every purchase. It talks about how Williams-Sonoma has helped establish the National Plastic Loose-Fill Collection Program, which has more than 3,500 strategically placed drop-off spots. These locations are convenient to local businesses, which can reuse the packaging fill. One of the company's reasons for choosing non-degradable plastic: "We pack a lot of fragile goods and know that plastic loose fill is the best cushion . . . meaning less broken merchandise . . . fewer customer service problems requiring product replacement and additional packing materials and shipping fuel." Makes sense. Another of the world's biggest users of polystyrene packaging in the past, McDonald's, has instead turned to recycled bags for its carryout food. The fast-food chain's latest effort for S.O.S. is composting its scraps and leftovers to cut down the volume of excess garbage.

Even the United States Pentagon has been thinking green. Beyond adding more trees and grasses around the geometric building and its parking lots, the February 1995 renovation detailed plans for acres of natural fiber carpeting and insulation materials, nontoxic paints (what took so long?), energy-efficient lights, and computers. It's been estimated that the environmentally good materials and new designs will pay for themselves in three years, due to energy savings.

It helps an S.O.S. cause to Click if celebrities get personally involved. In this junk-media world, it's the fastest way to get publicity. Ted Turner and wife, Jane Fonda, try to effect change by being members of the Environmental Media Association Board of Directors. Robert Redford lends his vast support out of the Sundance network by being president of the Institute for Resource Management and board member of the Environmental Defense Fund and the Natural Resources Defense Council. Sting works for the preservation of the rain forest, giving benefit concerts to raise money. (Our friend, Jessye Norman, graced the '95 edition, along with Billy Joel and Elton John.) Greenpeace has a CD for sale called Alternative NRG, featuring such stars as Annie Lennox, REM, and U2, which was recorded and mixed using solar power.

John Kennedy Jr. has been doing his share of civic effort to raise our S.O.S. awareness. In direct counterpoint to the tabloid sleaze that dominates our airwaves, the handsome Kennedy has hosted a pilot six-week local TV series, "Heart of the City." The shows were mini-profiles in courage, citing unsung heroes who have been doing their bit to clean up New York and its boroughs, in some small way helping to turn the oft-rotten Big Apple into a Golden Delicious. The promotion said it all: "They have not walked on the moon, won the World Series or been named Man or Woman of the Year by *Time* magazine. But they are Heroes. In a city some regard as heartless, they are the . . . Heart of the City."

Kids, too, pitch in with enthusiasm and a knack for getting news. And the impact is even greater when young children band together. There's the Earth Force Alliance, a group of national and international youth environmental organizations. Earth Force's recent effort, called "Go Wild for Wildlife," came directly out of the poll of 115,000 kids who voted that they felt wildlife preservation was the biggest issue right now. Earth Force has partnered with Nickelodeon in a joint project, the Big Help. Together, the two groups empower kids to become involved. In late '94, during the Big Help-a-Thon, kids pledged to volunteer 31 million hours to help improve our environment.

As much as individuals can help S.O.S., a company that sets up an ethical policy program influences its workers. Sets a good example from the top. Levi Strauss has a Global Environment Committee that clearly spells out its worker and human rights provisions. "A company's values—what it stands for, what its people believe in—are crucial to its competitive success. Indeed, values drive the business," Robert Haas, chairman and CEO of Levi Strauss, said in an interview in *Grassroots*.

One of the group's conferences, called Business for Social Responsibility, in October 1994, was well-attended by almost 300 companies and individuals. Its a crammed agenda covered such topics as "Social Responsibility Research," "Daycare in the Workplace," "Business and Children: An Agenda for Our Future," "Environmental Tools for Small Business," and "Recycling and Waste Management: Making It Pay." The conference's goals are far-reaching, to strive to change the fundamental tenets of business, making it sensitive to environmental impact and changing its values from pure profit to a socially-developed future with community involvement.

Among its members are Stride Rite, recognized for its liberal family-leave policy and inter-generational daycare center. Levi Strauss, Reebok, and Timberland have been praised for their concern about labor exploitation in Third World countries. These three companies try to make sure that any of their direct or subcontracted workers in Southeast Asia spend their job hours in a healthy environment under the protection of basic human rights. Timberland, in a tie-in with its successful hiking boots, has a policy to restore wilderness trails with funds accrued through its recycling efforts. The company has had an intense print campaign that called impressive individuals to our attention. The copy in one of the black-and-white ads reads, "An active volcano scorches the earth. An active person purifies it. Leading an army of young volunteers, Sarah Whitman wages war against the forces that poison the wind, water, earth and sky. Timberland is proud to honor someone who pulls on her boots and makes a difference. She's not a model. She's a model person."

Another well-intentioned company, WD-40, has set up a "Preserve Our Parks" Foundation that is funded by pennies from each sale of its famous stop-the-squeak household product. And a delicious company named Just Desserts has Clicked with its Garden Project, which hires and trains prison inmates to grow fruits and vegetables on city-owned land. Then the harvest is either donated to shelters for the needy or sold to local markets for recycled funding. Employees at Guess? pitched in with their own hands to help plant trees in the fire-scorched California mountains.

One ecology group, Conservation International, couples its save-the-environment thrust with acute business sense. It engages in "bio-prospecting," creating new ventures to provide local income to endangered areas. Besides its teriffic line of health and beauty products called "Secrets of the Forest" (the creamiest, dreamiest Wild Vanilla Lotion with orchid extracts), "CI" has encouraged the harvesting of Tagua palm nuts, which can be used as a perfect substitute for ivory—in jewelry, buttons, and carved figurines. For more information on this worthwhile organization, call 1-800-406-2306.

Animal Rights: Not All Bad News

Even though endangered animals are still disappearing, they're not going without notice—or a fight. The peregrine falcon is perching on the tops of New York skyscrapers and soaring around the helicopter lanes. Ospreys have returned to the swampy areas of the East Coast. On the beaches, piping plovers are still being run over by the increased traffic of four-wheel drives, despite the roping off of nesting sites. What about those famous spotted owls of the Northwest? The controversy was a classic, in that it pitted commerce against nature. The prevalent economic fear was that if the owls were saved, the timber communities of Oregon would become ghost towns. It was assumed that there would be a rippling wave of foreclosures, a crippling recession. "We'll be up to our neck in owls, and every millworker will be out of a job," the then President Bush forecast while campaigning in the region. But the calamity never happened. Even with deep curtailment of logging in the federally owned forests, Oregon posted its lowest unemployment rate (under 5%) in many years. One ex-millworker who had switched careers after going through the state retraining program said, "I never had any other options in my hometown, but the mill. Now, a whole new world has opened up."

The Florida Panthers, an NHL hockey team, is determined to save its namesake. Because of urbanization leading to habitat loss and other modern-day factors, the state's sleek panther population is endangered, with as few as under 50 animals left alive. The goal is to have hockey fans and local corporations pledge money to save the cats each time the goalie makes a "save" at a home game.

The newest wild animal that's reached the national spotlight, however, is the gray wolf. What a long haul it's been to bring the green-eyed creature back to the national park lands. The debates between environmentalists and the ranchers had ranged over two decades, hundreds of public hearings, opinions from six Presidents, dozens of Congressional Committees, and $12 million worth of studies for the wolf to be ready to return to Yellowstone. Federal biologists hope that the release of the predators to the area will restore the natural balance to control the tree-stripping moose, elk, and deer populations. Meanwhile, in the metropolitan New York area, three coyotes were spotted over the winter of '94–'95 in public parks. Hungry bears, too, have been seen foraging in populated areas, attracted by the availability of full garbage cans.

The Commerce Department is actively working to halt commercial fishing in almost 20% of the fertile grounds off the New England coast. This emergency action is targeted at protecting the schools of cod, haddock, and yellowtail flounder that are being rapidly depleted from one of the richest fishing areas in the world. Representatives of fishing and seafood industries agreed that steps are necessary to tend to the long-term health of the ocean's resources. In fact, some measures should have been taken as long as a decade ago, when the first shortages were just starting to emerge. But it's not too late for stern regulations.

An aftermath of the dumping that's going into our rivers, lakes, and oceans is a steep decline in fish safe to catch. In tandem with this comes the spread of mysterious algae growths. In nearby Long Island waters, we've had few sweet-as-sugar bay scallops for the past few years as a brown tide comes and goes. Pea-green algae have been choking off marine life around the Florida Keys. To properly protect the fishing and tourism industry around the Everglades and Florida Bay, the state would be obliged to buy back reclaimed farmland and completely flood it with fresh water. This proposed solution has caused a war between the two affected groups: the farmers who would be losing their land vs. the fishermen who are about to lose their livelihood. Hopefully, the powers-that-be will also consider the larger picture of the interdependent chain of life: algae and bottom grasses as food and shelter for whole schools of various fish and shellfish.

Watchdog citizenry has been influential in helping improve the conditions of all caged animals, whether it be at zoos (more natural habitats), circuses (more humane treatment), or at shelters/pounds (less euthanasia, more spaying). A foster care program that was started within the past few years at my pet organization, ARF (Animal Rescue Fund), in the Hamptons allows you to have a weekend dog if you can't commit to a full-time pet.

Benefits and Volunteerism

Environmental activism is not the only "saving" that's going on in the S.O.S. Trend. There's a serious interest in Volunteer Vacations, even a book with this title that describes programs to sign up for when you want to make a contribution to society. Listed are such tempting items as how to help the Audubon Society track migrating birds to how to volunteer for a stirring stint at a soup kitchen. Years ago, Lys's father, Allen, a surgeon/urologist, volunteered one month a year on the hospital ship, the *Hope*. He traveled to different ports of the world, where the ship would drop anchor, and he'd operate (from early morning to late at night) on many people who'd never seen a doctor in their lives. What happened to that floating mercy ship—an insurance liability casualty? And wouldn't it be wonderfully S.O.S. to send forth another? Or to accomplish the same result by a hospital airplane,

More Hope? For medical attention closer to home, more doctors (and other caregivers, like nurse practitioners) could donate an afternoon a week to the desperately needy.

Our friends lament that they barely remember the feeling of being invited to a party without having to write a check. Every foundation and action group has figured out that for a sum of anywhere from $35 to $500 a ticket, a charity benefit is the fastest way to raise funds for a good cause—whether it's Meals-on-Wheels, restoring St. Luke's Church, the Ladies Village Improvement Society, Legacy, Oddfellow's Playhouse, or whatever. The typical route these days is to offer something in addition to a charitable desire to give: a glimpse into the inner sanctum of a house that you've always been curious to see; a close face-to-face encounter with a very famous celebrity, such as tea with Barbra Streisand; or an auction of posh gifts and irresistible services, such as a tap dancing lesson with Gregory Hines (my friend Ayse gave me that for a birthday present).

Charitable giving used to be more a part of everyday life. In the movie *Little Women,* even though the March family was quite poor and needy themselves, the girls voluntarily gave up their coveted breakfast oranges and sausages to an even needier German family nearby. Acts of charity were considered a moral obligation and civic duty, not only for the upper and middle classes, but for the working class as well. Charity meant devoting time, money, and energy to better the lives of others. Certainly these principles will need to be reactivated with the cutting of certain governmental relief programs. Part of the problem is that people who fill out the simpler tax forms have no way of deducting their gifts. Money given to charity per family actually took a slight dip in 1993. The national average comes out to 2.1% of yearly income. How do you match up?

Part of "doing good" is also "spreading good" each day. Like a pebble tossed into a pond, goodwill and kind intentions fan out in ripples. S.O.S. can be something as simple as stooping down to pick up a piece of garbage on the street. Or slightly more complicated, such as organizing a group to clean up a beach, riverside, or highway shoulder. That's charity we can control. Wouldn't it be great if there were a universal S.O.S. 911—one number we could call from anywhere in the world to a central Save Our Society clearinghouse to point out an ecological problem and right the wrongs. We already have hotlines to report DWI and tax evasion. Why not extend the hotline concept into a socially responsive realm with volunteer dispatch teams and knowledgeable cleanup crews ready to swing into action?

We're on the threshold of great debates on ethics. Not since the heyday of ethical philosophy has there been such a focusing on what's Right and Wrong. What we have done in the past decades in business and in the community has resulted in a crime against society. How do we instill a sense of rightness—or what is badness—in today's youth? How do we get it back into journalism and all areas of communication? Into commerce? It's the hot topic and hot course at grad schools and colleges. More and more regional and national business organizations will be gathering together to debate issues of social and environmental responsibility. Much of this is consumer-driven. Many people, willing to put their money where their beliefs are, are tracking which companies are socially and environmentally responsible. Green consumers report that they are willing to green-spend more for products that they believe are better for the environment than for competing brands that are potentially harmful.

Maybe because of our Puritan bedrock or our good old American naïveté, we're responding at some gut level to protecting the underdog—and the underdog is the environment. Yet, if we become hard-edged, we'd realize that this tough blue ball of a planet Earth would most likely survive, even if our human species is dinosaured out of existence. Note that the Trend is called S.O.S., Save Our Society. Although it's deeply concerned with and deeply committed to saving the planet, this concept can be pushed to its ultimate conclusion: saving ourselves.

Since the press loves to call me the "Nostradamus of Marketing," I sometimes look up the predictions of the 16th-century seer. Much of his popularity is due to the translation from the original medieval French text. For instance, his sixty-second prediction, in *The Complete Prophecies of Nostradamus*, is:

Alas, what a great loss shall learning suffer
Before the cycle of the moon is accomplished,
By fire, great flood, and ignorant scepters,
More than can be made good again in a long age.

Now this was interpreted by the American, Henry C. Roberts, in the 1940s to mean:

> The cycle of the moon shall end when, on the last cataclysmic day, it shall fall on the earth; until then much misery shall happen due to the ignorance of men.
>
> Mankind becomes aware of the environmental damage to the planet during the 1980s and '90s; however, many scientists announce that it is too late. The rain forest and ozone cannot be repaired.

Poetic license? A cosmic reading, albeit on the pessimistic side.

The Click for the future will be making the world safe for ourselves and our children and protecting our known world. Probably the greatest challenge S.O.S. faces is having to decide what to save. It's a sad fact, but we can't save everything. Our resources are limited, so each of us will have to make choices. And all of our choices will reverberate through society. Will we continue to insist that our corporations produce environmentally safe products when companies south-of-the-border have less stringent requirements? What will be the substitute for the budgetary allocations needed to pressure for greener ways?

As Sinclair Lewis wrote long ago, "The trouble with this country is that there are too many people going about saying, 'The trouble with this country is . . . '" Threats and alarms only make people feel anxious and paralyzed. Laying blame and shame aren't very motivating either. Yet, even though doomsayers control the headlines, there have been success stories. There are vectors of change for the good. If we each make the effort, for real, relying on facts and not scare tactics—the results will become collective. It's not overwhelming. We're still here. We still can Click. Never give up hope.

PART THREE

HOW TO CLICK

CLICKSCREEN

MEASURING THE TRENDS

If we do not change our direction,
we are likely to end up where we are headed.
—CHINESE PROVERB

We are asleep with compasses in our hands.
—W. S. MERWIN, AMERICAN POET

Now that you've read the Trends, you've got a compass to the future. If you know how to read the signs, the Trends will point you in the right direction. That's the direction that our consumer society is heading. If you interpret them correctly, you'll find yourself on a direct route to a Click.

ClickScreen is the methodology by which BrainReserve measures any specific target—a service, product, or product ideas, marketing/advertising concepts, a business, an industry—against our 16 Trends to find a fit. It works. ClickScreen is at the core of our work at BrainReserve: We use ClickScreen as a reality check, a future test. In short, ClickScreen is the screening device needed for all GO or NO decisions.

First test your core idea against the ClickScreen, before you even go on to consider the rest of the basics—financing, location, family matters. You can use ClickScreen to evaluate your next career move, your choice of college major, an idea to expand your present business, a product you've designed or invented.

It's human nature to be tempted by a snap/flash idea that feels right—especially one you've had in the shower. We're all drawn to those options that a family member or co-worker applauds (they want only the best for us, right?). And we must admit that sometimes we are swayed, temporarily, by the options that a client supports or shoots down (how many valid idea balloons have been punctured by "My wife doesn't like . . . "). Yet, regardless of peer or power pressure, we've never been rash enough to ignore the basic tenet of BrainReserve: No Action Is Taken or Recommendation Made Without Undergoing a Stringent ClickScreen.

When you too face the really important question of whether your idea has what it takes to succeed (to Click), e.g., "Does this widget have a future?" ClickScreen is the filter through which to determine:

- Trend-worthiness: Is the idea/product/concept a good fit when matched against the Trends? Is it on- or off-Trend?
- Longevity: Will it keep up with the needs and wants of consumers over a long stretch of time or is it merely a response to a short-term fad?
- Viability: Does it appeal to the mainstream or just to a specific group? Is the audience segment big enough to make a loud Click?

We've found again and again that super-successful ideas are supported by at least four Trends. Most ideas fit snugly with one Trend (sometimes an ideal match), but to be worth pursuing, the idea must be in sync with several other support Trends. At Brain-Reserve, each idea must pass the acid test of four-or-more-Trends-is-a-GO, fewer-than-four-is-a-NO.

Here's how the process works: Write down a list of all the Trends vertically on the left-hand side of a blank piece of paper or on the computer screen. Head other columns, horizontally across the top of the page: Yes, No, Maybe, Possible Change. Title the page with a brief explanation of your idea. Take each Trend in turn and consider how well the idea is supported by that Trend. Ask yourself, "Is it a perfect fit with this particular Trend, a just-miss, or a never-the-twain-shall-meet?" If the idea seems to be on-Trend, look for ways to make it more so, to enhance the match-up. If it takes a stretch of logic to make the idea Trend-continuous, rethink it to add the necessary Trend-supporting elements. If the idea is Trend-adverse, don't just give up and go on to the next Trend. Instead, try to figure out what you would have to do to reshape it and make the concept Trend-friendly.

It's okay if a few of the Trends really don't apply to your particular idea (remember, only four or more Trends need to be strong). One or two may even be diametrically opposed, for societal Trends, like people, can be contradictory. Think about how the same person can jog five miles, then gobble down a pint of ice cream. Or Cocoon for weeks, then Outward Bound. After going through all the Trends, analyzing, refining, and refitting your idea each time, you should be satisfied that your original good idea has the potential to Click. The really on-Trend winners are obvious, as are the Trend-rejects.

At BrainReserve, we've successfully applied the ClickScreen (originally, a sit-around-the-conference-room brainstorming session named Discontinuity Trend Analysis) to a diverse range of targets, including launching the popular Bacardi Breezer, making a computer more user-friendly, growing a small real estate firm, and finding a new image for an urban mayoral candidate. We've used it over and over again to come up with on-Trend, long-lived, and viable solutions for many mainstream clients: new product introductions, product extensions and repositioning, corporate acquisitions, and new ventures. The lesson in every BrainReserve assignment is the same: If a company tries to bypass the ClickScreen or ignore the results without following the corrections, the end result may be an unwelcome Clunk instead of a satisfying Click.

Since Lys and I know the Trends so well, we go around and do a shorthand ClickScreen wherever we go. If traveling, we make a quick scan of the small stores (markets, clothing boutiques, liquor, and hardware stores), the pharmacies, the supermarkets, and the mega-stores to see what's new or different. In April '95, at a Marketing Trade Fair at the MesseCenter in

Herning, Denmark, Lys spotted something we'd never seen before: personalized tissue boxes (the disposable cardboard kind) and thought, "Egonomics, Cocooning, Fantasy Adventure, Small Indulgences, Being Alive, Down-Aging, 99 Lives, FemaleThink/ Mancipation—an almost-perfect Trend fit." (Can you figure out the whys?) The 50- or 100-tissue boxes can be tailored with a company name, logo, photograph, or message. One even had a snapshot of a bride and groom joyously across the front, sent as a cute thank you for the wedding gifts. The idea is sound—tissue boxes are always visible, always handy. The person we spoke to was an American, Robert Delgatto, who works out of a small town in the Netherlands.

To illustrate the ClickScreen methodology in detail, we'll go through the BrainReserve exercise of applying the Trend-by-Trend template to an industry that we all know well: BANKING. Along with the supermarket, banking is one of those everyday, universal experiences with which we're all familiar. And one that would be vastly improved by Trend corrections. In the case of banks and banking, familiarity doesn't breed contempt (well, maybe it does) as much as active avoidance and endless frustration.

Have you ever seen the banking image depicted on calendars from the '30s, '40s, '50s? The quintessential white-pillared, brick bank that was the center of a town. As friendly a place as the post office (another off-Trender). The grandfatherly banker who saved (or at least tried to save) your home and your business in times of trouble. But as familiar tellers changed into strangers, lines grew long, and rules became rigid, instead of fixing the inside problems, banks set up ATMs to keep the customers outside.

When we are forced into the inner sanctum, as happened at the local branch of the Bank of New York the other day, the indifference is chilling. The ATM, in a separate building, was malfunctioning and had a sign, "Please go and see a teller for your transactions." After I waited in line for fifteen minutes, the next available teller told me he couldn't give me money from my account with my bank card without a check, and that I should go off somewhere and find another ATM. Trying to be logical, I said, "Then you shouldn't have that sign out there." He merely shrugged and said he didn't even know the ATM was broken.

Look at what we're dealing with at banks today. Headlines blare that safe deposit boxes are suddenly not safe. When you really think about it, why would you voluntarily entrust your absolutely most valuable treasures and certificates to the weakest link in the bank? A basement (usually), far from the main traffic flow, and often covered by only one puny surveillance camera. The safe deposit section in the bank across from us was flooded by a water main break and everything on paper was soggily destroyed. The area is usually attended by someone extremely young (and resentful about being stuck there) or someone so ancient that basic functions, such as eyesight, are questionable. Are either of these age groups the best ones to judge whether your signature matches the card on file (how incredibly old-fashioned). No PINs, computer matches of fingerprints or voice or DNA—just a hastily scrawled signature. Con artists have been having a "well-kept secret" field day, cleaning out jewels, cash, and convertible bonds. Read the small print of your agreement. Most have clauses that absolve banks of any liability, unless extraordinary lapses of security occur. What do you think banks are doing now when they offer to sell insurance on the contents of your box? Hint: They know you need it.

And now they're telling us that, in another shift of responsibility, it's up to our diligent eyes to catch a forged check. Few banks are actually looking closely at checks or scrutinizing signatures anymore, unless in the whopping-figure category. One bank manager revealed that his bank only examined those written for $10,000 and up, and scanned only 1 in 350 for those less than $5,000. Amazing. Why fill out a signature card, you may ask? It's rare for most ordinary people to write out checks for $10,000 plus. Weren't you always sure that if you signed your check in a peculiar way, crossed something out, or made a sloppy numerical mistake, your bank would refuse the check? Test this out by signing someone else's name or leaving your signature off altogether. Banks blame it on the standard excuse of a time/labor shortage, allowing bundled checks to pass through, unchallenged. Result? Check fraud is rampant.

When it comes right down to it, what services do they still provide? The latest insult to consumers is getting charged to talk to a teller. Minute by minute, the average cost from the bank's point of view is about $2 to $3 for every vocal interchange. Some banks are giving you two free talks, by phone or face-to-face, before slapping on a fee. Or they're charging you if you use a teller for something that could have been done by machine. Check your statements to see if your bank has joined up with this new non-service-oriented kind of punishment. After all, extra service charges tacked on here and there are providing a $15 billion-plus income for banks today—and that's not small change.

Banks, in their defense, are saying that they are losing money on half of their customers. Especially good customers who keep more than the required minimum balance and whom tellers know by name (now looked at as a bank-management negative). To encourage faceless-banking, Citibank has decided to cut charges for almost all transactions done electronically, to reward those who voluntarily avoid teller contact and use their personal computers, telephones, or ATMs. Plus we just received a very curt notice that our friendly neighborhood bank on the corner of 57th and First Ave. is becoming a "fully automated, self-service facility." And regarding that joint safe deposit box that has been full of valuables since 1976, "your current lease will officially terminate" and "We ask that you come in to empty your box and return your keys." Even though Citibank said there was "no rush," they actually broke open the box, itemized the contents, and carted them away to some unknown bank vault on Wall Street. Doesn't feel good. Doesn't make us feel secure. Isn't this the only industry you can think of that is trying to drive away customers?

Also, while we're on the case, we deeply resent the separate lines for most transactions, the desks of "vice presidents" who are always away from their desks (on a break) or on the phone. We wonder why our "no fee" accounts bear so many fees and generally wish there was an alternative to banks as we know them. This reaction serves as a red flag at BrainReserve, alerting us that an alternative may be just about to emerge. And that's just dealing with the consumer. Don't get us started on what havoc banks wreak on small business owners, entrepreneurs—yes, even on large companies.

If we go over the Trends via a ClickScreen, we can pinpoint the problem areas that prevent most banks from entering the 1990s and then highlight the solutions that will enable banking to Click in and cash in on the future. This is an example of the "top layer" of a ClickScreen; identifying some problem areas and some possible solutions.

ClickScreen: The Banking Industry Trend-by-Trend

Cocooning

Neither banks nor ATMs feel like safe havens . . . from anything. Unless you have a PC, to get your banking needs met, you have to leave your Cocoon and appear in person, preferably at your own branch. Often your arrival coincides with everyone else's (lunch hour becomes crunch hour) or, worse still, conflicts with the bank's inconvenient hours of operation. Even when hours are flex, the schedule is confusing. Parking is a hassle. Off-Trend.

Clanning

Banks take us out of our Cocoons to impersonal ATMs, branches full of silent strangers, and account managers we've never laid eyes on before. Gone are the days when gold miners gathered at Wells Fargo Nevada Bank to empty the pockets of their Levi's of the day's haul of gold, sharing the lode and the lore. When was the last time you looked forward to seeing friends at the bank or meeting some new, like-minded folks there? Never. Off-Trend.

Fantasy Adventure

Unless we're missing something, there's nothing titillating, sensual, or magical about banks. Strange, considering that a bank's role is to facilitate access to money—and money facilitates access to dreams: a new car, an exotic trip, the longed-for kitchen renovation, a college education. Instead of dramatic excitement or aesthetic pleasure, most banks are somber monuments to monotony. Banking hasn't a shred of adventure. You can't bank on the road or on a plane. If you go on a long holiday, your bills pile up, unpaid. Off-Trend.

Pleasure Revenge

The somber, visit-to-the-principal's-office atmosphere of most banks makes us feel that we've been caught with a smoking cigarette and are about to be lectured to or punished. There's a lot of revenge in this experience and little pleasure. Off-Trend.

Small Indulgences

Can you imagine anyone saying, "Oh, I'm going to treat myself to a trip to my favorite bank. I really deserve it!" Not very likely. Few banks have progressed beyond being a "because I have to" experience, about as much fun as going to the dry cleaners— only not as pleasant. Off-Trend.

Anchoring

Banks are definitely not a stop on the ride to inner peace. We don't expect a bank to be a spiritual haven or to help us find our meditative core. On the other hand, it would be nice if banks weren't so aggressively wedded to the 1980s creed of more-greed-than-need. Off-Trend.

Egonomics

Except for those tiny name and/or address lines on our checks and our personal, super-confidential ATM codes (98% of us use our birthdays or a similarly easy-to-remember and easy-for-others-to-figure-out date), there is little personalization or customization in banking. Not in the monthly mailings, not in the telephonic or in-person service, and certainly not in the products. Having, on average, only three different kinds of checking options to choose from doesn't make us feel unique. Off-Trend.

Vigilante Consumer

All banking customers become Vigilante Consumers for their own self-interest (no pun intended). It doesn't seem that anyone else is keeping track of whether a deposit is really credited or if the interest on your line of credit is calculated correctly. (Don't worry, it's immediately adjusted upward when it's in the bank's favor.) If the smallest thing goes wrong, you're handled like a criminal.

In general, the discrepancy between the bank ads in the papers or magazines and the reality of the banking experience is also making customers "mad as hell." When the copy announces, "Your personal executive will expedite all your transactions,"

"Your financial partner will maximize your money's productivity," or "We work hard every day to earn our customer's trust," does this sound anything like what's happened to you, unless you're one of the super-rich? Security and caring are illusional. Needlessly Off-Trend.

Being Alive

Being Alive is about living better and joyfully, focusing on the present, and minimizing stress. Even when banks become more interactive and introduce added electronic banking services, there's a problem: People get even more anxious about trusting high technology to keep their money secure. Try as we can to be fair, there's no way that individual banks are contributing to reducing stress. Wouldn't you feel your blood pressure rise when you read a recent survey revealing that up to 50% of Adjustable Rate Mortgage charges have errors? Or when you found that you were paying a higher rate than your neighbor? Or when the prime rate went up and so did your credit card interest payments, but not your deposit accounts? Off-Trend.

99 Lives

The banking industry is not structured to accommodate or support your multi-function, multi-role life. "Don't ATMs address our need for time-saving and accessibility?" Yes, somewhat. But banking hours are limited and ATMs are both scary at night and broken down so often that our 99 Lives needs are not met enough. Not enough to make up for having to see different bank staffers for different tasks; not enough for the scarcity of occasions that any transaction can be started and completed in one sitting (or standing); and not nearly enough attention to our goals versus theirs.

And now that bank chain after bank chain is merging into colossal mega-banks and closing all superfluous branches, banking is getting *less,* not *more,* convenient. Off-Trend.

Cashing Out

You've Cashed Out and cashed into personal discovery— Click-seeking in a new, less-stressed environment. So what could go wrong? You could find yourself up against the Bank from Cashing Out Hell! Instead of recognizing your personal achievements and greeting you with a Welcome Wagon, the bank often treats you with an ominous air of suspicion. Unless you have an established period of residency and a regular well-paying job, you're eligible for little more than opening basic checking and savings accounts. Off-Trend.

Down-Aging

Although banks haven't changed much since anyone's youth, most of the warm and cuddly, nostalgic elements are gone: the sincere first-name welcomes; the passbooks clutched proudly as balances rose; the Christmas Clubs; the hokey calendars; the sound, look, and feel of permanence and security. In fact, from having to deal with the tiniest of small-print brochures to the most unintelligible tellers behind a cage, the child-in-us quickly ages. Off-Trend.

FemaleThink/Mancipation

Bankers, whether female or male, tend to think like, well . . . bankers. Most procedures, products, and promotions are designed only with the bank's direct goals of profitability/cost-cutting in mind. Definitely risk-averse OldThink. This narrowness of vision is unfounded and ultimately a loser. Until bank boards and top management include FemaleThinkers and Mancipated Males, until the specific service needs of every consumer group (parents, schoolkids, oldsters, travelers, entrepreneurs, etc.) are addressed and met, consumers will continue to lose. Off-Trend.

S.O.S.(Save Our Society)

A few banks—both local and national—do play a significant role in their communities and encourage employees to contribute as well. Most small banks, on the other hand, rarely appear on nonprofit donor or sponsor lists. They don't often offer matching gift programs or provide low-interest loans for stabilization, renovation, capital equipment, or low-income housing.

With the merger frenzy going on, there's a valid question whether the larger consolidated banks will continue established social-friendly policies. What happens when one bank holding company, such as Chemical, which has a liberal loan policy in poorer communities, merges with another, such as Chase Manhattan, which is reported to have a stricter approach?

In the environmental area, banking requires tons and tons of paper (usually not recycled) for loan applications, deposits, and statements. Over 6 billion checks are written in this country each year. Banks don't encourage or reward customers or employees to be conscious, concerned citizens. Off-Trend.

Icon Toppling

Bankruptcies (even the queen of England's own investment bank, the venerable 233-year-old Barings PLC toppled); disastrous real estate loans; the savings and loan debacle; mergers that leave thousands unemployed; never-to-be-repaid loans to repressive foreign regimes instead of financing for local, job-creating enterprises; employee fraud—the negative list is very long and needs to include the newest excess: making excessive loans to large corporations. Does that sound like a description of an admirable societal icon or more like an industry teetering on the edge of toppling. Off-Trend.

We knew banks were in trouble, but until we ran through the ClickScreen, we didn't realize how completely off-Trend the whole industry is. Before we leave Bad-News Banking (although, the more off-Trend, the more opportunity for correction), why don't you practice ClickScreening on a true consumer banking story. Read the anecdote below and list the number of Trends being illustrated or violated.

A very successful businesswoman, social activist, and philanthropist in her mid-40s had taken her newly adopted Chinese baby girl to her country home for an extended vacation. She had two accounts with Bank C (chosen for its proximity to her city office), one with a balance of $70,000 in it, collecting next to no interest, and one with approximately $10,000 in it, collecting no interest.

Soon after settling in, the baby became feverish and was diagnosed with mild pneumonia. After the flurry of doctor visits and prescription-filling, our friend discovered that she had left her checkbook in NYC. It may seem strange to those who live in the total world of credit cards, but in the country here many small-town services are paid for by personal check, so she drove 30 minutes to the nearest branch of Bank C. There, her anxiety was treated to a major dose of bank bureaucracy: "I'm so sorry, but without your checkbook, our rules are quite clear and can't be circumvented under any circumstances. We can only offer you two (two!) checks at a charge of $6.50 each. However, since we don't have your signature card on file, there will be a limit to the amount of cash you can withdraw."

Needing far more, she opted to drive the five-hour round-trip to NYC to get her checkbook. Now, with revenge thoughts for Bank C, she has actively sought a banking alternative.

Example of:

_____

Violation of:

_____

If you said that her life and actions illustrated the Trends of 99 Lives, S.O.S., Down-Aging, Cocooning, Clanning, Vigilante Consumer, and Icon Toppling, you have been a careful reader. If you also cited 99 Lives, Cocooning, Egonomics, and Anchoring as Trends being violated, you have definitely Clicked into the Trends.

Click Corrections

What would it take to make commercial or retail banks responsive to current and future consumer needs?

Believe it or not, the prognosis for banks is not hopeless. Nor is the solution quick or simple. (It rarely is.) But in fact, every time you say or think, "I really wish my bank would . . . wouldn't . . . offered . . . etc.," you are citing/discovering opportunities for improvement and competitive advantages that need to be considered and evaluated Trend-by-Trend.

One solution would be to study what "perks" the banks are offering their upscale customers. . . and copy them or downscale them for the masses.

The money levels may be different for the two groups, but the needs are the same. We all want banks to follow the three "Fs": be Fast, Flexible, Friendly. The prototypical bank of the future that has the best chance to survive and thrive needs to inspire confidence and loyalty. The corrections to the Click-Screen will sketch out an on-Trend bank. As you'll see, it could be called a Virtual Bank or TechnoBank, but those labels don't capture the additional ingredients of user-friendliness, a response to human needs, "when I want, where I want, how I want" banking.

The On-Trend Bank

Cocooning

Make the bank "a refuge from the storm." Preferential treatment and personal service. A commercial for NatWest Bank is on the right track when it shows a mother with a newborn child and announces that a service representative will make a house call to open a savings account in the baby's name. An end to rigidity (rules can be broken or at least bent by empowered employees). Perks for patronage.

Without ever leaving the cozy cocoon, every person can have easy 24-hour access to all account information, make deposits, withdraw, exchange currency, buy and sell securities, pay bills, get a hard copy of all transactions, including balance/budget updates. All interaction could take place through common home utilities (telephone/television) rather than computer. Or we could get a dedicated instrument like France's MiniTel, a telephone-linked home computer-device, for anything from banking to airline reservations. In a novel experiment, the First Direct Bank in Leeds, England, is the first 24-hour telephone-only bank. It is also the fastest-growing bank in Britain—half a million customers, not one branch.

Banks themselves could become cozier and more comfortable. Easy chairs, couches, desks instead of standing tables, TVs to watch, magazine racks, shoeshine stands. If lines are long, you could take a number, as at a deli, and be able to sit until your number is called. Often mentioned as one of New York City's best banks, the Republic Bank for Savings has live piano music at many of its branches, plus lower fees than most. Click.

Clanning

Banks responsive to the Clanning Trend are on the way to addressing Egonomics as well. (We often see that Clicking on one Trend is a surefire method to related Trend solutions.) The on-Trend bank would reflect its environment, it would be *like* a neighborhood. It would be great to create a town-square feeling around the bank. Have political speeches on a soapbox, much like Hyde Park Corner in London.

A powerful step is to staff the bank with people who literally speak the same language as the customers and who are more or less in the same age group. Or invite in groups with similar needs: first-time home buyers, women small-business owners, recent retirees or bereavement groups, home renovators/buyers/sellers, prospective parents. Or form a New Enterprise Club for eager entrepreneurs. Obviously, this can be done on the Internet, too. By being the catalyst for Clanning, the bank becomes a member of the Clan. Click.

Fantasy Adventure

A visit to a bank could be great fun and/or lead to fun and learning. For example, the lounge or waiting area would have video monitors on which to "visit" proposed vacation destinations, even select among typical hotel rooms. The bank's travel agency will make all reservations and book your flight, change your money, sell you EuroChecks, have money waiting for you at your destination, provide the credit card to charge all purchases with adequate, preapproved credit (gaining more airline frequent flyer miles), and, of course, make the loan necessary to pay for it all. Art and photography shows, home renovation seminars or videos, visits to the vault for schoolchildren, primers on Stock Market Basics or How to Write a Business Plan—the list is limited only by space. Click.

Pleasure Revenge/Small Indulgences

For perfect Pleasure Revenge and Small Indulgences, there could be a free beverage and coffee bar with diverse brewed coffees, herbal and exotic teas, cookies or chocolates, and (dare we dream) little high-fat ice cream cones in summer.

Banks might borrow an incentive idea from the you-never-know-when-you'll-win school of motivation (exemplified by slot machines and lotteries) and randomly hand out $5 or $10 cash-redeemable vouchers to customers. Ditto small monetary awards to anyone who's had to wait more than ten minutes.

Or overcompensate for mistakes made in your account: a bonus, a lunch voucher.

Does anyone remember when you were given an electric can opener, a toaster oven, or a small television to open a nice-sized savings account? How about something like a better rate (plus a little gift) now to encourage savings? Why should we get 1.25% on money in the bank when, with a little effort, we can get 8–9–10% elsewhere?

Best of all, the on-Trend Bank could be an enabler of small-sized dreams: If high-interest rates have precluded a major renovation on your home, then an easy-to-get mini-loan for a whirlpool spa or well-stocked workbench may bring enough satisfaction. Click.

Anchoring

No Virginia, money doesn't buy happiness. But the stress of financial problems is antithetical to a feeling of security and spirituality. Even Abraham Maslow's hierarchy-of-needs model states that economic needs must be met before one can aspire to higher states of self-actualization. So what does this have to do with on-Trend banking? Simply this: To the extent that a bank treats you with respect and understands your individual situation and needs, the closer you'll be to a firm Anchor. Your bank could help you in budget planning. Could check up on your projected Social Security payments. Advise you on investment research, alert you to idle cash. Click.

99 Lives

Mobile bank vans could be the Good Humor trucks of tomorrow. A mobile bank van would pass by your home, office, plant, or shop to bring small bills and make change, deliver cash/accept deposits. Offer free penny sorting and rolling. What a help for a small-business owner alone in his or her store. Or for those who are homebound or physically challenged. This bank-on-the-move could also drop off free overnight "rentals" for a line of video or CD-ROM seminars that explain everything from budgeting to estate planning.

Banks could throw their weight behind the movement to abolish prices such as $199.99; abolish pennies and require that all purchases be rounded off to the nearest even number, as the Dutch do. (While we're on the subject of money, wouldn't it be nice to have $2.50 coins, the way so many other countries have, and $500 bills for large purchases? And if we request an even bigger monetary change, we'd like our currency to come in different colors, maybe even different sizes, so it would be easier to tell $1 from $20 from $100 bills. Not too much to ask.) Cash machines could also offer more options: rolls of change, singles, hundreds, or even certified checks.

Of course, all these availabilities will be moot if we actually become a "cashless society," a concept finally on its way. A dozen large banks are testing computer-chipped cash cards, "electronic purses," that allow you to load money into the cards at ATM machines or by special telephone. You can then use the card to shop, pay bills, make calls at corner phones, ride the subways, without the bother of ever handling real money. Small fees will be levied both on the consumer who uses the card and the merchant that accepts it. In England, a similar "stored value" card system, called Mondex, is already in use. Meanwhile, we're still getting used to the concept of debit cards, which come preloaded (and prepaid) with an exact amount to spend.

Wouldn't it be helpful if the computer-driven banks could become more interactive: by signaling our answering machines or computers if our balances are getting low. There could be one-stop financial shopping and continuity among different sectors of the bank: real estate, insurance, mutual funds, educational needs, trusts, travel. And to save travel-time and cut back on lunch-hour lines, every large building or office complex could have its own "mini-branch." And what about dual or triple tasks: have video-tape rental/drop-off; dry cleaning; supermarket. What about 24-hour banking for one or two days a week? Click.

FemaleThink

Setting an example, there's the Grameen Bank that was started in Bangladesh by a future-thinker, Yunus Muhammad.

The name means "village," and the institution has created a village of goodwill by making small loans, averaging only $65, that have given hundreds of thousands of women enough startup capital to begin their own businesses. It's a shareholders' bank, basically controlled by poor and rural women. Together they are building a nation of entrepreneurs. When we interviewed Susan Davis, Executive Director of the Women's Environment and Development Organization (WEDO), which does women's issues advocacy at the United Nations, she told us, "When you're denied the tools or means to create self-employment, you're denied a basic human right."

Grameen is smashing the OldThink banking idea that you can only borrow large sums based on collateral or leveraging. This model is being spread around the world, to Malaysia, and to the United States. It seems that women are good risks—the repayment rate for loans is a very high 98%. Click.

Cashing Out

Instead of showing all bankers as the most extreme of buttoned-up employees, London-esque in their three-piece suits, why shouldn't the new "relaxed" dress codes invade banks too? Wear clothes more in coordination with the customers. Corduroy jackets for the country, cowboy shirts and Tony Lama boots for the West. Click.

Egonomics

Imagine calling, being online with, or entering a bank where you always have an assigned individual who knows your name and your history. Chase Manhattan is trying a version of this, having a client specialist (human) on 24-hour-duty who promises to update your personal history whenever you call, fax, or computer-send any interaction. But take that one step further and imagine that, whenever necessary, your "private banker" (that's what the really rich have) would shepherd you to the right specialist to address your current concerns—and that person takes care of you at once.

For customization on a larger scale, you should be able to tailor your own loan. You still pay the fees, but only specific ones based on your record. Whenever you wish, you can view your year-to-date revenues and expenses (posted by category), from the budget developed with the help of your bank liaison.

Or for little me-isms, why couldn't checks be computer-designed—the paper, the graphics, typeface, color, everything? You could have numerous individualized accounts that you can designate by code. These are used only for record-keeping purposes, since all deposited moneys earn the top possible interest.

At the appropriate times, your designated tax consultant can help you file your returns. As you get older, the print size of anything written automatically increases. Signature cards and the archaic procedures are long gone, and you're recognized at any bank or ATM anywhere in the world by means of voice print, facial thermogram (no two people have the same amount of heat radiating from blood vessels in the face), or eye retina—in a wink. Click.

S.O.S. (Save Our Society)

To help Save Our Society, banks should give used computer systems to schools in low-income areas; office equipment to senior citizen centers, thrift shops, or small business charities. Make community service/involvement part of every employee's job. Sponsor "Banking Fairs" at schools. Offer fewer points on a mortgage or drop a percentage point whenever customers donate to charities using their bank credit cards.

Environmentally, have "green" accounts with "no paper" for the ecologically correct. Slogan: "Don't Cut Down Trees, Push Buttons." Print checks on recycled paper. Offer an Environmental Affinity card through which small donations go directly to the Nature Conservancy, Greenpeace, or the Cousteau Society. Click.

Case proven. Banks can do a lot of little things to regain their positive image and Click into the next century. It's mainly a matter of stemming the anger against banks and changing the customers' attitudes. No industry can keep insulting its clients forever—without a rebellion. We all feel as if we have an inalienable right of respect for the privilege of handing over our hard-earned money for growth and safekeeping. We want our Friendly Bank back. We want our on-Trend Bank of the Future.

But the bigger issue here is the example of applying the ClickScreen. If you try it on your business, your idea, your life, you can see where anything—from an entire monolith of an industry to the smallest of business sketches—could possibly head. Use it as a tool to help make present-planning smarter, more focused—and more future-directed. If you relate it to your problems and challenges, as we just did, you'll be pointed in a Trend-true direction that will instinctively feel right. And whatever you do, you'll Click.

CLICKTHINKS

Vision is the art of seeing things invisible.
—JONATHAN SWIFT

We must never be afraid to go too far, for the truth lies beyond.
—MARCEL PROUST

You don't have to sit alone in an ivory tower or imitate Rodin's *Thinker* (elbow to knee/fist to forehead) and ponder "How to Click" by yourself. Get the best minds you know to help solve your future . . . and theirs.

Go beyond the expected. Don't be shy about creating a brainstorming session with friends, family, co-workers, mere acquaintances. First step: Make up lists of the most diverse people you know (or want to know), call and ask for a few hours of their valuable time. There is no such thing as failure here; all can contribute, all can benefit. Even though you're technically the focus of the gathering, each person will walk away with a gulfstream of ideas. When you tap into stimulating brain molecules, everyone becomes instantly energized. What's surprising is that often the glibbest talker is not the major contributor. Many times, it's the shy stranger who turns into the most imaginative, intuitive, original participant.

The process is fascinating and strange, since brainpower doesn't intensify by any known mathematical equation. Ten thinkers concentrating on one subject can race (much as the velociraptors in

Jurassic Park) to a better, sharper, more intense conclusion in one hour than one thinker in one hundred hours. Answers get even more interesting and more varied if the people-mix is mixed up enough.

The secret of success is having an impartial leader who stands (*not sits*) and jots down *all* the mumbo-jumbo (a brilliant idea may be buried for later retrieval). This moderator stays calm and reminds the group to headline answers, to stop telling rambling tales, to filter out any negativity, to push and probe in the quest to find the kernel of the solution.

Here are models that you can follow from a few ClickThinks that we conducted at BrainReserve. Then sit down and devise your own.

Moderator's Guide

ClickThink I: The Future

EXERCISE #1

Suppose that Sony has just introduced a new product called a "FutureCam 6," which allows users to look at the world in the year 2010 and take a picture of anything there:

- What scene or place would you take a picture of?
- Who would be in it?

Take a picture of the first "page" of the national newspaper (or whatever has replaced it) on New Year's Day, 2010.

- What are the five biggest headlines?

EXERCISE #2

Close your eyes, breathe deeply, and relax. Imagine that you are walking down a long, quiet hallway. On your left is a door marked "My Office, 2010." Now open the door and walk inside. Describe everything about the place you are in.

- Tell about the sights and sounds, the smells, if you like.
- What does the furniture or equipment look like, what is it used for?
- Are any other people there?

Now walk out of this room, and go farther down the hall. On your right is a door marked "Home, 2010." Walk inside and describe everything you see.

EXERCISE #3

Think back to when you were 20 years old.

- What was your fondest dream for the future?
- What is your fondest dream now for the year 2010?

EXERCISE #4

- How will you describe yourself in the year 2010?
- How will you describe your friends?
- How will you describe your enemies?
- What will be your greatest success?
- What will be your greatest failure?

EXERCISE #5

Think of your different "personas" and describe each briefly.

- Who are you today (include personal description)?
- Who are you on the telephone?
- Who are you/would you be on a videoconferencing call?
- Who are you/would you be on a computer bulletin board?
- Who are you/would you be on a Virtual Reality screen?

ClickThink II: Parenting

EXERCISE #1

Many societal "phenomena" will change the way parents think about and deal with their children over the next decade. What are these phenomena (cues)?

- Post-Boomer Baby Boomlet and their own Baby Bust: Trophy Babies, MOBYs (Mommy Older/Baby Younger), DOBYs (Daddy Older/Baby Younger), Increased Multicultural Adoptions.
- Crime.
- Drugs.
- Ongoing Recession.
- Eco-Problems.
- Dual-Income Families.

EXERCISE #2

Every generation has hot-buttons that cause an explosion between parents and kids. What are today's?

- Staying out late.
- Wild friends.
- Excess television watching.
- Grunge clothing/rap music.
- Computer games.
- Swearing.
- Cars.
- Smoking/drinking/drugs.
- Sex.
- Violence.

EXERCISE #3

- What will the "families" of Generation X look like?
- What will be the most important changes in parenting issues in the year 2010? Relate them to the Clicking Trends. Example:

  - Mid-'90s: Is your playground safe?
  - 2010 (Same question, use Trends to come up with possible solutions).
    - **Cocooning:** "Enclosed Playgrounds: Safe from Crime?"
    - **S.O.S.:** "Building a Home Playground from Recycled Soil."
    - **Being Alive:** "Protecting Playgrounds from Electromagnetic Currents."
    - **Down-Aging:** "Relearning Outdoor Play with Your Youngster."

EXERCISE #4

Identifications: What's the first single image (we call this a "badge") that comes to your mind when you hear the following names?

- McDonald's Happy Meals.
- Jell-O.
- Gap Kids.
- Fisher-Price Toys.

- Levi 501s.
- Nike.
- Marlboro.
- Mustang.
- Huggies.

EXERCISE #5

How can a family today become a "badge"? Describe what it would look like.

EXERCISE #6

What can one person (or a couple) do to make that image/ "badge" happen? Suggestions:

- Mentor the underprivileged.
- Take kids to workplace.
- Do homework together.
- Contribute to children's aid societies.
- Volunteer family time at shelters.

EXERCISE #7

What are the advantages and disadvantages of parenting? Think of ways to enhance the advantages, and lessen the disadvantages.

ClickThink III: Getting on Computer

OPENING EXERCISE #1

1. Take a moment to think about what life was like in the 1960s (or the '50s or '70s), and then give me words and phrases to describe "Women" and "Men" at that time (list separately).
2. Now do the same thing, but for "Women" and "Men" in the late '90s.
3. You are a computer whose name is Melanie or Max. Describe yourself.
4. The term is "Scary Technology." What would be the description (i.e., what frightens you about technology, what bad things could happen)?
5. You are making an extensive list of considerations before

you even begin shopping for your computer. What's on the list? (Cues: where/why/how/what.)

6. What services/products come to mind when I say the words:
   • Empowerment.
   • Control.
   • Luxury.
   • Freedom.
   • Safety.
   • Pleasure.

7. You are the owner/founder of a small "kitchen table" business, and you are writing a letter to be broadcast to your client list. What is your communiqué headlined?

8. You are:
   • A college student majoring in fine arts.
   • A sole proprietor dealing in marketing to consumer goods companies.
   • A small business owner dealing in landscaping services.
   How do you use your computer in ways that distinguish you from all other users?

9. Finish the sentence: "Going online is like . . . "

10. Immediate top of mind: As a consumer, what words come to mind when you hear:
    • LAN (local area network).
    • Integrated solutions.
    • Channels.
    • Mobile.

TREND EXERCISES #2

1. We're now going to play the old word game of Mix and Match. In this exercise, please be as wild and creative as you can possibly be. Consider the areas that are represented here, match them with three of the Trends and finish the sentence: "My computer is in tune with [Trend] because . . . " (Example: "The PowerBook is in tune with Fantasy Adventure/Wildering because it's portable enough to let me work in my tent, on my boat, or in my log cabin.") Trends:
   • Cocooning.
   • Fantasy Adventure/Wildering.

- Cashing Out.
- Egonomics.
- Small Indulgences.
- 99 Lives.
- Down-Aging.
- Clanning.

2. Hi-Tech Shopping and the Trends: What do the following Trends suggest about a good/bad shopping experience:
   - Cocooning.
   - Egonomics.
   - 99 Lives.
   - FemaleThink.
   - Small Indulgences.
   - Cashing Out.
   - Fantasy Adventure.

3. Service and the Trends: What do the following Trends suggest about good service/bad service:
   - Cocooning.
   - Egonomics.
   - 99 Lives.
   - Cashing Out.
   - FemaleThink.

4. In what ways can any of the technology and/or specific brands mentioned today help users Click into a new realm, a new plateau of business? Why? (Example: Desktop Video. A busy executive can join a conference on his or her notebook computer while sitting in an airport [99 Lives] or while at home [Cocooning]. The same service could let other members of the family tune in to a live broadcast or rock event [Clanning, Egonomics, Down-Aging].)

ClickThink IV: Opening a New Fast-Food Chicken Hut

WARM-UP
EXERCISE #1

- What was your favorite main-meal food when you were a child? Why did you love it?
- What was your least favorite main-meal food? Why did you hate it?

EXERCISE #2

Think of a food preparation that you have completed from start to finish within the last week, in all of its details (or your favorite recipe that you have brought). What was pleasant/un-pleasant about it?

EXERCISE #3

- Name your favorite texture in food: what does it remind you of?
- Name your favorite smell of food: what does it remind you of?

EXERCISE #4

List your favorite food for each time of the day: breakfast, lunch, snack, dinner. What characteristics make that food right for that part of the day?

EXERCISE #5

A famous tagline for a food product was "Shake and Bake." Think of other things that you might do to food in the preparation process, and come up with new taglines.

EXERCISE #6

Make a list of favorite flavor combinations.

TO HELP THINK OF NEW WAYS OF PREPARING CHICKEN
EXERCISE #7

You are the Minister of Meals on Calumer, a distant planet whose people share all of the best characteristics of what we imagine for Mid-Westerners on Earth: basic values, hardworking, family-oriented. An interesting fact about Calumer is that its inhabitants have, for as long as they can remember, eaten only one food: the Calumerian wog. They have eaten it at all ten meals of the day, all nine days of the week. Within the last decade, a terrible ecological disaster has befallen Calumer, and the wog population has died off. You have been sent to Earth to find a wog substitute, and your official contact, Julia Child, has suggested chicken. She presents you with a freshly plucked specimen. Your first reaction is amazement. You've never seen anything quite like it. What do you think of next?

EXERCISE #8

You look at the chicken. Describe it in the most flattering terms possible.

EXERCISE #9

If you could reinvent that chicken, what would you do (i.e., change its shape, color, texture, even rename it)?

EXERCISE #10

Think of foods that you have served with chicken. Now incorporate them so that they are included in the actual recipe.

EXERCISE #11

Use the flavor combinations from Exercise #6 to create new chicken preparations (cues: dips, sauces, coatings, stuffings).

EXERCISE #12

ClickTrend Exercise: Hand out lists of the Trends. Describe a chicken recipe or meal that goes with at least four of the Trends.

ClickThinks will help you fine-tune your dreams and redefine your desires. These questions can be used as a starting point or as a constant checklist along the way. Think of them as a tool to get you un-blocked, un-locked, un-frozen, and un-shut down. The real beauty of brainstorming is that ideas literally *storm* your brain.

We like to remind you that although it's possible to live without air for seconds, without water for days, without food for weeks, it's *not* possible to Click without a constant flow of ideas. And that fresh supply of creative energy, if we do say so, is the fastest, most direct way to bring on the *winds of change.*

CLICKTIME

We must use time as a tool, not as a couch.
—JOHN F. KENNEDY

And thus the whirligig of time brings in his revenges.
—WILLIAM SHAKESPEARE

ClickTime can be tricky. It's often not When You Click, but How You Click. There's a lesson in the lyrics of the clever Gershwin song, about how everyone laughed *"at Christopher Columbus, when he said the world was round . . . when Edison recorded sound . . . at Wilbur and his brother, when they said that man could fly. But ho, ho, ho, who's got the last laugh now."* It's not enough to act upon an idea that came to you in a "flash"—that might turn out to be just a "flash in a pan." You need to brainstorm your idea and look at it from every angle, every permutation, every Trend—to circumvent disaster. Think for a moment of all the monumental ideas, the important people, the ingenious products that have tripped into the abyss of Clicking Before Their Time . . . and have fallen flat on their proverbial faces.

Nimble-fingered inventor Johannes Gutenberg of Bible fame may spring to a few obscure-memoried minds. Remember, he was the one who discovered that by working with movable type (c. 1455), it was possible to print in one day what it took scribes a year to pen by hand. Problem was, Gutenberg may have been the first, but the timing was all wrong. Invention came way before need. The market simply wasn't ready (and he didn't do *any* market research). Medieval villages didn't have bookstores on their Main Streets and there was no Book-of-the-Month Club. Poor Herr Gutenberg went belly-up, bankrupt, kaput. Even a full fifteen years later, another printer lamented that he couldn't sell all the volumes that he was printing. About his stacks of overstock: "We're drowning in books."

Other notable lapses in time: The wheel was invented in 3480 B.C., but it took a man named Kirkpatrick MacMillan until 1839 to put one and one together and come up with the two-wheeled bicycle. In the 10th century, the Chinese cleverly concocted gunpowder (for fireworks), but it wasn't until the 14th century that man (supposedly a monk) figured out that gunpowder could fire a . . . gun.

Moral of this story: The earliest bird doesn't always get to keep the worm. Maybe you need to figure out a bigger, better, stronger, more calculating way to hold on to the prize morsel. Sir Freddie Laker was on-target, but off-timing with his defunct no-frills concept for an airline. Nowadays, everyone has copied his Skytrain principles, cutting down on hot meals (tossing you a cold ham sandwich and a bag of chips) or even cutting out *all* food on many flights. Now after thirteen years, Freddie's back with new plans to tackle the transatlantic skies.

He-men Charles Atlas and Vic Tanny were handsome hunks and good examples of early-on fitness gurus, but were too many years ahead of the sweeping phenomenon of Fitness Retailing. Compare their mini-world to Jane Fonda's or even Richard Simmons's with their library of videos, lines of workout clothes, step accessories, tapes. In the fashion arena, designer Rudi Gernreich shocked the world with his blatantly sexy bathing suits, but today the few-strings-attached suits would barely lift an eyebrow.

We can think of other things that started with a Big Idea, but stopped short of getting the Big Prize. For instance, the first plastic credit card that one could use to charge a multitude of indulgences, the Diner's Club (1950), lost out to the sheer scope of AMEX's green card; then even more so when Visa and Master-Card added their punch of starting tie-ins with airline mileage programs. Remember when Howard Johnson's orange-roofed "fast-food" chains with fried clam rolls and multiflavored ice creams were on every highway and byway? They've practically disappeared, replaced first by those Golden Arches, and then, you name it, everything from Taco Bell to Ben & Jerry's.

A classic cat-eats-mouse case was Coca-Cola and Royal Crown Cola. R.C. Cola was the first to come out with such innovations and consumer winners as aluminum cans and diet colas, only to watch them be swallowed up by the hungry giant, Coke. Now Coca-Cola is trying doing it again, copycatting the offbeat success of Snapple—with Fruitopia. Only Snapple is still holding on with its strong image and name.

People and their beliefs, as well as products, provide good examples of bad timing. One friend of ours, Carol Peters, the computer genius of daVinci's Time & Space, told us a sad tale about her grandfather. He was the respected dean of Yale Medical School, but also an outspoken advocate of socialized medicine. Senator Joe McCarthy, that unscrupulous ferret of suspected (nonproven) political disloyalty, went after him in his "witchhunts" and labeled him a "Communist." In the early '50s, this sort of accusation was tantamount to a guilty verdict. Nixon was the lawyer against him in the congressional hearings. Although her grandfather was eventually acquitted, he had already suffered the humiliation of being terminated from Yale and died shortly afterward, at age 50+, of a heart attack. Think of the tragic irony. Various programs on the government agenda today are close to his version of socialized medicine. The right of health care for all American citizens wouldn't raise an eyebrow now.

Nathan Pritikin was a perfect example of an early Clicker, a lone voice crying out in the health wilderness. Again, we go back to the 1950s, when the phrase "going on a diet" meant starving yourself and giving up breads and pastas (still called spaghetti then). Pritikin, although an inventor, was most brilliant about reducing complex ideas to simple concepts.

While reading volumes of WWII mortality data with his special military clearance, he made the astounding but basic correlation between heart disease and eating. Although genetics coupled with stress were thought to be the common denominator in heart-induced mortality rates, Pritikin noticed that these deaths actually declined an incredible 50% in England during the war (undeniably quite a stressful time).

Pritikin concluded that the element of change was the dietary shift due to food rationing. When the bombs were flying and the farmers were off in the trenches, the English population simply couldn't obtain their regular hearty portions of rich Devonshire cream, sweet country butter, strong cheddar cheese, thick slabs of prime ribs, and buttery Yorkshire pudding. All over war-torn Britain, many dinner tables were sparsely laden with undressed spuds and Brussels sprouts. Pritikin had more than a browser's interest in these mortality figures: at age 42, he had been diagnosed with a predisposition to heart disease and a too-high cholesterol count of 300 (although at the time, no one knew the correlation between heart problems and high cholesterol).

Thus, Nathan Pritikin started a campaign for a return to mankind's original diet: grains, vegetables, fruits. Low-fat, little meat. He followed his own advice, and his cholesterol fell to 110. Still, he was preaching to hostile ears. In the early '50s and '60s, this low-fat notion was considered beyond eccentric—it was considered downright crazy.

Both the government and educational facilities endorsed the marketing concept of Four Basic Food Groups (replaced only last year), feeding the military and schoolchildren unbelievably high-fat and high-protein meals. Early Weight Watchers diets allowed chicken livers sautéed in butter and thick cheese sauces. Another popular regime: the early Dr. Atkins's Diet sounded as if it were based on scientific fact, but it advocated well-marbled steak and one of the highest cholesterol foods, caviar, in its textbook, *Diet Revolution*. Most artery-clogging of all was the *Carbohydrate Gram Counter Diet*. "Enjoy Mayonnaise, Martinis, Bacon and Butter— And lose 10–15 lbs. a month!" declared the copy. "Like your Pork Chops and Chicken Fried? Forget about Calories. These and dozens of other usually 'forbidden' foods are yours."

Robert Pritikin (Nathan's son) was his father's first convert. While the rest of the immediate family stubbornly stuck to a richer diet, Robert, at age 5, began eating the same chewy and healthy foods as his dad. He grew to understand his father's belief that "we are dying of excesses, not deficiencies." Nathan started lecturing about health in the late 1960s, published his famous book, *The Pritikin Program for Diet & Exercise,* and in 1976, together with Robert, started the Longevity Center to train people on how to succeed on a low-fat diet in a high-fat world.

At the Center, people get an education about the pitfalls of dieting/dining. Since "finding food" is no longer a matter of survival, but a social activity, there are some basic rules. "The sedentary crave fats." "Healthy-sounding salads, if they come pre-dressed, are worse than a cheeseburger." "People who change their diet without exercising are more likely to fail." The Longevity Center is perfectly named: People who go there want to *live longer*. The Lourdes-like aspect of Pritikin comes from the amazing ability of one's body to respond quickly to a healthy diet. Hypertensives and heart patients may find themselves tossing out some of their drugs; adult diabetics may be able to forgo their insulin. Yet no one is expected to live like a saint. Robert Pritikin wisely knows that all of us have at least one favorite food we can't resist (well-done French fries, in my case). Emphasis is put on major areas of success, not occasional slips into bad behavior.

Our only question is, why aren't there state-of-the-art Pritikin Centers strategically located around the country? When the concept was born, it may have been too early, but it could Click now.

When I started my company, BrainReserve, I, too, had pushed the clock forward (as a futurist, that somehow seemed right). As I said, few businesses had any interest in Trend-predicting . . . until some of the predictions came true. While the small staff and I waited for today to turn into tomorrow, we used the time to refine our methodology, to expand our Trends, and predict, predict, predict what we envisioned for future consumers: what they would live like, what they would want, and what they would buy.

One of our 1980 predictions reported by I. Barmash in *The New York Times* turned out to be more than fourteen years too soon. We had said, "Watch for the little car laden with . . . razzmatazz, but good on mileage." However, ten years later, we still believed in the basic idea of a mini-car. In *The Popcorn Report*, we elaborated on it, exploring the car's Trend-worthiness in a marketing workshop called an "Extremism Exercise," in which every concept gets pushed "to the extreme" and then worked back to an acceptable place:

> . . . suppose you're an American car maker and the numbers are down. The extreme: nobody will buy your model anymore. Again, let the Trends guide you back. One option is to create a

Fantasy Adventure car that's a Small Indulgence, for people who have Cashed Out and don't need to travel too far. A friend of mine in the Japanese car business and I once invented a car which we whimsically called the PopSui, to be sold/serviced at supermarkets. The body of the car would snap together and have interchangeable seats—with unlimited color selection, even Dalmatian spots or zebra stripes (Small Indulgences, Down-Aging). The basic mix-and-match parts would always be in stock. The PopSui (Fantasy Adventure) would be wonderful on gas (S.O.S.), would be simple to repair (99 Lives), and would cost exactly $3,000 or 2 for $5,000.

Finally in March 1994, our dream car materialized in proto-type: the Swatchmobile, a co-venture from Mercedes-Benz and the Swiss watchmaker, ready for production in 1997. This egg-shaped micro-car will be inexpensive, fun, and smart. Over 45,000 orders have been preplaced for this two-seater vehicle that will zip around for 300 miles on one tank of fuel. But our question, wouldn't it be great if it came in the full spectrum of Swatch watch patterns? Have a "Keith Haring" car, a silvery "astronaut" car, an "underwater" neon-colored car?

Years ago, during the course of our BrainReserve project assignments, we used to get cranky when a client inevitably said, "We tried something like that a few years back, and it didn't work." To counter those words, we opened each presentation with a list of caveats. First qualifier was a small talk about timing. We started out by stating, "BrainReserve wishes to note and acknowl-edge that some of the new product directions come from ideas . . . *thought* of or *tried* before, but the *timing wasn't right.*" Just because an idea didn't fly before, we said, that doesn't mean it isn't viable today.

In reviewing a "new cracker" assignment that we worked on about ten years ago, we were astonished to find out that the focus groups nixed anything that mentioned "pesto" or "sesame," saying that they were "not familiar enough" and just "too esoteric." For that same assignment, we had also come up with the novel idea for a "mustard-flavored pretzel," which Eagle Snacks eventually developed and is so popular now. Another swell idea we had for a product that's doing well in sales today was the Mini-Croissant Cracker. Rereading our work from a decade ago, we noted that a few focus group participants raised the issue about the analog of the "distinct fresh bakery image of a croissant with the perceived inability of a cracker to deliver same." So much for that. Now isn't it about time for someone to rethink our idea of Cornbread Crackers—ones that look like miniature corn-on-the-cob and come in plain, buttered, or jalapeño pepper flavors?

Another new food product assignment from that same era proved just as alternately exhilarating and frustrating. We had so many bright ideas, for instance that "ketchup is one product that, except for packaging, hasn't changed over the years," and, hint, hint, wasn't it time to tinker with the rather dull sameness of this household staple? A few of our suggestions for adding some excitement: Ketchup with Sun-dried Tomatoes; Ketchup with Mushroom Slices; Extra-Chunky Ketchup; Ketchup with Jalapeño Peppers; Spicy Ketchup. These are mainstream ideas now, but fifteen years ago, they were considered "heresy." We also had conjured up Bagel Chips (now a staple); Breakfast Burritos (a 7-Eleven favorite); Crisp Chips, all-natural, crunchy vegetable chips (like Terra Chips today); pastas in an array of flavors/colors (tomato, beet, spinach, buckwheat); ten-calorie meringue drop cookies (much like Sweet Dreams today). Now what about tomato lollipops for healthy snacking? Or fresh-dated cereals in bags? Or the refreshing combination of fruit juice/yogurt drinks? And we still cherish the notion of soups with piggyback cans (similar to the Chun King line of Chinese dinners) holding crispy, crunchy toppings: croutons, wonton noodles; potato sticks, seafood crackers, corn chips, and last but not least popcorn. And we're still wanting and still waiting for someone to get these terrific products out on the shelves.

As Andy Warhol put it, "I'm always interested in the right things at the wrong time." Having a future vision about a product, a service, a company that was not only earlier but also very different from anyone else has taught us a valuable lesson. Some people lean on that old cliché, "Better late than never." You could draw a false conclusion from that, conversely thinking, "Better never than too early." But we think that the advice to follow should be, "Better early and wait than never at all." It's almost impossible to get the timing perfect. Don't even expect it. Just keep fine-tuning . . . until you can turn your idea into a coherent, credible, Clickable whole.

CAREERS AND CLICKING

Success is that old ABC—ability, breaks and courage.
—C. Luckman

Flashback: Ask any group of 6-year-old kids what they want to be when they grow up and they don't miss a beat. "An astronaut." "A doctor." "A fireman." "A cowboy."

Now flash-forward to the future. Let's see how these career choices would have turned out:

- The astronaut-wannabe's career didn't go into orbit, because NASA and the space program has been so down-sized. He's working as a ticket-taker at Disney's Space Mountain.
- The doctor is still paying off her $60,000 in student loans. She can't afford to go into private practice because of the high costs—setting up an office, buying the diagnostic equipment, paying for insurance. So she's taken an HMO job at a salary of $65,000 (making less than her father who never graduated college). As for her dream of being a caring, sensitive physician, she's encouraged to see as many

patients as she can in as little time as possible. In fact, she's actually penalized if those patients re-book often.

- The fireman is about to be laid off because the city where he works has gone through a financial crunch and privatized the fire department. His new employer is hiring new recruits for less than half the salary he's making. With a young child from a second marriage, and only a small pension, he's going to have to Click into the next act of his life pretty quickly. Otherwise, he's going to have a real emergency on his hands.

- The cowboy is doing just fine, thank you. He settled in Montana, worked on a ranch, saved his paychecks, and plunked down $100 an acre for land as far as he could see. Lately, land values in Montana have been skyrocketing— driven up by West Coast refugees fleeing smog, fire, floods, earthquakes, and a general toxic lifestyle. Now the land is worth $2,500 an acre, and our cowboy is galloping on "don't-fence-me-in" land worth 5 million bucks. Falling in love with cowboy movies as a kid certainly paid off.

The message is pretty clear. And pretty scary. Today, traditional career planning is just about useless. It's not just because we are in an era of rapid change. It's because the old structures and the old rules are being torn down right before our eyes.

We all know about the impact of technology. We all read about the tens of thousands of workers who have been laid off by Fortune 500 corporations (remember Icon Toppling). But part of us still believes that it's only temporary—that traditional American business will, like Rocky, stagger to its feet and triumph again. But unfortunately, life is not a movie.

Jeremy Rifkin, in his frightening book *The End of Work,* writes that "in the years ahead more than 90 million jobs in a labor force of 124 million are potentially vulnerable to replacement by machines." Remember those vintage 1950s fears that automation would take away your job? It may have taken forty years or so to happen, but the robots are on the march.

Harvard economist James Medoff depresses us even further with the gloomy information that there are 50% fewer jobs for unemployed people at every level than there were in 1985. Which means the chances of an unemployed worker re-entering the workforce in some traditional way aren't exactly rosy. A group called Exec-U-Net, out of Norwalk, Connecticut, has perfected a way of being prepared. Although the majority of its members who earn more than $100,000 a year fear they will get axed within the year, these networkers publish plentiful listings of job opportunities, compiled from companies and search firms.

What's driving the rampant job loss isn't necessarily that all industries are doing badly. The impetus can be blamed on corporate America's favorite buzzword: re-engineering. Re-engineering, the polite way of saying that because of efficiency through technology, companies can do more with less—and the less is spelled, Y-O-U A-R-E F-I-R-E-D. Union Carbide re-engineered its Danbury, Connecticut facility (its administration, production, and distribution operations) and cut 13,900 workers in the process—more than 20% of its payroll. And the plans are to cut another 25% by the end of the re-engineering phase. The projected savings: $575 million by this year. Nothing to sneeze at.

That's not an isolated example. It's being repeated across the country, in the Sun Belt, the Rust Belt—and with the pare-down-Big-Government leadership change in Washington, the Beltway. After all, who can argue with the ring of re-engineering: Be more productive. Cut the fat. Get lean and mean. Loss down, profits up. What CEO or Wall Street trader wouldn't love it?

But for the millions of Americans whose lives will be disrupted, careers truncated, security cracked apart, re-engineering is a devastating refrain. Troubling times lie ahead. The need to Click will be more urgent than ever before in their lives.

Can you re-engineer your own Click, even though you're a victim of forces beyond your control? You bet. Being fired can create a fire within, and you can actually Click into a job that's more meaningful and, yes, even more lucrative than the one you had.

Although we've called this chapter "Careers and Clicking," the reality is that the old-fashioned notion of a career doesn't exist anymore. In fact, the word "career" is as outdated as the word "typewriter." Remember the traditional path to success? Go to college. Get a job. Get promoted. Retire. That patterned sequence is part of the historical scrap-heap. We're in post-post-Industrial America. The truths self-evident are Re-Careering and Multi-Careering.

Your career path can no longer be looked at as a straight line;

instead it's a connect-the-dots puzzle. Even if you are one of the rare birds who stays in the same job, you can't expect to head in one direction. Even the interior world of the larger companies is changing. Instead of going either "up" or "out," workers are beginning to shift laterally from one department to another. Corporations have started to encourage that kind of sideways mobility. Stopping the Peter Principle in its tracks. Say, if an outstanding action-person was moved up to become a desk-bound executive—but moving paper wasn't his thing, wouldn't it be smart for him to cross the ranks and become the head of the construction crew, donning a hard hat and overalls?

This should be the model for the enlightened corporation—not to keep people on narrow tracks or in tiny boxes.

Even if you work for a large corporation, you can adopt a fight-back attitude, instead of just accepting the inevitability of being locked into a professional prison. Often, your first job at a large company was the luck of the draw. The first opening. At a magazine, it could have meant sales, not editorial. In insurance, claims, not sales. At a manufacturing plant, production, not personnel. So, look within. Are you stuck in a division that represents the past and is likely to be sold off . . . or dramatically downsized? Why wait for the pink slip to flutter across your desk?

Become your own In-placement Consultant. First, identify the most on-Trend activity that your company is involved in—that's where your future will be. Find out everything about the job that interests you most. Use your connections inside the company to gather the information. Present yourself as a candidate to Human Resources—or go directly to the division's management. Tell them you'd even be willing to take a pay cut for the opportunity.

Of course, re-inventing your career within your current organization is only one option. Luckily in America, there are multitudes of opportunities to finding a Click. We've established four categories of Career Clicks—the Conscious Click, the Unconscious Click, the Heart Click, and the Accidental Click. All effective, all valuable, and all possible.

The Conscious Click is what happens when you make a business decision or a career decision from a truly analytical perspective. You look into your own skills and your needs—personal, professional, financial. You study the BrainReserve Trends to see which industries and fields represent the best future. If you're running a small business, you analyze it and see where you can expand it via the Trends. And then you act.

The Unconscious Click is what happens when you're processing many possibilities, but on an unconscious level. Then, when the right idea hits, although it may seem sudden, in reality you've been working on it all along. We can't tell you how many people have used phrases with us like "a bolt from the blue," "it struck like lightning," and "the idea came from nowhere."

The Heart Click happens when you make a decision straight from your heart's desire. It's your passion, what you were really meant to do. Maybe you went off to business school or accepted a formal-type job because you were programmed to by your family, but you really wanted to write. Or sing. Or run a country inn.

The Accidental Click is what happens when one of life's twists and turns changes the ground rules of your life. Accidents, illnesses, sudden windfalls.

The Conscious Click: Finding the Future in the Present

The future doesn't arrive unexpectedly one day. It doesn't come unannounced, like a singing telegram. What-will-be-will-be enters our world slowly and gradually, calling attention to itself with dozens of flashing blips on our radar screen. We just have to be alert for them and know how to interpret what we see. That's the very essence of learning to identify and create opportunities that spring from the Trends.

Men and women have Clicked into careers of both monumental and modest proportions by learning to keep their eyes trained on Trends. Take the now-legendary Scott Cook. He and his wife couldn't find a money management software program that met their needs. Everything available was woefully inadequate—complex, confusing, and frustrating. At the same time, he saw the explosion in ownership of PCs, as well as the explosion of home businesses. The opportunity became evident. It wasn't marginal. It was huge.

And so was the result. Cook developed Quicken in 1982—simple, inexpensive personal financial software. It took the market by storm by seeing a need and Clicking into it. More than

8 million customers have bought into Intuit's Quicken, which now plans to make headway in the home banking field.

But don't assume that even with the most beautifully thought-out Click in the world, success will come without obstacles. Everyone has his/her share of struggles. Guts and gumption are critical ingredients for enacting the Conscious Click.

We also like the story of Make-Up Cosmetics Limited, the company that produces MAC. MAC was founded by makeup artist Frank Toskan. He began making his own cosmetics ten years ago because he wasn't happy with the colors he had to choose from on the market. Believing that earth tones were lacking and pinks were too prominent, he asked his brother-in-law, then a chemistry student, to help. Together, they whipped up some new pigments in his kitchen.

Today, MAC has Clicked big-time—it's one of the hottest companies in the cosmetics business. It expects sales to exceed $100 million in 1995, and Estée Lauder has recently announced that it will distribute MAC products overseas—the first time the cosmetics giant has ever distributed someone else's products.

And don't think for a moment that Conscious Clicking into a new career is only a younger person's game. The AARP (American Association of Retired Persons) estimates that 20% of its members "have serious plans to start businesses or at least work for themselves." My relatives Vikki and Gary Gralla envisioned their retirement as "going down a corridor with many doors to try. It's important to create a dreamlist of everything you plan to do. By retiring *to* something, you get to execute your dreamlist."

For instance, when the very wise Augusta Weber left the outskirts of New York City for a place in Sag Harbor, she was planning that this would be her retirement haven. A psychotherapist by profession, she decided that instead of stopping work "cold turkey," it might be smarter to hang up her shingle and see several patients, for a few hours or maybe one day a week. This rapidly grew to two full days, four days, six days. Augusta (whose name comes from Latin, meaning "imposing") took on associates, conducts groups, has a full-sized setup, the Harborview Counseling Center. Not content with that, she started an advanced program for therapy professionals (complete with brochures, advertising, and all), the Augusta Weber Institute—because there was a drastic need for one in this area. Now, fourteen years into her "retirement," Augusta (who handles some tough, "stuck" cases) is finally trying to figure out a way to take off two consecutive days each week.

Using the Trends

One way to see what emerging needs are not being answered is to use the Trends as your ladder. The results can be astonishing. Here's an example of what we mean. In the field of travel, if you combine Cocooning, Egonomics, and 99 Lives, you could come up with a *travel agent who travels to your house.* A new category of vacation planner who comes to your living room at your convenience and brings brochures, videos, information on the best means of transportation and hotels. Everything you'll need to plan a vacation. Think what an improvement this is over the usual haphazard way of planning a trip. Normally you need to call back and forth, do hasty research, and often face disappointment when you get to your destination.

We don't know if anyone is pioneering this concept, but with so many travel agents across America, it seems like a perfect way to Click into better service to your customers. Now that travel agents are facing a policy of reduced fees by many airlines as well as the threat of online delivery replacing the core function of a travel agency, this beleaguered group had better get innovative.

As we scan the careers of the future and approach the information superhighway, what we hear is a giant Clicking sound. Techno-America is creating enormous opportunities. There are openings for developing "content" for the vast reaches of cyberspace. For becoming an Internet guide to help struggling "Tech-Nots" get on board.

Another huge opportunity comes from the chance to sell products on the Internet. Bypassing traditional distribution methods, millions have the opportunity to Click with less investment than ever before. Other sources of career guidance are the online services themselves. America Online has a career center that gives you access to a counselor online, as well as the ability to search out data on potential employers. It's also a smart place to list your skills in the talent database.

Ever since we wrote *The Popcorn Report,* one of the questions that we are asked the most has to do with franchise opportunities. Everyone wants to get the jump on the next McDonald's. It's clear that with the explosion in home offices and telecommuting, businesses like Kinko's and Alphagraphics are in the right place at the right time. They are truly the Executive Sweet—offering just about everything a business requires. An interesting franchise opportunity called HQ Business Centers goes one step further, offering conveniently located, fully staffed office centers on a permanent or part-time basis. Whoever offers the best videoconferencing facilities will be a place to watch. Over 40% of the large corporations are already using videoconferencing, cutting back on travel by interviewing job applicants, holding focus groups, and conducting meetings with it. Think of how this will help smaller companies with tighter budgets.

But why not go one step further, and open a business with an original idea that may be the base of a brand-new franchising opportunity? Remember, today's household-name franchises started off as a local-something-or-other. Again, let the Trends be your North Star. Here are some startup opportunities we've brainstormed:

- You know there is an explosion of play centers across the country, places like the Discovery Zone and Gymboree. These safe, Cocoon-like environments appeal to parents as neighborhoods grow more dangerous. How about adding Fantasy Adventure to the play center concept and opening one with a theme—such as the Wild West or space travel. Or even Peter Pan or Alice in Wonderland. (We are guessing that Peter P. and Alice W. are in the public domain, so you wouldn't have to buy the rights.)

     Or take the Click one step further. Why not open entertainment centers for senior citizens? You could provide seniors with Virtual Reality rooms where they could meet their favorite old-time screen or TV stars. There could be media rooms, large-screening the great classics. An exercise space, with low-impact swings and trampolines and climbing paths. (In Down-Aging, there's a mention of centers for younger adults—but no one has targeted elders.)

- Although heading out to a restaurant can be fun, many families still prefer the warmth of a home-cooked meal . . . especially if somebody else did the cooking. Why not create a business that comes into the home and prepares a delicious, home-cooked meal (the ultimate Cocooning fantasy)? This new service would give families a choice of meals (including low-fat and vegetarian), would buy the necessary ingredients, prepare and serve the meal, and, the best, clean up afterward. A possibility for the first no-hassle holidays. To make this a "go," the service needs to be priced moderately—somewhere between the cost of Mom doing it herself and going out to a restaurant.

- The Vigilante Consumer—ever skeptical, ever doubting—provides the basis for a new business opportunity that we're calling Document Review. This new concept would supply experts who come to your house and complete a review of all your personal and business documents. It would be multipurpose: to make sure you're not getting ripped off in any way, to see that you're getting the most for your money, and to verify that everything is current and in order. This includes health coverage, car leases, insurance policies, phone services (so many people haven't signed up for the carrier's discount packages), mortgages, real estate taxes, credit cards . . . you name it. The payment structure is what makes this business so attractive to the consumer—no costs up front, but the business gets to keep 50% of the initial savings.

These three businesses have potential as free-standing operations. Even better, once you get them off the ground, they might be acquisition candidates for big companies willing to pay big bucks to entrepreneurs who've Clicked with breakthrough businesses.

Another option might be to go public. Steven Jacobs did. His concept, Starlog, which started in 1992, selling comics, science fiction toys and collectibles, is now a franchise chain with over $20 million in sales. "We went public with only one store open and raised $6 million," he recalls. "People believed in the concept." Why not? It's also perfect Down-Aging.

Another technique for developing a Conscious Click is to borrow from the success of one industry and transfer it to another. At BrainReserve, we call this Apply and Conquer. For example, over the last few years (as you may know from painful experience), mortgages have become incredibly complicated. Faced with migraine-inducing choices—fixed rate, variable rate,

30 years, 15 years, points, etc., you may have opted to turn to a Mortgage Broker to help sort through the alternatives. Mortgage brokering is one service business that fills an increasing need.

Look at other purchase decisions that have become complicated. Is there a need for a Car Lease Broker? Or an Electronics or Furniture Broker, to guide you through major home investments? Maybe an Arbor Broker? (Have you priced full-grown trees lately? Some good specimens can run about $25,000 each.) A Rose Garden Broker? A College Aid Broker? Or even a better edition of an Insurance Broker—only one who finds the *best* deal in the country, and then shares the commission with you (usually a hefty part of the first year's premium).

Peter Lynch, the investment guru, has a deceptively simple approach to stock picking. His books all pick up the same refrain: Buy what you know. Invest in companies you can understand. Go into the big discount stores and see what people are buying. That same basic philosophy applies to the companies in which you are considering investing your career.

If you're just starting out and want to Click into a career, consider what Kathy Reed did. Kathy had targeted Xerox as the company she wanted to work for, but the office in nearby Dallas said it didn't have any beginner-level openings. As the *Wall Street Journal* reported, ". . . she located the Kelly Girl office services Xerox used and said she only was interested in assignments at Xerox." She soon was placed as a temp and leaped rapidly into a full-time secretarial position. Of her first job, Kathy said, "Once you get it, you start networking and seeing what your opportunities are. You can't do anything from the outside looking in." In less than a year, Kathy was arranging trade shows and then was offered a prime job with the New Product Development team. "I thought I'd died and gone to heaven."

What's the bottom line? You can control your fate. Your Click. The Conscious Click proves that finding your path doesn't have to rely on a bolt from the blue. There are logical techniques you can use to apply the Trends and to Click yourself into a new reality.

The Unconscious Click: Insights from Foresight

Okay. Here comes the opposite of what we just told you. Clicking can reshape your career when an insight, a vision, or just a fantastic idea surfaces from the depth of your unconscious mind. Examples of the Unconscious Click include mega-successes of American business, such as that of Craig McCaw, who recently sold McCaw Cellular Communications to AT&T for mega-billions. Craig McCaw's epiphany—it suddenly occurred to him that the hordes of people stuck in traffic jams or zipping along in their cars would be perfect candidates for talking on cellular phones.

Or take the case of Howard Schultz, founder of Starbucks. As the *Wall Street Journal* commented, ". . . flashes of enlightenment often do strike at odd times and places." For Howard, it was a piazza in Milan. Impressed and intrigued by the phenomenon of the Italian cafe—where good coffee meets good conversation— he suddenly envisioned an American version of this noble tradition. But not all realizations are necessarily promising or even capable of being commercialized. So Howard applied some basic Trend thinking to his plan. He recognized that alcohol consumption was down, leaving former drinkers with no place to hang out (Clanning). He figured that Americans love Italian style and that love should transfer over to the Italian coffee bar concept. "It was Nirvana," he says now.

We're all familiar with the success that Starbucks has brewed up. And one man's Unconscious Click has been validated not only by his company, but by the entire coffee bar boom (reported in Pleasure Revenge). But are they growing too fast, and are too many people rushing into opening coffee bars without a clear business plan and a differentiated reason-for-being? There's a big difference between the bright Click of inspiration and the deadened Click of redundancy.

Often, an alertness to life is what lays the groundwork for a flash of insight. This is what happened to one of those smart young women in the traditional 1960s who seemed content, at first glance, simply being the mother of two small children and the busy wife of an accomplished man. Jacqueline Simon, married to Pierre, a most charming and successful French businessman, had a forced moment of introspection when she needed to consult a psychotherapist during a critical family situation. "The therapist was a truly smart woman," Jackie revealed, "who told me rather bluntly that despite my zealous devotion to my children, despite all our traveling and entertainment, she thought I had the most boring life of anyone she knew."

This startling sentence turned into a Click. It propelled

Jackie right into graduate school for a master's degree, where she realized two things: "I still didn't know enough" and "I wanted to contribute to making the world more comprehensible, for me and for others." She went on for a Ph.D. in Political Science, partly studying with the eminent Claude Lévi-Strauss. After getting her doctorate, the now incredibly non-"boring" Jackie works as U.S. Bureau Chief and Associate Editor for a high-brow quarterly magazine, *Politique Internacionale*, as well as being Senior Resident Scholar at the Institute of French Studies at New York University. A Click of Accomplishment, to be sure. But not her last one. Jackie added, "I'm just about ready for something else now. Having been through the process once, I know that's it going to happen again. It's purely intuitive."

These Unconscious Clicks don't just happen by chance. Sometimes there's a psychic rehearsal that plays on and on in your subconscious—only you have to look deep inside yourself to find your Click path.

Or, if you're lucky, the Click could be more surface, right before your very eyes—or as in the case of Andrew Tolmie, right under your very feet. Andrew, who resides in London, was floundering in his career path; first trying the advertising field, then the travel business. In trying to decide what he really liked to do, he came up with two choices: cooking and entertaining. Then it occurred to him, "Maybe people would like to rent out my flat for a business dinner, a cocktail party, a small wedding or extravagant feast." Andrew had landed on a rather novel idea for the Brits—a catering possibility out of his antique-filled home. He designed a mouth-watering menu, with such temptations as "tea-smoked shrimp in sesame oil, wrapped in spinach and chives" and "ginger mousse with lime and honey sauce," has a complete wine cellar, creates a regal atmosphere with flower-filled rooms and crackling fireplaces (telephone: 44-171-584-2300). A hospitable Click.

It's also important to keep in mind that a business venture that springs from an Unconscious Click can often be launched in your spare time. While you're still making a living at your nine-to-five job. Thanks to computers, telecommunications, laser printers, and the rest of the high-tech grab bag, a business can be set up in a matter of weeks. We've known dozens of people who've incubated their businesses this way, until it becomes strong enough to stand on its own.

The Unconscious Click can point you toward the rewarding, but intense (often insane) life of an entrepreneur. But there are many other career changes that the Unconscious Click can lead you toward. If you're locked into a job that grows more unsatisfying with each passing month, then you need to find the self-realization necessary to change direction. For instance, a friend of ours who was bogged down in the insurance business for fifteen years was out walking his dog one evening, when he looked at the end of the leash and realized what he wanted to become: a veterinarian. He worked out a plan (financially, relationship-wise) to go to vet school and dedicated the next six years working toward his degree. Today, he spends his days handling dogs, cats, birds, and the occasional amphibian . . . and has never been happier.

Many of us feel the tug of the Unconscious Click, but we don't always admit it—even to ourselves. We keep it repressed because we're fearful of the consequences. It means that we might have to toss our lives (and priorities) up into the air and let them fall in a different order. But your talents/skills are probably more transferable than you realize. If you've ever whispered to yourself, "Gee, if I could, I'd rather be doing X or Y" (fill in your blanks), think about latching on to that Click notion and running for dear life with it.

The Heart Click: Doing What You Desire

That "money isn't everything" is the oldest cliché in the book. But it's something that everyone has to come to individually. In the process of interviewing thousands of people for this book, we kept hearing this refrain over and over again. People talking about the wonder of being able to wake up each morning and do what they want to do. Sometimes, the getting to this point of real happiness takes almost unfathomable patience and an inner belief that secret dreams can happen. Tom Clancy worked for many, many years as a defense analyst (an "obscure" defense analyst, as the press likes to describe it) before he Clicked and became one of the world's most successful novelists. Tom Clancy knew that the real clear and present danger would be to ignore the true calling of his heart. His targeted focus and drive is what led him to the Click.

From the time we're children, we are thwarted in satisfying our deepest desires. We're stopped from snacking when we feel like it, swimming for hours on end, or even playing in the bath with our rubber duckies because we're told to "get serious and soap up." As a result, we turn into the kind of adults that accept compromise, compromise, compromise. Winding up in a career that our parents have dictated . . . or that followed from a series of unplanned circumstances. Either way, we end up Clickless.

But that scenario doesn't play out for everyone. Some lucky people manage to Click into a life of work that satisfies them in a profound and meaningful way. You can tell immediately when you meet people who derive that kind of pleasure from what they do—they radiate an inner harmony that's unmistakable. The phrase "found their calling" provides the right image—the ability to hear, amid the din and clatter of the world, the voice that's calling to you. Calling the sound of your future. The echo of your very own Click.

The good news is that it's never too late to experience the Heart Click. Nor is it ever too early. You can Click into a life of passionate pursuit any time you want. As the author James M. Barrie once said, "Nothing is really work unless you would rather be doing something else."

Berry Gordy, an American icon who founded Motown Records, always loved music. When he got out of the army, he decided to act upon his love and open a record store that specialized in jazz. But for many reasons (timing, finances, location?), it failed. Gordy was forced to find work at a Ford plant, where he earned $85 a week attaching chrome strips to cars (remember, this was the 1950s, when Chrome was King). To break the monotony, he used to compose melodies. In the evenings, he would hang out in Detroit's black nightclubs, peddling his music and meeting other singers. The Click break came when he crossed paths with Jackie Wilson and Smokey Robinson. Gordy had the insight, foresight, and just plain sight to recognize them as major talents and signed them up to start Motown.

Speaking of *strips* on cars, there's a man in Water Mill, New York, who found his Heart Click putting *stripes* on cars. Even though Steve Kistela had two loves—art classes in school and automobiles—he was preprogrammed to go into his father's construction business. Once, during his off-hours, he drove into New

York City to take a look at what was going on at the annual Auto
Show and became mesmerized by a live demonstration on the art
of pin-striping. Back on home turf, Steve purchased some enamel
paint and fine brushes and started drawing sure and steady lines
around his old refrigerator. Next, he practiced on his secondhand
car. Then on the cars of his friends. When he felt that he had
learned his craft, he announced his availability to local car dealers. Hence, a business called Classic Touch was born. He's busy
year-round and has even been called upon to pin-stripe and pin-
scroll lawn mowers (how Egonomics is that?). It's a Click career
for life.

Another Heart-warming Click comes from the story of a
growing company named Longaberger. Longaberger is a $300-
million business that employs 22,000 consultants, including the
person we talked to, Janice Topping Degatano from Monroe,
Connecticut, who loves the one-on-one selling of beautiful handmade baskets. In the 1970s, Dave Longaberger was thinking about
getting into the restaurant business. But because he was always on
the lookout for new opportunities, he had a habit of strolling
through the malls to satisfy his curiosity. As the "Longaberger
Story" recounts, "It was there he discovered . . . [something] that
touched his heart like no other product. He noticed basket displays in several stores. He would stop, pick up a basket and smile
as he thought back to an earlier time."

That earlier time was in the 1930s, when Dave's dad made
baskets during the Depression. Although he had closed his wicker
shop in 1955, he still hand-crafted an occasional basket until
1972. When Dave observed that his dad's baskets were ten times
better than these new ones, he decided to remake ones of the
same quality. A good combination for Cocooning and Small
Indulgences. Through this Heart Click, the Longaberger Company was born. Today, it is a highly successful company that
reflects the founder's deep values and integrity.

We looked at the career of a longtime friend, Amy Gross,
when she recently Clicked into running not one, but two major
magazines, *Elle* and *Mirabella*. Although she had been "pathed" by
her parents to become a doctor (as are her father and brother)
and was a pre-med major at Connecticut College, Amy veered
into writing because of a "chance" room placement next to my co-
author, Lys. Impressed by Amy's ability to ask penetrating ques-

tions, Lys, then editor-in-chief of the college newspaper, gave her the assignment of writing a feature story. Ultimately, Amy followed Lys to the editorial side of *Glamour* magazine, recalling, "We didn't have many job choices in those days, but we all understood that at the news magazines [*Time, Newsweek*], girls started out as either secretaries or researchers, so we opted for Condé Nast, which allowed us to write immediately."

Her career in magazines flourished. Amy next went to *Mademoiselle* to work for its Entertainment Editor, the "know-everyone" Leo Lerman. "It was very glamorous. I'd pick up the phone and it would be Marlene Dietrich. Or Leo would say, 'Amy, get me Cary Grant.'" She was eventually promoted to Features Editor of *Vogue* (1983). "It was thrilling. I got to see every new show, movie screening, ballet, galleys of new books. I walked around saying, 'I've got the best job in New York.'" Years later, Amy moved again, helping in the formation of *Mirabella*. Then along came *Elle*, with the title of Editorial Director, "meaning I was in charge of all text from the cover lines to the last page." A rare second chance presented itself when the owners of *Elle* were the purchasers of the folding *Mirabella*. Amy was put in charge of recapturing its original mission: to be a magazine for smart, competent women. How does she find her unique editorial voice? "I've always felt that I was editing just for myself and my friends. My work has always let me follow what I wanted to do." Heart Click, Click, Click.

What does this mean to you, if you're a little bit older than 20 or 25 and have drifted into a line of work that's as far from a Heart Click as you can get? It means stop, rethink your life, and find your Heartline.

It took David M. Battista of New York a few tries to find his Click. Even after completing medical school, he couldn't settle on a specialty that seemed right. Basically, although he was leaning toward pediatrics (loving the nurturing aspects), he wasn't keen on the all the blood and gore that came with kids falling out of trees or off their bikes. Undecided, David stopped practicing medicine altogether and switched over to pharmaceutical copywriting. After three years of being in advertising, he re-examined his options: What could combine his love of writing, his love of stories, and his love of healing? The answer: child psychiatry. Treating children as young as 12 months old for hyperactivity; listening and helping straighten out the already-damaged lives of

3- and 4-year-olds who've been abused. A real Click from the Heart.

Try to get in touch with those things that mean the most to you. We've heard about the Five O'Clock Club, a job search and career strategy network, whose director, Kate Wendleton, asks her clients to "list and prioritize their seven most rewarding life experiences, whether paid or unpaid." If you write those experiences down by yourself, you can measure how far afield they are from what you're doing now. And develop a game plan to bring your work and your passion closer together—so close that they can Click.

Following your passion doesn't mean that you have to leave the Trends behind. On the contrary. The trick is to take what excites you and "spin" it in such a Trend-wise way that you optimize your chances for success. This holds true whether you are searching for a career in corporate America or are about to embark on your own entrepreneurial adventure. Two entrepreneurs we know who are putting the Trends to good use are Pat Smith and Jeri Berger with their two small silk-flower companies, Very Romantic (arranged bouquets) and Silk Flowers by Geraldine. (Small Indulgences, Cocooning, 99 Lives, Anchoring, S.O.S., Egonomics.) Whenever asked if their beautiful silky Victorian roses or showy hydrangea plants are *real*, Pat and Jeri answer with their business motto: "They're Real, but Not Live."

Sometimes we can be undeniably successful at a job we love and still feel the need to Click into another challenge. Anna Quindlen seemed to have one of the most expansive, personally satisfying jobs in the world—an op-ed column in the *New York Times*. It gave her a platform to voice whatever earthshaking issues crossed her mind. Her column, entitled "Life in the 30s," was astute and sensitive, bringing a younger female sensibility to the middle-aged male ethos of the paper. Readers responded with fervor, and awards poured in. Rumors were that she would become the next Managing Editor. But then Anna announced she was quitting to write fiction. She summarized her Heart Click this way: "Every time I get comfortable in a job, I ask . . . what really terrifies you that you could do next. And this was it."

The lesson leaps out at us. Get in touch with your yearnings. Click into what you want, and what the world wants. It's the most powerful force on earth.

The Accidental Click: Like an Artist, Reshaping the Materials at Hand

Know that you may someday have to put aside the planning, the strategies, and the perfectly orchestrated Click path that you've developed. And be prepared to turn on a dime and Click with what life hands you.

In 1976, Anita Roddick's husband, Gordon, decided to fulfill his own dream of riding a horse from Buenos Aires to New York City (that's not exactly everyone's dream, but that's what makes horse races). That left Anita with young children and no resources. "Forget entrepreneurial dreaming," she related. "If I didn't make the money, the kids wouldn't be fed." Out of this accident of fate was born a company that has changed the face of retailing: The Body Shop.

Also in 1976, Andy Glanzman and his wife moved in with an elderly friend who needed to be looked after. Their friend's farmhouse was so primitive, it didn't even have electricity. So Andy started making candles. And he fell in love with the art. Today, Glanzman (who was once a rock guitarist) runs Northern Light Candles, a $4-million business that sells to more than 2,000 retail stores. Each one of the candles is hand-sculpted and signed by the craftsperson who molded it (Egonomics in action).

Flora Hanft, an advertising copywriter, had always been told that with her quick sense of humor, she could make it in "show business." Her break came, not from her particular brand of rib-tickling one-liners, but only after she became obsessed with following the O. J. Simpson case. Someone at a local radio station heard about the depth of her expertise and asked her to become the resident "O. J. Bureau," providing tongue-in-cheek commentary on the trial. Her role on the program expanded right away to fielding questions from call-in listeners. Now, stations in other markets have been contacting Flora about general cultural analysis, and it looks as if a radio career is on the horizon. An Accidental Click par excellence.

Actually, we had been wondering lately how many of the next generation will want to become lawyers. This is the first group who've been weaned on watching the live casts of the O. J. trial and nonstop Court TV. We've been hearing from so many parents who say that their little kids have been imprinted by legalese. No longer do they play Cops and Robbers or even Doctor and Nurse. They examine the stitching on their gloves or pretend that they're driving a white Bronco. One very young child, when asked if he knew O. J.'s last name, immediately said, "Trial." And a cartoon that we ripped out of a newspaper showed two toddlers tugging at a book, one crying, "I object," the other, "Out of order."

A freak Accidental Click happened to Dan Clark. It looked as if any possibility of any career for this college football star, who was about to be drafted by the Oakland Raiders, was over when he tragically became totally paralyzed (a situation from which he has partially recovered). Soon after his accident, however, he was asked to give a pep talk to a small rural high school football team. Reluctantly, the depressed former athlete decided to accept the offer. But when he faced the young players, Dan felt an internal Click. Based on that experience, Dan Clark has turned into a successful motivational speaker, very much in hand with Anchoring, now giving about four hundred talks a year to all different types of groups.

There's also Jo Waldron, who was born profoundly deaf. She developed a product called HATIS—Hearing Aid Telephone Interconnect System—that helps most of the 30 million hearing-impaired Americans understand voices on the telephone. Waldron's Click was supported by Phoenix Management, a company that assists people with disabilities. (If you've ever known anyone who can't hear, you realize how every little innovation helps. Such as the headsets now available in certain theaters and museums. Now, if only movieplexes would make them available.)

These few stories demonstrate that the opportunity to Click, often unpredictable, can even be found in adversity. Often, the difference between people who *seize* opportunity and those who don't is, in essence, the difference between people who *see* opportunity and those who don't.

To get better at seeing opportunity, start to envision solutions instead of obstacles. Remember, your next business opportunity could be sitting across from you at a meeting, a dinner party, a wedding. It happens every day. We live in the most fluid of all times when people can Click from one field to the next almost as easily as zapping with a cable remote.

Our final Click Thought of the chapter: It seems as if every week a different magazine or newspaper or TV show reports on the "Best Jobs of the Future." Our advice—ignore them. Or take them with a very substantial grain of salt. These so-called predictions look at the forecasts of the Federal Bureau of Labor's computer, based on the Federal Reserve and military spending, and simply report those findings. They're calculated on what's available today—not on the Trends. If you go by the Trends, the jobs will be obvious. America will need more childcare workers as more mothers go to work; more dry cleaners, more takeout-food establishments, more beauty clinics, and more manicurists, for the same reason. A given—more computer repairers. More homecare aides and physical therapists, as the population ages. Additional environmental experts, as natural crises become commonplace. Fewer receptionists and switchboard operators, as voice mail takes over. Less unskilled labor, as automated machinery replaces humans.

Some of the most exciting jobs of the future are the ones that haven't been created yet. As the *Economist* wisely pointed out, "Many jobs listed in the vacancy columns of today's newspapers—such as aerobics teachers, software engineers and derivatives specialists—did not exist in 1970." Want to Click into a career as a Personal Information Consultant—someone who helps individuals cope with and manage the information overload in their lives?

It doesn't exist yet—but it will. Because new fields are created when new technology creates new needs. Take the cellular phone industry or the computer-driven credit card industry, in which theft and fraud are literally costing about a *million dollars a day* because the thieves are consistently two jumps ahead of the technicians. It's hoped that the shortsighted solution for car and cell phones of punching in a longer string of numbers and PIN codes will be short-lived. What an opportunity for some techno-wizards to come up with brilliant yet marketable solutions to both stymie and catch the high-tech crooks.

It all ties back to our Click equation.

C for *C*ourage—the courage to embrace a changing world and find your place in it.

L for *L*etting Go—the act of leaving your fears and anxieties behind.

I for *I*nsight—the ability to look at the same landscape as someone else, and see something original.

C for *Commitment*—the internal reservoir that keeps you headed toward your personal promised land.

K for *Know-how*—your well-tuned skills and genuine depth of understanding that let you compete in a marketplace that doesn't tolerate mediocrity.

The Conscious Click. The Unconscious Click. The Heard Click. The Accidental Click. The four soundest, most grounded ways we know how to get re-energized and re-directed in this era of High Mobility. In this time when ideas and careers are moving at the speed of light, if you Click on the light switch, you can change your life forever.

CLICKGUIDES

MENTORING

A teacher affects eternity.
—H. B. ADAMS

Time-travel back to the ancient past. Your dad was the blacksmith in the village. You were his worthy apprentice. You were called William the Smith, son of Richard the Smith (or Molly the Baker, Cecilia the Candlestickmaker, in those role-defined days of yore) and all those in the hectarehood knew you as the Smithies. One generation passed bits of wisdom on to the next.

But nowadays, no one in the generational world before you has been a computer "morphing" expert or interactive television repairman. How do you apprentice? From whom do you learn? You either need to make a friend of the inventor or fervently hope that your direct supervisor is well-versed in the new technology. Ditto if you're the first female Catholic priest (not likely now) or female test pilot, or the first Mexican-American employed at a certain level at a company or . . . or . . . or the first in any position.

In Homer's heroic *Odyssey*, the best friend of Ulysses went by the name of Mentor. When the adventurer set out on his famous wanderings, Ulysses asked the trustworthy Mentor to take charge of his household and be the sole teacher of his only son, Telemachus. Thenceforth, anyone called upon to teach life's lessons has been known as a "mentor." In today's world, the base definition has been expanded to encompass any form of senior adviser as well as any role model. Now more than ever, everyone wants and needs mentorship.

Probe beneath the surface in any famous person's biography and you'll understandably find a mentor, a wise counselor, a steerer-in-the-right-direction. Aristotle had his Plato. Alexander the Great, his Aristotle. Leonardo da Vinci, his Verrocchio. Monet had Manet, then the tables turned, and Manet had Monet. Bertolt Brecht looked to Rudyard Kipling. John F. Kennedy, his father. Bill Clinton, his mother. Even the drip-and-dribble Jackson Pollock revered and learned from a homespun realist, Thomas Hart Benton. Composer Stephen Sondheim found an ideal role model at an early age, right next door, in his musical neighbor, Oscar Hammerstein II. (Hint: If you're lucky enough to live near someone talented, take full advantage of it.)

Mentors and the arts go hand in hand. Our most talented and close friend, Gerti Bierenbroodspot, a painter who has long been considered a "national treasure" in her native Holland, was mentored in her Art Deco painter/uncle Leo Gestel's atelier. There, by his easel, she reveled in his classic training: drawing, watercolors, oils. Her young adulthood mentor was from the Bauhaus school, and Arthur taught her the finer tricks of the trade: mixing her own pigments, grinding semiprecious stones into powder, gold-leafing, marbling, making thick oatmealy paper. Things that most artists no longer know (or care to know) how to do.

Sports figures, especially soloists, have built-in mentors in their coaches. Hands-on trainers who lavish attention, one-on-one. Think of the child gymnasts, the ice skaters, such as Oksana Bayul, who had to touch her coach's hands for luck before triple lutzing. Some tennis greats have real love-hate relationships, blaming a slip in the ranks on one trainer, a spectacular win on someone new. The father/instructor of the 4th-seeded French-Canadian star, Mary Pierce, was so controlling that he has been banned from the games.

Being mentored in business by an older boss, although quite common, often sets someone's work ethics and behavior for life.

In an interview, Rip McEldowney at MetLife talked about his first job at Citibank. Rip sought the banking field on the direct advice of his father: "The first step up the job ladder is a bank. Go there, learn how money works—how to borrow, how to use funds, how to leverage it—and you'll be fine in any other endeavor." There he met a mentor to interact with. "Fred Stecher was arrogant, almost abusive, like the lawyer in the movie *Philadelphia*, who kept saying, 'Explain it to me as if I'm a three-year-old.' He always urged me on, telling me, 'No, no, I don't get it. Help me, I don't understand.' When we were through, either he understood or I had to go out and get more information. Now I'm never too embarrassed to say that I don't know."

Ed Meyer of Grey Advertising learned other strengths from his mentor. Ed's business behavior was firmly rooted in "logic," while mentor Herb Strauss taught him the value of "emotional nourishment and understanding in business relationships." "His outlook was based on nurturing. Figuring out how to make people feel better about themselves. How through praise and jokes, people can be encouraged to participate and help in the evolution of an idea. He taught me that you can't push at people." This changed Ed, and the change has lasted through his career. "I now rely, more than ever, on feedback from those I work with, to help me develop new areas of interest, both for myself and for the company."

Mike Lorelli, president of Tambrands, credits his incredible work ethic to watching his father ("It was the behavior, more than the words"). Explained Mike, "He was always getting a jump on the day and turned me into an early bird. I get up at 4:30 every morning, run about four miles, work hard during the day, try to have fun doing it, and aim to get home early to see my kids." (Very on-target for 99 Lives, Being Alive, Mancipation.) As far as a real mentor, he targeted Roger Enrico, chairman of PepsiCo. "Rather than having a full calendar run his days, he purposefully held open empty time slots, so that he could add value wherever he felt it was best needed on a particular day. Roger also put competent people into place whom he trusted, in each of the basic blocks under him."

In the case of Dr. Patricia Allen, the noted Manhattan gynecologist grew up on a farm in a small town (pop. 4,200) in southern Kentucky and went to a one-room schoolhouse. "I was going to be a clinical psychologist because I never dreamed that I could be a doctor. My senior adviser told me to go on and study medicine and now I'm doing exactly what I was meant to do. I love my work." As someone who believes that "wisdom helps you Click" and that "you can't Click until mid-age," Dr. Allen is finding an increased appreciation for her mother as a mentor, as she herself gets older. "I'm just starting to enjoy the really feminine parts of me that I was always afraid of." She has started by thinking of her mom as "an artist of the domestic life." Dr. Allen explained, "My mother baked, kept a clean house. If a job had to be done, it was done. She showed the family how we were loved. Suddenly I can see the joy in my mother's life. "

John Greeniaus, President/CEO of Nabisco Inc. is a mini-mentor to many. He offers co-workers and friends (including me) support in the form of carefully-timed little notes, cards, and cut-out articles. Funny thing is that he always seems to know exactly what you're working on.

The act of mentoring often evolves into a strong chain of forged links. A good "mentoree" will want to be a good "mentor," repaying the debt by continuing the cycle of helping someone else Click. One of the most rewarding paths is mentoring the problem-plagued young: helping keep a kid in school, off drugs, off guns, off unsafe or unprotected sex. Mentoring means being part of the S.O.S. Trend—by volunteering to steer someone in the right direction.

There are all kinds of Big Brother/Sister (215-567-7000), helping-hand programs. Twinleaf, based in Bridgeport, Connecticut, pairs able retirees with vulnerable seventh and eighth graders, for tutoring and skills training. Or simply for a sympathetic ear and shoulder. Similar youth guidance programs are popping up around the country. The Greater Phoenix Youth at Risk Foundation starts kids off at camp, then puts them into a matched-up mentoring program. L.A.'s Fulfillment Fund has been running for sixteen years, mentoring the raw talent of junior high schoolers with trained volunteers.

Some advanced-thinking companies in the '80s set up in-house programs, especially geared to guiding women and minority employees along the fast lane. Unfortunately, in these streamlined '90s, many of the fund sources have dried up or the wise advisers have been urged into early retirement. However, some existing success stories have come out of Champion International Corp., which teams up senior-level managers with new employees; or from Dow

Jones, which sets up mentoring "squads" made up of diverse employees; or from IBM, which has seminars and brochures specifically for empowering women and minorities.

A few independent organizations stand out, such as Inroads, a national nonprofit organization targeted to helping black, Hispanic, and Native Americans find jobs in corporate America. SCORE, Service Corps of Retired Executives (800-634-0245) has executive volunteers advising new entrepreneurs, more than 250,000 annually—for free or at low-cost workshops. Focused on women and partially funded by the U.S. Dept. of Labor, the Leadership Foundation Fellows program was matching up twelve professional women with outstanding potential with chosen mentors in a one-year fellowship that includes a week at Harvard's JFK School of Government.

The bottom line for today is: Find your own sage. But beware the fickle or judgmental mentor. The word started by the Greeks can get misused or overused. Mentoring is not a short-term injection of hope or a hopscotch schedule of concern. A real mentor works with you, grooms you, fashions you, prods you, pulls and pushes over a period of time. Changes you and Clicks you into place. Bill Storts, a bright guy from Andersen Consulting, had some thoughts on this: "You can't say once a year that you are mentoring. The mentoring relationship is one of right and left hand with both sides working toward a common good. On the side of the mentor, it's very important that the mentor provides the mentoree with appropriate examples, structuring to be successful. On the side of the person being mentored, it requires a certain amount of loyalty and understanding to make sure there is a screening process of value so that things are put in the right context. There's an element of trust and suitability."

The "trust" word is key to mentorship. We learned about an interesting trust concept from reading the fine print on the menus at the sublime East–West coastal Japanese restaurants of chef Matsuhisa Nobu—called Matsuhisa in Los Angeles and Nobu in New York (our favorite place to dine in the entire country). They offer something called *Omakase* or Chef's Choice. *Omakerasu* means to trust (something to someone) or to let another person guide the decision making. To put it into another perspective, at this restaurant, it means that you can get a plate of soft-shell crab tempura rolls or crispy rock shrimp or steamed lobster on spinach, depending on what the chef wants to make for you. But in the larger scheme of things, *"omakase"* is a good word to capture the courage it takes to put yourself in someone else's hands. (Maybe the basic idea behind *omakase* could be transplanted to our schools: Wouldn't it be better to return to the *Little House on the Prairie* system of having *one* teacher stay with *one* group of kids for years, seeing them evolve, working on known problems, pulling out budding potential.)

As in a marriage, the hardest part is finding the right mentor/partner. Look to the obvious (teacher, boss). Then scan the field. To get the attention of someone very busy or distracted, you'll have to be ingenious, outstanding. How can you crack the shield around a person protected by a full-time secretary who won't even deliver a message from someone unknown? Send flowers along with a videotape of yourself. Offer a free service just to get under their noses (input their computer, paint their shutters). Anything to break the barrier. Do you recall what "Sidney Poitier's son" in *Six Degrees of Separation* did? Studied a certain family in depth, as if it were a college course, by memorizing details of their lives to the point of casual familiarity. Thus, he penetrated the inner sanctum, their home, by dropping a few intimate facts. If you were an ordinary person (i.e., not famous), wouldn't you talk to anyone who knew your grandmother's name?

Refer to the story that Dale Carnegie told in the business classic *How to Win Friends and Influence People*: "Years ago I conducted a course in fiction writing . . . and we wanted such distinguished and busy authors as Kathleen Norris, Fannie Hurst, Ida Tarbell, Albert Payson Terhune and Rupert Hughes to come to Brooklyn and give us the benefit of their experiences. So we wrote them, saying we admired their work and were deeply interested in getting their advice and learning the secrets of their success. Each of these letters was signed by about a hundred and fifty students. We said we realized that these authors were busy—too busy to prepare a lecture. So we enclosed a list of questions for them to answer about themselves and their methods of work. They liked that. Who wouldn't like it? So they left their homes and traveled to Brooklyn to give us a helping hand. . . . All of us, be we workers in a factory, clerks in an office or even a king upon his throne—all of us like people who admire us."

You can use the same attention-getting techniques to "beat

the odds" for getting into a tough school or a coveted job. Case in point: Our friend and 2-year-old Cece's mother, Vivian Shapiro, has a nephew, Brian, who majored in literature during his undergraduate years. "What can you do with English Lit., besides teach," he concluded. Meanwhile, since he loved building things, designing better bookshelves, etc., he dreamed about being an architect—but was told he first had to go back to take some courses in architecture so that his potential could be judged. Brian countered this requirement with his own inventive plan. He built scale models of his designs, photographed them, and put together a professional portfolio. On the basis of this, he was accepted at four top architecture schools.

A similar story happened years ago when a bright young Princeton student named Danny Gregory applied to BrainReserve for a job. He, like just about every other recent grad, had no practical experience. In response to our stock letter saying, "Send in your résumé," he created something novel and original. We received a bulky package containing a handmade book, illustrating in words and watercolor pictures a well-written story about what it would be like for a character named Danny Gregory, as a successful copywriter, to work at our company. Bingo, his fantasy came true.

The whole point of Doing Something Different is to challenge the excuse of not Clicking, to stop saying, "I can't change careers or do something I want, because I don't have any experience or the right qualifications." We say "Hurdles are put there to jump over." Or, the ClickLine: Where there's a will, there's a way in.

Seek and ye shall find a mentor to help you maneuver some of life's trickier paths. Erase the idea of standing alone and tall as a sunflower in a field. Leaning on a mentor can never be viewed as a weakness. It's very comforting to have someone to bounce even your wackiest ideas against (sometimes the most way-out ones are the best, but too far in the future). If you interview very successful people (as we did), you'll hear deep praise, intense loyalty, generous credit for the mentors who've assisted them along the way.

Whether you rely on a chosen person to impart a distinctive leadership style, to smooth out some of your jagged edges, or just to lend support in a time of crisis, the results of being mentored will provide you with a winning formula: extra clout and a two-way route to Clicking.

CLICKMESSAGES

EARLY WORDS OF
WORLDLY WISDOM

It takes two to speak the truth. One to talk, another to hear.
—OLD SAYING

People's perspectives on life are often set by an early phrase or oft-repeated message from someone important in their lives. A parent, a grandparent, a teacher, a boss. My mother, Clara Storper, used to say, "Don't let the bastards get you down." This echoed over and over again in my brain whenever I had to defend an idea that seemed too innovative, too novel, or too wild—and, in my case, this always proved to mean simply "too future."

On another tack, Lys's doctor dad, Allen Montague Margold, took an approach of total support, telling her, even writing her, "Keep your chin up, very very *high*." These words of influence have given her a sense of confidence and idealism that allows her to sit still for hours (years) writing these books. Actually, he ended all of his letters to her with a different motto-like bit of advice that fit the occasion. Suggesting that she "attempt to look for the good" in a stressful group experience, he signed off with "To adjust is the badge of intelligence." Lys's mother, Virginia, can also be considered a role model for the both of us. We often invoke her name, her vast energy, her endless beaus, her "age does not matter" attitude to remind ourselves about the power of positive thinking. She encapsulates it all by her "tomorrow's another party" philosophy or as the Beatles sang, "life goes on." The only aspect of her personality we can't seem to emulate is "never complain."

Some kind of early imprinting seems to be a meaningful element in people's success stories. Almost everyone we interviewed for *Clicking* could remember a word, a motto, an inspirational thought that not only stuck with them, but kept mantra-izing itself as their lives went on.

JESSYE NORMAN, OPERA STAR

Blessed with one of the world's most magnificent voices, this artist feels that the cornerstone of her success came from a phrase that her mother told her when she was only 12 years old (she was trying to practice a scene from *Macbeth* while her brothers teased her). The advice: "Just keep on going, Jessye." It always acts like a gentle push.

DIANE SAWYER, TV ANCHOR

Most people are surprised after meeting Diane Sawyer that she's not caught up with "power" and "being a celebrity." This naturalness probably comes from her father's three rules for life: "Be kind, be kind, be kind." To be on the receiving end of one of her warm and formidable hugs (as I was) is to understand how she translates belief into action.

JAMES MORGAN TOPPING, GENTLEMAN FARMER

James Morgan Topping, a young gentleman farmer from Wainscott, New York, had been a buddy of mine and Lys's for years. He raises exotic birds (including 1 wild turkey, 2 lovebirds, 12 peacocks, and 60 parrot finches) in his own beautifully handcrafted aviaries. His family credo is based on fierce individualism (they've been here since 1636). Jimmy's independent spirit (as strong and solitary as a tree) was reinforced by an oft-repeated saying of his grandfather's: "Partnership is a pretty poor ship."

GLORIA STEINEM, AUTHOR, FEMINIST

She's always found satisfaction in the feminist cause, guided in part from a life-lesson learned from her mother: "Don't let your possessions possess you." This one insight helped free her up for the more important things: a larger vision, a generosity of spirit.

LESLIE WEXNER, CEO, THE LIMITED

Stressing the value of making each one of the life-stages rich and fulfilling, his father once gave him this nugget of advice: "You don't retire *from*, you retire *to*."

WOLF SCHMITT, CEO, RUBBERMAID

Wolf's father was an early-on believer in a concept that has only now become acceptable: the power of visualization. The words that have guided Wolf since he was a very young boy: "Try to *see yourself* doing what you want to do, and you'll be able to do it."

SINEAD O'CONNOR, SINGER

This tough, sweet, reedy-voiced songstress so internalized a saying from her mother that she decided to make it the title of her last album, *I Do Not Want What I Haven't Got*.

LAURIE KAHN, EXECUTIVE VP, DIRECTOR TELEVISION PRODUCTION AT Y&R

It's especially important for a young girl to be boosted by words of encouragement by a father. Laurie's dad, Howard, prepared her for the competitive world of advertising (and the rest of life's trials) by instructing, "You can do anything you want to do."

NORA EPHRON, AUTHOR

She got her overall viewpoint about the way to look at things from her mother, who said simply, editorially, "Everything is copy." These three words have given her a particular perspective for relating every aspect of her life to her writing (even the negatives. Remember *Heartburn?*).

GLADYS JUSTIN CARR, VP AND ASSOCIATE PUBLISHER, HARPERCOLLINS AND EDITOR OF *CLICKING*

The far-ranging fields of interest and knowledge of our very wise book editor at HarperCollins probably came from her mother's smart words, which prepared her well for this world: "Always have options."

CHER, ACTRESS, SINGER, ENTREPRENEUR

Cher is someone who's Clicked so many different times and in so many different ways in her career, so it makes sense that Cher's mother taught her to take a long-range view. She said, "If it's not going to matter in five years, it doesn't matter now."

AYSE MANYAS KENMORE, BOARD MEMBER, REAL ESTATE MAGNATE

A part of our extended family (remember, we dedicated *The Popcorn Report* to her and her husband, Bob) and former BrainReserver, the well-loved Ayse is Turkish and heard this old proverb first from her grandmother in Istanbul, Safvet-Hanim, and later from her mother, Fazilet. Simply worded and very much to the point of her richly charitable life: "A thousand friends are too few, one enemy is too many."

JIM MORGAN, PRESIDENT, PHILIP MORRIS

In a kind of reversal of what would be expected forty years ago, his father spoke to his inner values ("It's not what you are, but who you are"), while his mother infused him with business advice. She explained about competitiveness: "In spite of the fact that everyone knows that there's enough to go around in the world, in reality, it's a competitive world and only people who are smart, work hard, and stay focused will ultimately win."

KATE NEWLIN, BRAINRESERVE

Kate learned her incredible 24-hour, 7-day work ethic from her father, Dale A. Newlin Sr., a retired Army colonel who fought in both World War I and II. He used to say to her: "If you work hard in America, you have to get ahead."

ADAM HANFT, PRESIDENT, SLATER HANFT MARTIN

One of my oldest friends in the business, Adam well remembers what he was taught by his college philosophy professor, "Never take 'no' for an answer, and most of the time, don't take 'yes' either."

CYNTHIA ROWLEY, FASHION DESIGNER

Her mother, an artist, told her, "Just create." And she steered Cynthia away from playing with coloring books, "because the outlines were already there."

SANDER A. FLAUM, PRESIDENT/CEO, ROBERT A. BECKER, INC.

Sander, my brother-in-law, once told me that he recalled his mother Rose saying, "Do a good deed daily." And every single day, Sander tries his best to follow this beneficent rule.

DAVID FINK, CORPORATE REAL ESTATE LAWYER

His grandmother, Bryna Poliacoff, a survivor of the Russian Revolution, who fled to Turkey, then emigrated to America and opened a famous Jewish restaurant in New York City's theater district, advised David that. "Life is short and changeable. Experience happiness in the every day."

RAY SMITH, CEO, BELL ATLANTIC

The clearest piece of advice that Ray Smith got from his mother was, "Get educated." Because neither of his parents went through high school (having to work instead), getting an education was the most important priority in his family. It was the path to being stimulated culturally and intellectually. (See "Kids and Clicking" for more of his story.)

JACQUELINE SIMON, PROFESSOR OF POLITICS

Closest confidant, dear Jackie told us about a phrase she learned from her mother, Rose "Lulu" Albert, specifically in reference to how to handle the ending of a love affair: "One nail drives out another." In other words, a new focus will help make you forget the past. This sound advice can also be applied to everyday disappointments, by reminding you that a new and better experience can replace every bad one.

LAUREL CUTLER, VICE CHAIR, FCB/LEBER KATZ

She always remembers and quotes the motto of the cultural club that her mother belonged to: "Culture is not a 'having and a resting,' it is a 'growing and a becoming.'"

ASH DELORENZO, BRAINRESERVE TREND DIRECTOR

Ash's Taurean father, Big Al Feinstein (see "ClickNames" for discrepancy in their last names) behaved in the least expected manner when things got tough. If he had a disastrous day in the stock market, he would take the family out to dinner, saying, "Anyone can celebrate when something good happens. It's when things go bad that we *need* to celebrate."

GERTI BIERENBROODSPOT, DUTCH PAINTER

Her mystic (and also Taurus-sign) father, Charles Theodoor, and her Bauhaus School mentor, Arthur Goldsteen, each taught her about spirituality, integrity, and art. But at one time when she was in her 20s, they sat together, facing her, and both instructed, "Continue what we've started." A directive, an inspiration perhaps, to the paintings she's creating now—those divine messengers, dream travelers, other-worldly angels, and celestial legends.

OLIVE WATSON, REAL ESTATE SALESPERSON, PHILANTHROPIST

Besides teaching the fearless (Little) Olive how to fly a jet and ski the highest mountain, her late father and IBM's great leader, Tom, used to give her sound advice. One of the wisest and most helpful for the challenges of life: "Stand up for what you *believe* in and be *prepared* to defend your position." A quiet, but firm voice of reason, Olive definitely was prepared—well.

JONATHAN CANNO, PRESIDENT AND CEO, EQUITABLE BAG CO.

His savvy, industrialist grandfather, Maurice Rosenfeld, the founder, in 1919, of the paper bag company that still provides the finest of shopping bags for every major store in New York, welcomed him to the firm with this tough advice: "Some people get heart attacks and some people give them. Make sure that you're one of the latter." A strong businessman as well, Jonathan listened carefully, but not wanting to cause any harm, he tempered the words to mean "Stay sharp and don't let anyone get the better of you."

MARY KAY ADAMS MOMENT, BRAINRESERVE

Her parents, Mary and Frank, soothed Mary Kay's young ruffled feathers when her older brothers teased her, saying, "Ignore them, they're probably just jealous." This advice has given her an excellent perspective. Although she understands not everyone is consumed by jealousy, Mary Kay realizes that most of the time, "it really is the other person's problem." And then she calmly, sweetly tries to help the culprit through it.

AMY GROSS, EDITOR, *ELLE* AND *MIRABELLA*

Is she the first dual-editor of two major-player magazines? She's had an amazing career, in that even though she's always worked for large publishing companies, she's been left to act, to make decisions, relatively on her own. This self-sufficiency came from the early teachings of her physician father, Joe, who told her, "Be your own boss, make your own meaningful work."

LIBBY PATAKI, NEW YORK'S FIRST LADY

The wife of New York's governor recalls a sage saying from her father-in-law at his produce stand. When a customer came in with a mild complaint about some recently purchased corn, the elder Pataki quickly threw a dozen new ears in a bag. Puzzled, Libby inquired about the wisdom of this, saying, "She was just giving you a song and dance." His reply was, "When you dance with your customer, she always leads."

JOYCELYN ELDERS, FORMER SURGEON GENERAL

She tells a similar tale, called "Dancing with a Bear," not only to her children, but also to the many young audiences she has addressed over the years. "When you're dancing with a bear, you can't get tired and sit down. You have to get the bear tired, so he'll sit down. Reach out and find other dance partners to help you wear out the bear." Good advice about the importance of cooperation—for all.

In thinking back, I also remember my grandfather, Isaac Storper, telling me and my sister, Mechele, "Everything you do is right." He was wrong, of course, but it made us feel loved.

If you recollect any specific words of wisdom that have urged you on or are pointing you toward a Click, e-mail them to us at Clicking@ ix.netcom.com.

KIDS AND CLICKING

How the twig is bent may be less important than
the way it bends itself.
—J. KRUTCH

Clicking isn't like swallowing a pill that will change your life
forever.

It takes nurturing—and Mother Naturing. Kids can
either have a series of little Clicks as they grow . . . or if born with
a special talent, they can burst forth with one of those cataclysmic
moments, a major *Wham!* life-knowing Click that can be developed and enhanced over the years.

The key to helping your kids find their C-L-I-C-K (remember
the acronym, "Safe-Cracking the Future") is to listen to them
and encourage them to tune in to their own voices early on
(Courage). Find out what they "know" about their futures already
(Insight, Know-how). Help them walk toward their best selves
(Commitment). And stay out of their way (Letting Go, on your
part; theirs, too). Kids can C-L-I-C-K *in any order,* as long as
they end up with a Click that's right for *them*—and not just wish-
fulfilling for *you.*

As we researched Clicking, we discovered a phenomenon we

called the Time-Released Click. So many success stories came from people who "knew" something special about themselves when they were children, even though they didn't act on it. How do you help your children figure out what's right for them? By taking them seriously when they tell you what's inside.

Twelve-year-old concert pianist Helen Huang has recorded Beethoven's First Piano Concerto and Mozart's 23rd Piano Concerto with the distinguished Kurt Masur, director of the New York Philharmonic. He talked about her virtuosity with the *New York Times*: ". . . she doesn't play as a child and she never tries to ask somebody if she was good. She knows." Kim Bond is also someone else who "knows." Kim was one of the pioneer girls to attend the tough Virginia Women's Institute for Leadership, which linked up with the "no-women-allowed" Virginia Military Institute. She had already achieved the distinction of being the first girl on the boys' wrestling team at her local high school. Bond attributed this quest for discipline as a way to try to build up the confidence needed to do well in her future career: neurology.

Click Speed Ahead

It's actually amazing how many kids speed ahead toward their goals, checking off one accomplishment after another. (There's a small group of Flash—or Flash-in-the-Pan—Clicks. They race toward fame, but can just as quickly flame out. The computer library, Nexis, is littered with stories of Wunderkids who are left to wonder what happened.) Thankfully, there are many successful types out there, creating firsts or new fields of business instead of hanging out at the malls. In fact, a recent study showed that just under 70% of teenagers today would like to start their own businesses (20% more than adults). Of this group of steady Clickers, we've tracked a few of the under-20 achievers.

Michael Simmons, CEO of Dataport Computer Services, founded the fast-growing telecommunications company at age 12. Brandy Norwood was signed by Atlantic Records at age 14; her song, "I Wanna Be Down," was at the top of *Billboard*'s R&B chart for weeks. Masoud Karkehabadi graduated from college at age 13, and is now researching Parkinson's disease. Another young genius has captured the title of "Youngest College Grad" in the history of America. Michael Kearney, who started talking at 4 months and reading at 8 months, earned his bachelor's degree in anthropology at age 10. Setting another record, Bala Ambati, at age 17, was the youngest medical school graduate. He had been scalded by boiling water as a toddler (in India), and felt comforted by the attending physician. "That's when I decided to become a doctor . . . to relieve human suffering." At age 3.

Evan Roberts, at age 11, turned his love of sports into a junior career as this country's youngest radio sports announcer. Westinghouse finalist Tracy Phillips invented a "talking wallet" for the blind. Her late younger brother, who was blind, inspired her to figure out a way for people to know what bills were in their possession—without seeing. And then there's Harvard scholarship student Lauralee Summer, who grew up in homeless shelters and welfare hotels, teaching herself to read and finding a "home" in library books. Her field of study now: Comparative Religion.

We read a compelling story about a young Chinese dancer, Zhongmei Li, who made the journey from a remote village, at age 11, to the Beijing Dance Academy to a performance in New York. In an interview by Jennifer Dunning in *The New York Times*, the fragile-looking Miss Li told how her parents were set against her auditioning as a dancer—pointing out her lack of training and the formidable competition. "'I went on a hunger strike,' she recalled. Her parents gave in, borrowing 200 yuan (about $24 now) for the ticket, and sent her on her way. She arrived at the academy to find thousands of children waiting to audition." But she danced. "When she made a mistake, she told the auditioners she had to start again. 'I had come so far,' she said. 'I wanted them to know I was a good dancer.' Out of 3,000 children, she was one of a handful chosen." That shows her determination. And she had even more of what it takes. "'We worked from 6 in the morning to 9 at night,' she recalled. 'I got up early to practice, before anyone else. But I had no alarm, so I put a string down the wall and tied it to my wrist.' The night watchman agreed to tug the string at 4 every morning."

Another early Clicker is Cynthia Rowley, the young fashion designer who won the prestigious Council of Fashion Designers of America's Award for New Fashion Talent. Looking back, she can pinpoint her self-knowledge exactly. "I made my first dress when I was 7. It was out of a giant brown paisley fabric and I would wear it every day, because it was 'my little outfit.' After that, I used to spread out on the floor and try to draw or cut around myself. Or I'd ask my Mom to trace me. I would come up with these wacky outfits. Eventually I went to school at the Art Institute in Chicago. Then one day, when I was 18, I met a buyer from the department store Marshall Field's, on a train, who admired what I was wearing and asked me to come to her office 'with my line.' So I dashed to the fabric store and quickly made five pieces by hand. She placed an order and that's how I got started."

Within two years, Cynthia Rowley had a whimsical pink-padded store in SoHo, a boutique section in Bloomingdale's, another store in Chicago, plans for places in Los Angeles, Tokyo, and Manila. Reflecting on her early vision, she commented, "There are two things I think about being a kid. How strong your personality is when you're little. And when people look at little kids, how they don't see what's really inside of them."

But those are the arts, you say. Those kids are different. How different is that story from the folk-tales of Abe Lincoln studying by candlelight or Joycelyn Elders walking barefoot for miles to get to school? And there's the ultimate Clicking recipe from J. Paul Getty: "Rise early, work late, strike oil."

One aside about practicing: It's been proven that those who push the limits, break the barriers, actually practice more. Lots more than those ranked slightly below their level of competence. The hours the stars put in are generally about 25% more than lesser talents. And the top excellers do added strategies, such as constantly studying videos of their opponents. We're talking about young chess players, swimmers, musicians, equestrians.

The Anatomy of a Kid's C-L-I-C-K

Remember, with some kids, the Click can be mixed: Sometimes the catalyst is the parent, or the teacher, or the coach, or a relative. It certainly takes Courage to see early *and* realistically just who your child is—and not get in the way.

There's Tiger Woods, the young ethnically-diverse golfer who is turning the tournament circuit upside down. His positive attitude came out of a negative (his African-American father's anger at his own treatment in golf), which helped create this teenage champion with his laserlike concentration. His father started him off early, hitting balls into a net while little baby Tiger would watch. According to his dad, this future golfer had an attention span of two hours when he was only 6 months old. At a certain point in his training, Tiger himself had to Commit to the Click (talent can't be forced). There was a clear moment when Tiger connected to the vision and began to claim it as his own. Now at the age of 20, Tiger wows the crowds with his beautiful form and accurate shots. He claims not even to strategize or plan or think about what he's doing on the green. Tiger just goes out there and does his best. His prowly, growly name helps.

That's the essence of the early-seeded Click. Sometimes it's just a process of "remembering what you knew" when you were very young and forgetting everything you learned in between. A quote from J. Robert Oppenheimer sums up this idea: " There are children playing in the street who could solve some of my top problems in physics, because they have modes of sensory perception that I lost long ago." And, if you're a parent, how do you help a young adult "remember"—and Click into it?

Turning Sleepwalkers into Clicks

So far, we've been looking at "winner" kids, the early ones who have acted on their potential to Click. But statistically, they're the minority. Many kids, if you ask them what they want to do, say, "I dunno." Even in the worst-case scenario, if your child insists upon pouting in a messy bedroom, is barely passing three subjects, and starts rolling his or her eyes at your every word, hold tight. There's a place in the cosmos for everyone. You just have to help them find their Click.

Even more worrisome to tuned-in parents is that smallest of subgroups, the Sleepwalkers. Those who seemed detached and unfocused. Other kids have their own ridiculing remarks to describe them: "There's a light in the window, but nobody's home" or "Not playing with a full deck." Do you just sigh, accept them for what they are, and let it go at that? First off, check out and check off the obvious medical/psychological work-ups, and then the less obvious, dyslexia, Attention Deficit Disorder, even Lyme disease (which makes one very tired). Often, the last in the class has some minor problem—even as correctable as bad eyesight—that is medically fixable.

Or it might be that some of the children who seem off in a world of their own—are. It may be a stranger place than most grown-ups comprehend. These kids could have discovered their own particular Click, only it's too many "Sigmas Out" of our interest zones. The point we're trying to make is that parents should take a fresh look at the wider world and not act on out-of-date judgment calls. In other words, don't squash a fertile mind.

Let's look at a hypothetical case. Say the son of a high-powered Chicago lawyer announces to his folks that he has decided to stop school and start a cottage industry that will craft Ecuadorean flutes. His parents' reaction? "Get back to your books." But if his parents would stop and investigate the market, they'd find out that ethnic musical instruments are some of the hottest items in international trade. Is this kid a dropout or a potential solid Clicker?

So even if your child is going through a purple-hair, pierced-nose-ring moment, don't despair. If all else fails, put on a Golden Oldie from the late '50s and tell her to "Get a Job." Lys got her taste of assertiveness training at age 11 when she worked on steaming summer days at Cappuano's Stand (known for the freshest corn-on-the-cob) in Norwalk, Connecticut. Her specific job: to say to the customers, "Please don't squeeze the tomatoes." To this day, she knows how to select the tastiest, ripest, absolutely best tomatoes—by scent alone.

And a little stand by-the-side-of-the-road is a good spot to learn from a wise saying: If life hands you lemons, make lemonade. But, we'd like to add, then market it, franchise it, and sell it to a major international conglomerate as a fresh fruit drink. Click.

Not Just Education, but New Ways to Learn

A growing element of the Kids and Clicking paradigm is technology. Every advance that's been made is something that kids take in their stride—and, unfortunately, many parents can't even begin to help out with homework. It might be that the meaning of education has been eroded over the years because too many have viewed the teacher as replacing parenting. In the world in which your children are going to be living, competing, and interacting, however, top priority must be given to reclaiming the education connection.

One way to do it would be to teach parents how best "to be parents." Lori Schiaffino, while working with BrainReserve, had an idea about setting up a major Parenting Mentor Program in schools across the country. In bimonthly sessions, a few pairs of experienced parents could take the time to coach single or struggling mothers and fathers, drawing them into a pro-active parenting relationship. There could also be "positive parenting pairs" to serve as role models.

There are some hopeful signals in the education turnabout. The in-school computer, a great leveler and great provider, certainly may be viewed as the key breakthrough in providing cultural literacy to children. (Every child can get access to *some* computer, whether in the classroom or at the Y or in corporate-assist plans.) Programs such as the Kids Web are off to a good start. They filter a vast amount of encyclopedic information, making it relevant and understandable for younger heads. *Ad Age* reports that very soon there will be close to 34 million children, ages 4–12, and that as the decade goes on, the littlest kids, by the age of 2, will begin banging out the alphabet (and random thoughts) with their chubby fingers on computers. Prodigy, America Online, and CompuServe have all geared up for this explosion of "baby literacy." Watch for the proliferation of online services (bulletin boards, chat rooms) for toddlers.

Big business has also stepped into the computers-for-kids circuit—contributing talent as well as dollars. For example, Ray Smith, chairman of Bell Atlantic, told me in an interview that he would like to be remembered as "the person who brought education into America's living room." He created a pilot study in a lower-income, mainly racially diverse school district in Union City, New Jersey. "We gave two computers to every classroom, put one in every student's home, and one in every teacher's home. They were all interconnected, were on the Internet, had e-mail and CD-ROMs of Microsoft Encounter, everything."

Within two years, the students' reading levels were raised significantly. "Homework being completed" is up by 85%. Absenteeism, for both students and teachers, has dropped to almost nothing. The school, which had been rated as being in the lowest 30 schools out of the 1,400 in New Jersey, is now the best school in its district.

Smith went on, "Not one of the computers has been damaged. And the most exciting thing to me is that when parents requested to be able to use the computers themselves, the teachers volunteered to come in on Saturdays." According to his figures, "50% of the parents showed up and spent the day being taught by their kids. Before the systems were in, there was hardly any communication between teachers and parents or kids and their parents. The change is fantastic. All we did was connect these people and they really started to Click." His goal? To provide this type of one-on-one computerized education at a cost of $300 per student.

Beyond such corporate efforts in public schools, there are also earnest attempts at better education through privatization and home schooling. (All to stimulate our kids into discovering the joy of learning, before they discover the joy of sex.)

A local and very special tale of "private" schooling comes from Courtney Sale Ross, who never actually intended to create a full-fledged school—but did just that. The Ross School in East Hampton, now in its third accredited year, ballooned from two girls in one grade to thirty girls in the fifth, sixth, and seventh grades.

The adventure of starting a school grew from a practical and philosophical seed when Steve and Courtney Ross planned an extensive family trip to Asia. They brought along a qualified teacher to instruct their third grade daughter and her schoolmate as they traveled through China and Japan. Although their on-the-move school had to be brought back to the United States because of her husband's illness, Courtney liked the basic concept of "world as a classroom."

This all translated into an unusual school: a core group that "travels" together, either electronically or physically, to the places they study. What makes the Ross School different is sometimes that when students open their schoolbooks to read about the French Revolution, they've also packed their suitcases and journeyed to France. Same goes for England, the Galapagos, and other points East and West.

"In addition, the girls get a rich learning experience out of the resources right here in the community," according to Patti Walton Silver, a mother of one of the students. "They're nature lovers which I think is due to getting them out of the classroom. One of the underlying mottoes of the school is 'Kids Teaching Kids.' When they come back from their trips, they exchange their perceptions and share their experiences. A group of girls went up to the Seneca Nation a year ago and bonded with the children there, many of them Native Americans, who, in turn, came back down here to visit. They are all teaching each other an important concept, that 'It's not school, it's life.'"

Next breakthrough for learning will be Educational Virtual Reality. Instead of having to travel physically through space, you'll be able to travel mentally through space—and maybe through time. Study the paintings at the Uffizi in Florence or take a lesson with Michelangelo. Walk around the Acropolis in Athens or get into a philosophical discussion with Plato and Socrates. Visit London's Globe Theater or learn dramatic structure from Shakespeare. You get the picture . . . explore with Magellan, experiment with the Newton or Madame Curie, recline on Freud's couch.

Epcot Center's Virtual Reality Lab now lets you experience Disney's highest-resolution VR invention (the best example of VR so far). Straddling motorcycle-like machines, with helmets and goggles on, we went on a magic carpet ride through the souk in Aladdin's city of Agrabah, occasionally crashing into villagers who would glare and shout, "Hey, watch where you're going," on a mazelike search for the "great golden scarab."

Already, much of the world is accessible by CD-ROM. And even real adventures can be shared by computer link-ups. In fact, a recent expedition across Antarctica was tracked daily by thousands of students. And the International Arctic Program has been set up so that the next husky-drawn team, led by an explorer named Seger, will have info posted on Econet and the Scholastic Network, so that an estimated 20–25 million children and adults around the world can follow its progress. By contrast, in 1909, when Admiral Peary discovered the North Pole, it was months before the news was tapped out by telegraph.

A friend of mine, Jerry Isenberg, who had been in the entertainment business and now is a professor/executive director for electronic studies at the University of Southern California School of Cinema-Television, has a long-range plan of taking a year's sabbatical in 1998 with his wife, Carole (see page 177), to work on expanding the concept of "distant education" for both high school and college levels. He explained, "If you were on a mountaintop in Tibet with a computer, a modem, and a CD and wanted to learn, you could do it—asking questions, taking tests, writing papers, attending lectures, seeing films, just as if you were in school. This will be the future."

In Oct. 1995, British Airways helped gather kids from all over the world to participate in an International Children's Conference. The idea grew out of the ten minutes allotted to kids to express their views at the 1992 Rio Earth Summit. Under the umbrella slogan, "Leave It To Us," the forum of several hundred 10- to 12-year-olds split into workshops to share ideas on the problems of the world. The end result: a charter by children for children was drawn up to give to all countries and the United Nations.

A $100-Billion Spending Spree

One of the clearest ways in which kids Click is cumulatively. They are a major market force—and they know it. It's estimated that they control about $100 billion of the nation's consumer spending and influence another $130 billion worth of purchasing power. Children are also major stockholders in many kid-oriented companies. The distributor of Mighty Morphin Power Rangers, Irwin Toy Company, has revealed that an amazing 60% of its shareholders are children. Getting shares of stock might not be every kid's dream of an ideal birthday present, but the appreciation is bound to grow—along with the stock's worth, hopefully.

Products aimed at talking to teens in their language (not talking down to them) will be a success. MTV, a major worldwide hit has got the patter down pat. Interestingly, in a survey done for the growing market of teen magazines, it's been determined that kids actually like to read ads—partly so they can rip them out and pester their parents (you can't do that with a TV commercial).

One evening this past winter, I happened to be sitting in the East Hampton Cinema, munching a junior-sized container of air-popped popcorn and waiting patiently as preview after preview came on before the feature. One of the previews was a clip about angry, extremely attitudinal under-20s, filmed with a swaying hand-held camera. The young woman in front of me leaned over to her boyfriend and said, "Oh look, a target flick. We're being marketed to."

This is the first generation of consumers who is growing up with a real sense of marketing, and it's requiring us marketers to do things differently. Our advice: Proceed at your own peril, if you intend to try to sell kids something or tell them anything. A better course of action would be to invite them into your place and listen to them. In *The Popcorn Report*, we advised companies to "Give kids a special 800 number (for age 18 or younger); Make them your pen pals; Hire children to sit on your Board."

In other words, don't underestimate the power of kids. It's children who can force their parents to stop smoking, to recycle, to buy (or boycott) certain products. And, we think, it will be the younger generation who will get their mothers and dads to vote (up from the shamefully low 36% in the last election).

An idea that Kate Newlin and I had been exploring was about conducting a "Kids' Election," letting them express their opinions about their own destinies. The kids' voting booths could be set up right next to the adult ones.

And there'd be online voting, too (through an e-mail code number). The twist would be that kids could vote *only* if their parents (and maybe even grandparents) were registered. Imagine the pressure.

To get this idea moved along, we envisioned setting up a bipartisan Kids' Committee that would rally the troops. A call-in number, such as 800-KIDVOTE, could be set up for anyone wanting more information. Will a Kids' Election happen? Maybe. Could it work to get more people to vote? A definite yes. It would serve as a multi-Click—in that all generations of Americans would be the winners.

Staying Clicked

To sum this up, the best way to ensure that your kid Clicks—in the present and in the future—is to follow our Click-o-gram.

Courage: See your kids the way they really are.
Letting Go: Shed your predetermined beliefs about their lives.
Insight: Try to remember what you were like as a child.
Commitment: Support your children every day. Even when it's tough.
Know-how: Give them access to your expertise—without stifling their dreams.

And let your kids Click their very own way. That's perhaps the toughest part of all.

HADTO³
VISIONARY CLICKING

You may say I'm a dreamer,
but I'm not the only one.
—JOHN LENNON

You see things and say "Why?"
But I dream things that never were;
and I say "Why not?"
—G. B. SHAW

People who Click with passion all say the same thing: "I HAD NO CHOICE." Call it an inner fire, true being, a life-throb, whatever—this driving force can start early and push someone headlong into his/her calling. We've named this kind of visionary Clicking: HadTo³, because we kept hearing the same answer over and over. "Why did I do it? Because I **had to, had to, had to.**" The beauty of this Bio-Drive is that it can happen at any time in your life; it has nothing to do with age, monetary level, educational status, societal achievement. You just have to recognize this Mission Inevitable and run with it. As trite as it sounds, the best advice is to "follow your dreams," or as Joseph Campbell said, "Follow your bliss."

We all know from history books and *Amadeus* that Mozart had no choice. He was an infant prodigy at the harpsichord, violin, and organ and had composed a first symphony and two operas before he was 12. Steven Spielberg started charging his friends to view movies when he was a small boy and then went on to create and direct films as a teenager.

Part of living your dream is being able to visualize it. When a reporter remarked to Roy Disney that it was sad that his brother never got to see Disney World, he answered, "Walt saw it and that's why we are seeing it. He was visionary." There's a growing business in helping people form a mental picture of inner amorphic forms. Sales of visualization videotapes are brisk. They cover the gamut from marketing/selling to shopping/smoking.

Coupled with a strong vision, there's often a chemical hunger that's ready to be tapped. Athletes are well-known for searching for the picture and zooming into that extra zone. There was Diann Roffe-Steinrotter who at age 26 was the oldest female in the Super Giant Slalom Olympic race at Lillehammer, Norway. Although she had the dry heaves before stepping into her bindings, she knew she had only a little more than a minute to Do It or Not. Diann stunned everyone by getting the gold—by being three-quarters of a second faster than the next closest skier. Another female downhill racer overcame her fear of that extra push by throwing herself out of planes in a parachute and skydiving. Point is, you can't stand like a bowling pin waiting for a strike to happen.

There are also visionaries who are bent on creating a better world. They Click on good deeds. A remarkable man, Deepak Chopra, M.D., is one such do-right person. He told us, "I have a purpose in my life. To heal. To create peace wherever I go." His pursuit of freedom takes an incredible abandonment of control, a letting go of societal norms. It also takes a monumental trust in oneself. He talks in a reassuring cadence: "I don't follow a schedule; I don't wear a watch; I don't have to be responsible to anyone; I've shed my need for control, for power, for approval."

This life of harmony was in direct contrast to his past position. In October 1980, he stopped for a moment to assess his stressful career. A successful internist, he recounted that he was constantly seeing between sixty and seventy patients per day. "It was purely mechanical. I felt like a drug pusher who had been given a license." At the same time, Dr. Chopra started looking for alternatives, reading about the intense lives of St. Augustine, Mother Teresa, and such, envying their freedom even more than their spirituality. With that background, he made the decision to change his life in one day.

Although Deepak Chopra can't seem to avoid success, he

now manages to stay loose from the power play. His phenomenal best-selling book of 1993, *Ageless Body, Timeless Mind*, is still going strong. He consults with a hospital complex in San Diego at the Center of Mind, Body, Medicine, teaching holistic healing techniques. "The weather is beautiful and the beaches are great," he concedes. He gives seminars on self-discovery and is advising the U.S. Olympic team. All the while, slowly, patiently, quietly, he's working to change the world. "I want to improve myself. If we all do this for ourselves and if there are enough of us, there will be change. A critical mass will be reached. Look at medicine. The hospital here has allowed some 'non-doctors' to go on staff. The NIH has given money to research Alternative Medicine; insurance companies are starting to recognize the value of acupuncturists. . . "

Part of this peaceful outlook comes from meditation. Deepak meditates for two hours each day (5–6 A.M. and 4–5 P.M.). He shared with us the essence of his Seven Spiritual Laws of Success, insisting gently, "If you do take heed of them, you will get you anything you want in life":

1. The Law of Pure Potentiality, where one must have the experiential knowledge of the spirit as a real force.
2. The Law of Dharma, a purpose in life; a realization that everyone has special gifts to give to others.
3. The Law of Karma, cause and effect. Or, what you reap is what you sow (this one is especially relevant to Click Thinkers). You have to be conscious of the choices you are making. (One aside: a friend of ours in Washington, D.C., Richard Socarides, also made this point. He observed that "little choices can lead to big results.") Deepak observes that as humans, we all have the innate ability to be "infinite choice makers."
4. The Law of Giving, simply "How can I help?" not "What's in it for me?"
5. The Law of Desire or Intention, being aware that inherent in every desire are the mechanics for fulfillment.
6. The Law of Detachment, meaning that if you really want something, you have to relinquish your attachment to the outcome. This is a deeper ideal than the sappy old cliché about "letting something go free, and if it comes back to

you it's meant to be." Chopra is saying be process-ori-
ented, not outcome-oriented.

7. The Law of Least Effort, or do less and accomplish more
(this was our favorite). Deepak Chopra spun this law with
basic charm. "Flowers don't try to bloom; fish don't try to
swim; birds don't try to fly, to migrate, to sing. The least
expenditure of energy does the most wonderful things."
His definition of nature is up-to-date. He calls it a "cosmic
computer," saying, "The universe is alive with intelligence
of infinite diversity, infinite organizing power, infinite
freedom."

Chopra has written fifteen books so far, with more in the
planning stages. His first novel, intriguing because it's about the
wizard Merlin, spans the centuries from medieval times to modern England. He explained that he felt that the element of magic
was missing in too many of our lives. In reminiscing about his own
childhood, Chopra recalled a time when tales were spun about
fantasy and wonder. He feels it's hard for kids today to capture
that mystery, that aura of bewitchery. "Except for maybe that one
day a year when you visit Disneyland, where can you discover a
sense of magic?" he questioned. So beyond his healing and his
work for peace on earth, Deepak Chopra defines a lighter, more
joyful mission to his life: "making people happy."

We also interviewed a second M.D. who, like Chopra, has
Clicked into a better space. Bernie Siegel's story reminds us of
our version of the song "Looking for Love in All the Right
Places." The author of many best-sellers, including *Love, Medicine
and Miracles* and his most recent, *How to Live Between Office Visits*,
came to realize a fundamental "wrongness" about the emphasis in
training in Western medicine. "Although in the business world
you study success, in the medical world what you study is failure
(dying)." As he practiced his profession, he eventually became
depressed and disillusioned. "The word 'doctor' means 'teacher,'
but no one teaches anymore. We are mechanized and treat disease, not people.

"Even the word 'patient,' which means a 'submissive sufferer,'
is a poor word. I don't want people to be 'good patients.' I want
responsible participants. When a patient asks a poignant, soul-
searching question, such as 'Does God want me to have cancer as

a punishment?' we are not equipped to answer," lamented Siegel. "We have to show our patients that disease is nothing more than the loss of health. When you lose an earring, you don't say 'God meant me to wear one earring, or if you can't find your car keys, 'God wants me to walk home.' We need to humanize medical education."

Siegel told us what he's calling his "new form of religion— UNDO." This stands optimistically for "Undo all the damage that has been done." Then he waxed pessimistic for a moment: "However, there may be no people left, because we are capable of destroying ourselves." Siegel went on about his basic and passionate philosophy of UNDO-ing. "When we say there's 'intelligent' life on this planet, we should be looking at the animals and at nature, not at humans. Also, it's not correct to say primitive vs. civilized anymore, because who knows which is which? The native cultures are the ones that respect the earth, respect their children.

"Use Your Passion," Siegel said, as a kind of life motto. "Stop thinking about yourself, and start thinking about your world. Find your way of contributing love to the world." Bernie Siegel makes everything sound so easy. His positive attitude is infectious. He tries to live his time giving love and experiencing joy, and trying to help others get in touch with their feelings. He recalled a telling incident about life choices that came from his family. Early in his parents' marriage, Siegel's father was at a career crossroads and sought advice from his wife, saying, "I've been offered two jobs— one in civil service that's safe and secure or one at Paramount that's more interesting but definitely risky." Her very wise answer: "Do what will make you happy."

This gentle, focused energy is the basis for Siegel's healing philosophy. "We can heal our bodies when we free ourselves of the guilt issue and say, 'Let's give it a shot.' After all, who is the ultimate winner? The one who's accumulated goods or the one who's accumulated happiness?" Bernie Siegel supplemented his underlying beliefs with a reading list of the works of Carl Jung, Joseph Campbell, William Saroyan, Thornton Wilder, Thomas Moore, Ashley Montague, and various volumes of Buddhist literature. He concentrated on poets and writers who felt pain or were pierced by sadness.

From that wealth of knowledge, he honed his simple, soulful

rules, which are pure Click guidelines: "If you want to change who you are, act as if you are that person. If you want to be more loving, act more loving." Bernie speaks with a lightness of being, mentioning his wife of forty years, Bobbie ("she's my best friend" and jokingly, "my biggest problem"), and their five children. He credits the longevity of their marriage to "love, commitment and humor." His parting words of advice: "Forgive yourself."

Tom Chappell, president of Tom's of Maine, is another study in good behavior. He and his wife, Kate, who's VP of Research and Development, started the natural hygiene company in 1970 with a loan of $5,000. They came to BrainReserve very early on (1980) to consult with us about a marketing position for their even earlier-on vision of selling all-natural products. Among their best-sellers, Tom's of Maine makes the most delicious spicy Cinnamint toothpaste.

The company today, headquartered in an old shoe factory in Kennebunk, employs sixty-five to seventy people. Everyone on staff must sign on to the company's eleven-part Mission Statement and eight-part Statement of Beliefs. One of the declarations concerns the environment: "To be distinctive in products and policies which honor and sustain our natural world." Another is even more sweeping: "To respect, value, and serve not only our customers, but also our co-workers, owners, agents, suppliers, and our community; to be concerned about and contribute to their well-being, and to operate with integrity so as to be deserving of their trust."

Tom Chappell feels he "has no choice." The most important thing, he reports, is doing something you believe in. The "emphasis on one word, creed (from the Greek word '*kardia*,' meaning 'heart and stomach'), is, by all means, not a new concept. It means that although your head does the planning, the core is your heart, your gut. You get to Clicking by experiencing the total right relation, accord. You've got to constantly find out who you are and work at things you're good at." Tom credits Paul of First Corinthians as his teacher. "He used his knowledge of the language and the values of his mosaic culture to talk about a new and higher value system. I use today's language of profit, boardrooms, market share, and cash flow, but these are not the reasons we work. The Higher Authority is Goodness."

It's interesting to examine the interaction of the company, its ethics, and its timing. The group of homespun products appeared years before the Return-to-Natural trend. Tom's of Maine was the forerunner of The Body Shop–type of honest disclosures, stating that its products contained "no saccharin, no preservatives, no dyes, no animal ingredients," and were "cruelty free." The company is one of the few .... that managed to migrate from small health-food stores to mass-market drugstores and supermarkets. This longevity and positivism come from deep within the family's clear philosophy and from Tom Chappell himself, who truly believes that "Life is a gift."

One aside: We remember reading an interesting idea from a newspaper interview with Kate Chappell, in which she was asked to describe a product she would like to invent (a perfect question for the head of R&D). One of her top-of-mind products was edible sandwich baggies. That Clicked into similar ideas we'd had at BrainReserve—lemon-flavored baggies to infuse and freshen leftover meats and vegetables—and one we'd come up with for an assignment for Dow—herb-flavored cooking bags that would add delicious taste to oven-baked meat loafs, chicken, ribs, whatever. What about pesto- or BBQ-flavored? What about a melding of Kate Chappell's edible idea and ours? Flavored ones that would melt or become part of the meal?

In studying the components of a HadTo³ person, we realized that it not only helps to have conviction, but it also helps to have a convincing voice. David Mixner, businessman, AIDS/civil rights activist, and an old friend of Bill Clinton's, sounds like an evangelist. His timbre is honeylike, coating each word with loving meaning. He told us his story over breakfast in Los Angeles. That he grew up in New Jersey, a farmer's son (not well-to-do), and learned to read at the public library. That he went to Arizona State University on a football scholarship, where he became swept up in the Vietnam anti-war movement. Martin Luther King's speeches helped pull David away from literature into activism, irrevocably showing him that a lone voice can create change.

Like King, David Mixner can stir an audience when he speaks. Part of the swaying power comes from his ability to remember whole passages of books (we are unduly impressed by that particular kind of "paragraph" memory). He reeled off a favorite Andrew Jackson quote: "One man with courage makes the majority." The aspect of singularity continues to intrigue him.

"So many people are terrified to do things without support. It's important to take personal responsibility for your own decisions." He points to his biggest personal failure, something he tried to organize in 1986, called the Great Peace March (based on King's idea that peaceful marching is a way of dissipating anger), which can only be summarized as "a cross-country flop with high aspirations." He sees it as a larger lesson, admitting, "I strayed from my ideals."

To restore his sense of equilibrium, he retreated to his love of books; rereading about past civil rights movements, the Irish and Italian, the Balkans and our South. Mixner noted, "Understanding history is essential for positive change. If you try to re-create history, you'll fail, but if you use it as a tool, it's invaluable. Look at past beliefs, not individuals, and adapt them to the 1990s world to see where we'll be in 1996, 2000, and 2020.

"I try to see things that others don't" (a good ClickLine), added Mixner. "And I would have loved to have been a pioneer, crossing this country in a covered wagon. My reward would be seeing that new valley before anyone else, even if only two seconds before." We concluded the interview with one of our favorite questions: "What would you title your autobiography?" David Mixner's reply: "That's easy; it would be *Destination Unknown*."

In an entirely different interview, Mixner's one-time co-worker, activist and author Torie Osborn, coincidentally had even more to say about the aforementioned and ill-fated Great Peace March. For Osborn, that negative experience, in retrospect, turned into a Clicking moment in her life. Until 1986, she had been moving merrily along, going from Middlebury College to getting her MBA in finance, as she steadily built up a certain professional confidence. Becoming involved in fund-raising as the communications director of the Great Peace March seemed like a logical extension of her personal beliefs and her career path. "It was a wonderful Utopian vision." Osborn explained, "We thought that having a moving mini-city of about 5,000 people marching across the United States for disarmament could change the world. I was so blinded by the desire to make it work that I lost my objectivity. Suddenly we were hundreds of thousands of dollars in debt. About 1,200 people got stuck in the Nevada desert. For a 'workaholic maniac,' I had to take a good hard look at what I had allowed to happen, but I emerged even stronger. Failure taught me a valuable lesson: After the fits and starts, suddenly you begin to glide. And I'm gliding now." Or as we call it, Clicking.

Another category of HadTo³ people are the ones whose life-drive revolves around deeds, not words. Ones who don't feel good in their own skin unless others are deriving some benefit from their actions.

One such good soul is a 74-year-old woman in Beverly Hills named Vera Brown. She Clicks by "giving back," saying it's the cure for illness, heartbreak, trauma, sadness. And it's the key for staying young. Vera made her early money by those simple inventions that are used mundanely in daily life: coated elastic bands for pigtails and ponytails, and rubber toe-spreaders used for pedicures (co-invented with her close friend, Lillian Chain). Handy little goods with big-volume sales.

Forty-one years ago, Vera joined a small charity group raising small sums for the March of Dimes. The members were invited to hear a lecturer talk about a far-off dream of running a camp for the blind. Captivated by this concept, the women forged ahead, getting donations of $5 and $10, and renting a store on Santa Monica where they worked with about eight children with impaired vision, teaching them reading and cooking on a Braille stove. This "dream" has grown into the Foundation for the Junior Blind, now serving over eight hundred youths.

Vera, whose work-life revolves around skin care products (mainly based on aloe vera, giving her the nickname "Aloe Vera Brown") and her salon (Vera's Retreat in the Glen) carries this beauty expertise over to her philanthropic life (she's developed an entire product line with instructions in Braille). She's also incorporated her message about the value of "looking good" and "self-esteem" into her work with runaway teens, abandoned children, the deaf, the terminally ill, and women with substance abuse problems (often coupled with homelessness). For this last group, she works tirelessly to help get them off the streets, cleaned up and clothed in *new* (not secondhand) clothes. These women then are treated to a Vera Brown Day of Beauty (facial, hairstyling, manicure, massage). Vera makes it her personal responsibility to get them signed up for a second appointment, feeling, "It doesn't do anyone any good to come in once and walk away. Forget it."

Her secret for happiness comes from a sunny, but not saccharine, outlook. "I love every day of my life. I start off every day by visualizing a big present at the end of the bed." In 1993, she was diagnosed with lymphoma, and is even turning this normally frightening news into something positive: a book whose working title is *Thank God, I Had Cancer.* Vera Brown explains her upbeat attitude: "This drive comes from a funny guy who sits on my shoulder and says, 'I'll give you exactly two seconds to be depressed; you are so darn lucky.'"

What is the ClickLesson to be learned from this? For all those who say that they're too busy in their careers to do anything for their souls, take note of these visionaries who have successfully integrated their paycheck and their heart's core. The pith of this idea is that you shouldn't wait to do what you want.

Sit down in a quiet place and think about your dream life. What would you be doing right now—if you could. Quit your present occupation and open a childcare center? Become a massage therapist? Create new computer software (Netscape mania)? Work in a boatyard? Be the executive director of a charitable organization? That would be a 100% change. Realistically, you could go for a fraction or even 50%. Hire the homeless in your company (and place them in whatever companies you deal with). Or work one day a week for a gardening center. We knew a New York advertising human-resources guy, Dick Kane, who truly loved everything about plants and flowers and trees. He started working with a local landscaping outfit here in the Hamptons, first on a very limited basis, then for two days a week, and eventually full-time, as he Clicked into his heart-career. There's an extra poignancy-point here, because he met an early death (in his mid-50s) and would never have realized his Click dream if, as originally planned, he had waited until his older retirement age.

Try this exercise some Sunday when you're not looking forward to your un-Click job on Monday—take an hour and visualize in detail what working at your Click job would be like. Write it down on a 3x5 card (or your electronic organizer) and keep it with you. Look at it at least three times a day. Each of the following Sundays, dedicate an hour toward making your Click job happen. Figure out your finances. Do your research in the library or in the field. Make some phone calls—to find people in a related line of business to question. Talk to your mentor, your "other," your best friends and family, yourself. And keep expanding your vision, week by week. Otherwise, it will just wither and fade away to another of those "I wished, I wanted" whine-lines. This very Sunday, dream yourself into your Click.

ZERO-TO-HERO

CLICKING THROUGH
FAILURE AND SUCCESS

Adversity is opportunity in disguise.
—OLD SAYING

There were time my pants were so thin,
I could sit on a dime and tell if it was heads or tails.
—SPENCER TRACY

Sure, it's easy to Click through success, but how on earth do you Click through failure? Isn't that an oxymoron? Mirror-opposite goals? That depends on how you define "failure." Unlike the one in the dictionary (a falling short; a deficiency or lack), our definition of real failure is not falling short or falling down, but remaining there once you have fallen. And not trying to get back up again. In the Broadway musical *Sunset Boulevard*, the aging movie star, played by Glenn Close, said, very theatrically, that she didn't like the word "comeback," but preferred "return."

A triumphant return does negate all those words-to-cringe-by: Canned. Canceled. Booted out. Disgraced. They all have a humiliatingly final ring, but as they say, it's not over till it's over. You can't keep a good person down. There's a ClickLesson to be learned in these clichés. What seems like an overnight hit usually hides many years of hard work—and often many nosedives. Click people take these stumbles in their stride and keep on going (often like stubbing your toe on the way to breaking a world record). Failure builds character, resiliency. Especially if you take the time to examine what you did wrong—and learn how to make it right.

How many names of executives who have snared the national headlines (for jolting reasons) can you think of in the count of ten? William Agee, Frank Lorenzo, Frank Biondi, Barry Diller; and the convicted ones, Michael Milken and Ivan Boesky. *Inc.* magazine ran an interesting poll that backs this up. Its survey of chief executives showed that 29% of them had prior business failures. And on average, CEOs had founded two other businesses each, and only about half of the former companies lasted. If you think about it, one of the heroes of American business, Henry Ford, had opened two earlier unsuccessful car companies before he Clicked with the Ford Motor Company and its assembly line in 1903. Inspiring, isn't it?

We're calling this roller-coaster ride Zero-to-Hero, with all its many permutations. You can go in both directions—success, failure, success, failure, failure, and so on. It's everyone's final wish, of course, to end on the success side, to go out in a blaze of glory. Richard Nixon serves as a good example of someone who couldn't have gone any higher—or fallen any lower. To be the first President in history obliged to resign, *scandalum magnatum*, to pack up and leave the White House and slink back home to San Clemente. Yet he ended his time on Earth as an elder statesman, respected and eulogized by many VIPs at his funeral. That's the basis of Hero-to-Zero-to-Hero. To get picky, we could go further to scan Nixon's life and chart his rocky road along the way. Serving as Ike's Veep, then losing to the more telegenic JFK, biding his time, then achieving a Hail-to-the-Chief win after a wait of eight years. Nixon himself talked about this: "Life isn't meant to be easy. It's hard to take being on top—or on the bottom. I guess I'm something of a fatalist. You have to have a sense of history, I think, to survive some of these things. . . . Life is one crisis after another."

How different was Nixon's attitude, or drive, from that of his Vice President, Spiro Agnew? From being chosen to be the second most powerful man in America, presumably adept at high-level maneuvering, he disappeared into the ether, never to be heard from again.

Bunker and Herbert Hunt, those infamous brothers, knew about crisis. As the quintessential rich Texans, they were always near the top of *Fortune*'s billionaire list, until they gambled big—and lost—on the oil and silver markets. Bankrupt, but not broke, and probably heading back up again.

Famous Amos is another one. Wally Amos succeeded in going from famous to infamous. The founder of the wildly successful Famous Amos Chocolate Chip Cookie Corp. twenty years ago, he opened his first store in Los Angeles on $25,000 and a variation of his aunt's cookie recipe. As the business quickly grew, Wally, a media star, was clearly more interested in promotion than management. Within ten years, he was losing hundreds of thousands on revenues of $10 million. And it just got worse and worse. He lost that company and the next one, Wally Amos Presents (based on hazelnut cookies), the use of his well-known name, his house—in short, he lost it all. But instead of skulking away, tail between his legs, the indomitable Wally is at it again, stirring up a batch of new cookies. Little low-calorie ones with chocolate chips, pecans, and coconut (sounds good), under the name of Uncle Noname (not very memorable). The ClickLesson here is that if you have a good product, yet are done in by a badly run company, by all means, try again—but next time, hire a smart businessperson.

Or get rid of a bad partner. That's what Dennis Wilfong did before he started over again. The inventor of the surge suppressor that controls energy flow and prevents the burn-out of computers and televisions, Wilfong had come up with a very necessary and good product, but unfortunately picked a lousy, financially questionable partner. To top off that business error, the company was featured on a rare badly researched "60 Minutes" episode that concluded that surge suppressors couldn't possibly work and were, in fact, rip-offs. The end of the company but not the end of the story. After a time of despondency and debt, Wilfong started baking the internal compound in his home oven and making the electrical suppressors in his garage. Orders came in, and his tiny company, Innovative Technology, took off. Sales in 1992: $12 million. Wrong partner, bad press, and you can still survive. It's a household staple now.

Ben Cohen and Jerry Greenfield, two hippie types who moved to Vermont to have fun, have miraculously managed to parlay one little scoop shop, opened in an old gas station in 1978, into a $150-million-a-year business with more than 600 employees and 100 franchisces. Of late, they rocked the business world when they decided to look for a new chief executive to handle the day-to-day management, so they could go back to what they liked best: tasting new flavors, developing new products, talking to customers, and doing good deeds. In their own oddball way, Ben and Jerry turned the job search into a "Yo! I Want to Be CEO!" contest, asking each applicant to write a hundred-word essay. First prize: the top job. Second prize: ice cream for life. While both founders are staying on the board of directors, Ben has turned over his daily duties to the new boss.

Ben and Jerry's story, one of the most-often-quoted American success sagas, started out with two misfits (in their words, "two fat nerds"). Jerry wanted to be a doctor, but was rejected by a total of forty medical schools. Ben left Long Island, bought a piece of land in rural Vermont, and made pottery that no one bought. Banding together, the friends from junior high decided to go into a food business. Should it be Ben & Jerry's Bagels? Ben & Jerry's Fondues? Ben & Jerry's Shishkebabs? Probably no Clicks there. Sensibly, those early ideas were rejected in favor of extra-chunky ice creams.

In an interview for the *New York Times Magazine* by Claudia Dreyfus, Jerry was quoted: "Ben is the creative one, the risk taker. Ben has often told me that he would rather fail at something new than succeed at something that has already been done before. That's a shocking concept to me. Also, as a team, we have a good sense of the absurd. The most immediate absurdity is that our business was started by two non-business people and it has reached such an exalted status in the ice-cream world." We would say, exalted status in any world. Real Zero-to-Hero.

Another CEO who is really an entrepreneur *in disguise* is Chris Whittle, whose big dreams and big schemes on new ways to educate America have had their ups and downs. Within a few short years, Whittle built up a $400-million empire that included such revolutionary concepts as Channel One, a televised news service set up to pipe current events, along with advertising (controversial), into the classroom; and the Medical News Network, which goes into doctors' offices. Underlying every venture is Whittle's basic premise: to let the sales of ad space pay for the more entertaining parts. Over time, he had either been involved in acquiring or starting up such diverse assets as *Esquire* magazine;

a Spanish-language magazine named *La Familia de Hoy;* two-minute TV programs for women, Momentitos; a women's pro baseball team; and the last, the Edison Project (turning public schools into private high-tech highs). Although his media company, Whittle Communications, has been broken up due to over-expansion and related debts; its ultra-posh Knoxville headquarters emptied and for sale; his many homes rumored to be sold off, too; Chris Whittle, the quintessential salesman, still has hopes of making money while doing good. He was quoted in *Newsweek* as saying, "It's like rodeo riding—you get thrown off, you get back on. It never crossed my mind I wouldn't just saddle back up again." And when that happens, the bow-tied Southern gentleman will be a Hero again.

Everybody in business (or out of business) would like to Click with a product like Microsoft. It's made Bill Gates the proud possessor of the incomprehensible sum of billions of dollars, plus allowed him single-handedly to change the Zero image of the computer nerd into one of a savvy Hero. Even on the television show "The Nanny," star Fran Drescher referred to Gates's elevated stature in her New York–ese French, *"Le Geek C'est Chic."* But is Gates relaxed, content, self-satisfied about his stratospheric success and ready to rest on his laurels? In a *Mirabella* article, a friend of his, Ann Winblad, gave this opinion about him: "Bill is driven by fear. Not the garden variety kind, but a deep, dark abyss. Pure dread that he will fail. What scares him is whether or not he'll end the has-been hot company." Somehow, this is very reassuring. If Bill Gates is scared, it's okay for *us* to be scared.

Sometimes when a product fails, it brings a person down with it. Sergio Zyman, the marketing strategist for the disastrous intro of New Coke, stayed around for a year, then quietly left to be a consultant (for seven years) on his own. We're not one to kick around old cans, but in an interview the day after the new version came on the market, my marketing instincts moved me to announce that "New" Coke was about "as welcome as changing the American flag." It was 1985, and in an effort to satisfy its sweet-toothed customers even more, Coke had dropped its 99-year-old formula—without checking with the consumer. What a shock to have a national classic disappear overnight. Fortunately, the Coca-Cola company had the business sense to react with fizz-speed (in two and a half months) and return the familiar-tasting

Coke to its loyal public. Billed as a giant marketing blunder, akin to the Edsel, the story has taken a Zero-to-Hero turn. Now Sergio Zyman is back at Coke and back on top with an even bigger job. And Coke has a double Click: double shelf space with New Coke and Classic Coke.

Older products stand a chance to be Hero-bound. Who out there remembers those weirdo products, Miracle Brush Lint Removers and Fishin' Magician, which used to be pitched on television in the '70s, pre-infomercial days? The company, K-tel, that hawked these gems went belly-up in 1985. Now the time has come to market the resurrected products again. CEO Mickey Elfenbein, nephew of the founder, is pushing the unique line of goods into Europe as well: Pump N' Seal Airtight Storage Makers, Firm Flex Exercise Machines, and Lustre–7 Car Wax. Another example of Sticking with the Click through bankruptcy—and a $60-million company is well on its way back up again.

Products themselves can run the full gamut from Zero-to-Hero-to-Zero-to-Hero too. One of the most challenging areas we work on at BrainReserve is the repositioning of existing products. After a certain timespan in the marketplace, many old standards need a face lift to succeed, if not survive. There's often a fine line between nostalgia and nothingness. Years ago, we re-looked at Bon Ami, a cleanser with a memorable image and tagline, showing a baby chick and the caption, "Hasn't scratched yet." The ecologically early product had even more going for it—its cleansing powder was so pure and so nontoxic that supposedly you could brush your teeth with it. We found out in focus groups and through the ClickScreen that its integrity, old-fashionedness, and honesty were still appealing to today's consumers who didn't want to see Bon Ami slickly updated.

Another product we helped reposition was the Shower Massage by Teledyne Water Pik. The gadget had run through its original splash introduction, then ever so slowly, the number of people interested in buying and installing the new type of showerhead began to dwindle. The answer to sluggish sales was as simple as isolating a positive attribute that fit Trend-wise, yet had been overlooked. In the Shower Massage's case, we found that consumers responded to an inherent benefit: When the jets were adjusted, it turned into a terrific stress-reducer. The Shower Massage became like a mini-spa, right in your home. A Click.

Bristol-Myers brought out Nutrament in 1961 as a quick supplement in a can for marathon runners, other athletes, and the skinny set who needed an easy way to get extra nourishment. By the '80s, sales were stagnant, except for certain ethnic pockets in big inner cities. Curious, the marketing and sales departments looked into the whys and wherefores of this phenomenon. It turns out that Nutrament had a secondary Hero position, as a cheap and nutritious meal replacement (under $2 a can) for the homeless/poor and a palatable diet for addicts who have a hard time with solid foods.

The building blocks of Legos suffered a tumble in popularity when everything became computerized, animated, and mega-fast. Now they're enjoying a renewed surge simply because it's a creative/destructive/creative way to play—a fundamental part of the growth process. Yo-yos, too, are having a revival. These ancient playthings from China went through a frenzy in the American '30s and '40s, when contests were held to see who could keep a yo-yo going the longest (without tangling), while doing certain tricks, like Walking the Dog. Today there's talk about making yo-yoing more legitimate, by raising the skills to the level of Olympic competition. Same goes for Ping-Pong.

Just in the last few years, a whole industry—the American car market, as well as the city of Detroit—was being written off as dying or dead. The cars had the reputation for being shoddy and inferior to the Japanese models, and even the workers were maligned as being sloppy and lazy. It simply wasn't considered "smart" to get an American lemon. But a rally of patriotism after the Gulf War to "buy American," coupled with advances in design and technology, have restored the sales. American cars are perceived to be sound and well-built, less costly to drive, and easier to service. A true Hero-to-Zero and back to Hero business.

Examples of Hero-to-Zero-hopefully-back-to-Hero in business are endlessly fascinating for the gossip makers in any industry. People are watched with envy as they climb up and watched with sadistic glee (especially if they have Big Egos) as they come a-tumbling down. Yet there's a begrudging admiration for the guts it takes to pick up and start all over again. Especially if you've been plastered all over the six o'clock news, the daily papers, and *People* magazine. Didn't we read at least 3 million words about Donald Trump? In the Clicking Trend of Icon Toppling, we've talked more about those big companies and institutions that have come crashing down.

In the highly visible field of commercial real estate, New York developer Bruce Eichner was a case study of a super–deal maker who became overextended in a dried-up market. Eichner had to watch as the banks reclaimed many of his office buildings and condos. Now the climate has changed and space is once again tight in Manhattan. But it seems as if Eichner has learned caution from the financial fall. His introductory venture created a slew of apartments over a giant Toys Я Us store. Another of his return engagements: a brilliant idea of turning a large Manhattan hotel into a time-sharing space. He's converting it slowly, floor by floor, so there's not much risk in losing.

Television, more than the movies or the stage, is one field where you're either a great success—or not. (It's lucky there are so many channels.) Cornelius Crane Chase, better known as Chevy, was a talk show host for about one minute. Reviewers called the show "a low moment in television," "disaster," "heinous." But the guy is funny and talented, and just needs another vehicle. Chevy, in a later interview, said, "I was unsure and it showed." Like the rock song, "I've seen fire and I've seen rain," it's possible to grow through that kind of experience. (Did you know that the phrase, "I've passed through fire," came from an allusion to the meltdown in gold refining?) Tom Snyder went through his ritual of fire, and came out unburned. After being replaced on NBC as a late-late host by Letterman years ago, he bided his time on CNBC and now has returned to follow Letterman on CBS. Musical chairs. Sally Jessy Raphael was supposedly fired twenty-eight times in her career. Another ex–talk show host is witty, witty, witty Joan Rivers. Now, in an attempt to share her tales of fortune and misfortune with others, Joan tells the audience of her how-to-be-happy seminar, "Realize that life is a movie and you are the star. Give it a happy ending."

One trying aspect to this Zero-to-Hero move is often how long it takes. Ventriloquist Shari Lewis and her homemade sock puppet, Lamb Chop, have a terrific stick-to-itiveness tale. They were first televised in 1960, canceled three years later, and retried for a short time in the '70s. Nothing, Zero. Many many moons later, in 1992, PBS took another look at the duo and aired the singing Shari and her precious Lamb Chop in their "Play Along" show every morning during the week. A Click. They're the third-favorite kids' show now, after "Barney," the purple dinosaur, and "Sesame Street."

Actress Brooke Shields had an early hit when she was a tender star in the movie *Pretty Baby*. And then she didn't do much she was proud of, until her recent Broadway debut as the tough talking, finger-snappin' Rizzo in *Grease*. In an article in *New York* magazine, entitled "Endless Comeback," writer James Kaplan remarked that Brooke's long string of mediocre movies "have run the gamut in quality from Y to Z," but praised her for "not flaming out. Not growing bitter and hard. Not robbing convenience stores or displaying her grown-up nakedness in *Playboy*." John Travolta, too, could be looked at as a Comeback Kid. After his fiery start as a sizzling 23-year-old disco king in *Saturday Night Fever*, he fizzled for years in a forgettable run of films, finally reappearing in a winning role as a pudgy, stringy-haired, 40-year-old in *Pulp Fiction*. After a repeat success as an ingenuous gangster in *Get Shorty*, his ask-per-picture is now: $23 million.

Another long dry spell happened to hefty rock star Meat Loaf, who Clicked into his first tremendous success in 1977 with his album *Bat Out of Hell*. After he sold an astounding 30 million copies, Meat Loaf's career went haywire with a disastrous combination of drugs, loss of voice, lawsuits. It took sixteen years to straighten things out completely and make a sequel, *Bat Out of Hell II*, which went platinum.

No one, however, waited longer for repeat critical acclaim than writer Henry Roth. At age 28, he published his first novel, *Call It Sleep*, the story of a Jewish immigrant, in 1934. Although it received excellent reviews, the book only sold a total of 4,000 copies. Thirty years later, it was rediscovered and reprinted as a paperback and successfully sold one million copies. In the interim, Roth had a colossal writer's block and supported himself in various jobs, such as a poultry farmer and an orderly in a mental institution. In 1994, after sixty years, Roth's second novel finally came out to high praises. Even though he recently died at 89, his complete series, called *Mercy of a Rude Stream*, is being published at a rate of one per year.

Those are the long stretched-out struggles. But think of the celebrities or politicians who have plunged from Hero-to-Zero in the space of one news flash. As opera great Jessye Norman told us, "Overnight is a very long time." Or as Marshall McLuhan summed it up for *People*: "A superstar is just another word for a sitting duck." Count the royals around the world who are in the firing range. But, in marketing terms, some big names or talents lose more than reputations. Beautiful Miss America Vanessa Williams had to give back her glittery crown when the pageant discovered she'd stripped for a spread in *Penthouse*. Her star-success came back, at even higher mega-wattage, with the well-received release of a Top Ten CD, a stint on Broadway as the lead in *Kiss of the Spider Woman*, and the best song, "Colors of the Wind," from the movie *Pocahontas*. Tennis star extraordinaire Martina Navratilova's coming out as a lesbian and her palimony suit with Judy Nelson did serious financial damage. She simply wasn't offered any of the lucrative advertising endorsements for any big-name products. Another Hero-to-Zero, ex-champion and ex-inmate No. 922335, Iron Mike Tyson, had an abusive fall from grace that cost him not only his freedom but also his big-time endorsements: $1.5 million from Diet Pepsi, $800,000 from Toyota, among others. Will another round of knockouts (in the ring only) as well as a dose of piety and religion bring them back?

In a heady reversal, going from Zero-to-Hero, supposedly washed-up George Foreman regained his heavyweight boxing title and his star status in 1994. To feel more like his formidable self, he went into the bout dressed in the same red trunks, now faded and out-of-shape, that he wore when he fought Muhammad Ali in 1974. Only this time in the ring, the 45-year-old Foreman weighed in at a hefty 250 pounds. Yet with one mighty right-hand punch, he knocked out his opponent, Michael Moorer (35–0) and caused one of the sport's great upsets. Savoring victory at his age, Foreman first spouted a line from Disney: "When you wish upon a star, your dreams come true," and then said, "This was for all my buddies in the nursing home and all the guys in jail." Next fight, Foreman vs. Tyson?

Mayor of the District of Columbia, Marion S. Barry, the crack-smoking, convicted felon, fell only briefly. Now re-elected to a fourth term, Barry was returned to his exalted place of honor by his constituency for one reason: By tending to the concerns of the people of Washington, D.C., especially the disenfranchised and the poor, he remained a *Hero* to them. Barry made an appeal to the voters, posing as the Ordinary Man, someone who "has been there and back, just like so many folks." That commonality was something that people could identify with. In typical irreverent American fashion, however, a rash of jokes surfaced, making up his so-called campaign slogans: "America's Most Wanted Mayor," "He'll Cut Drugs Off the Streets," and last, "Give Me Another Crack at It." To fight back, even though he was caught on tape in a criminal act, Barry's first line of defense was to blame others: the FBI and police for "framing him," the *Washington Post* for its coverage, Congress, and, for good measure, the white establishment.

Mayor Barry isn't the first to do this. It's an age-old habit of wrongly pointing a finger elsewhere. Does anyone recall the obscure story about the ancient Persian king Xerxes, who ordered a bridge built across the Dardanelles so that he could invade Greece? When the swaying span was swept away by tumultuous waves, an enraged Xerxes commanded his men to use flogging chains to inflict 300 lashes on the rebellious seas. This example can be referred to as the ultimate Exercise in Futility. Or pointing the finger of guilt in the wrong direction—away from yourself. Similar to what Yogi Berra once said: "I never blame myself when I'm not hitting. I just blame the bat. And if it keeps up, I change bats."

A big part of overcoming adversity, failure, or simply life's bumpy stretches is being able to take some responsibility.

As smart advisers say, admit it. Apologize, if need be.

Strength in Failure

It's often been remarked that the road to failure comes from underrating your competition or overrating yourself. Lys is always telling me that the word "genius" is overused. She read somewhere that Stephan Weiss, husband and creative partner/adviser of Donna Karan, felt likewise, saying something like: "If this is *great* and that is *incredible* and so-and-so is *genius,* what do you say when you come to a da Vinci and Einstein." Good point.

In a similar vein, colleges are starting to rethink their grading systems. There's no such thing as an "F" today. Failure simply does not exist. Stanford University's president, G. Casper, took the lead in calling for tougher marks. Not only was the dreaded "F" ban-

ished twenty-four years ago, but today, in most schools, there are
also very few "Ds" and "Cs" being given out. This "grade inflation"
has led to a weighty number of "A" and "B" marks. At Williams,
nearly half of the graduating class was sent off with honors, while
43% of Harvard's seniors were given prestigious "A" marks. In
addition, students had been given permission to drop a course,
right up to the day of the final exam, if they were not getting a
good enough grade. And then they could retake the very same
course without any of this paperwork trail showing up on an official transcript. (Is this why so many college students are in school
for more than four years these days?)

What's being proposed is a "W," which will signal Withdrawal.
And a new designation of "NP," for Not Passed, as a softer way to
say the Fail, Flunk, Forget It of days gone by. Stanford's president
wants to bring some reality and real honors back to the grading
system, warning, "To fail in some endeavor is something we all go
through. Unless you dare something and admit that you may fail,
you are living in an illusionary world." And it's important to
remember that we can't control the whole world.

That's a tough concept to swallow for all of us Type-A personalities. Because we are all graded in the real world. The "A" Team,
an "A" player, "A for effort," Top Gun, a Type-B personality. And
the new term from computer-ese, "to F6 someone," which means
"Delete." Harvard Medical School psychologist Steven Berglas has
identified a new behavior problem that he calls the "Success Syndrome." This manifests itself as a tendency to be self-destructive
after achieving success. In street slang this is known as "shooting
yourself in the foot." Some think that Clinton shows traces of this
trait. He had already gone the Zero-to-Hero route when he was
defeated once for the governorship of Arkansas. Then on to
Super-Hero as President. But his consistently high public-approval
rating lasted about one day. This seems to point to the fact that he
enjoys jumping the hurdles, instead of finding the smoothest
course.

In other words, there are some people who put themselves in
positions of high risk, looking for their Personal Best. Some test
themselves by climbing mountains (because they're there); others
challenge their limits by running a marathon. French philoso-
pher Albert Camus believed, "The struggle to the top is in itself
enough to fulfill the human heart. Sisyphus should be regarded

as happy." Before reading that particular quote, we always felt empathy for that poor guy in Greek mythology, the legendary Sisyphus who was condemned eternally to repeat the backbreaking task of having to push, push, push a huge stone up a hill, only to have it roll back down again—and then he would have to start the push again. Maybe Camus was right. Never-ending hard work—and a singular goal—can be glorious. There's another plus, for as we all know, a rolling stone gathers no moss.

One close friend of ours has spent his whole business life enjoying the challenge of the dare, rather than the comfort of an easy chair. Bob Kenmore started out at ITT, under the legendary Harold Geneen, as the youngest-ever vice president in charge of acquisitions. He was so good at spotting small, underdeveloped companies that he decided to split off on his own, putting together a deal to purchase Family Bargain Stores.

This started a cycle of parlaying one company's assets into buying another and another, until he built up a luxury-goods conglomerate. One highlight: Representing the New York Cartier, owner Kenmore was the actual person who raised his arms to be the winning bidder for Elizabeth Taylor's huge diamond at auction. That was fun, but having accomplished what he set out to do, Bob moved on. For as much as he liked being Chairman/CEO of a multinational company, he also wanted to explore two other worlds: academia and travel. To sum it up, Kenmore (and his wife, Ayse) went back to Stanford Business School for a degree, then taught at France's premier business school, INSEAD, and before returning here, circumnavigated the globe on a slow, bus-propelled journey. Then came the inevitable Flip. Back to the real business world, he quickly acquired Liberty Music on the East Coast (a Flip-Flop), then Krause's Sofa Factory in California, which had more than sixty stores, then an auto salvage chain in Los Angeles (a Flip-Click).

The most recent, but far from final venture on Bob's agenda, has been a plunge into the studying-buying-selling world of Renaissance- and archaeologically-inspired paintings. The point is, most people are too afraid to walk away from a job or a position and, as the cliché goes, just "chase the rainbow." But Bob Kenmore did, and found many pots of gold, from a reaping of handsome profits to creating a richer love life and a sharper mind.

Nobel Prize winner Kary Mullis had a simpler climb to the top of the mountain. He went straight up and then simply peaked. Or pinnacled. This biochemist, after cracking the way to reproduce DNA and being rewarded with the world's most prestigious honors and honorariums, declared that he was trading in his chemistry lab stool for a surfboard. Although his astounding technological breakthrough, known in scientific circles as PCR, forever changed the fields of anthropology, archaeology (the concept sparked *Jurassic Park*), diagnostics, and forensics (yes, the O. J. trial), Mullis states that he's never going back to the biotech drawing board. He plans to lead a life of indulgence—wine, women, and song—and then pursue his dream profession of becoming a writer.

In the same vein, we saw a blip on television about a man named Bobby Jacobs whose wife, Mary, urged him to "follow his dream." Known as the king of TV syndication (he earned over $3 million in one day), Bobby, age 45, apparently didn't even realize that he was bored with his life—until that verbal push. His dream? To Click as a country-western singer—and if drive counts, move over, Garth Brooks.

One good idea for ridding yourself of the *petit* agony of defeat comes from Carol Caruthers, a director at Price Waterhouse. She planned a party at which guests would be given "a second chance" to prove themselves at things at which they had once failed. If you lost your voice at the podium . . . or botched up a word at a spelling bee . . . or sent the golf ball into a sand trap . . . or tripped on the dance floor, you get a chance to do it right. In front of a friendly audience. Caruthers is a fighter who graduated from business school at 38, became a CPA at 39, and was hired at an accounting firm. She shares her philosophy with co-workers, saying, "People don't remember your mistakes; they remember what you made from them."

ClickLesson: Be Careful What You Wish For

Success is in the eye of the participant. Not the public. The definition of success changes depending on who's defining it. It's important to decide ahead of time what goals you are really after. Some pin-the-tail of success on personal relationships, others on a feeling of being in control of their lives. What do you want to

Click into: fame, fortune, happiness—or power? For instance, it will make a difference if you crave to be on *Fortune*'s "Richest in America" list. But think long and hard. Immense wealth can breed mistrust and be very isolating. Or if you want to be so famous that you're instantly recognized, just check it out with Paul Newman. Or Princess Di. No more privacy, you're constantly paparazzied with the anti-Click of macro- and micro-cameras.

In a *New York Times* article about lawyer Robert L. Shapiro, the writer talked about another "knife" in the O. J. case, "the serrated double edge of fame." That analysis continued: "By becoming the world's most famous lawyer, Mr. Shapiro also became its most studied, most picked-apart and, at least to some, its most exposed. He has proved Mae West wrong: Too much of a good thing can really be too much." And most interesting of all: "He now says unhesitatingly that . . . he regrets taking on the case and *would not do so again*. It's very, very hard to be scrutinized from the time you get up to the time you go to bed." Ladies and gentlemen of the jury, our case rests.

What can be gleaned from all these Zero-to-Hero-to-Zero-to-Hero examples is that, to paraphrase the saying, there are two kinds of failure: Those who dream and never do. And those who do and never dream.

If you don't risk-take, you can't make a mistake. But without mistakes, you can't grow strong. When you mess up, 'fess up. Be flexible. Just start all over again—and Click.

CLICKNAMES
WHEN EVERYONE KNOWS
YOUR NAME, YOU'VE CLICKED

The beginning of wisdom is to call things by their right names.
—CHINESE PROVERB

We're not trying to be funny. This chapter is really about the pros and cons of changing your name. It's a topic that most people are scared to talk about in an honest way. "Not politically correct," you might think. And we're definitely not saying that it takes a good name to Click. Every one of us can reel off a thousand examples of people who have Clicked with the most difficult of names. Maybe it's because we're Popcorn and Marigold that we have some strong opinions on the subject.

We say, if the name your parents gave you doesn't work for you or you simply don't like it, change it (think about how hard companies work on their brand names). Go for the name that's instinctively right, feels comfortable, expresses who you are. One that proclaims "I am" to the real you. For the most part, it's a given that certain public figures have a smoother time with a simple name; easy to pronounce, easy to remember. Why then shouldn't ordinary folk shed their old names and invent new ones, not for ethnic or religious disguises, but for the Click.

Americans who've only settled in this country over the last few hundred years seem overly wed to their given names. Just the other day, someone was lamenting that, because he was childless, it was "the end of the line" for his family name. Knowing that this name was only acquired coming through Ellis Island around 1910, we flippantly figured, "What a shame, to lose a lineage of, gulp, two generations."

The Hollywood star system knew the value of a name change: in the days when Archibald Leach became Cary Grant; Norma Jean Baker, Marilyn Monroe; and Bernard Schwartz, Tony Curtis. So have fashion designers whose names blanket ads and labels, such as Ralph Lauren, who was Ralph Lifshitz; or Halston, who was Roy H. Frowich. Writers switch and print with ease, from Samuel Clemens into Mark Twain, or Anne Rice, who pen-names also as A. N. Roquelaure.

A name change makes perfect sense if you're tired of constantly explaining an impossible spelling or if your name makes people break into giggles (Mr. and Mrs. Poodle, Noodle, or Strudel). What if Hamlet had been Egglet? The driver of the car that James Dean smashed his Porsche into in 1955 had the memorable name of Donald Turnipseed. A name may not translate well from another language. The name Belcher sounds too much like "something not done in polite company" in English, while in its original French, it has the lovely connotation of "bel cher" or "well-loved."

The ClickPoint is "Are *you* tired of it?" Some people are perfectly happy, or at least neutral, about a spelling-bee challenge (Zbigniew Brzezinski) or the definite oddities, such as the legendary Ima Hogg. Conversely, your name could simply be too plain or average for a flamboyant you. You might not want to be lumped into the other several million Smiths.

My birth name was Faith (Quaker overtones, with the inevitable tagline of Hope and Charity), Beryl ('30s movie-starish), Plotkin (my father's surname).

Perhaps my name change experience was unduly influenced by the fact that my lawyer mother never took the name of Plotkin, choosing to use her maiden name, Storper, her entire life. As I've said, when I was nicknamed Popcorn in my early 20s by my first boss, I liked the sound of it, the rhythm of it, the humor in it. And everyone had a comment about some aspect of my new name: Faith B. Popcorn. "What does the 'B' stand for, Buttered?" is one of the standard remarks, a real thigh-slapper. For all the jokes, no one ever forgets it. (See *The Popcorn Report,* page 100 for the Poppa Corne story.) My next name could be Trendar. There's no law against changing your name more than once.

When Lysbeth A. Marigold came to work at BrainReserve as Creative Director, she was ready for a name change. It's an organizational game here (which she started)—as you pass through the portals, you're scrutinized to see if your name Clicks with you. Her birth name was Margold, fine in itself, but it elicited no particular response, either pro or con. Except for constantly being introduced as Margolies, she was totally lukewarm about her name. After a fleeting flirtation with various spellings from Margot to the great French bordeaux, Margaux, she simply slipped in a skinny little "i." That one little letter changed something intrinsic inside herself (she says she feels happier, spicier, more marigold-ish) and in people's reactions upon hearing her name. It was a Click, prompting a sparkle of remarks like "What a pretty name," "Oh, that's easy, it's just like the flower," and so on. And with her first name, Lys, translating to "lily," she now has a double-flower name. We're not saying that it's a monumental life-changing alteration, but in one part of the whole-person-pie, a neutral was turned into a plus.

The bottom line is that names are not as sacred as you'd think. Last names, in total, are a rather modern invention. As late as 1800, in many cultures of the world, most people had only one name. Sadie, Abdul, Richard, Pepin, Isabella, Virginia, Hirohito, Gustav, or Nezih. Although family names first started in Venice in the 11th century, it wasn't until 1465 in England that King Edward IV ordered some of his subjects to take on a town's name (Sutton, Chester), a color (White, Black, Brown), or a trade (Carpenter, Cook, Butler).

Up to 10% of our last names found their origins in nicknames. Even the word "nickname" came from "ekename," or the added name. Look into church records in the Middle Ages, and you'll find that "pet" names simply evolved into surnames. A crafty person was called Fox; a tall guy, Longfellow; a happy-go-lucky or musical one, Whistler. Turks only got around to handing out last names in 1919 when Atatürk decreed that surnames were mandatory. The family of our best friend, Ayse *Manyas* Kenmore, picked the name of a nearby lake, Lake Manyasi. As people came through the gates here in the heyday of immigration, a flood of new names was produced, depending on the whim (or ear) of the record keepers.

Some political or religious stances on names have been stigmatizing . . . or empowering. In medieval Germany, Jews were required to pay dearly for Teutonic names, such as the costly Morgenstern (meaning Star of the Morning). In this century, when restrictions were imposed by the Nazis in the late '30s, all Jewish women were forced by law to take the name Sara, while all the men were mandated to become Israel. Even today, many German states require that a person's first name clearly establishes gender. And "Jesus" was ruled out as a proper forename by the courts. While in the United States, many African Americans have made both a religious and a political statement by replacing their bornnames with Islamic ones; including famous sports figures such as Cassius Clay, who became Muhammad Ali; or Ferdinand Lewis Alcindor Jr., now Kareem Abdul-Jabbar.

There's another whole category of those fortunate enough to be born with a memorable name. Prince, who has subsequently reduced his name to a symbol, was certified Prince Anthony Nelson, while Madonna was baptized Madonna Louise Veronica Ciccone. A cool couple from New Canaan, Connecticut, named Ladd and Molly Morgan, christened their son Lord. You can only have great expectations with a name like that. In much the same way, a name could influence a career. There are Doctor Docktor, a surgeon named Carver, and a veterinarian named Dr. Bird. And, of course, my dear pal, the aptly named James Lecesne, pronounced Le-Scene, is the formidable "performance-writer" who won the Academy Award for his short film *Trevor*.

Some names are just warming. Sportscaster Willow Bay has one. Her legal name is Kristine, but Willow was a prebirth nickname. Or Peaches Bass in the health field. Peaceful names like Marianne Faithfull, Brooke Shields, Dawn Mello, Heather Angel. Or pretty names: Lovelady Powell, who ran an antiques store in Sag Harbor, New York, and Cindy Lovelace (no relation to Linda), a New York lawyer who could change her proper Yankee image by shortening her name to the more off-hours Cin (Sin?).

In the extremely cute category, we have to mention a family

who all share the same nickname. Jerry and his wife, Jenny, referred to each other affectionately as Buddy, and when their first daughter, Elizabeth, was born five years ago, they decided to call her Little Buddy. Their next child, Caroline, was at first called Baby Buddy, which then changed to Sweet Buddy as she grew. Obviously, in that family, "every buddy" loves "some buddy."

On the other foot, certain names sound agitated. An artist in South Beach named Bobby Radical was selling T-shirts with an image of Florida in the shape of a gun. There's a tattoo artist named Emma Porcupine whose name conjures up the sharpness and swiftness of her needles. It was quite evident that Sid Vicious could come to a tragic end. And 19th-century English painter Richard Dadd may have been unduly influenced by his last name: O Dadd, poor Dadd, he went mad, murdered his dad and spent the rest of his life locked up in a lunatic pad.

Marriage can offer a slew of new problems. . . or relief. Unexpected combinations, such as Nina Weiner, LaVerne LeVine; shortcuts, Bill and Hill; or the change of ethnic identity at first take, such as our friend, Francesca Pitrelli, who ended up being referred to as Fran Freedman when she married Michael. Think of the prep school chum of Lys's, Carol Sippy, whose mother had to go through life being introduced as Mrs. Sippy.

Of course, wedding bells can also bring on golden opportunities for a quick, socially acceptable way to change a woman's not-liked last name for a better one. Or following the trend of the past decade, two partners in a vowed alliance can become hyphenated. Or even more "correct," last names of the betrothed partners can be melded or meshed. *The New York Times* announced the marriage of Valerie Silverman and Michael Flaherty, who merged their family names to go through life as the Flahermans. Our friends Marnie McBryde and David Fink have been talking about linking up, with the new name and intended progeny to be known as the family McFinks.

Recently the "About Men" column of *The New York Times Magazine,* entitled "My Maiden Name," explained one man's reasoning about taking his wife's last name. Although the writer had been born Sam Murray Howe, he opted to become Sam Howe Verhovek, because his large family was replete with many males (even a namesake nephew), while his wife's family was all girls with no one to pass down the Verhovek name. He went on to pon-

der how he would explain what "Howe" was. Not a middle name,
but a maiden name. He asked himself: "Now, can a man even
have a maiden name? The word 'maiden' shows up in the the-
saurus as 'earliest,' 'first,' 'original.' So, yes. Howe is my maiden
name." This very confident individual concluded, "And happily,
I can report, government computers from the U.S. Passport
Agency to the IRS have become totally gender-neutral on this
question. . . . a copy of our marriage license efficiently transformed me into Samuel Howe Verhovek in nanoseconds."

When Janet Siroto, BrainReserve's Creative Director, and her
husband, Jason Harper, lamented that there were no male offspring in her family to carry on the Siroto name, they made an
alternate decision. Jason would stay Harper, but their first-born
son would be called Milo Siroto. This confluence of names in one
nuclear family is fairly common in Latin countries, where children carry their mother's maiden name after their father's name.
In Iceland, the concept of passing down the specific family name
is nonexistent. If the father has the first name of Ivan, each one of
his daughters simply carries the last name of Ivans*dottir,* each son,
Ivans*son.* So in each family, brothers and sisters have slightly different last names that completely change with each generation.

Another idea for a name change is to look back to past generations. In Sweden, an executive we met was in the process of
dropping his father's name, Henderson, in exchange for his
maternal grandmother's name, Wildhouse. He explained it: "I
wanted to remix myself and it felt like the new me." Similarly, at
age 17, August Wilson, the double Pulitzer Prize–winning play-
wright, bought a used typewriter to try out all the various combinations of his given and family names. Somehow, being called
Frederick August Kittel or Freddie didn't seem to fit his vision of
himself as a serious writer. When he tried pulling out his own
middle name and paired it with his mother's maiden name, Wilson, that Clicked. August Wilson. The right sound for someone
who has the ability to poignantly capture a portrait of black Americans.

Divorce is an appropriate time for a woman to make an easy
switch back to her maiden name. It's usually a matter of filling in
a few forms—at no cost. Even going the legal route of name
changing doesn't have to cost a fortune. Although it varies from
state to state, basically you need to get name change forms from a

local courthouse, obtain a court date, run announcements in the newspaper, notify the state authorities and all other obligations (banks, credit cards, Social Security, financial assets), and, finally, get yourself a new driver's license and passport. Remarriage brings another opportunity and yet another set of names to the family mix. Upon the second union of their mothers, William Blythe disappeared and resurfaced as Bill Clinton, while Newton McPherson was shortened into Newt Gingrich.

In a way, it's harder and more confusing for friends and family if you decide to change only your first name. It's a difficult habit to break for all those people near and dear to you who are so used to calling out your name. It makes sense that the younger you are, the easier it will be to slip into accomplishing the change. It was tough when Lys's ex-sister-in-law decided to go from Harriet to Jennifer when she was in her mid-30s. At a graduation gathering at the University of Vermont for Lys's niece, the extended family members were calling out congratulations to "Harriet," while the newer friends kept greeting a person they called "Jennifer." To clear up the confusion, some of us who see her only at christenings, weddings, and funerals say "Harriet-Jennifer."

Eventually, if you're really serious about the name switch, it will stick. BrainReserve's Kate Newlin was named Pat when I started working with her a few years back. On the cusp of making some significant life changes, she decided to banish a first name that she never particularly liked. Her choice of Kate came in honor of a grandmother whom she adored. Although Kate was firm with anyone who, out of habit or laziness, slipped back into referring to her as Pat, it took some acquaintances a few months to get Kate down pat (oops). Yet now, only one year later, literally no one makes a mistake.

Actress Sigourney Weaver picked her fairly difficult first name, taken from an obscure character in *The Great Gatsby*, when she was only 13. Born with the name of Susan, she once commented in an interview that Susan seemed to belong to a "short" person and she was tall. Her parents, neither of whom go by their given names, reportedly had no trouble switching over to Sigourney. But even now, some childhood friends insist on calling her Susan, maybe as a way of bonding or keeping up the early ties. What echoes, if any, will Mia Farrow's kids have from her abrupt change of all their first names—going from Satchel to Sheamus; from Dylan to Eliza; and so on.

Architectural Digest's powerhouse, Paige Rense, started out as Patricia, but perhaps she had a premonition about her future relationship to a magazine (pages). As a young and quite distressed runaway teen, she decided on the name of Paige. There's a ClickLesson to be learned from a past interview with her in *New York* magazine. When asked if she ever thought—back when she was an usherette—that her house would be in *Architectural Digest*, she gave this understated reply: "I never thought I would have a house."

On the other side of the world, Mahoko Yoshimoto, the woman who wrote the international best-seller *Kitchen*, went for a Popcorn-like change, becoming known as Banana Yoshimoto. More than a name just for writing, her choice has an internal reason: "It suits me for going out in the world. It's sexless and it's funny."

Looking back to ancient history, the Romans had a preference for highly descriptive names—Agrippa, "feet-first"; Dexter, "right handed"; or Lucius, "light." On the *Mayflower* crossing, fifteen passengers were listed on the ledger as John, but there were also some way-out names: Remember, Love, Desire, Humility, Resolved, Peregrine, Oceanus (born at sea?) and Wrestling (a tough little fighter?). As a society, we're just coming out of an extremely conservative era of first names like Carol and Robert, Debbie and Dennis, Linda and Louis. For naming babies, we're starting to look back toward the more strictly biblical (Rachel, Moses) or to the family tree for Victorian flair (Belinda, Tad). Parents have been venturing out to pinpoint places on a map, with a definite swing toward names like Sierra, Paris, and India. Maybe geographic names are directives for creativity—for instance, we can think of three: the talented furniture designer Dakota Jackson, the clever performance artist Judy Chicago, and the intuitive television therapist Georgia Witkin.

Strong first names give a strong start to life. Look at all the focus put on Chelsea Clinton's name, apparently chosen because of her parents' fondness for the folk song "Chelsea Morning." Blunt, one-syllable words will be the badge of the late-'90s names. We know babies under the age of two called Geige, Quest, Cort, Pierce, Wren, and Lark. Lys's new daughter has the open, expansive name of Skye, with one of her Chinese names for her middle name—Qi, pronounced Chee, meaning life energy.

Many African Americans have created a cultural badge by selecting original names with unusual spellings: Shanelle, LaToya, LeRoi, Marletta, Shaquille. Once regional names were dead giveaways for immediate identification. Southerners were named Ida Mae and Beauregard, or took last names as first names: Ballard and Knox. Bostonians were often called Abigail or had Lowell Cabot or Quincy Adams somewhere in their birthright. You might consider another small change—spelling your given name crazily, phonetically, like the singers Phranc or Phred. Or all lower case, such as e.e. cummings or k.d. lang. Or dropping one letter without changing the pronunciation much, as Barbara Streisand did when she became Barbra, the Star.

For good or bad, popular movies have always been a source of inspiration; a rush of Ariels followed Disney's *Little Mermaid*, and we'll probably be meeting a rash of Simbas from the record-breaking *Lion King*. If you don't think a name can make a difference, ponder the fact that Margaret Mitchell's character Scarlett O'Hara was first called Pansy—and that *Pansy* was even the original title of *Gone with the Wind*. BrainReserve's male Trend Director was named Ashley because his pregnant mother had swooned over the Ashley Wilkes character from *Gone with the Wind*. But when Ashley became such a popular girl's name, he grew tired of the endless unsolicited mail addressed to a Miss or Mrs. Ashley Feinstein. We made it a highly satisfying (and fun) BrainReserve project to find a name that captured him better. Our first take was the cool-sounding Ashley Nashville, but we decided it was too country-western for his dapper persona. After a few joke takes, we all agreed that both his names should be changed. He should chop his first name to the more macho Ash, and switch over to his mother's maiden name for a more rhythmic, better balanced last name. He's now the dashing Ash DeLorenzo—and it suits him fine.

Beyond the importance of naming people the right names, there's an art and an industry to naming ideas, services, products, and companies. When we decided to call this book *Clicking*, we had a heart-stopping scare after we mentioned our chosen title and concept to a group that was putting together a new television entertainment show. They fell in love with it. Only at the last round did they drop the idea of using "Click" as the name of their NBC show and settled instead on another short, punchy word, "Extra." And luckily, it Clicked.

Most, if not all, companies go through the growing pains inherent in a name change as they get bigger or go international. Esso decided to go for the mysterious X-factor in Exxon. Others simplified down to initials, such as International Business Machines to IBM, American Telephone & Telegraph to AT&T, and Philadelphia Electric to PECO. We've seen a million commercials about their friends and family, but who even knows what MCI stands for? As advertising companies mixed and mingled, their names got so long that they had to become initialized in order to fit on a page. BBD&O and uh-oh. Of course, it's a well-known American trait to shorten, slice, dice, and devise new spellings for things. Note A&P, Rice Chex, Toys Я Us.

In 1994, almost one in eight companies changed its corporate name. The trend was toward more initials or tacking on some form of America or Technology. After the banking scandal, references to Savings Banks were quietly dropped. Mergers accounted for over half the changes, such as with Lockheed Martin or Northrup Grumman; or takeovers/buyouts, as Viacom from Paramount. A small phone company, Rochester Telephone, shed its one-focus image and took on a new market name with Frontier Corporation. The successful Boston Chicken (based on a winning formula of good taste, convenience, and value) decided to change its name to Boston Market to show its diversity of products—including turkey, meat loaf, and ham. Their particular Click was the ability not to be stuck in one place—but instead remain flexible and responsive to the market.

Cultural sensitivity can create problems with names. Certain words that are positives in English may have negative meanings in Japan or China or elsewhere. Global companies have to check that out. Dennis Carey of SpencerStuart reminded us about the introduction of Chevy Nova. The new model was being test-marketed in four cities, one being Miami—and was selling well everywhere but heavily-Latino Miami. In Spanish, "va" means "go," and coupled with "no," "Nova" meant "No Go." Not a brilliant name for a car.

Yet any product or corporate name change (to correct a mistake, for ease of remembrance, or simply as a power trip) becomes a costly provision. Often, name firms are consulted, focus groups are formed, press conferences are held, all printed materials from stationery to business cards are reprinted, and so on. It can run into the millions of dollars.

But as the Latins said, "*Nomen est omen*": "In name is power." And we say that the power of your name can help you Click. So be creative. Show your individuality, your uniqueness.

Put aside the schoolyard chant, "Sticks and stones may break my bones, but names can never hurt me." In business and in life, the *wrong* name may actually hurt or hinder you, while the *right* name (your soul name) can Click.

FUTURE TERMS

"When I use a word," Humpty Dumpty said in rather a scornful tone, "it means just what I choose it to mean—neither more nor less."
—LEWIS CARROLL

Nothing, surely, is more alive than a word.
—J.D. ADAMS

A Click language of new terms (some we've heard, most we made up).

Pick and choose those you'd like to use for fun, salting (and peppering) your speech now and in the future. Maybe a few are destined to make it to the dictionary—the way our past invention of Cocooning slipped into the everyday parlance of the media and of the streets.

B.C.: Before Computers.
B.T.: Before Technology.
Brailling the Culture: monitoring for a Trend pulse.
BrainJam: brainstorming session with a Trend base.
Burrowing: digging deeper in the Cocoon.
Career Regression: going down the ladder of success.
Children's Crusade: youngsters grouping together, in person or via the Internet, in order to save the planet.
ClickScreen: way to match your ideas against the Trends.

ClickTime: BrainReserve's newsletter (see page iv).
ClickTip: nugget of good advice.
Communal Clanning: chosen families, by bond, not blood.
Corporate Soul: ethics of a company that gives back.
CyberClans: people who connect by computer information.
CyberDiction: techno-language.
CyberScum: bad guys on the Internet.
DeTech: turn off your machine.
DialPain: phoning someone who gives you negative feedback.
Digerati: digital elite.
Dress for Depress: down-dressing fashions.
Dr. Juice Bars: idea for fresh, healthy juice drink stops.
Earlypreneurial: young self-starter confident about being non-corporate.
Fatal: an obsessive crush.
Female Realism: marketing without hype.
FlagWag: using patriotism to sway beliefs.
Foodaceuticals: future food/medicine combos.
FUD: fear, uncertainty, doubt.
FutureFocus: marketing technique to go to far-future, then backtrack into viable near-future.
God Squad: new religious fanatics.
Ground Zen: yoga-based calmness.
Hoffices: new business to set up home offices.
ITRW: CyberSlang for In The Real World (versus Virtual).
Kids' Election: youth pressure to register parents.
Living Wellness: new respect for all ages of life.
Millennium Shakes: fear of Apocalypse 2000.
MUD: multi-dimensional.
NanoSpan: concentration limit of a 99 Lives person.
NewLine Consultants: advanced computer helpers.
NPP: Non-Punctual Person.
Parroting: over-repeating.
Personal BillBoarding: wearing labels.
Propheteering: using religion to sell products.
Shouting: netting in ALL CAPS.
SITCOMS: Single Income; Two Children; Oppressive Mortgage.
Socioquake: transformation of mainstream America.
SoftTech: nothing too intense.
SourceSmart: restaurant chain serving healthy food where all sources are identified.

Tech-Knows vs. Tech-Nots: computer-savvy vs. computer-retard.
TechnoObsessed: state when being online interferes with life.
TechnoPreneur: new freewheeling, computer-biz whiz.
TeleTrance: calming phone experience (opposite of DialPain).
TrendSect: when two or more Trends meet, intertwine, or clash.
Up-Aging: getting old before your time.
Virtual Rape: sexual harassment online.
VS (Virtual Spirituality): next wave of Anchoring.
Zending: the Zen of spending. Paring down and selecting for
    soul satisfaction.
Zone Switching: Cashing Out to another dimension.

AFTER-FUTURE THOUGHTS

CLICKSTART INTO TOMORROW

In my end is my beginning.
—T. S. ELIOT

Weaving a net is better
than praying for fish.
—ANCIENT CHINESE PROVERB

The future moves so fast. What seems like a crazy hypothetical idea one moment, soon can turn into a reality. You have to be ready to buckle up and take the wild ride toward Tomorrowland. Information is gyring around our heads with macrospeed. The pandemic power of the World Wide Web has created a new sense of urgency into the world-wide marketplace. Coasting in cyberspace, gene swapping, even selecting whether to create a female or male baby — all are possible or on the brink of being so.

One thing for sure, the F-U-T-U-R-E doesn't hold itself back and wait patiently for us to wake up and act. Clicking into the Trends can save precious time by directing us away from something that's nothing and toward something that's really something. We firmly believe that the best measurement for a sound idea is not Good vs. Bad, not New vs. Old, but On-Trend vs. soon-to-be-Obsolete.

Now, right up to these last pages, we're still having future-future thoughts and more will pop up after the close of the book.

As the 16 Trends grow and spin, they're the distilled essence of what consumers everywhere are thinking, wanting, buying, dreaming about. And what they'll be looking for in the Future-Scape to come.

Age Countdown: If the secrets of your genetic blueprint can be deciphered and your expected longevity predicted, more or less, what will happen to fitness programs, the whole homeo-pathic market of vitamins and herbs? A bottoming out? Or will hope spring eternal?

Invisible Helmets: As pollution worsens in major cities, from L.A. to Mexico City to Beijing—we could be donning indi-vidual breathing bubbles around our heads. Not necessarily the hard "fishbowl" types that astronauts wear in outer space, but more flexible and form-fitting. A kind of Saran Wrap protection against free-floating toxins. The helmets will have all the advanced communication technology built-in. Or, in less pol-luted areas, we'll wear designer CitiMasks to filter our breathing. When pure air and clean water become precious commodities, there will be lotteries with specified-term supplies for the top winners.

Life Companions: Instead of engineering a "perfect tomato," why not concentrate on a strain of dog and/or cat breed that can last up to a human lifetime. More wet kisses, fewer tears.

Orphans Online: What about starting a central, global com-puterized adoption register to keep track of all the babies and small children waiting for homes. No politics, just a helping hand for innocent kids. An on-target charitable opportunity for Bill Gates (he has the resources, the money, the reach) to give back earlier than he's planned. This idea could work for abandoned pets, as well.

Center-City Living: As more people open their own small, entrepreneurial businesses at home (as more than 2 million did last year), emptied-out office buildings should turn residential. Or empty commercial space could provide shelter for the urban poor and homeless, or could be a space for elder/childcare. Now, if only there were a way to open those sealed office windows.

Superstore for the Disabled: With an estimated 20-million-plus Americans disabled to some extent and an aging population, isn't it time for a Home Depot/Toys Я Us-type of mega-store where you can find everything in one place: amplified telephones, voice trans-lators, etc.

Knowledge Chips: Someday, there will be tiny computer chips that you can buy or rent—to insert/implant into one of your own brain-chambers that's been made ready by surgery. Think of all the applications. You'll be able to speak fluent French or Chinese for a business meeting, a vacation, or forever. Or you can recite love poems when you go a-wooing. Or you'll be able to comprehend a television repair manual when your set goes on the fritz. Or you'll jump in and instantly know how to play golf/tennis/croquet—although you'll only excel as much as your muscle tone allows.

DNA Matchmaking: Using genetic research into health and personality traits, you can be matched with a potential spouse, fine friend, or business partner who fits with your gene pool. The Japanese are already doing it with blood types.

Catavans: A melding of the catalog and the van—large vehicles will roam neighborhoods and demonstrate/sell a range of goods, to purchase on the spot or order for next-day delivery. This fills a need-niche between the mall (time-consuming, hectic) and the mail-order catalog (can't try/touch, impersonal).

Show 'n' Tell: Schools will be hooked up with closed-circuit TV live inside prison walls, to show and tell kids exactly what it's like "on the other side." No romance. It will serve as a strong deterrent and encourage youngsters to stay straight.

Cheating Crisis: Since the Internet will give students an unprecedented opportunity to "borrow" homework from other kids ("Quick, e-mail me a book report on *The Great Gatsby*"), new educational cops will have to patrol online.

Spiritual Opportunities: We'll see a noteworthy rise in employment in the "spiritual" industry. If the CIA can turn to psychics, why couldn't mayors, judges, CEO's work through mediums and channelers to help figure out which people/products/companies to hire/acquire, who is good/bad . . .

More Steps: Anticipate more Twelve Step programs, as a way of connecting. MOA (Mail Order Anonymous) for catalog junkies; IA (Internet Anonymous) for people who can't get offline; even more general CA (Communications Anonymous) for those who are overly attached to cellular phones, car phones, beepers, faxes, e-mail, multiple lines, Call Return, voice mail. Or even worse, just plain call to listen to someone's message machine who isn't home or invade another's voice mail.

Penmanship: As a reaction to the domination of computers, flowing, show-offy handwriting with swirls and twirls will be the new status symbol. With the effect of different aromas down to a science, our pens will emit scents to make us more creative or boost our memory.

Pfff—Safe: There will be a portable spray for flash sanitation—to provide peace of mind by sterilizing dishes, cutlery, toilet seats, needles, etc. Especially good for on-the-road.

Sleep-Breaks: Naps will be a necessary part of the workday, as the rest/relaxation quotient is proven to help us live longer. There will Cocooning pods with filtered aromatherapy in every home and office, plus you'll be able to rent them for quickie snoozes when you travel.

No More Nightmares: New laser therapy, under the guidance of a knowledgeable psychotherapist, will be able to erase hideous memories or trauma. You'll no longer have to spend tortured years reliving child abuse, rape, or horrible accidents. Conversely, the enflamed area of the brain that produces the impulse to rape or commit child abuse could be blasted away by laser pinpointing.

Vows and Vows Again: Divorce may continue to decline, but so will traditional marriages as some try more unusual arrangements. Communal marriages. Bigamy, trigamy, quadrigamy. Serial marriages, with starter marriages as the first tryout, a ceremony down the road to initiate kids.

Population Control: In densely populated countries, boys and girls will be "contracepted" at birth, then activated after being granted approval (for good conduct, strong familial instincts) later in life. This same method of activation can even be used to re-start an older woman's hormones, postmenopause, if she so desires to wait for motherhood until post-career.

Compu-Plates: New microprocessor technology allows for instant calorie and nutritional computation at each meal, even in restaurants. Sensors and scans will weigh and calculate the calorie/fat/vitamin count of breakfast, lunch, or dinner.

Communication Booths: The phone booth of the Year 2010 will still be located at convenient street corners but will have a port for plugging in your computer as well as quick connections for picking up and sending e-mail or faxes.

Presto, Chango: Breakthroughs in hologram technology will create an instantly changeable world of home decorating. You'll be able to "faux decorate" and dwell in completely different looks—say, country French or stylized Art Deco—by simply pressing a button.

Do-It-Yourself Plastic Surgery: Aging Baby Boomers will be able to purchase home use medical appliances that can erase fine lines and wrinkles right in the privacy of home.

Goggles-to-Go: Special computer goggles can pick up your video game of choice, using wireless technology and a portable joystick. At your whim, you can play anytime, anywhere, any game you want.

A Generator in Every Home: Small, low-cost generators will become as popular as microwave ovens and air conditioners, cutting our dependence on big utility companies.

MicroChurches: Following the marketing precept of "fish where the fish are," churches, synagogues, and New Age services will open mini-branches in corners where people congregate—at malls, sports arenas, beach parking lots, Price Costcos.

Mass Security: As crime worsens, the need for housewatchers, car watchers, and bodyguards (today's escorts of choice) will grow. An opportunity for large insurance companies to expand and offer such services. Or maybe trained local neighborhood-watch groups will carry tranquilizer guns.

On-Your-Block TV: The growth of fiberoptics and the Internet will let ordinary American households create their own television shows. You'll be able to tune into neighborhood talk shows, real situation comedies, and maybe (we hope), live and sparkling brainstorming sessions.

By figuring out How-to-Click, you'll have realized that ideas never stop flowing (which is why the Trends may change, but never really end). Each day, we bolt up and face an onslaught of events, mindsets, and products that imprint our lives and alter our perception of tomorrow—endlessly providing the chance to Click into Completeness. Clicking into:

- Finding a purpose—and living it.
- Turning fear into strategy.
- Adapting Societal Trends Into Personal Opportunities.
- Visualizing where you and your future meet.

In the future, all these ideas will be in the present. That's fodder for thought. If you'd like to share some of your ClickThinks, you can become interactive by calling us (212-978-9999), writing us (c/o HarperCollins, 10 East 53 Street, New York, NY 10022), faxing us (212-481-9595), e-mailing us at Clicking@ix.netcom.com. . . . or by simply beaming us up.

Start Clicking

A LOOK AT
THE FUTURIST,
THE WRITER,
THE ARTIST:

Faith Popcorn, the Futurist (with Sissey Miyake).

Lys Marigold, the Writer.

Gerti Bierenbroodspot, the Artist (self-portrait).

C L I C K A R T

Q: Why is this book illustrated?
A: For two sound reasons.

1. Because we loved the idea that, in the past, most books came with illustrations and decided that drawings would be an instantaneous way to convey the future.
2. Because we were lucky enough to ignite our special friend, Gerti Bierenbroodspot from Amsterdam, so that she would apply her skill, enthusiasm, vision, and un-matched professionalism to this task.

Although in real life Bierenbroodspot (or GBB, for short) is a classical European painter, she deftly morphed into an illustrative mode for this project. After the three of us (me, Lys, and GBB) put on our thinking caps, we concocted icons or symbols that captured the essence of each chapter. Then, Bierenbroodspot trudged off to her ice-cold studio in East Hampton, New York, to elaborate, embellish, and build upon the core ideas. Delving deep into her subconscious, she has created an entire whimsical world of flora and fauna and folks on Trend, with some of the menagerie such recognizable creatures as lizards and chipmunks and others purely fictitious fantasies, such as pobbles and quangle-wangles.

Known primarily as a master surveyor of the frescoes of Pompeii, the labyrinths of Crete, the royal tombs of Egypt, the red monuments of Petra, and the ancient carvings of Palmyra, the talented Bierenbroodspot Clicked anew with this book, even designing the cover and painting the celestial-sky background for it, too. Born under the sign of Taurus with Sagittarius rising, Bierenbroodspot works magic with her strong left hand, a fine blending of inks and watercolors and a signature scattering of 24K goldleaf.

Bierenbroodspot has done the murals in the State House in Maastricht (where the European Union was signed), ballet decor for Balanchine, and the dining hall of a new Carnival Line cruiseship, and she has had major one-man shows in Paris, Amsterdam, Brussels, and New York. She was honored in December 1994, when Queen Beatrix of the Netherlands brought a retrospective of her work to Amman, Jordan, as the official state gift to King Hussein (who promptly bestowed a knighthood on Bierenbroodspot).

As Lys once wrote about her in the catalog of GBB's Native American series, *Songs of the Shamans*, "The gift of Bierenbroodspot is that she can capture a moment in history, a chiseled image in the flow of time, turning one brief second into eternity." For that and for what she added to *Clicking*, we eternally thank her.

R E A D I N G   L I S T

This is the BrainReserve reading list. Unless you're a professional Trend forecaster, you probably don't need to read or scan everything we do. A good plan would be to rotate your subscriptions. Alternate *Newsweek* with *Fortune, Elle* with *Women's Wear Daily, People* with *Entertainment Weekly.* If you're a Baby Boomer, take an occasional look at a Generation X publication, and, conversely, try reading *Longevity* even if you feel you're going to live forever. Cover all the bases, not every day, necessarily, but at least to try to keep up with what's going on today. It will help you to visualize and be prepared for tomorrow.

BrainReserve Reading List

General Interest/Information
Cristina
The Economist
Hispanic Under Thirty
Modern Maturity
New York
Newsweek
Psychology Today
Time
U.S. News & World Report
Vanidades

Women's Publications
Allure
Elle
Essence
Family Circle
Good Housekeeping
Harper's Bazaar
Ladies' Home Journal
Mademoiselle
Mirabella
Victoria
Vogue
W
Women's Wear Daily
Working Mother
Working Woman

Men
Details
Esquire
Gentlemen's Quarterly
Men's Health
Men's Journal

News
El Daily News
Financial Times
Herald Tribune (European
    edition)
Le Monde
New York Observer
New York Times
USA Today
Village Voice
Wall Street Journal
Washington Post

Science
Discover
Omni
Science
Science Digest
Scientific American

Health
American Health
Fitness
Health
Longevity
Men's Health
Prevention
Self
Shape

Food/Liquor
Bon Appetit
Cook's Illustrated
Eating Well
Food & Wine
Food Arts
Gourmet
Vegetarian Times

Home
Architectural Digest
Country Living
Elle Decor
House Beautiful
Martha Stewart Living
Metropolitan Home
This Old House

Travel/International
Arena
Condé Nast Traveler
Elegance (Netherlands)
Harper's & Queen
I-D
Marie Claire
Soviet Life
Time Out
Tokyo Journal
TransPacific
Travel & Leisure

Entertainment/Gossip
Bark
Billboard
Buzz
Entertainment Weekly
Hola
In Style
Interview
National Enquirer
People
Premiere
Rap Sheet
RayGun
Rolling Stone
Source
Spin
TV Guide
Us
Vanity Fair
Variety
Vibe

Literary/Art
Art & Antiques
Atlantic Monthly
Grand Street
Granta
Harper's
Journal of Popular Culture
New York Review of Books
New Yorker
Paris Review
Publishers Weekly
Quarterly: New American Writing

Business
Business Week
Delaney Report
Entrepreneur
Far Eastern Economic Review
Forbes
Fortune
Inc.
Japan Economic Journal
Nikkei Weekly
Smart Money
Worth

Politics
American Spectator
George
Manchester Guardian
Mother Jones
Ms.
Nation
New Republic
Politique Internationale
Reason
Washington Spectator

Environment
E: The Environmental Magazine
Earthwatch
Mother Earth News
World Watch

Newsletters and Trade Publications
Advertising Age
Adweek
American Demographics
Berkeley Wellness Letter
Boycott Quarterly
Brandweek
Chain Drug Review
Consumer Confidence Survey
Consumer Reports
Crain's New York Business
Food & Beverage Marketing
Food Marketing Briefs
Harvard Women's Health Watch
Iconoculture
John Naisbitt's Trend Letter
Manhattan User's Guide
Market Watch: The Wines, Spirits
   & Beer Business
Marketing News
Mayo Clinic Health Letter
National Home Center News
New Product News
Supermarket News
Tufts Nutrition Letter

Gay/Lesbian
Advocate
The Blade
Curve
Diva
Genre
Men's Style
Out

New Age
East West
Family Therapy Networker
New Age
Tricycle: The Buddhist Review
Whole Earth Review
Yoga Journal

New Tech
Home PC
MacWorld
PC World
Wired

Offbeat
Coffee Journal
High Times
Libido: The Journal of Sex and
    Sensibility
Monk: Public Diary of the
    Pilgrim's Journey
New York Press
Paper
Plain
Project X
Utne Reader

Youth Market
Dirt
Might
Sassy
Seventeen
Sister 2 Sister
YM (Young Miss)
YSB (Young Sisters & Brothers)

Online
scan.scan.scan

As we've said, in addition to reading, we see just about every interesting new movie (plus quite a few duds) and Broadway, off-Broadway, and off-off-Broadway plays. We cover the culture closely, going to lectures, art shows, museums, concerts, and cabarets. And, of course, we spend a lot of time in front of the tube, watching, taping, and digging for Trends.

I N D E X